Comedy Italian Style

Dino Risi and Vittorio Gassman (Photo courtesy of Dino Risi)

Comedy Italian Style

The Golden Age of Italian Film Comedies

Rémi Fournier Lanzoni

continuum

NEW YORK • LONDON

2008

The Continuum International Publishing Group Inc
80 Maiden Lane, New York, NY 10038

The Continuum International Publishing Group Ltd
The Tower Building, 11 York Road, London SE1 7NX

www.continuumbooks.com

Printed in the United States of America

Library of Congress Cataloging-in-Publication Data

Lanzoni, Rémi Fournier.
Comedy Italian style : the golden age of Italian film comedies / Rémi Fournier
Lanzoni.
p. cm.
Includes bibliographical references and index.
ISBN-13: 978-0-8264-1821-0 (hardcover : alk. paper)
ISBN-10: 0-8264-1821-X (hardcover : alk. paper)
ISBN-13: 978-0-8264-1822-7 (pbk. : alk. paper)
ISBN-10: 0-8264-1822-8 (pbk. : alk. paper) 1. Comedy films–Italy–History
and criticism. I. Title.
PN1995.9.C55L36 2008
791.43'6170945–dc22

2008029672

ISBN 978-0-8264-1822-7

A Kristin, Simon e Henri

Table of Contents

List of Illustrations

Frontispiece: Dino Risi and Vittorio Gassman

1. Totò (Ferdinando Esposito) in Mario Monicelli's *Cops and Robbers* (*Guardie e ladri*, 1951)
2. Alberto Sordi (Cencio) in Luigi Zampa's *Ladro lui ladra lei* (1958)
3. Totò (Ferdinando Esposito) and Aldo Fabrizi (Brigadiere Bottoni) in Mario Monicelli's *Cops and Robbers* (*Guardie e ladri*, 1951)
4. Vittorio Gassman (Gerardo Latini) and Mario Scaccia (the jeweler) in Dino Risi's *Love and Larceny* (*Il mattatore*, 1959)
5. Richard Basehart (the secretary), Franco Fabrizi (the chauffeur), and Broderick Crawford (the bishop) in Federico Fellini's *The Swindle* (*Il bidone*, 1955)
6. Alberto Sordi (Alberto) in Federico Fellini's *I vitelloni* (1953)
7. Dino Risi and Federico Fellini in 1957
8. Carla Gravina (Nicoletta), Vittorio Gassman (Peppe), and Renato Salvatori (Mario) in Mario Monicelli's *Big Deal on Madonna Street* (*I soliti ignoti*, 1958)
9. Vittorio Gassman (Peppe) and Marcello Mastroianni (Tiberio) in Mario Monicelli's *Big Deal on Madonna Street* (*I soliti ignoti*, 1958)
10. Jean-Louis Trintignant (Roberto Mariani) and Vittorio Gassman (Bruno Cortona) in Dino Risi's *The Easy Life* (*Il sorpasso*, 1962)
11. Saro Urzì (Don Vincenzo Ascalone), Stefania Sandrelli (Agnese Ascalone), and Lina Lagalla (Francesca Ascalone) in Pietro Germi's *Seduced and Abandoned* (*Sedotta e abbandonata*, 1964)
12. Alberto Sordi (Alberto Innocenzi) and Serge Reggiani (Ceccarelli) in Luigi Comencini's *Everybody Go Home* (*Tutti a casa*, 1960)
13. Luigi Comencini on the set of *Everybody Go Home* (*Tutti a casa*, 1960) with Carla Gravina and Serge Reggiani

37. Giancarlo Giannini and Laura Antonelli in the episode "Signora, sono le otto" in Dino Risi's *How Funny Can Sex Be? (Sessomatto*, 1973)

38. Alessandro Momo (Ciccio) and Vittorio Gassman (Fausto Consolo) in Dino Risi's *Scent of a Woman (Profumo di donna*, 1974)

39. Giancarlo Giannini (Mimì) and Luigi Diberti (Pippino) in Lina Wertmüller's *The Seduction of Mimi (Mimì metallurgico, ferito nell'onore*, 1972)

40. Giancarlo Giannini, Lina Wertmüller, and Mariangela Melato on the set of *Swept Away (Travolti da un insolito destino nell'azzurro mare d'agosto*, 1974)

41. Bruno Zanin (Titta Biondi) and Maria Antonietta Beluzzi (the tobacconist) in Federico Fellini's *Amarcord* (1974)

42. Nino Manfredi (Nino Garofalo) with a fellow Italian immigrant in Franco Brusati's *Bread and Chocolate (Pane e cioccolata*, 1974)

43. Alberto Sordi (Guido Tersilli) in Luciano Salce's *Il Prof. Dott. Guido Tersilli, primario della clinica Villa Celeste convenzionata con le mutue* (1969)

44. Alberto Sordi (Romeo Proietti) and Anna Longhi (Augusta Proietti) in the episode "Le vacanze intelligenti" in Alberto Sordi's *Dove vai in vacanza?* (1978)

45. Alberto Sordi (Giacinto Colonna) and Rossana Di Lorenzo (Erminia Colonna) in *A Common Sense of Modesty (Il commune senso del pudore*, 1976)

46. Alberto Sordi

47. Philippe Noiret (Giorgio Perozzi) and Ugo Tognazzi (Lello Mascetti) in Mario Monicelli's *My Friends (Amici miei I*, 1975)

48. The rescue operation of the Tower of Pisa in Mario Monicelli's *My Friends II (Amici miei II*, 1982)

49. Vincenzo Crocitti (Mario Vivaldi) and Alberto Sordi (Giovanni Vivaldi) in Mario Monicelli's *An Average Little Man (Un borghese piccolo piccolo*, 1977)

50. Alberto Sordi (Peppino), Silvana Mangano (Antonia), Bette Davis (Amalia), and Joseph Cotten (George) in Luigi Comencini's *The Scientific Card Player (Lo scopone scientifico*, 1972)

51. Stefania Sandrelli (Donatella) and Alberto Sordi (Monsignore Ascanio La Costa) in the episode "L'ascensore" in Luigi Comencini's *Quelle strane occasioni* (1976)

52. Ugo Tognazzi (the professor), Miou-Miou (Angela), and Gérard Depardieu (Franco) in Luigi Comencini's *Bottleneck (L'ingorgo: una storia impossibile*, 1979)

53. A scene from Luigi Comencini's *Bottleneck (L'ingorgo: una storia impossibile*, 1979)

Acknowledgments

Dino Risi and his films inspired this project, and I extend my deepest gratitude for his warm enthusiasm each time we met and discussed commedia all'italiana and for graciously offering one of his personal photographs for the cover of this book. He will be greatly missed, personally and professionally, his passing coming in the final stage of this book project. Many thanks to Mario Monicelli who also welcomed an interview and support for this study. I am honored to have been hosted in Rome by Furio Scarpelli, who granted an engaging discussion on the origins of the commedia, and also by Carlo Verdone who offered an informative and enthusiastic conversation about its profound impact on a new generation of directors. Among the numerous people who have helped me throughout the development of this project, I would like to thank Evander Lomke, former senior editor at Continuum, without whom this publication would never have been possible. I would also like to thank David Barker, editorial director at Continuum, who took over the project with great interest until its completion, along with Amy Wagner, copyeditor, Gabriella Page-Fort, publishing services supervisor, and Max Novick, production editor. *Comedy Italian Style* greatly benefited from the expertise and passion of my longtime friend, Corrado Corradini, who, thanks to his unlimited knowledge of Italian cinema as well as his appreciation of linguistic subtleties, was able to reveal some of the enigmas of Italian humor. I am also indebted to Peter Bondanella for endorsing the book project and, as always, for giving me some invaluable feedback on Italian cinema. His book, *Italian Cinema*, which I first read in 1996, remains an inspiration. I would also like to express my gratitude to Jean Gili, who agreed to meet with me in Paris and shared his vast experience with Italian comedy. Many thanks to Danielle Hipkins, who generously shared an article she wrote for a film conference in London in October 2006. I would like to extend my gratitude to Fabrizio Corallo and Gioia Donati for helping me getting in touch with several key figures in the Italian film industry in Rome. For the documentation of this volume, I am indebted to Elisabetta Chiarotti, Rosaria Alba, and Antonella Felicioni from the Centro Sperimentale di Cinematografia in Rome who helped to locate valuable photographs, Andrea Amatiste from the Istituto Luce in Rome, and also to Maria Cidda and Umberto Cicconi from the Archivio Allori in Rome. In addition, I would like to express my sincere gratitude to the staff of the library at Elon University library, with a special nod to Lynn Melchor, interlibrary loan coordinator, Sandra Kilpatrick, acquisition specialist, and Lynne Bisko, non-print librarian, for their rare aptitude for patience in light of my numerous unusual requests. Many thanks to Ilaria Cecchi from Archivio Reporters Associati in Rome, who offered her assistance on several photographs, and Ron Mandelbaum from the Photofest Archives in New York; to Giovanni Feliciotto from Taormina, who provided several films on DVD, as well as to the personnel from the Iconothèque at the Cinémathèque Francaise in Paris. On a personal note, I would like to thank my brother Jérôme for his technical assistance with photographs, as well as my cousins Rossana and Bruno, who many years ago screened several important Italian comedy films for me in their home in Milan. Many thanks to my friend Sandro Picchietti, with whom numerous hours were spent watching *Amici miei* endless times and Giacomo Bartoloni Saint Omer (il Sassaroli). My everlasting thanks also go to my father, Jean-Jacques, who always communicated his passion for Italian cinema and, in particular, for Federico Fellini. As a young child growing up in the seventies and discovering this new cinema, I developed a parallel fascination, which today is expressed in concrete form. At last, I am very happy to thank, as well as to dedicate, this book to Kristin, my wife, whose patience once more has made this project possible thanks to her knowledge of both English and Italian.

Introduction

The purpose of the present book is to reintroduce some of the most prevalent and representative Italian film comedies of the 1960s and 1970s to English-speaking readers and spectators. For decades, Italian comedies from this period, called comedy Italian style or *commedia all'italiana*, have been known through a handful of critically acclaimed productions, those that had the good fortune of commercialization outside Italy usually following an international prize, such as Pietro Germi's stylistically innovative *Divorce Italian Style* (*Divorzio all'italiana*, 1961) and its unprecedented Oscar for Best Screenplay in 1963. However, such international recognitions, too sporadic in time, have tended to hide the immense number of productions made in Italy during the two decades. One of the primary goals of this publication is to provide readers with a comprehensive panorama of comedy Italian style, beginning with the late fifties and continuing until the late seventies, in tandem with an in-depth investigation of how these films functioned within a society in an economic and social state of flux. This sophisticated comedy movement, led by a group of prolific screenwriters and promoted by outstanding actors and directors, successfully convinced popular audiences and film critics of the quality and value of comedy as a cinematographic genre. In fact, its inherent ability for collective observation and what appeared to be a noticeable disregard for morality made films of the *commedia all'italiana* an accurate social barometer and a powerful tool to mirror the time's struggles within Italian society and its many calamities.

An important point to note is that the definition of the *commedia all'italiana*, awkwardly translated in English as comedy Italian style, could lead readers and spectators to an indistinguishable terminology conundrum since *commedia all'italiana* remotely evokes the literary period known as the *commedia dell'arte* (which, as will be noted in a moment, influenced it in specific ways) as well as the postwar commercial genre known as *neorealismo rosa*. Therefore, it is important to note the chronological constraints of the *commedia all'italiana* (1958–1979) as well as its directed thematic interests. More a movement than a genre itself, comedy Italian style consistently presented a prevailing dose of social satire using popular comedic elements to represent contemporary Italian society. For the above-mentioned reasons, this study does not include films such as Steno's highly popular *An American in Rome* (*Un americano a Roma*, 1954), the *Don Camillo* saga, the innumerable films featuring Totò, Vittorio De Sica's *Marriage Italian Style* (*Matrimonio all'italiana*, 1964), Mario Monicelli's *L'armata Brancaleone* (1966), Alberto Sordi's *Stardust* (*Polvere di stelle*, 1973) and *Smoke over London* (*Fumo di Londra*, 1966), or Luciano Salce's *Fantozzi* series whose endless sequels hit the national box office from 1975 to 1996, among others; these films never belonged to the *commedia all'italiana* movement.

The movement drew inspiration from a number of sources, uniquely combined and in varying ways, to reflect the mood at the time and consistently result in an unpredictable tragedy (i.e., from television, commercial cinema, and reality itself). One of the sources of *commedia all'italiana* is the above-mentioned literary movement, the *commedia dell'arte*, but it was equally inspired by popular culture and directly confronted the religious, economic, political, and social angst of the changing climate in Italy.

The present volume examines the evolution of the genre and its thematics in chronological order. It is divided into three parts, each part corresponding to a decade (fifties, sixties, and seventies), and further subdivided into chapters. Each chapter offers the historical context, a discussion of the genre development, and a consideration of the period's most representative directors, films, and actors. Chapter one, "The Forerunners," explores the different inspirational sources of Italian comedic elements in films from its introduction at the turn of the twentieth century. More than just an adaptation or review of theatrical comedies, Italian film comedies included a range of influences, from their very own *commedia dell'arte* tradition of social satire to the influence of Hollywood comedies of the silent era, as well as the *Telefoni Bianchi* comedies from the prewar Cinecittà era. While actors often came from the stage of the *Avanspettacolo*, this chapter also emphasizes the role of seminal screenwriters who for the most part had collaborated in the production of satirical journals like the *Marc'Aurelio* in the 1930s.

Chapter two, "The Age of *Neorealismo Rosa*," narrates the development of Italian comedy during the postwar era and in particular the influence of neorealist cinema and its subsequent *neorealismo rosa* movement on popular audiences and comedy filmmakers. One of the most crucial sections of the present volume is the explanation of the fundamental differences between *commedia italiana* and *commedia all'italiana*; this careful delineation is made through a study of the work of Mario Monicelli and Steno's *Cops and Robbers* (*Guardie e ladri*, 1951), Federico Fellini's *I vitelloni* (1953) and *The Swindle*

(*Il bidone*, 1955), and of course, the influential *Big Deal on Madonna Street* (*I soliti ignoti*, 1958), making a strong impact on the community of future authors. The second part is called "The Years of Euphoria and the Commedia all'Italiana" and begins with chapter three, "Italian Comedy in the 1960s," a section that offers an overview of Italy during the years of the economic miracle or the so-called *boom economico*. This section offers a detailed synopsis of the Italian film industry in the 1960s through an examination of the role of state censorship during these years of profuse cinematographic productivity and innovation as well as an investigation of the reasons for the success of the *commedia all'italiana*. In addition, the second part of the chapter explores the so-called "art of getting by" in the *commedia all'italiana*, representing the prototype of modern Italian comedic characters. Chapter four, "The Protagonists of the New Comedy Style," is organized around the most important filmmakers of the early sixties whose emblematic productions are the most representative of the new comedy in Italy. The list includes directors Dino Risi and his vivid social satires like *The Monsters* (*I mostri*, 1963) and *The Easy Life* (*Il sorpasso*, 1962), Mario Monicelli whose comedies often dealt with historical narratives like *The Great War* (*La grande guerra*, 1959), Luigi Comencini and *Everybody Go Home* (*Tutti a casa*, 1960), Pietro Germi with two seminal comedies centered on the south, most notably with the internationally acclaimed *Divorce Italian Style* (*Divorzio all'italiana*, 1961), as well as directors like Alberto Lattuada with *Mafioso* (1963), Antonio Pietrangeli's *The Magnificent Cuckold* (*Il magnifico cornuto*, 1964), and Luigi Zampa's *Il vigile* (1960). The third and final part, called "The Final Act of the *Commedia all'Italiana*," begins with chapter five, "Italian Comedy in the 1970s," and introduces a detailed analysis of the political situation during the "Lead Years," then shifts to examine the Italian film industry of the 1970s and the economic dilemma within the cinematographic industry that resulted in the deregulation of media laws and the subsequent greater presence and importance of television. In addition, this chapter focuses on Italian comedy following the economic boom with a careful eye to what Ettore Scola's filmmaking and his emblematic discourse of cynicism accomplished as well as how Marco Ferreri's inclination for the "grotesque style" exerted an influence on other Italian filmmakers, even outside the realm of film comedy. Finally, Chapter six "The Last Protagonists," presents the most important productions of the last decade, many of which were often mistaken for dramas due to the high level of cynicism, unconventionality, and tragic endings. The main protagonists of the final decade represented, although each with idiosyncratic humor, a scathing portrait of an amoral society; these include Dino Risi by now the most expert comedy filmmaker, Lina Wertmüller with her own exuberance and cinematographic virtuosity, Federico Fellini who accomplished a successful return to comedy, Alberto Sordi and his humanistic vision of social comedies, Mario Monicelli with the treatment of difficult subjects, and finally Luigi Comencini with his usual depth in terms of composition and narrative structure.

In an effort to acquaint English-speaking readers with some of the most emblematic dialogues and place in relief Italian humor of the *commedia all'italiana*, I have placed translations of film dialogues within the book. Because most of the original screenplays are not available or simply have never been published, I directly transcribed the dialogues from visual supports (mainly DVDs) and then translated the excerpts (with the assistance of film and language experts) into English, maintaining intact as much as possible the meaning and nature of Italian humor (instead of transcribing English subtitles which are often restrictive and inaccurate or translating faithfully the words).

Whereas Continuum and the author have made every effort to identify holders of copyright materials used in this book, in some particular instances this was not always possible, and we would like to extend our sincerest apologies to any copyright holders whose rights we may have unintentionally missed. If any omission exists, Continuum welcomes suggestions, and when possible will include them in any future editions of the work.

Part One

Before the Advent of the
Commedia all'Italiana

Chapter 1

The Forerunners

The purpose of this first chapter is to offer a panoramic view of the different functions of traditional Italian comedies with respect to their recurrent and influential effect on the *commedia all'italiana*, also known as comedy Italian style, which surfaced between the late fifties and the early sixties. The secondary objective is a demonstration that the *commedia all'italiana*, although deeply rooted in historical conventions, radically differed from its ancestors: the prewar *telefoni bianchi* and the *neorealismo rosa* of the postwar era.[1] The reasons for this radical transformation were several seminal and propitious contemporary events: the irresistible wind of change caused by the advent of the economic boom, the widespread distribution of television and resulting dynamics between small and large screen, the initial decline of state censorship over the film industry maintained for a decade by the Christian Democrat administration, and finally, exceptional artistic dynamics created by phenomenal actors, screenwriters, and filmmakers. Entirely original and idiosyncratic by nature, comedy Italian style was able to synthesize not only a new lifestyle, but also a national identity and a unique cinematography, which triggered an immediate enthusiastic response among popular audiences. With secured success at the box office, and growing support of producers, the *commedia all'italiana* successfully moved forward to become the financial backbone of the entire Italian film industry for well over the next two decades.

The Origins of Italian Comedy

The volume's central discussion answers seminal questions on the *commedia*'s identity to gain a more comprehensive vision of the genre, including the following: What is the fascination and influence of cynical comedies, social satires, and grotesque parodies? What is the relationship between comedy and narratives?

Why do Italian comedies almost always include a minor yet significant dose of (un)predictable tragedy? Do Italian satires merely represent the product of literary ingenuity or the visual record of a quotidian human experience? Can a fictive comic tale have any significance with regard to morality, human psychology, or any other realm of philosophical reflection? Can a narration or screenplay enlighten the readers/spectators about the complexities of human struggle? As Italian film historian Aldo Viganò once wrote, "There are two faithful sources of inspiration for Italian pop culture: lyrical opera and *commedia dell'arte*."[2] Therefore, it comes as no surprise that for Anglo-Saxon spectatorship, the Italian comic mind, heir of a long tradition of literary realism, is based on a combination of authentic dramatic narratives contradicted by comic situations.

Finally, the following reading of the present volume needs an imperative semantic clarification. Neglected by many film historians, the subtle differentiations between the different phases of evolution related to Italian comedy deserve today a long-awaited explicit articulation, which will shed light on the numerous and confusing labels attributed to the respective époques of the Italian comedy. The first that comes to mind is the prestigious *commedia dell'arte*, the ancient art of satirical theater from the Italian Renaissance, which often serves as a point of reference throughout the present volume, as it is the historical source of inspiration for the large part of Italian comedies. Second, the term *commedia italiana* often corresponds to the conventional bourgeois comedies of the postwar era, usually dominated by slapstick humor, many of which belong to the *neorealismo rosa* period. Finally, and most importantly, the term *commedia all'italiana*, also called "comedy Italian style," designates comedies from approximately 1958 to 1979 that all share a common denominator: a new type of ruthless social satires through the lens of cynicism and grotesque. Therefore, for the sake of the present study's comprehension, it is crucial for the reader to bear in mind the above-mentioned terminology.

Before any attempt is made to draft definitions of comedy Italian style and conceptualize its principles, it is important to keep in mind that Italian humor has always shown inherent interest in faithfully observing reality and society while simultaneously presenting a "de-sacralizing" vision of the world. For centuries, Italian comedies have functioned as vehicles for social satires that ultimately represented the dark aspect of human nature and society's evils. The golden age of Italian comedy, the *commedia all'italiana*, asserted itself at the very end of the 1950s to blossom in the 1960s and ended as a principal genre at the end of the 1970s.[3] The phenomenon, the most prolific Italian cinematographic movement considering the number of long feature films produced in two consecutive decades, was the unexpected result of decades of long culmination from political and socioeconomic aftermaths. In his article "Le istituzioni del comico e la forma-commedia," Maurizio Grande underlined the constant dilemma for comical protagonists—between acceptance into society and their rejection from it—through four different thematic contents of comedies: narratives linked to the integration into society, narratives linked to the forced adjustment to social norms, narratives linked to concealed identity, and narratives linked to lost innocence.[4] One could easily superimpose an ensemble of subgenres to Grande's categorization: comedies of societal customs, social satires, musical comedies, romantic comedies, burlesque comedies (including farces and vaudevilles), among others. However, in order to better understand the authentic nature and evolution of Italian satirical comedies, and despite the above-mentioned categorizations, the present volume will privilege both chronological and thematic approaches.

Throughout the centuries of prolific national history, Italian popular culture has always valued humor as the ultimate weapon of wit; an impressive achievement if one considers the innumerable cultural referents to Italian humor around the world. Whether in the medieval conventions of short stories dear to Boccaccio's *Decameron* and his strong vein of irony or sarcasm, or Renaissance taste for farces like Machiavelli's *La mandragola* (1524), or the *commedia dell'arte* with Carlo Goldoni (1707–93), the so-called *beffa* (Italian medieval farce) has been at the epicenter of Italian comedy writers' modus operandi.

As previously mentioned, the primary intention of this chapter is to present the main traits that constituted Italian traditional comedy before the advent of the *commedia all'italiana* at the end of the 1950s. The goal is then to introduce some of the most prominent aspects of film forms, narratives, and history that contributed to the formation of the comedy genre between 1945 and circa 1958. Asserting that Italian comedy (as opposed to the *commedia all'italiana*) indirectly took its roots from the ancient Greek comedy is certainly nothing new, as the characterization during its development in history and its connection to its first early modern rendition with the medieval farce, also known as the *beffa,* and, of course, the *commedia dell'arte* after the sixteenth century, has been the center of much scholarly research. And it is precisely this improvisational theater, which for more than four centuries has shaped and defined Italian humor and comedy until the present. Filmmaker Mario Monicelli (b. in 1915), author of numerous comedy films over the course of seven decades, gave a persuasive definition of the ancient tradition, stressing the importance of the combination of laughter and despair as an omnipresent theme in Italian comedy:

> This is truly part of the Italian tradition; it's something that comes from the *commedia dell'arte*. *Commedia dell'arte* heroes are always desperate poor devils who are battling against life, against the world, against hunger, misery, illness, violence. Nevertheless, all of this is transformed into laughter, transmuted into cruel joking, in mockery rather than

wholehearted laughter. This approach belongs to a very Italian tradition that I have always defended.[5]

The *commedia dell'arte* was not only known for its astute protagonists who successfully and happily trespassed on established social rules or for its legendary use of masks and improvisation, but also for its inherent ability to promote prolific dialogues, a quintessential dynamic of the artistic performance. The *commedia dell'arte* of Arlecchino, *servitore di due padroni*, was in a certain sense conjuring misery and injustice by evoking the possibility that he could refuse the established order and established forms of power. Though limited in its audience scope, the *commedia* discourse was a flickering light of hope, soon perfected by Molière (1622–73) and later Carlo Goldoni (who despite the improvement brought to the genre, institutionalized its dynamics and consequently fossilized them into literary conventions).[6] Whether satire, parody, farce, or even simple burlesque comedies, contemporary Italian humor has excelled in its popular proliferation by effectively transforming any given dimension of ridicule into a sophisticated work of derision. During its two glorious decades, comedy Italian style possessed an inherent particularity, as it appeared to be a genre without a myth or rather mythical paradigm (unlike Westerns, Peplums, or historical films, which all included it), as Italian film scholar Aldo Viganò noted:

> Unlike Westerns, horror films, musical comedies or melodrama, comedy is in fact a genre without mythological characters and places. Its main referent is never something archaic and universal, but rather is linked to quotidian life and [harsh] reality.[7]

Indeed, the examination of the specific uses of humor in the *commedia* provides a thorough understanding of the role of the films and their intended focus on the vicissitudes of Italian individuals struggling in daily life through the advent of modernity and economic changes (as Totò often liked to remind film critics "misery is the script of true comedy"). This introduction illuminates the present perspective on this under-explored yet extremely popular entertainment genre, and the profound disposition of Italian satires to provide sociological interrogations, introspective examinations, and perhaps to reveal its indifference (or excess of critical distance) towards the film medium itself.

According to Ettore Scola, "The *commedia all'italiana* comes from anonymous parents, but we are all sons of the *commedia all'italiana*."[8] Coming from one of its most prolific writers, this *battuta* implies the unfathomable dimension of the origins and its endless quest for the original creators. The many varieties of comic disciplines would certainly constitute too vast and diverse of a field for an introduction to this genre. Therefore, it is from the absence of emotional and historical background (or mythical entourage) that the new comedy Italian style created its very own tradition, straight from the daily reality of the booming sixties, such as in Vittorio De Sica's *Il boom* (1963), Dino Risi's *A Difficult Life* (*Una vita difficile*, 1961), or *The Easy Life* (*Il sorpasso*, 1962).

The Silent Era and the Prestige of Hollywood Comedies

Evolving into the third largest film industry (far behind France and the U.S.) due to its organizational atomization and lack of centralized structures, Italian silent productions were mainly dominated by an inclination toward historical reconstitutions (i.e., Mario Caserini and Eleuterio Rodolfi's *Last Days of Pompeii* [*Gli ultimi giorni di Pompei*, 1913] or Enrico Guazzoni's *Marc'Antonio e Cleopatra*, 1913). Italian comedies of the silent era were characterized by the success of the *Cretinetti* series (authored and interpreted by French actor André Deed before World War I) and the so-called "*comica finale*," a popular subgenre usually presented after the screening of long feature films of cinematographic shows. One of the popular comic genres was burlesque comedy, whose culmination extended from the invention of the cinematograph (1895 in Lyon, France) to the last years of World War I. The best representative was dramaturge and screenwriter Lucio d'Ambra (1880–1939) who collaborated with many filmmakers, including Carmine Gallone, an immensely popular professional. With silent productions such as *Il re, le torri, gli alfieri* (1916), *Wives and Oranges* (*Le mogli e le arance*, 1917), *Il girotondo degli undici lancieri* (1919), all directed and written by d'Ambra, a new influential style became popular among general audiences (reportedly inspiring Ernst Lubitsch himself). However, over the course of a few years, d'Ambra's appreciation slowly diminished with the Italian public for its lack of renewal and ambition, as his style was often compared to *commedie leggere* (a slightly pejorative term to describe less innovative narratives meaning in Italian "light" comedies). The silent film era was described as a very codified art, and therefore did not possess much leverage for innovation, which explains why Italian comedy was never prolific nor competitive during these early years (i.e., with the exception of Alessandro Blasetti's *Sole!* in 1928, and Mario Camerini's *Rotaie* in 1929 being distributed abroad). Unlike France, which did not have a similar multidialectal situation but benefited from an important production of silent film comedies, Italy was gifted with many different regional vernaculars and therefore dialect comedies had to wait for the advent of sound in order to flourish. The *battuta* or comic line made its beginnings on the large screen and served as a catalyst for popular audiences to remember a film for its memorable line rather than physical feats of skill.

Two actors can be labeled as the modern forefathers of the future comedy Italian style. Famous in part due to his play entitled *Nerone* (1917), and later in Alessandro Blasetti's film version *Nerone* (1930), Ettore Petrolini

(1884–1936) developed an artistic significance with the long-time neglected farce genre reminiscent of the *commedia dell'arte*. In this pioneering "sound" satire on the excesses generated by the lust of power, Petrolini's multiple personae were able to coax and elude the censorship of the Fascist regime. Along with Petrolini, Raffaele Viviani (1888–1950), the other celebrated albeit short-lived protagonist of the Neapolitan theater scene, specialized in comedy rooted in the lower depths of society (far from Eduardo De Filippo's bourgeois comedies, as for instance with Alessandro Blasetti's *La tavola dei poveri*, 1932). Since the golden age of the *commedia dell'arte*, tragic and comic elements had never been so close. In these days, comedies not only depended on genuine feats of skills and other physical tours de force, but were also regulated on precise comedic timing. The crescendo preceding a liberating *battuta* had to be synchronized to the right moment: a second too late or too early and an entire scene could lose its effect, miss its point, and ultimately let a film fall into oblivion.

The silent era eventually came to an end in the late twenties with the first talking pictures from America (Alan Crossland's *The Jazz Singer*, 1927), bringing a wind of change to all European national cinemas. In 1930, Gennaro Righelli's *La canzone dell'amore*, based on a short story written by Luigi Pirandello (1867–1936), coincidentally named *In Silenzio*, opened the way for many successful musical comedies, as it was also the very first Italian "talking" motion picture film to be released in Italian theaters the following year. With the urgent need to reestablish themselves with the Italian cinema industry, many veteran Italian filmmakers and comedy authors found inspiration from comedies made in Hollywood. Inspired by the American comedy tradition made famous by Howard Hawks' *Bringing Up Baby* (1938), Ernst Lubitsch's *Ninotchka* (1939), Frank Capra's *It Happened One Night* (1934), George Cukor's *The Philadelphia Story* (1940), or later Billy Wilder's *Some Like It Hot* (1959), Italian comedies of the prewar era maintained a similar cinematography, albeit in their own style, many of which ranged from character-driven absurd humor to compilations of clever gags.[9] Some similarities are worth noting, such as the happy ending so characteristic of Hollywood comedies in the late 1930s and subsequently implemented in the *telefoni bianchi* comedies (literally known as "white telephones"). In addition, protagonists evolved in an Italy rather unknown to popular audiences, one in which money, luxury, and fictive romance stood light-years away from the spectatorship's quotidian life. In a similar manner to its American counterpart, Italian comedy protagonists rarely dealt with money concerns on screen (with the exception of Camerini's *I Will Give a Million* [*Darò un milione*] starring Vittorio De Sica in 1936).[10] Perhaps the most compelling difference that persisted between the two national comedy styles was the predominance of the notion of an attainable "dream" in Hollywood narratives, whereas Italian comedy offered more realistic endings; though neglected in the narratives, social elements and their ineluctable consequences eventually regained their relevance at the end of Italian films. With the prestige of Hollywood comedies reaching out to Italian writers and producers, a strong element of choreography surfaced in new comedies of the sound era, inspired by musical comedies, and their inherent theatricalization of the plot, all converging toward a greater cinematic sophistication.

The Prewar Era, Cinecittà, and *Telefoni Bianchi*

Italian cinema in the thirties was dominated by the omnipresent censorship of the Fascist regime, and when it was not solicited, most filmmakers, like Mario Camerini or Alessandro Blasetti, took upon themselves an even more disconcerting resolution of self-censorship. Although comedy would have been the only genre to possibly outsmart the wheels of Mussolini's censorship, no significant production could claim such a feat.

Romantic comedies, melodramatic cinema, and sophisticated narrations inspired by the refined comedies made in Hollywood all came from the same mold; these comedies stood light-years away from the contemporary hardships encountered by Italian popular audiences. The "a-temporal" approach to narration clearly defined the new comic genre of the decade in Italy. Following the Fascist regime's modest and temporary conquest of colonial victories in Africa (Ethiopia in May 1936 along with the protectorate of Libya, Eritrea, and Somalia), the government drove Italian popular audiences toward new allegorical horizons: fictionalized realities became the norm and blurred the then current political realities. In addition, the scarcity of innovation and the lack of thematic diversity contributed to the temporary stagnation of the comedy genre.

Mussolini's decision to implement a partial ban on the importation of Hollywood films (January 1, 1939) left Italian comedies with little or no competition; in response, Hollywood's major distributors—MGM, Paramount, Twentieth Century Fox, and Warner Bros—withdrew from the Italian market in protest. Despite the unusual international climate that favored a strategy of "easy escapism," the decade produced some fine Italian comedies. The revelation came from a young Neapolitan actor, Vittorio De Sica, who quickly proved to become the prodigy of the prewar era. He was featured in Mario Camerini's *What Scoundrels Men Are!* (*Gli uomini che mascalzoni*, 1932) followed by similar successes in *I'll Give a Million* (*Darò un milione*, 1936), *Mister Max* (*Il signor Max*, 1937), and *Department Store* (*I grandi magazzini*, 1939). With the exception of Camerini's cinema, which displayed a modest attempt to satirize, all the comedy films of the decade employed the same model: mundane bourgeois comedies that had few innovations or unexpected twists.

This era of the so-called *telefoni bianchi* ("white telephones"), which began in 1937 and ended in 1941, was defined by a period of political jubilation as well as a popular euphoria with the rediscovery by middle-class Italians of the possibilities for entertainment (in great part generated by Fascist propaganda). Consequently, the entertainment industry, and cinema in particular, were the first to benefit from this emerging trend, which also corresponded with the inauguration of the mythical Cinecittà on April 28, 1937. The short-lived phenomenon could best be epitomized by an artistic orientation to display, more or less forcefully, a glamorous cinematography that included at least one scene of a luxurious interior with protagonists using the emblematic white telephone, symbol of wealth and elegance as opposed to the common and ordinary black telephone. Once again, many filmmakers felt compelled to self-censor and consequently turned their expertise toward a so-called "light comedy" style that included the artists' comic *battute*. With World War II, the wind changed, and Italian popular audiences began to realize that these comedies no longer corresponded with their expectations, in terms of entertainment, and the phenomenon disappeared as quickly as it had surfaced a few years earlier. Alessandro Blasetti's *Four Steps in the Clouds* (*Quattro passi fra le nuvole*, 1942), which heralded the advent of the first neorealism elements in comedies, confirmed the trend of the moment to search for tangible answers rather than inaccessible dreams.

The *Marc'Aurelio* and the New Screenwriters

Italian satirical comedies, unlike the French and the Anglo-Saxon, had the unique ability to observe signs of the time without artistic concession. The compelling observations of postwar-era Italy revealed the difficult, quite humoristic apprenticeship of democracy as unprecedented political events evolved with an ever-increasing speed. As World War II came to an abrupt end, and as Italy prepared for its colossal reconstruction effort, the question of popular entertainment remained predominant in its relevance to the evolution of culture among Italian popular audiences.

One of the primary concerns of film scholars was the preoccupation of the genre's literary origins. In the case of the *commedia dell'arte*, the answer, as previously mentioned, evoked the ancient literary source as an evident inspiration in its form and content, while *commedia all'italiana* seems to be just the opposite. As a matter of fact, one could take this idea further along by arguing that indeed no contemporary literature can rightly claim exclusive paternity of the new comedy genre since most of its inspiration came from oral sources. With the exception of satirical journals, the entire paradigm came from the people and meet its literary elite. Director Mario Monicelli describes the fundamental nonliterary dimension of comedy Italian style:

> Most likely, *Un borghese piccolo piccolo* is not a *commedia all'italiana*. Above all, coming from a novel from [Vincenzo] Cerami, it did not have

that intention. It became a *commedia all'italiana* only because it has been interpreted by Sordi.[11]

Italian satirical publications were one of the important bases of development of comic films during the first part of the twentieth century. One of them, the *Marc'Aurelio,* founded in Rome in 1914, was a prosperous satirical magazine, which included many renowned collaborators during the Fascist years of the 1930s, such as Vittorio Metz (1904–84) and Cesare Zavattini (1902–89). Its success triggered the creation of similar periodicals, like *Bertoldo,* begun in Milan in 1937 by Giovannino Guareschi (1908–68) and Giovanni Mosca (1908–83), and later, the *Candido* in 1945, which produced a long series of *vignettisti caricaturisti* (caricaturists) whose caustic and nonconformist satirical humor was extremely popular among the Italian middle class. These prewar-era years became important as the moment when a new modern comic mind took shape, entirely original and extremely fertile in comedic appeal. Vittorio Metz himself defined the new comedy style:

> We Italian humorists stand out from French and what is considered English humor, since for years we have evolved on a completely different field. Our [humor] is animated, dismaying, fulminating, a violent comedy that has the rare quality to reach easily both intellectuals and the people.[12]

Thanks to its surrealist tone, the *Marc'Aurelio* avoided much government censorship, as the bulk of its satirical caricatures were taken from everyday life or chronicles of daily newspapers. By the end of the decade, it had a prosperous turnout of 400,000 copies per edition, and was in its own way a medium of resistance to fascism, as with subtle persuasion it was able to convey a humor underlying the fictitious integrity of the Fascist press. The *Marc'Aurelio,* though benefiting from a national prestige, had to compete with other publications such as *Il Travaso, La Tribuna, Don Basilio, Calendario,* or *Bufamario.* From this unprecedented concentration of talent, a new generation of screenwriters was born, whose particularity did not emerge from the traditional mold of cinematographic critique but rather a literary background, already comfortable with transformation of the content of quotidian reality into witty vignettes. After the war, most of them entered the Italian film industry to collaborate on screenplays for the neorealist comedies, a genre in high demand. Screenwriters like Vitaliano Brancati[13] (1907–54), Achille Campanile[14] (1899–1977), Oreste Del Buono (1923–2003), Federico Fellini[15] (1920–93), Alessandro Continenza[16] (1920–96), Ennio de Concini[17] (b. 1923), Ennio Flaiano[18] (1910–72), Ruggero Maccari[19] (1919–89), Marcello Marchesi[20] (1912–78), Steno[21] (1915–88), and Ettore Scola[22] (b. 1931) met regularly in public places and in one particular bar, the now famous "Otello della Concordia," in via della croce in Rome.

Interestingly enough, the momentum of the satirical publications as well as the interest in the tradition of *avanspettacolo* diminished during the post-war era before falling into oblivion at the end of the 1950s, coincidently corresponding with the sudden advent of the *commedia all'italiana* on the big screen. It was precisely the *avanspettacolo* (comic shows presented before a live audience in between two feature films), a subgenre of comedy/theater, that gained visible notoriety between the 1930s and the first years of the economic boom. Heir of the *teatro di varietà* (variety shows), the *avanspettacolo* was designed to entertain popular audiences before the screening of the main feature film, hence its brief duration. Because of the unpredictable nature of the comic challenge, the genre was never considered an authentic protagonist of the comedy scene, though it was the springboard of many artists like Ettore Petrolini, the forerunner of the genre, and also Erminio Macario (1902–80), Totò (1898–1967), and Renato Rascel (1912–91), among others.

Notes

[1] These comedies also evoke, for the most part, a sense of remote past that directly recalls the image of an anarchical medieval time, much like Boccaccio's *Decameron* and the famous *beffa* (medieval farce).

[2] Aldo Viganò, *Commedia italiana in cento film* (Genoa: Le mani, 1995), 11.

[3] Dino Risi was the first filmmaker to openly criticize the new label generated by the Italian critique. The main contention was based on the fact that the title *all'italiana* denied the Italian specificity of what was done before: "Perché questo giudizio limitativo, riduttivo? Le commedie prodotte in America si chiamano commedie americane, quelle che facciamo in Italia su delle situazioni e dei problemi nazionali, chiamamole commedie italiane e basta. I critici amano le etichette, le formule che spesso si rivelano odiose, nocive e il più delle volte improprie." ("Why such a limiting and reductive judgment? Comedies produced in America are called American comedies; the ones we do in Italy on problems and situations of national scale, let's call them Italian comedies, and that's it. Critics love labels, formulas that at the end prove to be awful, negative and most of the time inappropriate." Translated from Italian by the author.) Claver Salizzato and Vito Zagarrio, eds., *Effetto commedia: teoria, generi, paesaggi della commedia cinematografica* (Rome: Di Giacomo Editore, 1985), 205.

[4] Maurizio Grande, "Le istituzioni del comico e la forma-commedia," in Ricardo Napolitano, ed., *Commedia all'italiana* (Rome: Gangemi, 1986), 37–54.

[5] Jean A. Gili, *Italian Filmmakers' Self-Portraits: A Selection of Interviews* (Rome: Gremese, 1998), 75.

[6] Although arguing that the *commedia dell'arte's* primary origins could possibly be traced back to Aristofane, Cratino, and Eupoli certainly makes sense; it however does not correspond to the subject of the present volume.

[7] Translated by the author from Italian: "A differenza del Western o dell'horror, del musical o del melodramma, la commedia è infatti, un genere privo di mitologia.

Il suo referente principale cioè, non è mai qualcosa di arcaico e universale, ma ha sempre a che fare con il quotidiano e il contingente." Aldo Viganò, *Commedia italiana in cento film*, 12.

[8] Translated by the author from Italian: "La commedia all'italiana è di genitori ignoti, ma siamo tutti figli della commedia all'italiana."

[9] Standing far away from mainstream Hollywood comedies of the time, the comedies of Charlie Chaplin (*The Gold Rush* in 1925 or *Modern Times* in 1936) were a rare exception, since its humor was partly based on an acute observation of life and its tragic outcome.

[10] Located in France for the present purpose.

[11] Translated in English by the author from Pietro Pintus' *Storia e film: Trent'anni di cinema italiano (1945–1975)* (Rome: Bulzoni, 1980), 149: "Molto probabilmente, *Un borghese piccolo piccolo* non è una commedia all'italiana. Oltre tutto, essendo tratto da un romanzo di Cerami, non aveva quell'intento. E' diventato una commedia all'italiana solo perché è stato interpretato da Sordi...."

[12] Translated by the author from Italian: "Noi umoristi italiani siamo fuori dal binario della comicità francese e da quello del cosiddetto humor inglese e avanziamo da anni su di un terreno del tutto diverso. Il nostro è un tipo di umorismo acceso, sconcertante, fulminante, un umorismo violento che possiede la rarissima qualità di arrivare facilmente sia all'intellettuale che al popolo." Ricardo Napolitano, *Commedia all'italiana*: *Angolazioni controcampi* (Rome: Gangemi, 1986), 23.

[13] Vitaliano Brancati's collaboration for screenplay includes Luigi Zampa's *Difficult Years* (*Anni difficili*, 1948), *The Art of Getting Along* (*L'arte di arrangiarsi*, 1955), and Steno and Mario Monicelli's *Cops and Robbers* (*Guardie e ladri*, 1951).

[14] Achille Campanile's collaboration for screenplay includes Alessandro Blasetti's *The Anatomy of Love* (*Tempi nostri*, 1954).

[15] Federico Fellini's collaboration as a writer also includes Alberto Lattuada's *Variety Lights* (*Luci del varietà*, 1950), among many other films.

[16] Alessandro Continenza's prolific collaboration as a writer includes Mario Monicelli's *Totò Looks for an Apartment* (*Totò cerca casa*, 1949); Mario Mattoli's *Neapolitan Turk* (*Un Turco napoletano*, 1953); Steno's *A Day in Court* (*Un giorno in pretura*, 1954) and *An American in Rome* (*Un americano a Roma*, 1954); Antonio Pietrangeli's *The Bachelor* (*Lo scapolo*, 1955); and Dino Risi's *Love and Larceny* (*Il mattatore*, 1959).

[17] Ennio de Concini's collaboration as a writer also includes Mario Monicelli's *Totò and the King of Rome* (*Totò e i re di Roma*, 1951); Mario Camerini's *Sunday Heroes* (*Gli eroi della domenica*, 1953); and Dino Risi's *Weekend, Italian Style* (*L'ombrellone*, 1966) and *The Treasure of San Gennaro* (*Operazione San Gennaro*, 1966).

[18] Ennio Flaiano's collaboration in screenwriting also includes Luciano Emmer's *Paris Is Always Paris* (*Parigi è sempre Parigi*, 1951); Federico Fellini's *I vitelloni* (1953), *The Swindle* (*Il bidone*, 1955), and *La dolce vita* (1960); Alessandro Blasetti's *Too Bad She's Bad* (*Peccato che sia una canaglia*, 1954); Dino Risi's *The Sign of Venus* (*Il segno di Venere*, 1955); Federico Fellini's *Boccaccio '70* (1962) for the segment "Le tentazioni del dottor Antonio"; and Gian Luigi Polidoro's *Run for Your Wife* (*Una moglie americana*, 1965).

[19] Maccari's impressive list of collaborations would be difficult to summarize due to the exceptional number of partnerships mainly with Dino Risi and Ettore Scola. Some of his most important works include Steno and Mario Monicelli's *Cops and Robbers* (*Guardie e ladri*, 1951) and *High Infidelity* (*Alta infedeltà*, 1964); Giorgio Simonelli's *Accadde al commissariato* (1954); Giorgio Bianchi's *Accadde al penitenziario* (1955) and *Count Max* (*Il Conte Max*, 1957); Dino Risi's *Love and Larceny* (*Il mattatore*, 1959), *The Easy Life* (*Il sorpasso*, 1962), *The Gaucho* (*Il gaucho*, 1965), *The Monsters* (*I mostri*, 1963), *March on Rome* (*La marcia su Roma*, 1963), *Complexes* (*I complessi*, 1965) segment "Una giornata decisiva", *The Priest's Wife* (*La moglie del prete*, 1971), *How Funny Can Sex Be?* (*Sessomatto*, 1973), *The New Monsters* (*I nuovi mostri*, 1977); Luigi Zampa's *Roaring Years* (*Gli anni ruggenti*, 1962); Antonio Pietrangeli's *The Magnificent Cuckold* (*Il magnifico cornuto*, 1965), *The Visitor* (*La visita*, 1963), *The Girl from Parma* (*La Parmigiana*, 1963), *I Knew Her Well* (*Io la conoscevo bene*, 1965); Ettore Scola's *Let's Talk About Women* (*Se permettete parliamo di donne*, 1964), *The Devil in Love* (*L'arcidiavolo*, 1966), *Down and Dirty* (*Brutti sporchi e cattivi*, 1976), and *A Special Day* (*Una giornata particolare*, 1977); Mauro Morassi's *The Success* (*Il successo*, 1963); Franco Giraldi's *Big Baby Doll* (*La bambolona*, 1968); and Luigi Comencini's *Bottleneck* (*L'ingorgo: Una storia impossibile*, 1979).

[20] Mario Mattoli's *Imputato alzatevi!* (1939); Mario Mattoli's *Totò al giro d'Italia* (1948); Mario Monicelli and Steno's *Totò Looks for an Apartment* (*Totò cerca casa*, 1949); Luigi Comencini's *The Emperor of Capri* (*L'imperatore di Capri*, 1949); Carlo Ludovico Bragaglia's *47 morto che parla* (1950); Camillo Mastrocinque's *Totò, lascia o raddoppia?* (1956); Edoardo Anton and Carlo Infascelli's *Follie d'estate* (1963).

[21] Steno's production as a writer also includes Mario Monicelli's *Totò Looks for an Apartment* (*Totò cerca casa*, 1949), *A Dog's Life* (*Vita da cani*, 1950), *Totò and the King of Rome* (*Totò e i re di Roma*, 1951), *Cops and Robbers* (*Guardie e ladri*, 1951), and Mario Mattoli's *The Firemen of Viggiu* (*I pompieri di Viggiù*, 1949).

[22] Ettore Scola's contribution for screenwriting and dialogues can be found in Steno's *An American in Rome* (*Un americano a Roma*, 1954); Antonio Pietrangeli's *The Bachelor* (*Lo scapolo*, 1955), *The Visitor* (*La visita*, 1963), *The Girl from Parma* (*La parmigiana*, 1963), *The Magnificent Cuckold* (*Il magnifico cornuto*, 1964), *I Knew Her Well* (*Io la conoscevo bene*, 1965); Giorgio Bianchi's *Count Max* (*Il Conte Max*, 1957); Nanni Loy's *Il marito* (1958); Luigi Zampa's *Roaring Years* (*Gli anni ruggenti*, 1962), *Follie d'estate* (1963); Dino Risi's *Love and Larceny* (*Il mattatore*, 1959), *The Easy Life* (*Il sorpasso*, 1962), *The Monsters* (*I mostri*, 1963), *March on Rome* (*La marcia su Roma*, 1963), *The Gaucho* (*Il gaucho*, 1965), *Complexes* (*I complessi*, 1965) segment "Una giornata decisiva", and *The New Monsters* (*I nuovi mostri*, 1977); as well as his very own *The Devil in Love* (*L'arcidiavolo*, 1966), *Drama of Jealousy* (*Dramma della gelosia: tutti i particolari in cronaca*, 1970), *The Most Wonderful Evening of My Life* (*La più bella serata della mia vita*, 1972), *We All Loved Each Other So Much* (*C'eravamo tanto amati*, 1974), *Down and Dirty* (*Brutti sporchi e cattivi*, 1976), *A Special Day* (*Una giornata particolare*, 1977); and Luigi Comencini, Nanni Loy, Luigi Magni, and Mario Monicelli's *Goodnight, Ladies and Gentlemen* (*Signore e signori, buonanotte*, 1978), *The Terrace* (*La terrazza*, 1980).

Chapter 2

The Age of *Neorealismo Rosa*

Far from being an ephemeral interlude in cinema history, Italian neorealism (1943–52) was able in just a few years to define a new vision of the world through the seventh art, by focusing on the representation of reality with an unprecedented visual meticulousness. Its intellectual integrity and force not only drove many filmmakers to adopt and apply its artistic point of view for other genres (drama, comedies, documentaries, and so forth), but it also represented the only cinema worth exportation for other spectatorships at the end of the 1940s. Comedy was also at that time a vector for new cinematographic concepts. As Mario Monicelli described it, neorealism was not the only way to put twenty years of hardship and misery behind, and in its own way, humor on the big screen could move crowds, albeit not with the realistic vision of Vittorio De Sica's *Bicycle Thief* (*Ladri di biciclette*, 1948) or Roberto Rossellini's *Germany Year Zero* (*Germania, anno zero*, 1948), but it opened new perspectives to the popular audience. As Mario Monicelli stated, "Laughter became a chance for redemption, a liberating experience, the losers' voice that was rising against the social rules."[1]

Neorealism and *Neorealismo Rosa* in Question

According to French historian Jean Gili, the new observation of reality through a sensible social conscience during the wake of World War II broke new ground in the intimate rapport between Italian comedy and social conscience: "Neorealism put the comedy genre back on a road it should have never left, if it were not for twenty years of Fascism: the observation of Italy's social problems by humor, irony, satire."[2] Caught between a film genre and a cinematographic movement, Italian neorealism, against all odds, served as a vehicle to reorganize and conceptualize a genre almost abandoned by most talented comedy filmmakers. In 1945, Italian general audiences were experiencing a serious "deficit in laughter," but despite the non-comical nature of neorealist cinematography, the latter was able to inspire countless comedy filmmakers. This connection to neorealism is obvious with the legendary scene in Roberto Rossellini's *Open City* (*Roma, città aperta*, 1945) where Don Pietro Pellegrini (Aldo Fabrizi), a priest working clandestinely for the resistance, hits an old man with a cooking pan in order to keep him silent while nearby German soldiers search the building. This episode became the emblematic scene par excellence of what neorealism had to convey toward future genres self-proclaimed as heirs of its legacy. For screenwriter Rodolfo Sonego, the comedy element even in the darkest tragedies such as Rossellini's *Open City* was acting as a safety valve, a device without which no narrative could fully operate in the spectator's mind. As Italian film scholar Pietro Pintus explained:

> The comic element becomes the catalyst for the evil present inside the narrative material. Probably, [it is] a necessity not only for the author but for the audience that leads to building humoristic solutions in order to digest this evil, this tragedy.[3]

One of the prominent filmmakers directly inspired by the neorealist movement was Luciano Emmer, with *Domenica d'agosto* (1950) and *Le ragazze di Piazza di Spagna* (1953). Both films, coauthored by screenwriter Sergio Amidei (1904–81) and inspired by parallel narrative structures reminiscent of Rossellini's *Paisà*, presented a multitude of characters that energized the screen with a new *comicità* generated by situations that mixed collective experience with individuality. Another example was Mario Monicelli's *Totò Looks for an Apartment* (*Totò cerca casa*, 1949), an early film dealing with a contemporary issue whose implications were urgent social issues (the question of housing in those years of the postwar era). Vitttorio De Sica's *Miracle in Milan* (*Miracolo a Milano*, 1951), though not a comedy per se, uniquely added a fantastic dimension to a comedic narrative. Though the film included a myriad of visual innovations, it was never considered part of the *neorealismo rosa* (romanticized comedies through the lens of realism) as it appeared in most anthologies of Italian comedies, since its tone and style clearly differed from mainstream popular comedies of the decade (a forerunner of magic realism rather than *commedia all'italiana*). In addition to the above-mentioned comedies, it is important to point out some other comedy experiences whose commercial release as well as artistic achievement contributed to the history of Italian comedies. These films include Gennaro Righelli's *Down with Misery* (*Abbasso la miseria*, 1948), Luigi Zampa's *L'onorevole Angelina* (1948), Monicelli's *Vita da cani* (1950), and Steno and Monicelli's *Guardie e ladri* (1951)—the latter will be studied further in this introduction.

As the box office of the decade revealed, the comedy genre was highly popular in the postwar years, as many filmmakers invested time and money in order to produce popular comedies (i.e., Totò made 64 comedy films between 1945 and 1960 and a total of 107 in his entire career). Unlike many other comic actors, Totò's films always included a social background that depicted an element of misery inherent in Italian society's lower class. One example, illustrated in Monicelli's *Totò cerca casa*, brilliantly depicted the tragedy of homelessness and severe unemployment. As evident as the present connection with the neorealist movement may be, the immediate postwar era is still remembered to this day for its exceptional neorealist productions rather than the comedies themselves.

Concomitantly with the conclusion of the neorealist experience, a new comedy flavor surfaced under the label of *neorealismo rosa*, and gained importance and recognition from Italian popular audiences. This comedy style never was, nor was intended to be, a subgenre of neorealism, though the name may bring confusion (the first reason that comes to mind being its remote interest in social and political issues). In addition, the new comedy style was limited in its organization, themes, and artistic development; dependent on conventional narrative frames; and rarely in tune with the social economic and political contemporary background. *Neorealismo rosa* came from a combination of neorealism (for lead actors) and *avanspettacolo* scenarios (for supporting roles). Unlike neorealism, which began before the end of the war, *neorealismo rosa* originated at the beginning of the 1950s to compensate the neorealist artistic preponderance (though only a small minority of Italian moviegoers saw the neorealist masterpieces at a time when "sad" films were not commercially successful). So the question of a potential reaction may be better explained in terms of inspiration rather than opposition. The roots of *neorealismo rosa* should be examined with the same method as for neorealism: as a reaction to the war and two decades of fictionalized propaganda. As Ettore Scola explained:

> During those years, as a possible reaction to neorealism, to its grave and tragic films on Italy destroyed by bombs and poverty, the first Italian comedies were characterized by superficial films, which used anything to make people laugh but were not completely honest.[4]

Scola is right in his assertion that *neorealismo rosa* wanted to move away from the patterns of neorealism, even though at the end it appeared to be a reaction to prewar comedies (1930s as well as 1940s) more than a reaction to neorealism. The *neorealismo rosa* definition could be best described as an authentic observation of pseudodramatic reality through a comic lens. One of the characteristics attributed to the new *neorealismo rosa* was its prominent element of *qualunquismo* (indifference), reducing social issues to the trivial or remote background. Sentimentalism was usually at the basis of the plot, the inexorable love intrigue as a primary narrative element, as for instance, in the manifesto film from Luigi Comencini entitled *Bread, Love and Dreams*

(*Pane, amore e fantasia*, 1953), followed a year later by *Bread, Love and Jealousy* (*Pane, amore e gelosia*, 1954) starring Gina Lollobrigida and Vittorio De Sica. With such casts, the new genre was far from the precepts of neorealism, since their productions used very few nonprofessional actors.[5] Another major difference with the preceding movement was the substitution of a sociopolitical investigation by a custom satire heavily based on national or regional characterizations, as for instance, in Vittorio De Sica's *The Gold of Naples* (*L'oro di Napoli*, 1954).

Coincidentally, it was during these years of commercial success generated by the *neoreaslimo rosa* that the Italian comic cinema experienced an unprecedented distortion of its own nature by associating with a movement rather than a genre, which in theory had little in common with centuries of comedy tradition. While many old-school filmmakers happily embraced the movement (Alessandro Blasetti, Mauro Bolognini, Camillo Mastrocinque, Vittorio De Sica, or Luigi Comencini, who later joined the cause of the *commedia all'italiana*), a few young directors kept a critical distance from the movement. Although very slow in its expansion, this artistic change brought the simple desire to establish a much sharper vision (i.e., Mario Monicelli and Dino Risi), a new point of view that watched society and its social evils under a microscope. The horrors of war, the devastations, and the endemic misery rapidly brought Italian audiences to reality and confirmed the deceitful content of two decades of Fascist propaganda

Totò (Ferdinando Esposito) in Mario Monicelli's *Cops and Robbers* (*Guardie e ladri*, 1951)

as well as escapism. As a matter of fact, *neorealismo rosa* never was intended to be a transgression of neorealism; on the contrary, far from being a last interval of its process, it was actually the logical evolution of a genre that had never been able to experience success on a critical level.

Under the leadership of Mario Monicelli or Dino Risi, many filmmakers understood that taboo subjects or politically incorrect materials, which could not be faithfully represented on the screen through drama, were in fact partly achievable through comedy. The Italian public, which was not necessarily inclined to openly discuss certain subjects (i.e., sexuality, adultery, or religion), was receptive to the same delicate matter as long as it could adopt a convincingly derisive point of view. So in the early years of the postwar era, and in particular the period subsequent to the establishment of the Christian Democrat government, censorship took new targets to eventually assert itself more powerfully. As paradoxical as it may appear, Fascist censorship was less active as authors exerted a higher level of self-censorship. The Christian Democrat censorship was therefore more aggressive against filmmakers and producers, requiring sometimes twenty cuts in one single feature film (the case of Mario Monicelli's *Totò and Carolina* [*Totò e Carolina*] in 1955). As a consequence, comedies of the 1950s greatly suffered from state censorship, which in many cases prevented the freedom to depict social injustices, with their burden of situational absurdity often indirectly incriminating the responsibility of the Christian Democrat order. This explains in part why so many producers, anticipating a secured investment with Totò's persona and his unalterable national popularity, never dared to change the course of his art direction, thus remaining limited in their social commentary (adding more farce to his acting repertoire was therefore the safe thing to do).

In light of the omnipresent limitations, many comedy authors experienced great difficulty differentiating themselves from the "sophisticated" comedies of the preceding decade (i.e., Mario Bonnard's *Before the Postman* [*Avanti c'è posto*, 1942]). The result was light comedies with little critical substance to offer. So was there a conscious effort from the perspective of the screenwriters to bring a significant dose of nobility to the genre? A pertinent question indeed when taking into consideration that up to that date the genre was destined to amuse popular audiences in need of quick entertainment given the difficult reality of the postwar reconstruction effort. Furio Scarpelli commented on the ephemeral aspect of immediate postwar comedies, arguing that authors were convinced that the comic films were to last a season, a summer at least, and fall into oblivion for eternity since no playback devices existed at the time: "Had we known that years later critics would reexamine them, perhaps we would have made them differently.... We would not have written things so lightly, just to laugh."[6] Here, in all modesty, Furio Scarpelli failed to mention that the exceptional quality of comedy writers rapidly compensated the lack of time required to prepare the filmmakers' screenplays.

Despite all the novelty brought by *neorealismo rosa*, Italian comedy of the mid-fifties was still very far from the advent of the *commedia all'italiana*. The collective humor of the 1950s, also known as *commedia corale*, continued to dominate the large screen with the exception of Totò, whose individuality had always made himself his "own genre." Despite the reconstruction efforts collectively congregating Italians from all regions and all social origins, the new country remained very much an individualist nation, where spontaneous gatherings remained scarce (besides in the work or social sphere). As pointed out by British historian Paul Ginsborg:

> In other regions, especially the Veneto and some parts of Lombardy, the strongest tradition of collective action and solidarity was a Catholic one, of mutual aid and cooperative societies. In many parts of the South, and not only the South, the only forms of collective action were feast days and pilgrimages.[7]

Along with the predominance of collective humor, the conventional patriarchal apprehension about women's sexuality and its social promotion was evidently more and more present within Italian comedies. Camillo Mastrocinque's *Totò, Peppino, and the Hussy* (*Totò, Peppino e la malafemmina*, 1956); Alessandro Blasetti's *Lucky to Be a Woman* (*La fortuna di essere donna*, 1956); Mario Costa's *Arrivano i dollari* (1957); Vittorio Sala's *Costa azzurra* (1959); Mauro Bolognini's *Wild Love* (*Gli innamorati*, 1955); Giorgio Bianchi's *The Moralist* (*Il moralista*, 1959); Vittorio De Sica's *The Gold of Naples* (*L'oro di Napoli*, 1954); and Antonio Pietrangeli's *The Bachelor* (*Lo scapolo*, 1955) are just a handful of examples representing female sexuality still struggling to break new ground in terms of identity and representation, still remote from what will be obtained less than a decade later. This characteristic was all the more pertinent since masculinity[8] was also associated with childhood. As Maggie Günsberg wrote on comedy:

> The comic association of masculinity with childhood in a number of comedies, especially in its propensity for play rather than work, and in its toying with consumerism, might be taken as an indication that Italy was not ready to deal with the rapidly spreading consumer culture.[9]

The comedies of the 1950s presented distinctive narratives, all of which included numerous equivocal situations, quid pro quos, travestiments, personality exchanges. In a nutshell, and to paraphrase Enrico Giacovelli's phrase, they corresponded with an *imborghesimento della commedia di borgata* (a growing element of bourgeoisie in non urban comedy).[10] While the urban settings inspired countless comedies, new locations began to surface with the "beach comedy," midway between the pseudopastoral style of comedies of the postwar era and the future urban fast-paced comedies of the economic boom (adventurous comedies heralding the future era of consumerism, first-time romantic affairs, extramarital relations, discotheques, partial nudity, implicit sexuality). Alberto Lattuada's *The Beach* (*La spiaggia*, 1954), starring French heartthrob Martine Carol, was an example of the trend. Though prominent at home, the Italian film industry could not compete abroad with foreign industries and exported a relatively small number of long feature films. In light of this economic situation, most producers had no other choice but to concentrate on a national audience, choosing to illustrate the quotidian of their existence on the large screen. After the boom of the 1960s, many producers also became distributors. For many filmmakers, it was a major setback for creativity and their margin for freedom. By being compelled to satisfy popular audiences, producers were less attentive to the filmmakers' request and more concerned with popular spectatorship trends (i.e., the request for more erotically charged motion pictures).

The decade never saw a real proliferation of political satires. Two exceptions were Luigi Zampa's *The Art of Getting Along* (*L'arte di arrangiarsi*, 1954) that indirectly alluded to the capacity of politicians to adapt and reinvent for the different political *époques* of modern Italy, and, of course, the most famous of all political satires, the *Don Camillo* saga, a political farce rather than satire, exemplified by the myth of Peppone and Don Camillo in Julien Duvivier's *The Little World of Don Camillo* (*Il piccolo mondo di Don Camillo*, 1952), followed by his own *The Return of Don Camillo* (*Il ritorno di Don Camillo*, 1953), Carmine Gallone's *Don Camillo's Last Round* (*Don Camillo e l'onorevole Peppone*, 1955), and *Don Camillo: Monsignor* (*Don Camillo monsignore ma non troppo*, 1961), and finally, Luigi Comencini's *Don Camillo in Moscow* (*Il compagno Don Camillo*, 1965).

A Special Case in Italian Comedy: Totò

Considered by generations of moviegoers as the greatest Italian comic actor of all time, Antonio de Curtis (1898–1967), nicknamed Totò "*il principe della risata,*" like many comedy actors, benefited from great success and public acclaim in Italy while never experiencing international fame. Despite an undisputable physical talent for slapstick comedy due to a unique mimetic performance reminiscent of Buster Keaton and Charlie Chaplin, the Neapolitan actor was not always innovative, as many of his films included a series of repetitive stunts and gags adapted for the large screen. In 1937, he set the tone for his future personae with a brilliant lead performance in a long feature film, Gero Zambuto's *Fermo con le mani!*. The defining moment of his career occurred in the 1940s when he crossed the path of review writer Michele Galdieri, in addition to iconic actress Anna Magnani (Roberto Rossellini's *Roma, città aperta* in 1945 or Luigi Zampa's *L'onorevole Angelina* in 1947). To his credit, Totò was convincingly able to project on the screen the stereotypical image of the southerner, poor and used to the art of getting by, reused and perfected by the *commedia all'italiana* in the 1960s. With a true talent for improvisation on the set, Totò possessed an inherent anarchical profile, in the end, delivering an unexpected narrative, and eventually bringing confusion to the pre-established order. Due to a growing eye disease, which after 1957 seriously hampered the development of his career, the actor was progressively compelled to abandon the theater scene. Slowly Totò accumulated identical roles, everlastingly recycling his comical genius that was often associated with Peppino de Filippo in numerous farces. It was his small, but providential appearance in Mario Monicelli's *Big Deal on Madonna Street* (*I soliti ignoti*, 1958) as Dante, a different role for him, which marked a turning point in his career as well as the comedy of the 1950s. Many film historians viewed this historical collaboration as the symbol of the "*passaggio del testimone*" from the postwar generation (Totò, Memmo Carotenuto) to the new one, the future protagonists of the *commedia all'italiana* (Vittorio Gassman, Marcello Mastroianni). While some of these film historians erroneously associated Totò with the *commedia all'italiana*, his career mainly included comedy of the postwar era, since he rarely contributed to the emergent movement/genre in the 1960s. Most filmmakers preferred the fresh talent of Vittorio Gassman, Nino Manfredi, or Ugo Tognazzi. Protagonists of the *commedia all'italiana* imposed characters filled with preponderant negative traits such as *cattiveria* (malevolence), hypocrisy, vanity, cowardness, a paradigm indeed far from Totò's universe, best illustrated by Alberto Sordi in Dino Risi's *The Widower* (*Il vedovo*, 1959) or Antonio Pietrangeli's *The Bachelor* (*Lo scapolo*, 1955). Totò's most important performances, all of which remained outside the *commedia all'italiana* movement, included Mario Mattoli's *Totò al giro d'Italia* (1954); Carlo Ludovico Bragaglia's *Totò le Moko* (1949); Luigi Comencini's *L'imperatore di Capri* (1949); Mario Mattoli's *Totò sceicco* (1950); Monicelli's *Totò and the King of Rome* (*Totò e i re di Roma*, 1951); Steno and Monicelli's *Cops and Robbers* (*Guardie e ladri*, 1951); Vittorio De Sica's *The Gold of Naples* (*L'oro di Napoli*, 1954); Monicelli's *Totò and Carolina* (*Totò e Carolina*, 1955); Mauro Bolognini's *You're on Your Own* (*Arrangiatevi!*, 1959); Alberto Lattuada's *La Mandragola* (1965); Dino Risi's *Operation San Gennaro* (*Operazione San Gennaro*, 1966); and Pier Paolo Pasolini's *Hawks and Sparrows* (*Uccellacci e uccellini*, 1966). From variety shows to *avanspettacolo*, Totò's films have been watched by immense popular audiences (mainly in Italy), which is over 270 million spectators; an unequaled performance to this day.

The 1950s comedies were also characterized by the growing tendency to display behavioral contradictions (more and more mental rather than physical). The case of Luigi Zampa's *Ladro lui ladra lei* (1958) illustrated the evolution of Italian humor now mature enough to utilize the dialectal duality (a humor based on immediate discrepancy between dialect versus standard Italian) mixed in the same scene in order to produce the intended comic relief. One of the most emblematic scenes of the decade comes from this film; Cencio

Alberto Sordi (Cencio) in Luigi Zampa's *Ladro lui ladra lei* (1958)

(Alberto Sordi), an expert crook dressed as a cardinal of the Church, scheduled to meet a businessman in order to help him send money illegally to Switzerland, stands at a window from an ecclesiastical library to authenticate his credibility. However, outside his accomplice Cesira (Sylva Koscina), the woman who is to alert him of the businessman's arrival, is being verbally harassed by two young-sters on a scooter. Cencio, who sees no other choice, asks the two ruffians to leave her alone in proper ecclesiastical Italian. They both obstinately refuse and engage in provocative behavior toward the clergyman, who is now compelled to curse at them in Roman dialect in order to scare them away: "e bisogna che ve ne annate! Mannaggia!" ("Get the hell outta here!") Though the stratagem works, Sordi remembers that he is still inside a crowded library filled with ecclesiastical members who at this moment all stare at him in utter disbelief.

During the second half of the decade, a few postwar comedies were characterized by a common desire to take the comedy genre away from its neorealist roots. Some of them, like Nanni Loy's *Il marito* (1958) or Antonio Pietrangeli's *The Bachelor* (*Lo scapolo*, 1955), adopted plots closer to quotidian reality and began to engage in a strategy of social and gender commentary as a main priority. At one point, scenarists and filmmakers realized that a stronger comedy was needed, one that would prove to both popular audiences and producers alike that the underlining negative aspects of modern Italian society and consumerism were a way to both entertain and bring social responsiveness to the public eye (Pietro Germi's *Divorzio all'italiana* and the question of the south, which will be developed in the next chapter). One emergent aspect of comedy was the implementation of an unusual dose of cynicism. Although still very remote from the *commedia all'italiana* of the 1960s, cynicism and irony were in a way the best advocate to evoke reforms for Italian society and impose a self-examination of its own humankind. As screenwriter Furio Scarpelli recalled:

> Everyone from our generation makes that kind of cinema, giving a great part to irony. Irony is part of the tragedy of life; it is necessary to narrate it…. Why have so many friends and students uselessly endured trying to make their cinematographic story convincing? Because sometimes, inside, these incitements lack these enrichments, this boiler, this engine…. What replaced this impulse is what was called in Italy a psycho-sociological progress, that is to say, to give value to what you are, to narrate one's self. It is very difficult to discover the abyss that exists between this self-consciousness, this exhibition, and its use to achieve works that talk about others and interest them.[11]

Differences Between *Commedia Italiana* and *Commedia all'Italiana*

Even though the *commedia all'italiana* may be considered by the nonspecialist a subgenre of Italian film comedy, the genre/movement actually surpassed Italian comedy in terms of critical and popular success, both national and international. The key to the performance was in large part for its authors to transpose successfully the personal and common struggle of the average Italian into a product of national appeal (i.e., the vicissitudes of Communist journalist Silvio Magnozzi in Dino Risi's *A Dificult Life* [*Una vita difficile*, 1961], forced to compromise his ideals to survive economically, thus representing in emblematic scope the story of millions of Italians in the early years of the economic miracle).

The new developments brought by the *commedia all'italiana* were numerous. Because attempting to classify their importance would be an endless task, one should point out that the most important discrepancy between postwar comedy and the new *commedia all'italiana* was the level of social observation and its subsequent engagement. If the "light comedies" of the 1950s as well as the ones that emanated from the *neorealismo rosa* era did not carry with them a social implication toward the already conquered popular audiences, the new comedies of the 1960s were just the opposite. Comedy Italian style's primary intentions were both to serve the purpose of entertainment as well as to incite a validation of social satire from the spectators' point of view: not just humor for its own sake, but also a certain level of intellectual reflection on society, politics, and humanity. As film historian Lorenzo Quaglietti wrote in 1963 in the journal *Cinemasessanta*:

Recently, Italian film comedy has gone through a complex transformation. Many low quality products with gratuitous and provincial humor seem to have disappeared from our screens to make room for more ambitious works that report with great interest their attention on the most paradoxical aspects of Italian reality.[12]

Comedy Italian style was born step by step through a social and political conscience (from the Italian comedy) that initiated the stamina and leadership of screenwriters such as Cesare Zavattini (1902–89) and Sergio Amidei. They were able to conjugate drama and irony in a comical manner without losing the ultimate target of social commentary. However, it is important to remember the preponderant influence of Sergio Amidei, who collaborated for the neorealist adventure with cineastes such as Roberto Rossellini and Vittorio De Sica for *Open City* (*Roma città aperta*, 1945), *Shoe-Shine* (*Sciuscià*, 1946), *Paisan* (*Paisà*, 1946), *Germany Year Zero* (*Germania anno zero*, 1947), or *Stromboli* (*Stromboli terra di Dio*, 1949). In the late 1950s, while the new comedy style became reality, Amidei experienced a second wind and wrote for *Big Deal on Madonna Street* (*I soliti ignoti*, 1958), *Generale Della Rovere* (*Il generale Della Rovere*, 1959), *Roaring Years* (*Anni ruggenti*, 1962), *Il medico della mutua* (1968), *Il prof. dott. Guido Tersilli primario della clinica Villa Celeste convenzionata con le mutue* (1969), *Why* (*Detenuto in attesa di giudizio*, 1971), and *An Average Little Man* (*Un borghese piccolo piccolo*, 1977). Indeed, with the new comedy style, laughter was no longer the only objective for screenwriters, producers, and directors as they began shifting their focus toward cultural stimulus, even triggering a social consciousness to the popular audiences.

Furio Scarpelli explained that comic films of the 1950s were in large part made to satisfy producers and a public with a dire need to be entertained and forget the hardship of the immediate postwar era and the painful effort of reconstruction.[13] But what characterized comedy Italian style in the 1960s was its resemblance to political films (similar to Francesco Rosi's *Hands Over the City* [*Mani basse sulla città*, 1963] or Elio Petri's *Investigation of a Private Citizen* [*Indagine su un cittadino al di sopra di ogni sospetto*, 1970]) in terms of documentation and the journalistic approach to the subject in their investigation of reality. Consequently, filmmakers and screenwriters felt the need to be more assertive and give a substantial political and social message within the content. From this, the *commedia all'italiana* was born, and laughter was able from now on to take a different shape and content. However, the new style was criticized on occasion for its forceful approach to contemporary problems without suggesting a salutary exit to viewers. The absence of didactic conclusions, a trademark of the new comedies, was also a reminder of the profound dislike for morality from authors. Only years later did spectators fully appreciate the authenticity of the screenplay as well as the importance of their performance. For the first time, Italian comedy, unlike the bourgeois comedies of the preceding decade, improved the depth of the narrative discourse by exposing the confrontation between amoral protagonists and a quotidian reality abandoned by civil values. The second predominant distinction between the two cinematographic *époques* was without a doubt the presence of cynicism. The advent of the new comedies at the end of the 1950s, following *Big Deal on Madonna Street* (*soliti ignoti*), implemented a new dimension in the narrative, which ultimately established cynicism and cruelty as a legitimate cinematic ingredient. The old vision of reality of postwar Italy's reconstruction effort had been seen through the infantilized glare of generations of conventional filmmakers, whereas the vision of the economic boom was all of a sudden scrutinized through the adult lens of cynicism and composure. Dino Risi, who like many filmmakers successfully made the transition between both cinemas, explained his position in defense of cynicism.

> In my opinion, cynicism is not a defect, it is not a negative attitude; it is a way of saying things as you try to get to the truth, without prejudice and without compromise. Cynicism is a very beautiful way of looking at reality, without pretending, without hiding anything.[14]

One of the predominant characteristics of the rapport between popular audiences and actors was the process of identification that for several decades never experienced much change; the comic hero often communicated a positive message to the audience (with a visible absence of sarcasm). One of adaptation and insertion into a society, as cruel as it may have been, was the unavoidable background of the narrative. On the other hand, the new comedy of the 1960s allowed the public to identify with a more human comic protagonist, filled with defects and even an unprecedented dimension of malice, even cruelty. Hence the explosion of Alberto Sordi's character type and the unconditional fidelity the Italian popular audiences granted him until the end of the seventies. Monicelli's views on sentimentalism were also explicit as he considered it "an element that I or the *commedia all'italiana* hate."[15] In this respect, one can go as far as to say that the comedies of the 1950s proposed a comic protagonist oftentimes as victim (i.e., Marcello Mastroianni, the victim of Sophia Loren's deceitful tricks in Alessandro Blasetti's *Too Bad She's Bad* [*Peccato che sia una canaglia*] in 1954) whereas a decade later the new comedy Italian style of the 1960s preferred to emphasize the cruel and sarcastic nature of the comic hero. While the comic protagonist of the economic miracle eventually experienced hardship and despair, he/she was also able to express a new dimension, unknown a few years before. Mario Monicelli underlined the potential brutality of the new comedy.

> We thought about filters, customs, chronicles, current affairs to unmask weaknesses and subterfuges, flaws and pettiness of everyday people, turning upside down common truths and destroying myths, with malice

and no mercy, since the *commedia* is mean, even ruthless. With this objective, verisimilitude takes on a decisive role. It is a demand but also a weapon for our battlefield.[16]

In other words, the malice and psychological ruse no longer corresponded with the ancient art of getting by. Something had radically changed in the Italian comedy, and it no longer was enough to be funny for a character to be labeled a comic actor; it was also necessary to display a dimension of possible cruelty in order to fit in the new format of the *commedia all'italiana*. This phenomenon explained in part the longevity of actor Alberto Sordi, who through the entire postwar generation, followed by the economic miracle as well as the lead years, always embodied the image of the non-sentimentalized Italian prototype with whom a large majority of Italians identified.

One way to summarize the difference between traditional comedy and *commedia all'italiana* is the fact that the new comedy style included significantly more dramatic elements in its narrative strategy, as Jean Gili called *Amici miei*, the manifesto of Italian humor of the 1970s, a "perfect blend of farce, derision, and deep despair."[17] As the postwar comedies were more dedicated to a political correctness, the new *commedia* never respected its precepts, adding even more physical and psychological unease to the story for the viewers. If the 1950s were based more on slapstick and physical humor, the new comedy of the 1960s connected with a psychological humor, pointing out the human cost caused by a country involved within a hasty modernization: solitude and alienation of the individual as the first effect of the consumerism era. Monicelli recalled his position on society's nightmare as a filmmaker:

> One of our favorite targets has always been individualism, generous in words and avaricious in actions, an element present in many protagonists ready to criticize institutions, social hierarchy, common places, but then irremediably crushed by a reality to which they had to abide.[18]

The old-school comedy generated a humor based on a collective humor rather than an individualistic one, more theatrical, more physical, more sentimental, more willing to solve the fundamentally irreversible differences between main characters. To summarize, it usually attempted before the epilogue of the narrative to solve some elements of social hardship through a potential reconciliation and ultimately an "integration" into society. As for the new comedy of the 1960s, the message preferred to target the social contradictions of Italian society and emphasized its costly aftermath for the individual. Monicelli explains his choice to cast Alberto Sordi for *An Average Little Man* (*Un borghese piccolo piccolo*, 1977), which beyond the comic presence of the Roman actor allowed the audience to identify with the ordinary protagonist and eventually with his transformation into a revengeful murderer.

I treated the subject in a violent and mature mode, but I chose Sordi, not Volontè. Sordi is the most loved man by Italians, the actor that entertains them, the prototype of the *commedia all'italiana*. I inserted him in this story to elicit shock in order to demonstrate how easy it is to become a monster when one wants to take justice into one's own hands.[19]

If the content was evidently visible, the form was also going two separate roads. The happy ending, emblematic of Hollywood's sophisticated comedies, found in the comedy of the 1950s its corresponding tone with many Italian productions, such as Alessandro Blasetti's *Peccatto che tu sia una canaglia* (1954) showing Marcello Mastroianni and Sophia Loren reconciling their differences with a final kiss (heralding a happily ever after), or Luigi Comencini's *Bread, Love and Fantasy* (*Pane amore e fantasia*, 1953). On the contrary, the comedies of the following era were notorious for abruptly putting an end to the narrative progression, thus avoiding embarrassing or unwanted reconciliation (with protagonists, society, or even the public). To offer a few examples: Mario Monicelli's *The Great War* (*La grande guerra*, 1959) showed Alberto Sordi and Vittorio Gassman executed by an Austrian firing squad minutes before the Italian army liberated their position; Dino Risi's *The Easy Life* (*Il sorpasso*, 1962) ended with the abrupt accidental death of Jean-Louis Trintignant caused by Vittorio Gassman's reckless driving on the costal highway; Pietro Germi's *Divorce Italian Style* (*Divorzio all'italiana*, 1961) ruined Marcello Mastroianni's honeymoon hope with Stefania Sandrelli as she seductively flirts with the sailor on board; in Marco Ferreri's *The Conjugal Bed* (*L'ape regina*, 1963), Ugo Tognazzi's death was caused by his wife's sexual appetite; in Franco Brusati's *Bread and Chocolate* (*Pane e cioccolata*, 1973), Nino Manfredi walked through a railway tunnel back to Switzerland, a country with no future in sight for him, or Mario Monicelli's *Amici miei* ending with the sudden death of Perozzi, to offer a few examples. In this respect, the filmmaker's responsibility stopped at the end of the narrative and therefore was not supposed to engage on a moralistic enterprise often the case in Hollywood cinema. As Dino Risi reminds us: "Spectators must form their own opinion…. Morality is only a behavior. One cannot identify it a priori out of necessity: neither categorical nor hypothetical."[20] In other words, for the new filmmakers of the *Commedia* generation, morality and its cinematographic rhetoric were never to be part of humor and this explains why the new satire, with (tragically) open ending questions, consequently represented a substantial change when compared with the postwar comedies. Another differentiation in form was the interest comedy Italian style promoted for the use of regional dialects at the very center of its comical dynamics. Pietro Germi's Sicilian comedies, for instance, created an unprecedented linguistic phenomenon, that of uniting the Italian language thanks to the originality of screenwriters and dialogists into a meta-language or pseudodialect, accessible and understandable for the popular Italian audiences across the twenty regions of Italy (just as television had

Totò (Ferdinando Esposito) and Aldo Fabrizi (Brigadiere Bottoni) in Mario Monicelli's *Cops and Robbers* (*Guardie e ladri*, 1951)

achieved a decade before). Therefore, since the dialectal presence was necessary (and in some cases overused) in order to upgrade the *comicità* in comedies, it was no surprise to see Roman dialect appear as the dialect of predilection for comedy Italian style of the 1960s, which was not the case necessarily for comedies of the postwar era. This domination came in large part from using Rome as the shooting location for many comedies at the time, as well as the attraction the capital city created for the collective imagination, epitomized by an infinite source of satirical material against the abuse of bureaucracy and government in general. Despite the dominance, other dialects also experienced national recognition: Sicilian with Pietro Germi's *Divorzio all'italiana* (1961), *Seduced and Abandoned* (*Sedotta e abbandonata*, 1964), and Alberto Lattuada's *Mafioso* (1962); Veneto dialect in Pietro Germi's *The Birds, the Bees and the Italians* (*Signore & signori*, 1965); Lombard with Elio Petri's *The Teacher from Vigevano* (*Il maestro di Vigevano*, 1963); and Roman dialect in a myriad of films such as Luigi Zampa's *Il vigile* (1960), Dino Risi's *Il sorpasso* (1962), *Una vita difficile* (1961), *The Monsters* (*I mostri*, 1963), and Luigi Comencini's *Everybody Go Home* (*Tutti a casa*, 1960), among others. During the postwar era, dialects added color and verve to the comic lines, and later in the 1960s, dialects were used as a narrative element. Interestingly enough, the use of Tuscan dialect, long neglected by comedy authors, made its comeback in the mid-seventies with Monicelli's 1975 *My*

Friends (by chance, since Germi, the original author of *Amici miei,* had decided to set the story in Bologna). According to Monicelli, the choice of transferring the location to his native Tuscany was appropriate in light of the spirit of the humor involved in the *boccacesque beffa*: "The Tuscan spirit basically is never sentimental; it consists of a certain cynicism, a certain skepticism."[21]

The Forerunners of the Comedy Italian Style

Steno and Monicelli's *Cops and Robbers* (*Guardie e ladri,* 1951) was the very first significant link between neorealism and the future *commedia all'italiana*. In the guise of a conventional comedy, the film was more than a simple tale of "hide and seek"; it became an early manifesto of the comedy Italian style promoting the opposition of extremes as the core of the plot. The subject written by Piero Tellini,[22] the screenplay by Ennio Flaiano, Vitaliano Brancati, as well as Steno himself, followed the vicissitudes of professional crook Ferdinando Esposito (Totò) and police officer Bottoni (Aldo Fabrizi). Following a complaint from an American tourist who was sold a fake ancient coin at the Forum, the police are after Esposito. After a long escape scene, which begins in the busy Roman traffic and ends in the surrounding suburbs (*borgata romana*), the crook manages to disappear, leaving the *brigadiere* Bottoni responsible for the evasion. As a consequence, he is discharged from the police force. In the meantime, the thief's family befriends the police officer's family, and a complicated series of *quid pro quo* begins. This unwanted "reciprocality" was a novelty as both protagonists, though standing at the opposite of the moral spectrum, shared their inner difficulties with one another and realized, much to their surprise, that they were identical: having difficulty paying the rent, family problems, the future of the children, the reconstruction of Italy (at the time, this unprecedented dynamic created severe criticism from the government promoting a climate of Catholic conformity). More importantly, in *Guardie e ladri* the very incipient element of the future comedy Italian style surfaced with the confrontation of two opposite characters like Totò and Aldo Fabrizi and the promotion of each comical protagonist's individuality (as opposed to the *corale* element of the conventional comedies). Perhaps the most powerful moment of the film was the symbolic ending, as both thief and policeman procrastinate their inevitable arrival at the police station, a symbol of unjust fate (surreptitiously symbolized by Saint Peter's cupola in the background).

Dino Risi's *Love and Larceny* (*Il mattatore,* 1959) put into the spotlight the growing success of two con artists and petty swindlers (Vittorio Gassman and Peppino De Filippo) who impersonate a multitude of individuals in an assortment of make-up disguises and costumes. Straight from the theatrical tradition of *commedia dell'arte*, this film, however, differed in its content in light of its social commentary. After years of dramatic performance on stage and on the big screen (Giuseppe De Santis' *Bitter Rice* [*Riso amaro*] in 1949), Vittorio Gassman was finally able to demonstrate his comic skills in this virtually one-man show, a vaudeville performer with tremendous acting abilities. The film, whose screenplay was written by Sandro Continenza and adapted by Sergio Pugliese from an original story by Age and Scarpelli, exemplified in a condensed version centuries of the art of getting by, which heralded the future *commedia all'italiana*. The most noteworthy scene was the moment Gerardo (Vittorio Gassman) uses a complex stratagem to "effortlessly" steal a diamond ring. For this, he convinces the jeweler himself that the next-door pastry shop owner will bring him the money a few minutes later (she eventually will bring him twenty-six pastries rather than twenty-six thousand lira). Dino Risi's skill was premonitory for the future *commedia*'s style; he captured the subtle ironies in the behavior of melodramatic protagonists, successfully joining theatricality and cynicism via an unsympathetic modern lens.

A couple of years following the production of Federico Fellini's first comedy with *I vitelloni* (1953), the maestro explored new grounds of comedy apart from the archetypical molds of popular laughter by injecting a tangible dimension of cruelty, satire, and sarcasm.[23] Decisively ahead of its time, Fellini's *The Swindle* (*Il bidone*, 1955) inspired countless authors as his vision and methods were imitated a decade later by the great masters of the 1960s comedy Italian style. With a screenplay and story by Ennio Flaiano and Tulio Pinelli, Fellini narrated in a "serio-comic" manner the struggling life of Augusto (Broderick Crawford), an aging con man dedicated to regaining redemption from a life of crime and deception as well as providing money for his daughter's education, which as a father he failed to deliver her entire life. With his accomplices, his main fraud assignment is to extirpate money from poor peasants of the Lazio region. As he poses as a Roman Catholic bishop, along with his accomplices Picasso (Richard Basehart) and Roberto (Franco Fabrizi), they knock at people's doors and with the help of their robe's prestige, they secure their victims' attention and respect. The benevolent clergymen, "official emissaries from the Catholic Church," begin their scam by

Vittorio Gassman (Gerardo Latini) and Mario Scaccia (the jeweler) in Dino Risi's *Love and Larceny* (*Il mattatore*, 1959)

revealing that the peasants are the proprietors of a hidden treasure buried on their property, as an unknown criminal confessed on his deathbed to have buried a chest by a tree on their property. The confessor's final will is to bequeath the treasure on the condition that he receives five hundred masses celebrated in his memory. With the help of the peasants' obscurantist belief, they collect the money their victims can gather in order to pay for the masses, and leave them ecstatic, though with a fake and worthless treasure. Unlike most contemporary gangster films, Fellini's *Il bidone* examined the element of loneliness and the social detachment of the individual versus Italian postwar society through a sardonically humorous comedy. In his reexamination of misguided existence, Fellini offered a profoundly moving testament of the inherent honesty of the human heart. This time, the innovation came with a strategy of social and psychological observation laced with omnipresent comedy. In a riveting finale, the courageous love for an ignored daughter ironically condemns and redeems the main protagonist.

With Mario Monicelli's *I soliti ignoti* (1958), an innovative type of comedy was born, as the director turned away from the conventions of earlier films. Instead of comic films of the 1950s, which featured protagonists with theatrical masks and an apparent emphasis on their characterization, the basis of Monicelli's humor was directly the result of a clear and elaborate scenario (Suso

Richard Basehart (the secretary), Franco Fabrizi (the chauffeur), and Broderick Crawford (the bishop) in Federico Fellini's *The Swindle* (*Il bidone*, 1955)
Photo courtesy of Centro Sperimentale del Cinema

Alberto Sordi (Alberto) in Federico Fellini's *I vitelloni* (1953)

Cecchi d' Amico usually working for Luchino Visconti, Sergio Amidei, Rodolfo Sonego, Age and Scarpelli, Ettore Scola, and Ruggero Maccari).

The term *soliti ignoti*[24] ("the usual unknown suspects") was a journalistic phrase to identify and designate the unknown perpetrators of thefts. Originally conceived as a caricature and intended to parody non-mainstream French *polar* films (Jules Dassin's *Rififi* in 1955), the film quickly evolved toward a pioneering comic experience liberated from the *farcesque* dimension of the usual *scippi, scippatori, imbroglioni, ladri, borsaioli, tagliaborsi, marioli* (Italian lexicon, to no surprise, possesses an extensive and unusually prolific spectrum of terminologies regarding thieves). However, Monicelli offered a very different perspective, as his art direction chose a much more comedic avenue. Unanimously considered a seminal transition movie by film historians, *I soliti ignoti* went far beyond the scope of traditional satire creating an innovative homage to B series film noir while paying tribute to its serious-minded antecedents to establish an entirely new direction for the comic genre. In addition, the film incorporated new tragic subjects—namely death. The scene, however, was edited during the montage in high speed in order to attenuate the gruesome death of a mobster boss falling under the tramway.

The film's premise shows Cosimo (Memmo Carotenuto), a notorious burglar, being sent to jail following a failed car theft. His accomplice Capannelle[25] (Carlo Pisacane) scours the town to find someone to take the rap for him with a 100,000 lira compensation. He eventually finds Peppe (also known as Peppe il Pantera, Vittorio Gassman), an inept boxer in need of quick cash who turns himself in at the police station. Unfortunately, the

Dino Risi and Federico Fellini in 1957

inspector, far from being convinced, puts him in jail too. Under the pretence of being sentenced to years (he is actually scheduled to exit the following day), Peppe gains the confidence of Cosimo and extirpates from him the secret information of a future heist at the Monte dei Pegni, a local pawn shop whose safe is located next to an empty apartment. While the access into the apartment appears relatively easy, no one in the clan is able to crack a safe. So they decide to talk to Dante Cruciani (Totò), a near-senile safe expert who agrees to teach them the basics in the art of safe robbery. In the meantime, Cosimo, thanks to general amnesty, gets out, determined to vindicate himself. However, following another missed theft, he is run over by a tramway and dies instantly. The group of incompetent petty crooks begins to organize for what they swear will be their ultimate assignment. The team includes Mario (Renato Salvatori)—a young womanizer who falls in love with the beautiful Carmela (Claudia Cardinale), the overly protected sister of Ferribote (Tiberio Murgia), a jealous and hot-headed Sicilian who keeps her locked up at home, preoccupied with safeguarding her virtue—Tiberio (Marcello Mastroianni) a "cameraless" photographer overwhelmed with a crying baby while his wife finishes her sentence in prison for cigarette smuggling, and Capannelle, a toothless old man who seems to be more on the hunt for food than for money.[26] The goal, to extract the keys from the young woman (Carla Gravina) who lives in the apartment (next to the pawn shop), goes awry as Peppe gets sidetracked with his own romantic entanglements. Finally, the thieves gain access to the apartment and the long-awaited moment can occur. Their first attempt to drill through a wall fails when they hit a water pipe and flood part of the apartment (this scene inspired Woody Allen in *Small Time Crooks* more than three decades later). Finally, after hours of enduring labor, they slowly dig a hole inside the wall, but realize, much to their utmost dismay, that they just destroyed the wall of the kitchen of the same apartment. Resigned to their own fate, they leave the house in the early hours of the new day and separate only after having filled their stomachs with pasta and *ceci* instead of having filled their pockets with jewelry.

The film's principal source of comic relief was evidently based upon the fundamental incompetence of the crew. To achieve the level of an unprecedented

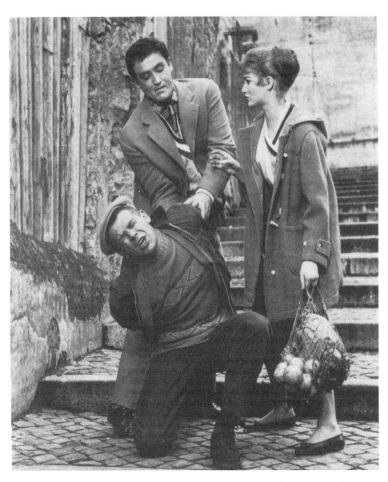

Carla Gravina (Nicoletta), Vittorio Gassman (Peppe), and
Renato Salvatori (Mario) in Mario Monicelli's
Big Deal on Madonna Street (*I soliti ignoti*, 1958)

sustained comedy, the producers were reticent to cast Vittorio Gassman, since his career in theater had confined him so far to serious roles and offered no guarantee for success in a leading comic role. Monicelli's selection of Vittorio Gassman was fought for months by producers who saw in the Genovese actor a theatrical representative too serious for the role and whose film career had been dominated by his past villain roles (i.e., De Santis' *Bitter Rice* [*Riso amaro*] in 1949). Once officially chosen, Gassman's facial expression was slightly altered to accentuate the comic effect: a low-rise wig displayed a short forehead and a pronounced speech impediment. In addition to the fortunate casting of Gassman, Monicelli also imposed his choice of Totò (backed by the popular success of his legacy but not necessarily from film critics) and discovered the talent of Claudia Cardinale who, born in French Tunisia, did not know how to speak Italian at the time of the shooting.

Monicelli directed the initial robbery sequence judiciously. During a "safe cracking" lesson, Totò teaches the inexperienced and disaster-prone candidates how to manage a successful career in bank robbery (the attentive spectator could see Monicelli officially pass the relay of comedy from the hands of Totò to the new generation of future comic actors here). This picturesque scene allowed the story to define the latent disasters and their inevitable unraveling, immediately establishing a humorously subversive tone. The subsequent robberies confirmed this, with one disaster after another. With the skill and calculation of expert engineers, the want-to-be thieves must pull off the heist with meticulous, intricate planning and preparation. Together they research the locales, devise a

Vittorio Gassman (Peppe) and Marcello Mastroianni (Tiberio) in Mario Monicelli's *Big Deal on Madonna Street* (*I soliti ignoti*, 1958)

plan, and rehearse it to perfection, mixing without any kind of limitation dark humor and comic farce, juxtaposing a dramatic element of the narrative with a "liberatory" gag. The presence of slapstick comedy was also in high profile with the pawnshop scene where Cosimo points at the cashier a gun concealed under a newspaper asking "la conosci questa?" Unaware of his ill intentions, the cashier grabs the gun, examines it attentively, and gives it back to him, offering 1,000 lira for it. Cosimo, speechless by the humiliation, runs away. So one may ask why *I soliti ignoti* does not quite belong to the comedy Italian style? While many historians do consider it the founding stone of the movement, one could argue that it simply was too early to fully belong to the genre. Shot in 1958, it was not part of the initial aftermath of the economic miracle as subsequent films were, by virtue of their timing in history. In addition, its unhappy ending, though heralding many more imitations, was still far from the quintessential tragic ending like Dino Risi's *Il sorpasso*, where the accidental death of the main protagonist was unexpectedly displayed.

However, *I soliti ignoti* remains a turning point, announcing the impending revolution of the new comedy style. In its content, too, the novelty was tangible. From this narrative that allowed occasional intervals of slapstick farce (gushing water and wrong wall demolition), the experience took an abrupt, radical shift into social criticism, a stance that virtually no other comedy filmmaker had taken before Monicelli.[27] With the denunciation of a society of leisure caught in its contradictions, the film displayed urban poverty able to withstand the onslaught of a new modernization in the boom years. One of the final thoughts of the film came from Tiberio, as he reminded them of the fatality of their line of work: "Rubare è un mestiere impegnativo, ci vuole gente seria, mica come voi! Voi, al massimo, potete andare a lavorare!" (Stealing is a demanding profession; it is for serious people, not like you! You guys, at the most, can go and work!) The film clearly borrowed some of the neorealist aesthetics and emphasized humanity to accentuate a sense of subversion and to give the narrative a genuine social dimension. On the other hand, the film's dark, smoky atmospheric look implemented a great noir feel, with a realistic urban background (i.e., the shots of Roman suburbs with their wet streets in the 1950s were worth a nostalgic glance). The presence of neorealism in supporting roles could also be noticed in the presence of children and their immediate loss of innocence, such as the scene in which Capannelle asks neighborhood children for help in a poor zone of Rome's periphery[28]:

Capannelle: Tu conosci un certo Mario che abita qua intorno? (You know a Mario who lives around here?)
Bambino: Qui de Mario ce ne so' cento. (There are hundreds of Marios here.)
Capannelle: Si, va bene ma questo è uno che ruba... (Ok, but this one is a thief...)
Bambino: Sempre cento so'. (Still there are hundreds.)

The story ended in cruel disillusion as the final scene showed the trap of industrialization closing in on them as the men are driven to what resembles forced labor. The failure of the enterprise heralded the forthcoming social and economic fights, which would eventually take place a decade later in Italian society. The myth of forced adaptation, as described by Maurizio Grande,[29] here takes shape under the voice of Capannelle: Ma ti fanno lavorare sai! (They will make you work, you know!) Though still the expression of a choral humor (as opposed to the 1960s style centered on the individualism of the protagonists) with a comedic series of mishaps and slapstick bungling, the film was built around the theme of failure, anticipating the future expectations of overly ambitious individuals who filled the comedy Italian style theme of materialism and greed following the economic boom. The film reminded Italian popular audiences that the country was still far from turning the page of the reconstruction effort; hasty modernization and its unrealistic dreams of quick wealth were a premonitory step toward disaster ("the poor stealing the poor" was in itself authentic proof of social inquisitiveness, which was re-explored two decades later by Ettore Scola in *Down and Dirty* [*Brutti, sporchi e cattivi,* 1976]).

As in movies with dialects, one of the noticeable comical mechanisms of *I soliti ignoti* was the unique juxtaposition of different regional dialects within the group dynamic: Peppe used a Roman dialect and painfully tried to imitate a Milanese accent to impress his future conquest Nicoletta, who herself spoke with a thick Veneto accent; Capannelle spoke with a Bolognese accent; Ferribotte and Carmela spoke Sicilian; Mario and Tiberio spoke Roman; and finally Totò spoke in his usual Neapolitan tongue. This clever interaction of dialects within the script created an emotional bond between popular audiences and the movie, differing from mainstream comedies, which usually limited regional accents to secondary comical functions.[30]

In 1959, French critics celebrated the film and indirectly influenced their Italian colleagues who had originally expressed mixed feelings about the film, thus creating a delayed positive response from Italian spectators. In addition, Piero Umiliani's music score, a fast-paced jazz music, added an innovative touch. In 1959, the film earned an Oscar nomination for Best Foreign Film. In 1985, Amanzio Todini's disappointing sequel, *I soliti ignoti vent'anni dopo*, included Vittorio Gassman, Marcello Mastroianni, Tiberio Murgia, as well as the same group of screenwriters who collaborated during the first version in 1958. In addition, the film was the subject of a couple of Hollywood remakes, including French director Louis Malle's *Crackers* (1984) starring Sean Penn, and more recently, Anthony and Joe Russo's *Collinwood* (2002) with George Clooney in the role of Dante Cruciani.

Due to the seminal effect of Monicelli's *I soliti ignoti* on the community of comedy filmmakers, screenwriters, and even producers, the rapid expansion of the new comedy style began to take shape by the end of the decade. An innovative era was about to begin, including twenty years of exceptional prosperity for a genre already used to fighting for its survival. The deserved success was also due to the collective nature of its representation of Italian life and, in particular, of the predominance of several screenwriters who consistently provided sound quality to the plot and dialogues that gave life to an exceptional crew of supporting actors.[31]

Notes

[1] Translated by the author from Italian: "La risata diventava una possibilità di riscatto, una forma liberatoria, la voce dei perdenti che si leva contro le regole sociali." Sebastiano Mondadori, *La commedia umana: conversazioni con Mario Monicelli* (Milan: Il Saggiatore, 2005), 20.

[2] Translated by the author from French: "Le néoréalisme relance la comédie dans la voie qu'elle n'aurait jamais dû quitter si n'étaient passés par là vingt ans de facisme, la voie du traitement par l'humour, l'ironie, la satire, des problèmes de la société italienne." Jean A. Gili, *La comédie italienne* (Paris: Union Générales d'édition, 1978), 89.

[3] Translated by the author from Italian: "Il comico diviene come catalizzatore di molti mali che sono all'interno del tessuto narrativo. Probabilmente, una necessità non soltanto dell'autore ma della platea che conduce alla costituzione di soluzioni umoristiche per poter digerire questo male, questo tragico." Pietro Pintus, *Storia e film: Trent'anni di cinema italiano (1945–1975)* (Rome: Bulzoni, 1980), 182.

[4] Translated from French by the author: "Pendant ces années, peut-être par réaction au néoréalisme qui donnait des films graves, voire tragiques, sur l'Italie détruite par les bombardements, sur la pauvreté, la première comédie italienne était caractérisée par des films assez superficiels, qui faisaient sans doute rire, mais qui justement dans ce but utilisaient tout et n'étaient pas tellement honnêtes." Michel Ciment, "Entretien avec Ettore Scola," *Positif* 543 (May 2006): 92.

[5] Vittorio De Sica's tenacity to use nonprofessional actors was made legendary when he refused to cast Cary Grant in the role of Antonio Ricci despite the financial support of American producer David O. Selznick.

[6] Translated by the author from French: "Si on avait su que des années après la critique les aurait revus, examinés, peut-être qu'on ne les aurait pas fait ainsi…. on n'aurait pas écrit des choses aussi légères, juste pour rire." Jean Gili, "Entretien avec Furio Scarpelli: L'ironie fait partie du drame de la vie," *Positif* 543 (May 2006): 96.

[7] P. Ginsborg, *A History of Contemporary Italy: Society and Politics 1943–1988* (London: Penguin, 1990), 22.

[8] About the overpowering omnipresence of masculinity in Italian comedy, Dino Risi offered a rather direct confession, yet not quite politically correct, regarding his preferences in terms of comedic protagonists: "I've spoken of actors because I've usually always made masculine cinema, a cinema of actors. Of course, I've also directed actresses and developed a good rapport with some of them. The female roles in my films that I've made, it's true, have always been a little on the side. I had these four actors whom

I worked a lot with, Sordi, Gassman, Tognazzi, Manfredi and also Mastroianni, these five actors. The first four appeared in almost all my films and so the stories centered around male characters. They were the heroes. Women were always slightly in the background." Jean A. Gili, *Italian Filmmakers' Self-Portraits: A Selection of Interviews* (Rome: Gremese, 1998), 87–89.

⁹ Maggie Günsberg, *Italian Cinema; Gender and Genre* (Basingstoke: Macmillan, 2005), 71.

¹⁰ Enrico Giacovelli, *La commedia all'italiana* (Rome: Gremese, 1990), 27.

¹¹ Translated by the author from French: "Tous ceux de notre génération, nous faisions ce genre de cinéma en donnant une grande place à l'ironie. L'ironie fait partie du drame de la vie, elle est nécessaire pour le raconter.… Pourquoi tant d'amis et d'élèves ont-ils souffert inutilement pour faire tenir debout une histoire cinématographique à raconter? Parce que parfois, à l'intérieur, manquent ces incitations, ces enrichissements, cette chaudière, ce moteur.… Ce qui a remplacé cette impulsion, c'est ce qu'on appelé en Italie un progrès psycho-sociologique, à savoir donner de la valeur à ce qu'on est, se raconter soi-même. Il est très difficile de découvrir l'abîme qu'il y a entre cette conscience de soi, cette exhibition, et l'utilisation qu'on doit en faire pour réaliser des œuvres qui regardent les autres et les intéressent." Gili, "Entretien avec Furio Scarpelli," 97.

¹² Translated by the author from Italian: "La commedia cinematografica italiana ha subito in questi ultimi tempi una complessa trasformazione, sembrano ormai scomparsi dai nostri schermi gli squallidi prodotti di una comicità gratuita e provinciale, per cedere il passo ad opere più ambiziose, che rivolgono, con sempre maggior interesse, la loro attenzione agli aspetti più paradossali della realtà italiana." Lorenzo Quaglietti, *Cinemasessanta* (1963).

¹³ Gili, "Entretien avec Furio Scarpelli," 96.

¹⁴ Gili, *Italian Filmmakers' Self-Portraits*, 82.

¹⁵ Translated by the author from Italian: "Il sentimentalismo è un elemento che sia io o la commedia all'italiana odiamo." Pintus, *Storia e film,* 152.

¹⁶ Translated by the author from Italian: "Pensavamo al setaccio, il costume, la cronaca, l'attualità per smascherare debolezze e sotterfugi, piccolezze e difetti della gente della strada. Rovesciando luoghi comuni e abbattendo miti, senza pietà e con cattiveria. Perché la commedia è cattiva, anzi spietata. In questa ottica la verosimiglianza assume un ruolo decisivo. È un'esigenza ma anche un'arma nel nostro gioco al massacro." Mondadori, *La commedia umana,* 15.

¹⁷ Gili, *Italian Filmmakers' Self-Portraits,* 74.

¹⁸ Translated by the author from Italian: "Uno dei nostri bersagli preferiti è sempre stato l'individualismo generoso di parole e gretto dell'animo di molti personaggi pronti a criticare le istituzioni, le gerarchie sociali, i luoghi comuni, ma poi irrimediabilmente schiacciati da una realtà a cui erano costretti a inchinarsi." Mondadori, *La commedia umana,* 22.

¹⁹ Translated by the author from Italian: "Ho trattato l'argomento in modo violento, maturo, ma ho scelto Sordi, non Volontè. Sordi è l'uomo più amato dagli italiani, l'attore che li fa divertire, il prototipo della commedia all'italiana. L'ho inserito

in questa storia per provocare uno shock a chi avrebbe visto, perché rifletesse come è facile trasformarsi in un mostro quando uno si vuol far giustizia da sé." Pintus, *Storia e film,* 50.

[20] Translated by the author from Italian: "Sono loro gli spettatori che devono trarre le conseguenze…. La morale è solo un comportamento. Non la si può identificare a priori con alcun imperativo: né categorico né ipotetico." Caprara, *Mordi e fuggi: La commedia secondo Dino Risi* (Venice: Marsilio, 1993), 8.

[21] Gili, *Italian Filmmakers' Self-Portraits,* 74.

[22] Piero Tellini also wrote screenplays and dialogues for Alessandro Blasetti's *Four Steps in the Clouds* (*Quattro passi fra le nuvole,* 1942); Mario Bonnard's *The Peddler and the Lady* (*Campo de' fiori,* 1943); Luigi Zampa's *L'onorevole Angelina* (1947); and Eduardo De Filippo's *Side Street Story* (*Napoli milionaria,* 1950).

[23] French comedies, heirs of the theater tradition dear to Marivaux and Molière, have always experienced a rather difficult passage from comedy to tragedy within the same narrative, which was not the case of the *commedia all'italiana* (nor was it with the forerunners such as Fellini's *Il bidone* and *I vitelloni*). Italian comedies, unlike many other national cinemas, have rarely been the victim of rigid classification of their genre, which could have prevented authors, filmmakers, and producers to even conceive a film interfering with several genres concomitantly. French comedies of the postwar era (with rare exceptions such as Autan-Lara's *La traversée de Paris*) were well defined as comedies and rarely involved a dramatic element functioning as the driving force of the film's humor.

[24] The original title of the film was *Le madame* following the nickname given to police officers in the Roman dialect of the postwar era.

[25] In light of the new wave of comic actors, Capannelle interpreted by Carlo Pisacane was an authentic rendition of *commedia dell'arte* with a unique facial expression announcing already the prolific utilization of supporting roles in the future *commedia all'italiana.*

[26] Carlo Pisacane, the actor who played the part of Capannelle, was a Neapolitan actor. Because of his pronounced accent, Nico Pepe dubbed him in order to obtain a genuine Bolognese accent in postproduction.

[27] Monicelli likes to remind cinema historians of the difficulty encountered on the set with fellow writers and producers. For instance, the pressure from screenwriters Age and Scarpelli, as well as producer Franco Cristaldi, to add extras in to the exterior scenes in order to show a more Roman background known for its friendly and animated streets. Instead, Monicelli insisted on following cinematographer Di Venanzo's orientation for a less realistic Rome, thus displaying fewer extras.

[28] Translated by the author from *I soliti ignoti's* original screenplay.

[29] Maurizio Grande. *Abiti nuziali e biglietti di banca: La società della commedia nel cinema italiano* (Rome: Bulzoni, 1986), 52.

[30] Many spectators from popular audiences therefore could hardly identify with protagonists gifted with great acting talent, impeccable diction, and mastery of the Italian language.

[31] These supporting actors included Aldo Fabrizi, Pepino de Filippo, Nino Taranto, Mario Riva, Vittorio De Sica, Walter Chiari, Marisa Merlini, Saro Urzì, GianMaria Volonté, Tiberio Murgia, Renato Salvatori, Carlo Pisacane, Daniela Rocca, Leopoldo Trieste, Lando Buzzanca, Aldo Puglisi, Claudio Gora, Catherine Spaak, Lea Massari, Franco Fabrizi, Ornella Muti, Eros Pagni, Gianfranco Barra, Monica Vitti, Gastone Moschin, Bernard Blier, Adolfo Celi, Anna Longhi, Elena Fabrizi, Tano Cimarosa, Ada Crostona, Alvaro Vitali, Ciccio Ingrassia, Duilio del Prete, Enzo Cannavale, Rossana di Lorenzo, Memmo and Mario Carotenuto, Romolo Valli, Riccardo Garrone, among many others.

Part Two

The Years of Euphoria and the *Commedia all'Italiana*

Chapter 3

Italian Comedy in the 1960s

The Italian film industry of the 1960s produced some of the most recognized auteur films of international acclaim, with works like Michelangelo Antonioni's *L'avventura* (*L'avventura*, 1960); Federico Fellini's *La Dolce Vita* (*La dolce vita*, 1960); Pier Paolo Pasolini's *Accattone!* (*Accattone*, 1961); or Visconti's *The Leopard* (*Il gattopardo*, 1963). Italian auteur cinema as a genre gained visibility thanks to the recognition acquired at European film festivals such as Cannes and Venice as well as the Academy Awards; Sophia Loren received an Oscar for her role in Vittorio De Sica's *Two Women* (*La cociara*, 1961), and both Federico Fellini's *8½* (*8½*, 1963) and Vittorio De Sica's *Yesterday, Today and Tomorrow* (*Ieri, oggi e domani*, 1964) won Best Foreign Film in consecutive years. Italian film comedies, however, with the exception of Pietro Germi's *Divorce Italian Style* (*Divorzio all'italiana*, 1961),[1] were not intended to reach international audiences (France was the exception due to its historical ties to Italy as well as the explosion of coproductions between the two film industries).[2]

According to British historian Stephen Gundle, in the early years of the economic boom, Italian cinema was more than just an entertainment device in parochial or communal theaters; it was also an "agent of social change... a factor of considerable importance: an educator, a source of new ideas and the mediator of the passage to novel and unfamiliar modes of living."[3] But more than simply exhibiting facets of new Italian urban character types in visual form, Italian cinema, and comedy *all'italiana* in particular, adopted the role of observant sociologist as it promoted social consciousness. Depicting countless unfulfilled desires and fruitless hopes of Italians during the troubled years of the "economic miracle" (1959–64), the new comedy contributed in its own way to change the face of modern Italy. With authentic material extracted directly from quotidian reality, comedy filmmakers such as Dino Risi, Mario Monicelli, Marco Ferreri, Luigi Zampa, Alberto Lattuada, Antonio Pietrangeli, Pietro Germi, among others, were able to provide the public with the opportunity to rediscover itself through mostly unglamorous portrayals. According to comedy authors, and in particular screenwriters such as Agenore Incroci and Furio Scarpelli (mostly known as Age and Scarpelli), Ruggero Maccari, Ettore Scola, and Rodolfo Sonego, satires of the economic boom had little social bearing on contemporary Italian society (whether on a sociological or political level), but rather exerted a strong psychological influence through a sarcastic manner in affirming the little faith they placed in the dark humanity they intended to depict. Directors like Pietro Germi, Dino Risi, and Marco Ferreri made it their expertise to illustrate the root causes of social decadence in Italian cities and its peripheries. Their innovative methods utilized real-life situations, never before attempted during postwar comedies, to perform an analytical form of "social autopsy." The newly popular *commedia all'italiana* was about to write one of the most important chapters in Italian film history.

Italy During the Years of the Economic Miracle

Although collective memories of the 1960s in Italy are increasingly vague with time, the era is best remembered as a historical moment of economic euphoria followed by the first symptoms of a generalized social and cultural malaise. Marking a clear break from the preceding postwar decade, the sixties announced the end of the age of social consensus and shared values. The reconstruction efforts of postwar Italy with its capitalistic economy provided the lower middle class with purchasing power and, therefore, access to mass consumption and a lifestyle never before experienced (Italy became the seventh most industrialized country at the turn of the new decade): affordable automobiles, travel and leisure, television, and the resources to pursue a university education for the younger generations. The relationship between man and work changed profoundly as well. In this new economic era, an increasing number of Italians no longer worked primarily to earn for their basic needs, but also to "consume." Due to the new demand in this economic climate, there was an important surge of workers migrating from southern Italy into the industrial triangle (Genoa, Turin, Milan), thus creating a demographic unbalance for years to come. Catholicism also experienced a dramatic shift when the papacy of John XXIII and its Second Vatican Council opened its doors to the world and modernity. Feminine emancipation became a greater reality following the ambition of new political coalitions (*centrosinistra*) allowing women to gain respectability at the work-place as well as in the family nucleus, eventually obtaining the law on divorce in 1970. Finally, the 1960s are remembered as an era of intense social unrest, financial scandals, student protests, and as the prelude to one of the darkest episodes of modern Italian history: the *anni di piombo* (the "lead" years), which introduced political terrorism.

The Italian Political Life

From a historical perspective, Italian political life of the 1960s did not stand in contrast to the other decades of the postwar era. The constant succession of ephemeral governments storming through Palazzo Chigi confirmed the flawed nature of the political system (the constitution mainly), and the incapacity of its national leaders to bring continuity to the economic conjuncture. The fifty-nine different political administrations in the sixty years since the establishment of the Republic in 1946 clearly illustrated the inadequacy of the constitution and the institutions in general, and the 1960s, under the leadership of Prime Ministers Amintore Fanfani or Aldo Moro, were no exception.

The principal political party to control the endless succession of different governments was the Christian Democrats, often described as the heavyweight political force of postwar Italy since its legacy lasted an unprecedented, and as of yet, unequalled forty-four years (1948–92). Created in 1942 by Alcide De Gasperi, along with Giulio Andreotti, Aldo Moro, and many other liberal political leaders, the party's main goal was to act as a mediator between social classes in order to bring the country's entrepreneurship to the level of a market economy. Despite its liberal vision and reformatory perspectives, the party gradually moved away from its optimistic precepts to a more conservative position by the end of the 1950s. With the beginning of the economic boom looming large, the Christian Democrats were obligated to act in concert with the growing influence of the left-wing factions within their own political force, headed by Amintore Fanfani. In 1963, the party line officially relocated its strategic position toward a *centrosinistra* (center-left coalition supported by the PSI or Partito socialista italiano).[4] Perhaps the party's strength, but also its greatest weakness, came from the fragmentation of its ideological trends and ideas, most of the time giving its political engine constant rejuvenation from within, but also at times creating divisions and even episodes of temporary paralysis.[5]

In 1958, the second Fanfani government announced its ambition for social and economic reforms, striving for a more equitable distribution among the classes of its national revenue, in particular for the lower middle class, along with the long-awaited nationalization of the energy industry (to that date, still monopolies run by five regional companies). After the season of reforms was over in the mid-sixties and many promises remained on paper and were never put into place, the party entered its first phase of gradual decline. By the last years of the sixties, a widespread desire for social and economic reform began to elicit a deep and accumulated social malaise. This manifested itself with students' protests, workers' strikes, coincidentally natural disasters (i.e., floods in Florence),[6] and more poignantly, the devastating effects of terrorism, begun in 1969 and continuing into the seventies, a period known as the *anni di piombo* (see chapter 5). In addition, the gap between southern and northern Italy considerably worsened as the south continued to develop at a much slower pace, intensifying new immigration abroad similar to the first wave at the turn of the century (c. 1872–1920). Many points of contention remained on the sociopolitical agenda: the overdue increase of wages, welfare provisions, reorganization of pensions, the reduction of working hours, the need for public housing, and the organization of labor laws (known as the *statuto dei lavoratori* in 1970).

A year after the events of May 1968, which had reshaped France's political horizons, a similar movement took place in Italy, connecting for the first time university students with workers from the big industries. Orchestrated by the three main national trade unions, CGIL (Confederazione Generale Italiana del Lavoro), CISL (Confederazione Italiana Sindacati Lavoratori), and UIL (Unione Italiana del Lavoro), and energized by the powerful emblematic slogan *potere operaio* ("power to the working class"), demonstrations of force took shape in large cities of the north, including numerous attempts to occupy major factory plants. Serious incidents took place in September 1969 (known as *l'autunno caldo*) at the Fiat manufacturing unit in Turin, with sabotage actions in various assembly lines that destroyed thousands of cars. Consequently, after five days of useless mediations, twenty-five thousand workers saw their employment suspended. The following three months of intense social confrontations deeply affected Turin, by then in a state of total paralysis.

Social unrest was quickly followed by a separate phenomenon in Italy: the emergence of terrorism. From 1968 and until 1975, some 4,385 actions of violence (including 63 homicides) took place against politicians, all over Italy, but in particular in Milan, Turin, and Rome. December 12, 1969, the massacre of Piazza Fontana occurred: a terrorist attack on the National Bank of Agriculture in the center of Milan, where sixteen people died and fifty-eight were wounded. Within the same hour in Rome, another bomb exploded in the underground passage of the Banca Nazionale del Lavoro along with two other bombs in different places in the capital city, resulting in seventeen more wounded individuals. In total, there were five terrorist attacks in Italy on the same day within an hour, forcing the country to violently enter a new phase of its modern history, a dreadful decade marked by the scourge of terrorism which would climax in 1978 with the assassination of Christian Democrat Aldo Moro (see chapter 5).

The Years of the Economic Boom

The end of the 1950s was an unparalleled episode in Italian economic history, one of momentum that began to change the fossilized rules of society: the economic miracle. This phenomenon came from two combined political factors: the success of the Marshall Plan, which required public companies to produce materials at low cost to private sector enterprises as part of the country's reconstruction effort, and the newly created E.E.C. (European Economic Community),[7] which facilitated Italian exports to the rest of Western Europe.

In 1958, after years of the state controlling productive assets, Prime Minister Amintore Fanfani (the second term for Fanfani)[8] embarked on an ambitious program of economic and social reforms. In an effort to stimulate its disorganized industry, which had fallen prey to many financial scandals (i.e, the banking scandal involving Gianbattista Giuffrè, also known as *Il banchiere di Dio*, or the scandal of the Leonardo da Vinci airport in Rome involving major fraudulent activity),[9] it encouraged the development of rural enterprises and private businesses, liberalized foreign trade and investments, relaxed state control over prices, and, most importantly, heavily invested in selected large industrial productions. As the economic boom became a reality, the industrialization of the country adopted an unprecedented pace in Italian modern history, and its frenetic growth rate, along with the one in Germany, resulted as one of the most spectacular on a European scale. 1960, the peak of the boom, was a record year for the Italian PIL,[10] or *prodotto Interno Lordo*, the equivalent of the GDP or Gross Domestic Product. Between 1958 and 1962, the index of industrial production experienced a progression of 90 percent, as did the per-capita income. Sectors like the automotive industry, precision mechanics, and metallurgical corporations were at the forefront of the country's industrial endeavors. Large, successful companies such as Edison, Olivetti, Pirelli, Montecatini, to name a few, announced record growth while automobile production quadrupled in those years (148,000 cars came out of the assembly lines in 1958, and by 1962, there were 760,000). Low salaries and concentration of capital enabled large industries to remain competitive in an international market and were, without a doubt, the two main factors that facilitated this provisional growth.

Coincidentally, the year of the centenary of Italy's unification fell during a period when economic discrepancies between the north and the south brought about dramatic aftermaths, such as the average income of the northern population becoming double that of the south.[11] Postwar immigration out of the country and migration within were no longer sporadic but had become a pandemic mass transfer phenomenon; by the late fifties, the colossal internal migration provoked unprecedented demographic imbalances in the north and economic cataclysms in the south.[12] Legions of young people suddenly abandoned their rural origins, depopulating entire villages and regions, in order to seek fortunes in the prosperous industrial triangle of the north and occupy low-income high-rises, already in short supply in the suburbs,[13] that juxtaposed the nearby industrial complexes (1.3 million Italian workers moved to the north between 1958 and 1963) in which they then worked. The exodus abroad from 1951 to 1955, also unplanned, included some 1,366,000 Italians who had left their homeland for economic reasons; this continued, and from 1956 to 1960, the movement intensified to include another 1,739,000 and from 1960 to 1965, 1,556,000, resulting in a grand total of 4,662,000 immigrants who had left Italy for abroad. Each day an average of one thousand Italian nationals would cross the border to perform humble manual labor (i.e., 387,000 for the year 1961),[14] and as expected, the south proved to be the most affected: in 1961 alone, Sicily lost 460,000 of its residents.[15] This massive exodus toward an advanced industrialized society left rural Italy in a desolate condition, as its rural population went from 41 percent of the national population in 1958 to 14 percent in 1963.

After several years of national euphoria and intense industrial production, the economic miracle began to decline in the early months of 1964,[16] the first year of concrete difficulties, as salaries could no longer contend with uncontrolled price inflation.[17] Even with the government's new control of the large energy companies in 1962 with the second Fanfani administration, the deficit could not be rescued. The remaining years of the decade proved to be less productive as mass consumption stalled and economic stagnation settled in, only to fuel growing social unrest; these conflicts became the central focus of the political scene.

Consumerism, Automobiles, and Status Symbols

The sudden advent of consumerism *all'italiana* of the early 1960s was a preponderant ingredient of the economic miracle. It could be best epitomized by the Italian family depicted in Dino Risi's tale "L'educazione sentimentale," the first episode of the feature film *The Monsters* (*I mostri*, 1963), a social satire that opens with the protagonist (Ugo Tognazzi) and his son having breakfast at a local bar, buying ready-made snacks for school, then driving to class in a brand new Fiat 600, while his spouse conveniently shops at the local supermarket. The access to consumerism, whether on screen or taken from reality, was now decisively embedded in Italian quotidian life with its newly implemented supermarkets, cigarette vending machines, public phones, beach bars equipped with jukeboxes, discothèques, etc. These new conveniences offered a direct and continuous invitation to consume, promoting a new image of Italy, far from the traditional rendition of postwar Italy. As transformations in consumer habits, both qualitatively and quantitatively, became a reality, vacationing quickly surfaced as a new popular trend: no longer a luxury, it was a right owned by all Italian working families who could now explore the coasts of Italy during summer vacations.

Figure 1: Yearly spending by general audiences (billions of lira)

Year	Theater	Cinema	Radio/TV	Outdoors
1960	8,191	120,987	48,631	14,298
1962	8,376	132,471	56,641	15,521
1964	11,383	151,699	79,080	19,422
1966	13,559	165,305	95,162	23,851
1968	14,143	170,618	111,836	29,128
1970	16,534	181,896	123,513	33,925

source S.I.A.E.

Consumerism also took shape more immediately than the newly created *autostrade*, infiltrating most Italian homes in the form of a mass consumer medium: television. With its prolific commercialization, the new home-based leisure redefined the concept of communal entertainment as well as popular culture. In just five years (1958 to 1963), the percentage of Italian families that owned a television set jumped from 12 percent to 50 percent (similar to other consumption goods such as refrigerators from 12 percent to 58 percent and washers from 3 percent to 25 percent). Starting on January 3, 1954, Italy's first regular national broadcast aired from the RAI studios in Turin, reaching at the time 24,000 television sets; by 1961 it had reached 2,761,000; 4,400,000 in 1963; and 6,044,000 in 1965. Although considered the longtime adversary of the cinema industry, due to the economical nature of its broadcast and communal qualities (neighbors being able to gather around a single TV set), television was actually an adopted theme among comedies of the boom era. Far from avoiding the theme of television, comic films took advantage of the popularity of television broadcast among Italian popular audiences and featured its manifestation on many occasions. Film historian Giacovelli wrote, "It is not television that diminishes cinema, but rather cinema itself that diffuses and enlarges television and its myth."[18] Indeed, films such as Luigi Zampa's *Il vigile*, representing Sordi and Sylva Koscina during the popular *Il canzoniere* and its mythical presenter Mario Riva, Camillo Mastrocinque's *Lascia o raddopia*, and even satires such as Dino

Jean-Louis Trintignant (Roberto Mariani) and Vittorio Gassman (Bruno Cortona) in Dino Risi's *The Easy Life* (*Il sorpasso*, 1962)
Photo courtesy of BIFI

Risi's *The Monsters* (*I mostri*, 1963) with the episode *L'opio dei popoli* depicting a husband (Ugo Tognazzi) "glued" to the screen watching his favorite show late at night while his wife (Michèle Mercier) entertains her lover in the next-door bedroom, all directly strengthened the status of the emerging new medium.

Along with television, the advent of the "affordable" automobile as a good of mass consumption was to revolutionize the image of postwar Italy, bringing it to the level of the modernized countries of Western Europe and ultimately initiating a materialistic era that included a four-wheel common denominator. While opponents to modernity focused on the automobiles' environmental pollution as well as the escalating record of accidental deaths, the large majority of Italians welcomed Fiat, Lancia, Alfa Romeo, Maserati, and, of course, Ferrari as powerful cultural symbols of individualism, prosperity, personal freedom, and, most importantly, mobility. The success spoke for itself: the number of cars in Italy rose from 342,000 in 1954 to 5,472,000 in 1965.[19] Many contemporary filmmakers viewed the car as a formidable emblem that represented "the sign of the times" and its future mystical legacy for many generations to come. Dino Risi's *The Easy Life* (*Il sorpasso*, 1962), *A Difficult Life* (*Una vita difficile*, 1961), *The Monsters* (*I mostri*, 1963); Antonio Pietrangeli's *The Magnificent Cuckold* (*Il magnifico cornuto,*1964); Luigi Zampa's *Il vigile* (1960); and Francesco Rosi's *I magliari* (1959), among others, faithfully reproduced the psychological effect that the automobile created on the collective imagination. In addition, these films revealed the male obsession with the car's shape, prestige, and what it signified, disclosing the shifting perceptions of Italian masculinity, more and more enslaved in a materialistic lifestyle. Part of the driver's equipment included the unavoidable driving gloves, leather loafers, red horn charm hanging from the rearview mirror for good luck,[20] a magnetic miniature saint (often Padre Pio) attached to the dashboard and accompanied by a magnetic sexual innuendo, such as the "*Sii prudente. A casa ti aspetto io*" ("Be safe. I am waiting for you at home") magnet of Brigitte Bardot as seen in Dino Risi's *Il sorpasso.* These accoutrements that were a part of many vehicles (much like the fragrant tree in NYC taxi cabs) are further outlined in an episode from *I mostri* called "Vernissage" that depicts Ugo Tognazzi installing (almost ritualistically) all of this "collateral" equipment in his new Fiat before exiting the car dealership.

In 1958, Fiat introduced what would soon be labeled the "car of the century" in Italy, the *Cinquecento* (Fiat 500). This tailor-made vehicle not only transformed the luxury good into an affordable conquest for mass consumption, but it would also gradually replace the scooter and send the mythical bicycle back to ancient chronicles (the purchase of an automobile being less than ten monthly wages at the time). Along came the Alfa Romeo Giulia in 1962 (which had introduced the Giulietta in 1954), a car that would become extremely popular with the upper middle class. With the exponentially growing number of vehicles on national roads, the first segment of the "Autostrada del Sole" (approximately 100 kilometers) was inaugurated by Prime Minister Amintore Fanfani in December 1959 (the

Figure 2: Road accidents in Italy per year

Year	Accidents	Deaths
1960	275,993	7,680
1970	220,850	–
1980	175,786	–
1990	161,782	–
2001	–	6,682
2003	225,141	6,015
2005	225,078	5,426

source ACI (Automobile Club Italia)

final chapter of the project ending in October 1964 with a direct connection between Milan and Naples). From now on, even the most modest tourism vehicle would take anyone from Milan to Parma in just over one hour, inciting thousands to use their free time in a newly conceptualized manner.

Coincidentally, toward the end of the reconstruction effort, taking place in the preboom era, new labor laws allowed Italian workers to spend more time at home. To many men, the novelty seemed to generate empty time in an empty space, a sort of "forced leisure," with the often difficult task of appearing as the emblematic *capo famiglia* without a given task: an unexpected demasculating process that disrupted the deeply rooted patriarchal society. Therefore, many men, young and old, welcomed the advent of the "affordable" automobile in order to "escape" the family sphere for leisurely pursuits, flamboyantly represented in Dino Risi's *Il sorpasso* as Bruno Cortona (Vittorio Gassman) transgresses the road signs in search of thrill and adventure until the tragic ending on the coastal highway.

While the Italian administration for years had attempted in vain to implement a long overdue set of *codice della strada* (road regulations), it finally adopted one on June 15, 1959, making it the last Western country to endorse such laws. This decision was realized due to the enormous rising death toll on the roads, a direct consequence of the exponential increase in motorized vehicles in circulation in Italy (twenty times more cars on the roads in just over a decade). The newly emerging infatuation with speed quickly took its toll on Italian youths, as countless victims filled road statistics for years to come (even with a maximum speed of 100 km an hour like in the case of the Fiat 600). As a framework for this analysis, 1960 was the worse year in Italian history, setting an unprecedented record with 275,993 accidents (including 7,680 deaths).[21]

The Presence of Catholicism

At the end of the 1950s, Italy, unlike much of Western Europe, remained a fervent Catholic society, deeply anchored in its traditions; this was due in large part to the ubiquitous presence of the Roman Catholic Church and the control exerted by the *Sant'Uffizio* (Holy Office) of the Vatican in national politics. Its precepts, despite the difficult postwar years and the rapid growth of secularization in the north (Emilia-Romagna and Tuscany), continued to promote a certain Manichean vision of the world. Vividly illustrated in Fellini's *Il bidone* (1955) or Dino Risi's *I mostri* (episode of "The Testament of Francesco"), the Italian people's trust in and dependence on the Roman Catholic Church was resolute. One example, which illustrates the authoritative moral stance of the church, was the practice of coercive measures such as the denunciation and excommunication of politically active atheists, Communists, and philosophers, among others. In 1958, and under the initiative of the secretary of the Holy Office, Cardinal Alfredo Ottaviani, the practice of excommunicating Communists, begun in 1949 by Pius XII's pontificate (1939–58), was renewed and extended to include Christian Democrats, specifically Silvio Milazzo[22] and his fellow political officials who had allied themselves with the Communist Party in order to win the 1958 regional elections in Sicily.

By the end of the 1950s, Italy was Europe's fastest growing economy, and for the Church, the economic wind of change and its subsequent boom triggered preemptive initiatives from the old institution. Although deeply involved in modern-day politics, particularly with the Christian Democrat Party, the Catholic Church's main preoccupation was centered on its interminable combat against contemporary heresies such as the promotion of divorce, premarital sex, contraception and abortion, and their potential consequences on Italian moral as well as quotidian values (i.e., the concept of family as the basic social unit on which both society and state were founded). The position of the church was all the more complex in that its very foundation was slowly losing ground with a diminishing attendance of churchgoers: if 69 percent of Italians attended church services in 1956, just two decades later, in 1979, only 32 percent attended.

Following the death of Pope Pius XII on October 9, 1958, the cardinals' council elected Monsignor Angelo Giuseppe Roncalli (1881–1963) to become Pope John XXIII on October 28 of the same year. The pontiff was chosen by his peers in order to maintain the political status quo and keep the current course of the Church and its involvement in politics on track. Little did they know that the new leader of the Church would do just the opposite. He became the first pope to leave the walls of the Vatican,[23] addressing new spiritual concepts by inviting the faithful and the "nonbelievers" to collaborate (he received the Soviet ambassador and several leaders of the Communist world at the Vatican in special audiences).[24] His welcoming and open persona undeniably broke down barriers to the Holy City, the very heart of Christianity, provoking a true "earthquake" that—to reuse his own expression—heralded the "sign of the times." However, John XXIII's true legacy was the Second Vatican Council. After four years of preparation, the Ecumenical Council of the Roman Catholic Church was inaugurated in October 1962 (and concluded under Pope Paul VI in 1965). This historical council, involving 2,494 advisory prelates, bishops from 86 different countries of the 5 continents, produced 16 documents, one of which, the Constitution on the Sacred Liturgy, authorized the vernacular to promote greater accessibility and hence, attendance, substituting Latin with the modern languages of all Catholic countries around the world; in addition, it allowed the priest to turn to face the faithful during the Mass, no longer turning his back to face the high altar. On April 11, 1963, the encyclical "*Pacem in Terris*" became a crucial document that promulgated a "universal peace in truth, justice, charity and liberty" and is remembered as one of the great texts in the history of the Church, one that clearly marked a defining moment in the new precepts of Catholicism and the "disappearance of the monolithic character that had predominated in the pre-Conciliar period."[25]

In addition to the Council, remarkable developments occurred in tandem with the rapid modernization of the country: in particular, the liberalization of the press and loosening of censorship. On December 7, 1966, the Vatican published the new charter of the *Sant'Uffizio*, which announced the abolition of the "Book of the Index of the Forbidden Books." This drastic shift away from censorship was all the more impressive since the index was created by the Counter Reformation doctrinal intransigence soon after the advent of the press and "heretic" publications in the sixteenth century. Nevertheless, the church was still holding a strong grip on the press and indirectly on Italian families. At the beginning of the economic boom, the Catholic press was still very powerful, with more than 1,800 publications,[26] including the prominent magazine *Famiglia Cristiana*,[27] which reached 5 million readers in 1960 (acutely portrayed in Pietro Germi's *Seduced and Abandoned*).

Catholicism and its cultural framework were therefore rapidly changing and so was Italian society, as illustrated later in this chapter with featured films

Saro Urzì (Don Vincenzo Ascalone), Stefania Sandrelli (Agnese Ascalone), and Lina Lagalla (Francesca Ascalone) in Pietro Germi's *Seduced and Abandoned* (*Sedotta e abbandonata*, 1964)

such as Pietro Germi's *Divorce Italian Style* (*Divorzio all'italiana*, 1961), *Seduced and Abandoned* (*Sedotta e abbandonata*, 1964), and Dino Risi's *The Monsters* (*I mostri*, 1963). The *compromesso storico* (historic compromise) was no longer an intellectual debate engendered by "men of good will." It was an actual shift in cultural orientation that shaped the future of Catholicism and allowed a plurality of ideological canons whose effects, strangely enough, coincided a few years later with the social cataclysm of 1968–69.

Patriarchal Society and Feminine Emancipation

While the 1950s remained a patriarchal society in which the woman's role was primarily centered on the maintenance of the household and the education of children, the 1960s, on the other hand, was the decade that witnessed emancipation for Italian women who for the first time expressed a determined refusal to accept their marginalized position.

On September 20, 1958, the newly voted Merlin Law (named after Senator Lina Merlin who had fought for the bill for more than an entire decade) entered in force throughout the country, closing down over 560 active houses of prostitution that accommodated no less than 2,700 prostitutes. Following the example of France in 1946, the new regulation forbid prostitution in brothels, decriminalized prostitution if practiced privately, and criminalized those who exploited prostitutes or led women into prostitution.[28] But far from abolishing the effect of prostitution, the closing of these houses nationwide (Italian brothels had been under state control since 1883) had the opposite effect: the public, highly visible display of prostitutes now practicing their trade. As paradoxical as it may seem, the determination to close the doors of brothels actually put prostitutes out onto the street, the new place for solicitation for decades to come. Strangely enough, a man's engagement with a prostitute was an "acceptable indulgence" with Catholic priests due to its rate of recurrence, a "regular offense" that could be absolved during confessional.

Feminine emancipation came with the progress made in terms of birth control and the commercialization of the contraceptive pill in 1967. While it had been available in the international market by 1958, and while legal in Italy, it had not been commercialized there due to the inherent respect of Catholic precepts concerning sexuality and Christian bioethics. Consequently, no pharmacist at the time was disposed to go against the omnipotent Catholic moral: even Pius XII on September 12, 1958, a few days before his death, defined it as "immoral," for whoever manufactured, sold, or used it. The turning point came on April 21, 1967; following long deliberations, the Higher Council of Public Health (Consilio Superiore della Sanità) gave a favorable verdict for the use of the pill, which was the first step toward the removal of restrictive norms on the commercialization of contraceptive drugs on Italian territory. The encyclical of the Pope was gradually considered an inappropriate interference by many observers that eventually extended to include some traditionally conservative voters. Likewise, as moral codes were changing in Italy, the Catholic priest lost credibility for many, especially when evoking God as the solution for all intimacy problems within couples. The Church's reactions to the new impulses of open sexuality in the sixties made it appear more and more incompetent to many young Italians.

Nevertheless, the legal system made progress for women's rights as old patriarchal barriers fell down one after the other. In 1965, in Acalmo, Sicily, Franca Viola, a woman who survived an eight-day kidnapping involving rape and violence, became the first woman to refuse the concealment of her "dishonor" and the so-called *nozze riparatrici* or reparatory wedding. Despite enormous pressure, she challenged public opinion and her condition as "dishonored," which was grounded in old patriarchal traditions, and she openly denounced all the perpetrators. On December 17, 1966, the verdict that came from Trapani's courthouse sentenced the kidnapper to fifteen years in prison and four years to his accomplices. Unfortunately, the victory was ephemeral since her family, following a series of death threats, had to leave Sicily. However, this case proved that the subordination of Sicilian women no longer had to be a concealed matter subjugated to the ancient rule of *omerta* (the implied law of silence), powerfully illustrated in Pietro Germi's *Seduced and Abandoned* (*Sedotta and abbandonata*, 1964).

One of the most important moments in the movement for new social reforms was the law on divorce. In October 1965, and following two fruitless attempts to propose a vote in 1954 and 1958, the divorce bill was first presented at Montecitorio. As the feminist movement gradually became of national interest, diversionary maneuvers surfaced to avoid debate on the issue of divorce.[29] In 1970, Loris Fortuna introduced his proposal for new legislation on divorce to the parliament, along with Antonio Baslini, supported by the PCI, the Radical Party, and the center-left coalition, but strongly opposed by the conservative line of the Christian Democracy. The new legislation, officially known as *legge 898*, which legalized and regulated divorce,[30] was approved on December 1, 1970, following a national referendum whose outcome was to astound the entire political class at the time (Catholics and laics included): 19.1 million constituents voted in favor while 13.1 voted against (Sicily along with Sardinia were the only regions of the south to vote for divorce in the 1974 referendum; see Chapter 5). A last attempt to abrogate the law was made under the form of a new referendum (May 12 and 13, 1974) with an impressive 87.7 percent participation rate, resulting in a 59.3 percent majority opposed to the abrogation of the law. Despite its victory, the feminist movement's battle was far from over as the question of abortion was soon to be addressed, fundamentally symbolizing freedom for women, without state control and much less religious influence.

From a sociological point of view, the patriarchal-based society of Italy witnessed the proliferation of new lifestyles and new customs, many of which were directly imported from Anglo-Saxon cultures. Partially emancipated from Latin heritage and Catholic morality of the postwar era, behaviors within all social strata were no longer exclusively shaped by the precepts of tradition and religion, but rather conditioned and affected by the new popular entertainment forms, such as television, sports, and cinema. In fact, many Italians, like the character of Roberto played by French actor Jean-Louis Trintignant in Dino Risi's *Il sorpasso* (1962), gradually discovered that beyond the public spheres, which required adaptation to specific social norms (marriage, career, possession of status symbols), lied an aggressive society in constant evolution, little concerned with morality, oblivious to history, and even less connected with its future.[31] Moreover, the presence of the nouveaux riches, eager for material gain, along with the loss of prestige regarding intellectual professions (faithfully rendered in Mastronardi's novel *Il maestro di Vigevano*, 1961), further affected society's values.[32]

In addition to the euphoric inclination for materialistic consumerism, Italian society experienced some unknown symptoms of social alienation within the new urban population. In the growing peripheries of Milan or Rome, the depersonalization of individuals excluded many from traditional community landmarks. Loneliness, anonymity, poverty, unresponsiveness of the society, interpersonal conflicts expressed with violence and civil litigation, *incomunicablità* (incommunicability was the famous terminology first used in Antonioni's films), all contributed to the atomization of Italian society.[33] And it was precisely the lack of social connections, inherent in a capitalistic society, which rendered the newly urbanized population particularly susceptible to the influence of modern mass media, specifically cinema and television. Historian Stephen Gundle underlined the unprecedented nature of the medium by stating, "Its role in providing the unifying myths of a society that politically was still sharply polarized meant that on the face of things, the cinema was well placed to shape change."[34]

Italian Film Industry in the 1960s and State Censorship

The 1960s faced an unprecedented challenge in terms of communication and information: new means of media communication (television, radio, cinema) rapidly gained coverage all over Italian territory while the government, as well as the Catholic Church, no longer able to control its growth within the law, experienced a major setback. The issue of censorship—moral, religious, and/or a system of controls over artistic innovations and popular consciousness—was at the forefront of public and political debates. As a result, the early years of censorship reached a visible climax in its rapport with the film industry. Threats and intimidations emanated from the Church, and the Christian Democrats controlled censorship commissions; authors and filmmakers had little choice but to comply, using auto-censorship on their screenplay or, for the most daring artists, using comedy in order to dodge traditional censorship, an uncertain guarantee.

Censorship in the cinematographic panorama of pre-boom Italy was nothing new for spectatorship and filmmakers. The earliest institutionalized form of state censorship goes back to a law adopted in 1913, Article 785, which forbade the projection of silent films offensive to the moral sensibilities of the time. A few years later, in 1919, a decree (Article 1953) allowed the censorship commission to confiscate suspect scripts (*Commissione per la Censura Cinematografica presso il Ministero dello Spettacolo*). During the Fascist era, censorship took on a new function, beginning in 1934 with the creation of the *Direzione Generale per la Cinematografia*. After the war, it began to adopt a role in a formative rather than cognitive function. The so-called "instruction" of popular audiences, led by the notorious *Sottosegretario* Giulio Andreotti,[35] also author of the no less notorious quote "I panni sporchi si lavano in casa" ("it is better to wash dirty laundry at home") was by then the quintessential role played by the censorship commission during the 1950s. In the postwar period (c.1945–58), censorship continued, written into the new Italian Constitution of 1948 with Article 21 (freedom of thought/*libertà di manifestazione del pensiero*), which prohibited what was perceived as bad moral values. Beginning on April 21, 1962, with the implementation of Article 161 and continuing into the present, the *Ministero del Turismo e dello Spettacolo* has regulated the content of film production (the law eliminated preventive censorship on theater and literature).

The fight against hedonism and so-called decadent values in the early years of the economic boom could not be better illustrated than with Federico Fellini's *La dolce vita* (screenplay by Flaiano and Tullio Pinelli), which was released in theaters in 1960. The voice of the Vatican, *l'Osservatore Romano*, invited the court to take a firm stance against the film, which according to the press was promoting immoral values, vice, and idleness; their protest reached a level of outrage unknown to this date, publicizing the film as unacceptable, especially since it was set in Rome, the seat of Catholicism, according to the *ministro dello spettacolo* Umberto Tupini (DC). Ironically, despite the warning of the government, which called Fellini's artistic vision a "scandalous subject, negative for the formation of Italians' civil conscience," *La dolce vita* not only won the *Palme d'or* at the Cannes Film Festival on May 20, 1960, but also rose above conservative values, allowing the world to see a new face of Italian cinema.[36] In a similar manner, Michelangelo Antonioni, far from being spared by the state commission, saw his master copy of *L'avventura* confiscated for "obscenity" and promoting values counter to family traditions. Marco Ferreri, a regular target of the state commission, also experienced countless cuts from *The Conjugal Bed* (*Una storia moderna: l'ape regina*, 1963) and the final version of *The Ape Woman* (*La donna scimmia*, 1964).

Because of the constant presence of Hollywood cinema displaying imbedded consumerism habits, the recent influence of the French New Wave, and *auteur* cinema in general, Christian Democrat governments of the early 1960s had to be, to a certain extent, more dismissive than ever before. Its uphill battle was against a filmmaking in a constant quest for new references and always trying to emulate contemporary life through its social and behavioral novelties. One could argue that the level of censorship in the early sixties was even higher than the numerous restrictions orchestrated during the Fascist era due to the challenge brought by the new filmmakers (led by filmmakers such as Pasolini, Antonioni, or Ferreri). As a matter of fact, when comparing Italian popular audiences of the immediate postwar era and the ones from the boom, it seems that the latter had clearly become an informed spectatorship, since viewers had by then familiarized themselves with Hollywood cinema and developed a filmic proficiency in differentiating cultural paradigms.

At the end of the postwar era, the configuration of communication and entertainment in Italy was quickly taking new shape as newspapers and radio were substituted, in part, by the frantic development of television all over the country and the growing interest for a cinematic culture among general audiences. So how was the economic conjecture of the Italian film industry in the early years of the 1960s? To some extent, the industry experienced a rather sound prosperity in many aspects of its productivity, as Cinecittà's production was going full swing with an average of almost 230 Italian films produced or coproduced each year and 700 million tickets sold (the record being 819 million sold in 1955; see Chapter 1). On the distribution level, Italians were able to have decent access to the cinematic medium, as they attended an average of two movie viewings monthly (in the mid-1950s), more than any continental European nation at the time. With an average of 650 million admissions every year, Italian moviegoers were without a doubt among the most engaged viewers with their national cinema, as well as foreign feature films, at the end of the decade, which corresponded to twice the European average of the time; a performance all the more impressive since at the same time some neighboring national film industries, such as the French, experienced increasing hardship in retaining its spectatorship in theaters (in the early sixties over 10,000 cinema theaters were active in Italy, four times more than today).

Figure 3: Box office numbers and income in the 1960s

Year	Spectators (in millions)	Income (in million lira)
1960	745	120,987
1961	741	125,650
1962	729	132,471
1963	697	140,518
1964	683	151,099
1965	663	159,080
1966	632	165,306
1967	569	164,265
1968	560	170,618
1969	551	179,210

source S.I.A.E.[38]

Because of the huge box-office success of Italian comedies, Hollywood films were somewhat momentarily marginalized in the 1950s and 1960s (with, however, a steady comeback after 1976). At the beginning of the sixties, Italian productions were still inferior in number when compared to Hollywood cinema on its national market (160 Italian productions versus 194 American productions in 1960) and interestingly enough, this trend quickly inverted for the first time a year later to see the margin continuingly grow between both national industries. Whereas Italian productions represented 32 percent of the national market in 1960 (trailing American films, which were leading the market with 38 percent), a decade later they were leading their own market with 48 percent (leaving American films far behind with 27 percent). A success all the more impressive in that it intensified throughout the 1970s (see Chapter 5), the only national cinema in the Italian market to actually experience a progression in numbers. At their peak in the mid-1970s, Italian films time and again earned a majority of box-office receipts in Italy, while Hollywood productions represented less than a third of total receipts. At the end of the 1970s, this equilibrium had more than overturned, since Hollywood cinema had already made slow but continuous progress in Italy as well as the rest of Europe (i.e., in 1970, American productions represented 29.3 percent of the Italian market, and in 1983, 41.6 percent).[39]

Within this broad context of market-based strategies, the reasons for the increasing competition between Italian films and those produced by one of its many several trading partners and national cinemas, such as France and of course Hollywood, were mainly a strictly internal (or national) phenomena. Indeed, Italians loved to go to the theaters more than anyone else in Europe. In the year 1960, Italians' budget for movies was by far the most important one, with 57 percent of the entertainment choice; 3.8 percent was for theatrical and musical representations combined, 6.7 percent was for sport events, 23 percent

Figure 4: Italian and international film productions in Italy (1960s)

Year	Italy	USA	France	UK	Others	Total
1960	160	194	24	39	84	501
1961	205	155	37	44	93	534
1962	245	148	42	37	83	555
1963	230	173	38	34	151	626
1964	290	152	29	47	70	588
1965	203	150	16	41	60	470
1966	232	141	20	31	42	466
1967	247	127	37	40	57	508
1968	246	167	55	30	91	589
1969	249	142	30	22	73	516

source S.I.A.E.

was for the radio and television registration. This visibly indicated that half of the funds spent on entertainment were for the cinematic medium (almost ten times more than outdoor activity).

At the other end of the distribution, the statistics were also eloquent, revealing a clear inclination for Italian general audiences to favor national productions and coproductions. In 1960, half of the Italian public went to see Italian films and only a third went to Hollywood films. A decade later, the number of spectators who went to Italian films grew even larger, reaching two-thirds of general audiences (65.1 percent of the national box office in 1971) while American films continued to experience a decrease.

Italian film comedies, especially the *commedia all'italiana*, along with Spaghetti Westerns and Peplums,[40] were clearly supporting the entire industry, as their successful box-office records guaranteed substantial benefits and indirectly boosted confidence for Italian producers and authors. The most successful comedies each year were regularly seen by over a million spectators, as for instance Mario Monicelli's *The Great War* (*La grande guerra* with 1.7 million spectators in 1959), Luigi Comencini's *Everybody Go Home* (*Tutti a casa* with 1.1 million in 1960), Pietro Germi's *Divorce Italian Style* (*Divorzio all'italiana* with 1.2 million in 1961), Dino Risi's *The Easy Life* (*Il sorpasso* with 1.3 million in 1962), Vittorio De Sica's *Marriage Italian Style* (*Matrimonio all'italiana* with 2.3 million in 1964), Mario Monicelli's *For Love and Gold* (*L'armata Brancaleone* with 1.8 million in 1966), Dino Risi's *The Tiger and the Pussycat* (*Il tigre* with 1.2 million in 1967), or even Pietro Germi's *Serafino* (3.0 million in 1968).

On an economic level, production companies came and went at an unusually high frequency. This phenomenon revealed both positive and negative implications for the film industry of the time: on the one hand was a healthy

Figure 5: Box office in Italy in the 1960s between the main national productions

Year	Italy	USA	France	UK	Others
1960	50.6	35.6	2.1	4.9	6.8
1961	47.3	38.5	2.1	8.2	3.9
1962	52.2	36.6	2.4	4.7	4.1
1963	42.0	42.3	3.1	4.5	8.1
1964	50.4	38.9	1.4	6.0	3.3
1965	49.3	36.0	1.1	10.4	3.2
1966	49.7	30.3	1.4	5.0	13.6
1967	54.2	28.4	7.1	7.0	10.5
1968	55.6	29.0	5.0	2.8	7.6
1969	61.7	28.8	1.6	3.9	4.0

source S.I.A.E. in percentile

industry whose high volume guaranteed economic momentum, and on the other was a latent fragility in light of the lack of continuity, echoing an obvious overproduction. While film comedies made the most revenue at the box office, and indirectly sustained in a large part the Italian productions, several important film companies encountered economic hardship in the middle of the decade, such as Titanus, which dramatically reduced its production of featured films after commercial disasters of costly motion pictures (i.e., Luchino Visconti's *The Leopard* [*Il gattopardo*, 1963]), and Lux in 1964.[41] In a now market-based industrial economy, this phenomenon was essentially masked by the successful flourishing of coproductions, particularly with France, as almost half of Italian productions were coproduced at the end of the decade. As film scholar Peter Bondanella described, "The decade between 1958 and 1968 may in retrospect be accurately described as the golden age of Italian cinema, for in no other single period was its artistic quality, its international prestige, or its economic strength so consistently high."[42] Italian cinema and its industry, therefore, were successful on many different levels: productions, exhibitions, and, more importantly, on an artistic level, as *auteur* films were able to guarantee international fame while the comedies *all'italiana* provided a much-needed economic and financial stability.

Alberto Sordi (Alberto Innocenzi) and Serge Reggiani (Ceccarelli)
in Luigi Comencini's *Everybody Go Home* (*Tutti a casa*, 1960)
Photo courtesy of BIFI

Luigi Comencini on the set of *Everybody Go Home* (*Tutti a casa*, 1960)
with Carla Gravina and Serge Reggiani
Photo courtesy of BIFI

The Art of Getting By and the *Commedia all'Italiana* of the 1960s

The *commedia all'italiana*, a national cinematographic patrimony for some and
an exclusively masculine genre for others, served for many years as the principal economic strength of Italian cinema. Internationally known by the work of
filmmakers such as Mario Monicelli, with his seminal *Big Deal on Madonna
Street* (*I soliti ignoti*, 1958), Pietro Germi with *Divorce Italian Style* (*Divorzio
all'italiana*, 1962) and *Seduced and Abandoned* (*Sedotta e abbandonata*, 1964),
but also Dino Risi with *A Difficult Life* (*Una vita difficile*, 1961) and *The Easy
Life* (*Il sorpasso*, 1962), the genre revealed many acting talents during this
decade and confirmed the future legacy of picturesque icons such as Alberto
Sordi, Nino Manfredi, Vittorio Gassman, and Ugo Tognazzi, all of whom
depicted the Italian resilience in the utmost idiosyncratic manner.

While constantly omnipresent in the collective imagination of a newly modernized Italian society of the 1960s, these comedies could very well be considered
unadulterated renderings of Italian people, whose country underwent fundamental transformations at the time. Consequently, the inherent pessimism of many
comedy filmmakers began to pervade their films and their social visions, heralding a new type of cinematic anxiety and outrage. Cynicism, irony, malevolence,

and cruelty all composed a series of devices—mostly employed in dramas—that when used in Italian comedies triggered just the opposite reaction: humor.

To obtain a decent comprehension of Italian satirical humor, the identification and exploration of the various functions of the so-called *arte di arrangiarsi* (or the art of getting by) is essential. This emblematic presence is particularly noticeable in satirical comedies with respect to its recurrent and influential evocation of the remote past that directly recalls the image of an anarchical medieval time, dear to Boccaccio's *Decameron* and the famous *beffa* (medieval farce). At the same time, however, I will argue that although rich in cultural and historical traditions, these satires broke with the conventions of the postwar-era comedies (best described as *commedie piccolo borghese*, even labeled *neorealismo rosa*).[43] They were profoundly shaped by the economic boom of 1959–64 and triggered a desire, for the average Italian, to join modern economic transformations. With the first signs of economic recovery in sight, the themes of comedies changed, introducing, for instance, capitalism, speculation, provincialism vs. consumerism, and the evolution of migration from villages to large city suburbs. Through a critical observation of customs, the new social satires demanded actors to resemble reality (as opposed to the popular characters taken from stages of regional theaters), and rather subconsciously to involve popular audiences with humor and the new *arte di 'arrangiarsi*, which unavoidably brought the Italian character to the attention of the rest of Western Europe and quickly—to some extent—the rest of the world. From now on, Italian comic actors were to forge an unambiguous "masculine" individuality based essentially on a new approach to modern society and the art of dodging the new order, the new "deal."

Often called *il supergenere* by Italian film critics (a genre that included many others), Italian comedy orchestrated its own myths inspired by the past and the then present-day quotidian life.[44] In Mario Monicelli's *Big Deal on Madonna Street* (*I soliti ignoti*, 1958), the use of the traditional "art of getting by," interpreted by Marcello Mastroianni stealing goods at a flea market, heavily based on physical expression, vaudeville, and theatrical rhetoric, was still very much obvious at the end of the fifties. So the coming of the new comedy style, *commedia all'italiana*, turned away from this type of traditional comedy. One goal for the new screenwriters was to mutate the basic physiognomy of Italian comedy and the fossilized image of the *arte di arrangiarsi*. Often misconstrued as exclusively a direct descendant of *commedia dell'arte*, which is rather restrictive (i.e, the robbing of a camera at a marketplace like in *I soliti ignoti*, the art of pickpocketing, or *Guardie e ladri* in which Totò, master con artist is selling a fake ancient coin to an uninformed American tourist visiting the forum in Rome), the "art of getting by" was in reality adaptation rather than exploitation. As a matter of fact, *l'arte di arrangiarsi* can be considered the very early prototype of Italian film comedy: the phenomenological representation of an individual trying to get by at any cost, even if he/she must make significant moral compromises: examples include outsmarting the legal system, changing political parties, infidelity in marriage, or concealment of identity as exemplified by the character of Alberto Sordi in Luigi Comencini's *Everybody Go Home* (*Tutti a casa*, 1960) forced to change and hide his own identity numerous times in order to survive the anarchical situation in Italy in the wake of September 8th events.

The Innovations of Commedia all'Italiana

According to semiologist and film historian Maurizio Grande, the "art of getting by" was a clear product of a *cultura dell'adattamento* (a culture of adaptation)."[45] As early as the end of the 1950s, the new comedy style regularly included a large collection of different plots all containing the element of quotidian survival, indirectly evoking the pseudo heroism of the art of getting by—inherent in the Italian way of life. Grande also argues that too often the image of that art was visualized into a collective skill, a phenomenon linking the individual to society:

> The so-called art of getting by is nothing more than a lurid mechanism in order to dodge one's own misfortunes, a way to adopt a new persona in an attempt to save face. In other words, the art of getting by is the art of deceit and of pretense, a supreme art to fool oneself before even tricking others, until reaching catastrophic fury through comical self-defamation that transforms the daily routine into malaise and failure.[46]

The evolution from visual feats of skill to more sophisticated cultural manifestations on the screen coincided with the coming of the new comedy in Italian cinema. If many of the comic protagonists of the 1950s based their humor on absentmindedness and strong idiosyncratic wittiness (i.e., Totò and Fabrizi, among others), the trend became inverted during the next two decades. In the sixties and seventies there was a deeper psychological element to the actors' comic expression, and a clear desire to resemble, or give the impression of resembling, contemporary spectators. Whereas the comedies of the 1950s included an "art of getting by" based on collective humor,[47] which often, if not always, offered a final reparatory consensus, the 1960s displayed it from a different angle, based this time on individual humor. The *commedia all'italiana,* known for its choral qualities, was now turning into a *satira all'italiana*, a self-deluding satire of the individual.

The typical comedies of the postwar era could be best described as comedies of inclusion as opposed to the *commedia all'italiana*, which preferred the representation of a single individual excluded from society or social order. From the *telefoni bianchi*[48] of the late 1930s to the *neorealismo rosa*[49] of the 1950s, a dimension of reclusion and melancholy was perceptible within the comic protagonists along with their immutable and expected destiny.

One famous illustration of this element of consensual perception is Monicelli's *Guardie e ladri*, from 1951, with two famous actors of the postwar era: Totò and Aldo Fabrizi. Totò is a thief caught by a police officer (Fabrizi). However, during the long pursuit, both of their families have befriended each other, making it difficult for the policeman to take Totò to jail. Even though the roles and behavior seem to be exchanged for a moment, the conclusive outcome is still the expected one. This film clearly belonged to the traditional comedy genre and to the *neorealismo rosa* movement, and not the *commedia all'italiana*.

With the hopes of reconstruction for a country, which at the time was still mainly agricultural, the comedies of the *neorealismo rosa* rarely reevaluated institutions, such as the government, and used the typical stereotyped protagonists, such as young idles, police, politicians, thieves, and pickpockets. For the old-fashioned comedies, by nature conformist in their depiction of socio/political life, everyone at the end of the day could potentially be a good person for society. French film historian Jean Gili called it, "comedy of consensus that aims at ironing out society's contradictions."[50] In contrast, the following decade was just the opposite: disillusions of a nation poorly or too quickly rebuilt, prey to fast-paced industrialization. With the end of the economic boom looming, pessimism became the major tone, since the individual was able to see for the first time that behind the social masquerade[51] lay hypocrisy, frustrations created by the society of consumption, compromises, and corruption. Consequently, comedy directors invested in stories of presentiments, euphoria conjugated with consciousness of fragility, of impending doom. One of them, Dino Risi's *I mostri*, was a seminal film, "a point of no return," since it clearly screened a new type of comedic dynamic: the film offered no integration, no inclusion; instead it flirted on a recurrent basis with tragedy and even entered the realm of the grotesque as

Vittorio Gassman in the episode "Che vitaccia!" in Dino Risi's
The Monsters (*I mostri*, 1963)
Photo courtesy of Dino Dino Risi

Ugo Tognazzi, teaches his young son (Ricky Tognazzi, his actual son in real life) the important lessons of life—not to trust anyone, to dodge the legal system, and to be street smart before anything, that is to say, to be *furbo* (a very powerful adjective in Italian). So unlike the postwar comedies, all of the traditional values were dramatically reallocated, if not overthrown.

The Role of Morality versus Satire

Because the naïve optimism of the postwar era was quickly replaced with a rational pessimism from the posteconomic boom, the role of morality and consensus became gradually obsolete. Interestingly enough, in most comedies *all'italiana,* a final judgmental and moralistic sentencing was absent at the end of the narrative, leaving spectators free to decide (even with the often biased camera point of view commiserating with the unfortunate protagonist). Film historian Aldo Viganò, author of a biography on Dino Risi, explained this new approach to narration and this tendency or conscious choice to give no concession whatsoever to sentimentalism:

> He [Risi] does not speak with the Catholic language of sin, of forgiveness, or even resignation, nor the Marxist tone of solidarity of the classes or revolutionary fight, but rather as an entomologist who studies beings of science without separating the good from the bad, the allies from the enemies. For this, the consequence of atheism brought to an extreme, Risi does not have the primary quality that critics look for in an artist, that is, the willingness to change the world.[52]

As one of the most extreme performances of the time, the film *The Monsters* represented an apogee of cinematic cruelty through the eyes of a filmmaker attentive to the moralistic content of its narration and not, as many critics have falsely understood, the moral itself. The homeless (Vittorio Gassman) who saves the few lira he has to attend a soccer game (La Roma, of course!) and leaves his struggling and hungry family behind; the corrupt deputy in Parliament (Ugo Tognazzi) who, aware of a gigantic financial scandal, finds ways to avoid being informed about it; the unfaithful wife cheating while her husband is glued to the TV set; the *mediatic* monk obsessed with his physical appearance before a television program; in other words, the problematic nature of normality and conformity in society viewed through the eyes of satire. These "monsters" were essentially a social product, a consequence of abnormal but logical situations. But these characters were also victims, which behind the mask of vulgarity and grotesque, were to find a way out only through tragedy.

In Dino Risi's *Il sorpasso*, Bruno Cortona (Vittorio Gassman) tries to take advantage of the outcome of a car accident, allowing humor and tragedy to mix in a manner radically opposed to what was done a few years before with traditional comedy. As he arrives at the site of the accident, he does not know that the truck driver has died in the crash, his body is lying on the ground under a sheet. We, as the spectator, come to this realization at the same moment as Bruno.

Again this subtle visual and sensorial orchestration corresponded to a new and persuasive exploration into the realm of the grotesque. Risi truly gave a revealing "sense of measure" in the direction of his actors (as well as instigating an inherent sense of sobriety in the narration), dosing out the comedic element that directed the spectator to reflection or self-reflection without imposing a moralistic position. One of Risi's objectives was to make a peremptory link between a scene taken from a comedy and a scene taken from everyday life, or, more specifically, between man's vice and virtue. A constant spectacularly visual dilemma, often depicting the Italian individual caught between adhesion and repulse, assonances and dissonances, the example of *Il sorpasso* was a clear study of customs finally liberated from the logical dimension of its plot, of continuity, and, for the first time, free to go beyond the socially proscribed ethic.

So what about morality? Risi's morality was well known to have come from reality itself even in its crudest and cruelest form. From the confrontation among characters and against regulations of society came a morality that did not fit the Catholic ethic or the laity's. It is therefore a fair assessment to say that the morality was a fair competition between individuals (openly amoral) and a daily reality, which contributed to a desacralization of the values, behavior, and customs of Italian society during the economic boom.

The Art of "Arranging" Narration

Unlike many cinematographic movements, the "art of getting by" and on a larger scale the *commedia all'italiana,* never took its inspiration from a contemporary literary influence, nor political creeds. Mario Monicelli explained: "The *commedia all'italiana* became very important in the world by inventing all of its themes, all of the situations and characters."[53] In its structural organization, the originality was also a predominant strength with three principal elements appearing in various modes. First, the confrontation of opposites: the juxtaposition of antithetical elements has always been a guarantee of comedy. For instance, in *A Difficult Life* (*Una vita difficile,* 1961), the unresolved conflict is between Sordi, a Communist journalist filled with social ideals immediately after the creation of the Italian Republic and engaged in an uphill battle against the Christian Democrat administration, and his wife (Lea Massari), who would rather compromise and live a normal existence. The center of interest lies in the human dimension of both parties, with each character "ceding" something to the other. This frequent juxtaposition of opposite characters, such as Gassman and Trintignant in *Il sorpasso,* provided the core, the dynamics without which the "comicità" could hardly function in what was a usually improvised narrative predisposed for "spur of the moment" patterns. For example, in the film, two character types contrast with one another: Vittorio Gassman as the shallow gregarious womanizer infatuated with his *Lancia coupé*, and Jean-Louis Trintignant as a reserved law student fixated on his forthcoming bar examinations. In Monicelli's *The Great War*, the northern versus southern, Gassman as Milanese and Sordi as Roman, leads unavoidably to a discrepancy of "cultural" values and linguistic confusion through regional dialects. Again, the same pattern can be noted in Risi's *The Monsters*, with Ugo Tognazzi, the impulsive and reckless father, teaching his innocent five-year-old son the important lessons of life—his own style—with a rather unusual motto: *bisogna farsi furbi* (one needs to be clever and never to trust anyone). The scene with Ugo Tognazzi driving his son to school epitomized the new value of the "art of survival" featuring two conflicting, yet interdependent individuals caught up in circumstances where no one can leave the other.[54]

The second element is the protagonist's social adaptability. This second element was characterized by the protagonist's unusual movement from a familiar social milieu to another, unfamiliar one, this time including a new referential paradigm (cultural, linguistic, or social). As a result, the central character was often compelled to adapt to the new awkward situation, a quandary, which logically triggered a series of frictions and ultimately frustration. In Dino Risi's *Il sorpasso*, Roberto, all of a sudden lured away from his desk and the preparation of his law school exams more or less against his will, spends two frantic days with Bruno, filled with new emotions and eventually drama. Roberto, symbol of the average postwar Italian, respectful to the social order,

Vittorio Gassman (Giovanni Busacca) and Alberto Sordi (Oreste Jacovacci) in Mario Monicelli's *The Great War* (*La grande guerra*, 1959)

Alberto Sordi (Otello Celletti) and Vittorio de Sica (Mayor of Rome)
in Luigi Zampa's *Il vigile* (1960)

legal system, and resigned to his own fate, his own future in society, is here
challenged by the spontaneity and apparent modernity of Bruno, who represents
the Italy of the economic boom, and its dimension of euphoria, materialism, and
carelessness. The conclusion of the narration manifested itself in an extremely
powerful allegorical manner involving an "unexpected" death.[55]

The third element is the delayed harmonization. The "art of getting by" ends
when protagonists find stability and when the process of synchronization is done
despite insurmountable obstacles. An unbalanced situation in need of equilibrium
was the stereotypical pattern. An innovator in the genre of the "road movies," *Il
sorpasso* adopted a pseudo-picaresque development by the inherent mobility of its
narrative content: a sports car moving from place to place and bringing two opposite characters eventually together. The comedy usually ended when all protagonists had been integrated in the narrative itself: when a balance has been reached,
the story has been told. Again in Risi's narrative, the young Roberto finally opens
up to his new friend Bruno and confesses that he has just spent the best two days
of his life. It is at this moment of synchronization that the story shifts to find a
rapid closure (involving death), since the dramatic function has been fulfilled.

The structure of the *commedia all'italiana* was also one of many innovative
narrations: the linear storyline of the postwar era began a process of disintegration. The change actually occurred with the fragmentation of the narrative.
The anecdotal style with gags, episodes, caricatures, sketches, and paradoxes all
converged to create a present-day, highly convincing drama with seemingly collateral episodes. Perhaps undervalued as a "present tense" phenomenon of current affairs as well as a lack of appreciation for the new narrative configuration,
comedy Italian style was misjudged and underestimated (as neorealism was in

its time), and only valued a decade later primarily by French film historians, and still to this day asserts the modernity of its narrative uniqueness.

The "old school" comedies of the postwar era began to lose ground among popular audiences, since they rarely represented in their narration a socially unique individual, but rather a group of individuals in a unique situation, as in for instance Camerini's *Gli uomini, che mascalzoni* (1932), Steno and Monicelli's *Guardie e ladri* (1951), Fellini's *I vitelloni* (1953) and *Il bidone* (1955), De Sica's *L'oro di Napoli* (1954), and many others. The transformation was unavoidable with the move from traditional comedy to a new comedy, figuratively but also in effect from the remnants of the former one. New narratives were now moving away from the process of fragmentation of the old storyline format to focus only on a facet of the plot and no longer on the plot itself. And that is precisely why the *commedia all'italiana*—distancing itself from the *commedia dell'arte* tradition—began to appear on the big screen with a brand new profile: "episode films" such as Dino Risi's *The Monsters* (1963).

By the same token, but on a different register, Dino Risi's *Il sorpasso* was a good representation of the new trend among filmmakers to carefully organize a "fragmentation" of the narrative conjugated with a present tense and no particular logical progression to the storyline: in other words, a series of sequences or takes, all supporting the phenomenological representation of the *epos quotidiano* or "everyday life epic." During a scene from *Il sorpasso*, Bruno Cortona (Vittorio Gassman) illustrates the "art of getting by," in his own words, with fragments of life not always connected with the logical progression of the narrative frame. He describes to Roberto how he, as a social chameleon, will always be able to change professions and adapt to any difficult circumstances in life:

Roberto: Is it true you work for refrigerators?
Bruno: Sure! It's my field, but it's not doing very well. If tomorrow the market saturates, I will change. You understand? I worked dozens of jobs. Let's say if tomorrow antique furniture is hot, well, I start searching the country, and I will find an eighteenth-century chest. If painting is hot, I will find a Guttuso and so on….
Roberto: Then nuclear missiles hit us and you rent an atomic shelter?

The *arte di arrangiarsi* can also be characterized by a unique mode: according to Aldo Viganò,[56] it was "a first-person narration recited in the third person." A rather subjective piece of reality (the mindset of one single protagonist confronting society accentuated by the charisma of the 1960s actors) was observed through the objective lens of the filmmaker within a collective look. The usual contradiction between the represented object or individual and its/his actual representation was the main dynamic of the new comedies. Since the protagonist had to constantly "arrange himself" in order to survive in the rapidly growing society as well as the pressure of consumerism, the dissociation between protagonist and spectator eventually disappeared, leaving the spectator projecting his own self on the screen, realizing that he too could be a Vittorio Gassman or an Alberto Sordi. The spontaneity of their actions, in other words, the demeanor on the screen, made emblematic actors such as Sordi, Manfredi, Tognazzi, or Gassman distant from daily reality. But the proximity of their psychological content, their moral representation gave the audience an opportunity to judge them as if they were comparable, and consequently the old gap that existed for decades between protagonists and spectators began to close. The narrative framework of the *arte di arrangiarsi* was directed on a quotidian paradigm easily recognizable, where spectatorship could relate and capture every stylized sign through individual or collective existence. In other words, spectatorship was able for the first time to capture and relate to the easily recognizable references of their daily life.

Humor, therefore, was prompted by the fact that the spectator was compelled sooner or later to become spectator of himself, and consequently, the laughter was usually accompanied with a sensation of *disagio fisico*—to use Aldo Viganò's phrase—or physical and moral discomfort. For the filmmakers of the *commedia all'italiana*, to be a protagonist in life was clearly a dramatic experience by essence often inscribed in a scenario of helplessness and degradation. Therefore, in order to observe life with full objectivity and with the required critical distance of the spectator often meant to transform drama into comedy (i.e., Germi's change of mind with *Divorce Italian Style* at the origin scheduled to be shot as a tragedy). Comedy Italian style proved, unlike the old school comedies of the fifties, that humor could be successful outside the usual rigid structures of comedy genres like vaudeville or French comédies de boulevard (Fédeau, and so forth).

In conclusion, we could ask ourselves the following question: why is this mode of observing social and cultural changes no longer mainstream cinema in Italy today? The visual analysis of reality finds once again a better reception through conventional narration—being either literary adaptation, auteur fictions, or documentary style features. Films of the 1960s, and in particular the ones from the *commedia all'italiana*, will remain a rare attempt in Italian film history to establish a real and direct contact with the Italian public, exhibiting a playful reinvention of the quotidian, and daily existence.

Far from being a picaresque experience, these seminal films were often fragmented pieces of narration, witnessing a humanity that acknowledged its own flaws, its own limitations. Indeed, protagonists always seemed to compromise and ultimately betray their own existential ideals. That is precisely the reason why one should bear in mind that the goal of *commedia all'italiana* was primarily to seduce Italian popular audiences rather than convince contemporary film critics. For Risi, "comedy is just a mode to translate tragedy into a spectacle without boring the public."[57] In other words, life, like filmmaking, did not have a proper mission nor preset function. The translation of human behavior into images in motion translated the aspect of immediacy and ultimately reality: the coexistence of tragic and comic with, at the end, freedom given to the viewers to bring their own experiences and interpretations.

Notes

[1] Pietro Germi's film was a celebrated international hit with an Academy Award for Best Screenplay, a nomination for Best Actor in a Leading Role (Marcello Mastroianni), and Best Director in 1963.

[2] Dino Risi had a record twenty-three coproductions with France only. Like him, many Italian filmmakers collaborated with the French film industry, such as Marco Ferreri (eighteen films), Luigi Comencini (eighteen films), Mario Monicelli (seventeen films), Mauro Bolognini (fourteen films), Ettore Scola (fourteen films), Steno (fourteen films), and Alberto Lattuada (twelve films).

[3] Stephen Gundle, "From Neo-Realism to Luci Rosse: Cinema, Politics, Society, 1945–85," in Zygmunt Baranski and Robert Lumley, eds., *Culture and Conflict in Postwar Italy* (London: Macmillan, 1990), 196.

[4] It was the first time the Socialists had agreed to enter a center-left coalition since 1947.

[5] The Vatican exhorted the Christian Democrats to identify and dismiss the left-wing Catholics leaning toward an "open dialogue" with the Communists.

[6] On November 4, 1966, a dreadful flood affected many northern cities bordering the great rivers: Florence, Venice, Trent, Siena, with enormous damages in Piemonte, Lombardy, Liguria, for the most part. Among the cities with the most damage was Florence, submerged by almost ten feet of the Arno water with incalculable devastation to the priceless artistic patrimony along with thirty-five fatal casualties, hundreds of injured, and twelve thousand homeless.

[7] Today's European Union.

[8] Fanfani's first government lasted just but a few days from January 18 to February 8, 1954.

[9] One of Italy's most dismaying banking scandals was associated with the name of Giambattista Giuffrè, also nicknamed the *banchiere di Dio* (the banker of God), who was arrested for financial fraud on August 20, 1958, generating one of the greatest and unusual scandals of the century. Over the course of several years, in the provinces of Emilia Romagna and in the Marches, Giuffrè was able to convince an important number of incredulous parishioners with the endorsement of priests and bishops to whom he promised annual interests between 25 and 100 percent, pledging a prompt short-term reimbursement. As rumors got around the different parishes, hopeful candidates approached the banker with all their savings in hand. For more than a decade, Giuffrè's financial transactions had no legal existence per se, but nonetheless he was able to secure countless loans informally and personally. Giuffrè's fame and "generosity" was even seen as divine philanthropy. The Italian government awarded him with the title of *Commendatore* and the Vatican with the

title of Knight of the Holy Sepulcher. But in the spring of 1957, the pyramid scheme came to an end, as the unscrupulous banker never reimbursed any loan nor did he reinvest the borrowed capital. The Vatican Council finally cut ties with Giuffrè, but it was too late, as thousands of small investors had lost part or all of their savings. Another financial scandal, which also reflected the confusion of the times, was related to the construction of the new airport, Leonardo da Vinci, inaugurated in Fiumicino in occasion of the Olympic Games on August 20, 1960 (the games of the XVII Olympiad). Just six months later, however, it was revealed that the soil of the airport and surrounding area was unfit for use. Due to the imbroglio, the price of the land suddenly had jumped to 250 percent and the costs for the reconstruction were five times more than anticipated.

[10] The Italian PIL passed from 23,200 billion lira in 1960 to 55,900 billion in 1968 and the national consumption from 14,788 billion in 1960 to 64,569 billion in 1968.

[11] The north refers to the so-called industrial triangle in the northwest of Italy between Genoa, Milan, and Turin.

[12] Beautifully written in novels such as Beppe Fenoglio's *La Malora*, 1954; or Italo Calvino's *Marcovaldo*, 1963.

[13] Fellini's *La Dolce Vita* (1960) was filled with numerous images of these buildings under construction, which were very much symptomatic of the country's rapid physical transformation.

[14] 142,000 Italian workers in Switzerland; 114,000 in Germany; and 49,000 in France.

[15] Puglia lost 410,000 of its residents as well; Calabria 345,000; Campania 345,000; Abruzzi 175,000; Basilicata 131,000; Sardegna 135,000.

[16] This was the year when workers began the great protests in order to ask for increased pay wages and subsidies for unemployment.

[17] 1964 was the first year of the cool down illustrated by many belated industrial inaugurations, also called "cathedrals in the desert" (i.e., the inauguration of the gigantic siderurgical complex in Taranto concomitantly with the decline of the demand on international markets).

[18] Translated by the author from Italian: "Non è la televisione a mettere in scatola il cinema, ma il cinema a diffondere e ingigantire la televisione e il suo mito." Enrico Giacovelli, *La commedia all'italiana* (Rome: Gremese, 1990), 112.

[19] In the years 1963–65, Fiat sold an average of 650,000 cars per year; Alfa Romeo 50,000; Lancia 27,000; Ferrari 250; Maserati 250.

[20] *Il corno* (the bull horn), the symbol of fertility from Greek mythology, due in part to its phallic features (the bull being commonly associated with abundance and fertility) has the power to keep away evil and other calamities.

[21] Comparatively, the number of accidents during the economic boom was clearly of a greater number when compared with 1993, and its 148,032 accidents (including 6,288 deaths) among a circulation of 35 million cars. With 2.5 million cars in circulation in the year 1960, the death rate was consequently much greater than today's.

[22] Silvio Milazzo (1903–82) was an Italian politician as well as an agricultural industrialist. His career was mainly remembered for his election to president of the Sicilian

Region in 1958, with a highly controversial coalition between the Unione Siciliana Cristiano Sociale, the PSDI, the PLI, the PRI, and the Movimento Sociale Italiano, with the support of the PSI and the PCI. This political strategy proved successful, as it managed to oust the Christian Democrat usual government with important consequences on national politics. The phrase *"milazzismo"* is still used in the political jargon to define original political alliances between the left and the right.

[23] Giovanni XXIII was indeed the first pope to travel around Italy as he took the train on October 4, 1962, to Loreto and Assisi, first venue of the pontifical authority since Pius IX left for the last time since 1857.

[24] For the first time in history, a pope of the Roman Catholic Church agreed to receive a ranking Soviet leader (Aleksei Adzhubei) and asked him to deliver a message directly to Nikita Khrushchev.

[25] Percey Allum, "Uniformity Undone: Aspects of Catholic Culture in Postwar Italy," 94.

[26] Allum, "Uniformity Undone," 85.

[27] *Famiglia Cristiana*, a prominent weekly national magazine, has been promoting Catholic values for Italian families since 1931. At times, the publication was able to reach one million copies all over Italy. As paradoxical as it may appear, critics emanated by Italian conservatives have accused the weekly magazine of promoting Communist ideas to the detriment of traditional Catholic values (i.e., Silvio Berlusconi's refusal to give an interview to the magazine during the 2006 elections).

[28] The new law was promulgated thanks to the initiative of former prostitute and national figure Marthe Richard.

[29] In Protestant countries, the return to the customs from the Old Testament consented to introduce the divorce regulated like the wedding from the civil right. In Catholic countries, the Council of Trent reconfirmed instead the indissolubility of the wedding and denied the divorce. Reintroduced in France by the Revolution and subsequently legalized by Napoleon, it was once banned by the French Restoration, to finally be reintroduced in 1884 in France.

[30] The practice of divorce already existed to some extent, as affluent couples and their legal representation were able to exert influence in order to present valid motives in order to obtain the annulment of a marriage.

[31] Transgression, an omnipresent theme in countless Italian comedies, was not only a social movement. It was also physical, as illustrated by the new tendency to ignore road signs, or other fellow drivers, as well as marital, with its concept of extramarital affairs in terms of consumerism; a dimension resolutely far from values of postwar Italy.

[32] According to historian Penny Sparke, after the early fifties, "the concept of modernity, associated increasingly with ideas of comfort and luxury, rather than with necessity, became an increasingly important element within an essentially 'bourgeois' culture of the home." This phenomenon was all the more significant in that it coincided with Italy's accession to the reality of the newly created European market. Penny Sparke, "Design, Ideology and the Culture of the Home," in Zygmunt Baranski and Robert Lumley, eds., *Culture and Conflict in Postwar Italy* (London: Macmillan, 1990), 232.

[33] Interestingly enough, the isolation of Italian urban populations caused many feelings of exclusion, in great part caused by social alienation. At the same time, the family

unit, as an indirect consequence, became more important than ever, and as a result more women, against all odds, began to earn the status of fulltime housewives.

[34] Gundle, "From Neo-Realism to Luci Rosse," 217.

[35] Born in 1919, Giulio Andreotti was involved in many governments of the postwar era: in 1947 as *Sottosegratario alla Presidenza del Consiglio* in the different De Gasperi governments, then as Minister of the Interior (governments Fanfani, 1954), Minister of Finance (governments Segni and Zoli, 1955–58), Minister of Treasure (governments Fanfani, 1958–59), Minister of Defense (governments Segni, Tambroni, Fanfani, Leone, and Moro, 1959–74), and Minister of Industry (governments Moro and Leone, 1966–68). Andreotti was seven times *Presidente del Consiglio* (1972–73, 1976–79, 1989–92), the equivalent of Prime Minister, and Secretary of State from 1983 to 1989. In 1991, he was elected state senator for life.

[36] One facet of the postwar Italian cinema was a general attraction with physical, almost graphic representation of the body from *auteur* cinema to the comedies *all'italiana* as film scholar Geoffrey Nowell-Smith underlines: "Although Italian films of the 1950s were more sexually explicit than American films of the period (still regulated by the ludicrous production code), their morality was primitive." "Tradition, Backwardness and Modernity," in Zygmunt Baranski and Robert Lumley, eds., *Culture and Conflict in Postwar Italy* (London: Macmillan, 1990), 58.

[37] S.I.A.E., *Lo spettacolo in Italia, Statistiche 1995* (Rome: Pubblicazione SIAE, 1995), 102.

[38] In 1960, the Italian public went to see 41 percent of Italian films and 46 percent of American films. Ten years later in 1970, the same public went to see 59 percent Italian films and 30 percent American films. S.I.A.E., *Lo spettacolo in Italia,* 175.

[39] In the mid-sixties, the popularity of the Peplum genre was quickly replaced by the Spaghetti Westerns genre among popular audiences.

[40] In the timeframe of thirty years, Lux produced a total of 170 feature films and distributed over 300 films.

[41] Peter Bondanella, *Italian Cinema: From Neorealism to the Present* (New York: Continuum, 1996), 142.

[42] The predecessor of the comedy Italian style was labeled "*commedia italiana*" (opposed to *commedia all'italiana*), also known as *commedia piccolo borghese* from the thirties to the fifties (*commedia rosa* or *neorealismo rosa*). The immediate postwar years were dominated by slapstick comedies (Totò, Aldo Fabrizi, Rascel), political comedies (Luigi Zampa), *neorealismo rosa* (Luigi Comencini, Renato Castellani, Luciano Emmer), as well as some remnants of *telefoni bianchi* (Mario Camerini).

[43] Unlike other genres such as dramas or even traditional slapstick comedies (i.e., *telefoni bianchi*).

[44] Maurizio Grande, *Il cinema di Saturno* (Rome: Bulzoni: 1992), 65.

[45] Translated by the author from Italian: "La cosiddetta arte di arrangiarsi non è altro se non l'epico inarcarsi del soggetto comico sulle proprie disgrazie, un modo di sfigurare la propria faccia quanto più si tenta di salvare le apparenze. In altre parole, l'arte di arrangiarsi e l'arte di mentire e di fingere, arte suprema di ingannare se stessi prima

ancora degli altri; fino a raggiungere nell'auto-diffamazione comica un furore catastrofico che trasforma la routine quotidiana in epica del malessere e del fallimento." Grande, *Il cinema di Saturno*, 71.

[46] With rare exceptions, like the comedies that promoted Totò, who as main protagonist dominated the plot with little room for any other supporting roles.

[47] *White telephones* were Italian comedies of the 1930s that included a strong element of escapism to distract popular audiences from the harshness of daily life, thus representing stories taken from glamorous social milieu featuring emblematic white telephones.

[48] *Neoralismo rosa* were comedies with a realistic social picture, inspired by the neorealist background involving the working class of society whose protagonists struggle in the daily existence, such as Comencini's *Pane amore e gelosia*.

[49] Translated from French by the author: "la comédie de consensus qui vise à aplanir les contradictions d'une societé." Jean Gili, *La comédie italienne* (Paris: Henry Veyrier, 1983), 8.

[50] Here the term "masquerade" is used as a synonym of the omnipresent Italian concept of *perbenismo,* or social respectability, an unquenchable source of inspiration for screenwriters of the *commedia all'italiana.*

[51] Aldo Viganò, *Dino Risi* (Milan: Moizzi, 1977), 10.

[52] "La commedia all'italiana è diventata importantissima nel mondo inventando tutti i temi, tutte le situazioni, tutti i personaggi." Pietro Pintus, *Commedia all'italiana: parlano i protagonisti* (Rome: Gangemi, 1986), 148

[53] During the next decade (1970s), Italian comedies clearly maintained the same function, following the same outlined wit like that in *Profumo di donna* and the unpredictable interaction between two opposed characters.

[54] In a similar manner, the relationship resembled that of the retired colonel Fausto Consolo interpreted by Vittorio Gassman in *Profumo di donna* and Ciccio played by Alesandro Momo through their journey down to Naples.

[55] In other words, to tell a story in a subjective manner that is at the same moment represented from an objective camera angle or as Aldo Viganò explained in the present quote "narrato in prima persona e messo in scena in terza persona." Viganò, *Commedia italiana in 100 Film* (Genoa: Lemani, 1995), 14.

[56] Translated by the author from Italian: "Per me, il comico non è che un modo di tradurre la tragedia in spettacolo senza annoiare il pubblico." Valerio Caprara, *Mordi e fuggi: La commedia secondo Dino Risi* (Venice: Marsilio, 1993), 1.

Chapter 4

The Protagonists of the New Comedy Style

At the beginning of the 1960s, Italian films conquered the Italian market in both production and distribution. That unprecedented success in Italian film history was due to the combination of several concomitant factors: the stagnation of Hollywood films in Italy, the rise of new charismatic Italian authors, the development of the economic "miracle" and its climate of euphoria, the financial backing from producers, and most importantly, the momentum of experienced screenwriters such as Sergio Amidei,[1] Ruggero Maccari,[2] Rodolfo Sonego,[3] Age and Scarpelli, Luciano Vincenzoni,[4] and Ettore Scola.[5] These writers were at the very heart of the *commedia all'italiana*, and how they illustrated the defects of a nation in rapid transformation undeniably privileged the cynical vision of human nature. As film scholar Peter Bondanella states:

> Perhaps no other nation's popular culture so consistently dared to display its worst features and to subject them to such a hearty laughter. It was ultimately an act of artistic courage, as well as sound business practice, to make such films, and they deserve an honored place in Italian film history alongside neorealist classics, which at one time had functioned as the cutting edge of progressive thinking of Italian popular culture.[6]

In the early sixties, many of the above-mentioned screenwriters brought to light new symptoms of Italian society's woes through comedic situations. Combining hyperrealistic narratives with a mood of cynicism, they successfully led spectators away from a linear sense of logic and no longer asked conventional questions about the plot. Instead, they pursued an unprecedented psychological dimension in their films that included a mix of reality with the grotesque; social monstrosity was pictured while frantic hysteria created by the pace of modern life was underscored. These screenwriters, true architects of the *commedia all'italiana* and its success, gave Italian cinema some of the best pages of its history.

Dino Risi and the Art of Caustic Satire

Dino Risi (1917–2008) played an integral role in the establishment of the *commedia all'italiana*: he directed over ninety feature films, the majority of which he cowrote both the screenplay and dialogue. Risi's break came in 1940 when he met Alberto Lattuada, who invited him to serve as assistant director for *Giacomo the Idealist* (*Giacomo l'idealista*, 1942), directed by Lattuada, and *Old-Fashioned World* (*Piccolo mondo antico*, 1941), directed by Mario Soldati. After World War II, Risi made several successful short films on his own; one of them, *Buio in sala* (1948), attracted the attention of a prominent Italian

Dino Risi

producer, Carlo Ponti. Risi also participated in the elaboration of scripts, such as Steno and Monicelli's *Totò and the King of Rome* (*Totò e i re di Roma*, 1951) and Mario Camerini's *Sunday Heroes* (*Gli eroi della domenica*, 1952). He became a national figure of Italian cinema thanks to *Poor But Beautiful* (*Poveri ma belli*, 1956), but it was with *The Widower* (*Il vedovo*, 1959) that he made the transition from the light comedy of *neorealismo rosa* to the caustic satires. Among the countless actors and actresses Risi cast over the years, his protégé was Vittorio Gassman, the most important actor in the director's career, starring in fifteen films, including *Love and Larceny* (*Il mattatore*, 1959); *The Easy Life* (*Il sorpasso*, 1962); *The Gaucho* (*Il gaucho*, 1963); *Scent of a Woman* (*Profumo di donna*, 1974, Oscar nomination for Best Screenplay in 1976); *The New Monsters* (*I nuovi mostri*, 1977, Oscar nomination for Best Foreign Film in 1979); and *Dear Father* (*Caro papà*, 1979).

A *Difficult Life* (*Una vita difficile*, 1961) was Risi's first long feature film labeled *commedia all'italiana,* as it marked a transition from his preceding comedies like *Il mattatore* (1959) and the physical characterizations and impersonations performed in it by Gassman. In an attempt to classify this work, the question of genre was still very much relevant; the film included several key dramatic episodes, and although using a conventional narrative, he deformed it with satire and comic intermissions. The public easily identified with the protagonists, who mirrored on the screen the drama and experience of quotidian life: moral miseries, social contradictions, and the art of getting by. This process of the audience's identification with the film's protagonists was a distinctive feature of the new comedy, unlike other preceding movements.[7]

Alberto Sordi (Silvio Magnozzi) on the beach in Viareggio in
Dino Risi's *A Difficult Life* (*Una vita difficile*, 1961)

A good example of the thematic evolution of Italian comedy was illustrated by Risi's choice for a story in *Una vita difficile*, one that combined historical drama and political satire. Like many of his fellow filmmakers (i.e., Mario Monicelli for *La grande guerra* and *I compagni*; Luciano Salce for *Il federale*; Luigi Zampa for *Anni rugenti* and *L'arte di arrangiarsi*), Risi paved the way toward a new style of historical fresco that represented the story of many Italians with this film. This phenomenon of historical introspections, somewhat neglected during the era of neorealism as well as the years of the *commedia italiana* of the 1950s, came back to life during the first years of the new decade. Following the success of Mario Monicelli's *La grande guerra* (1959) and Luigi Commencini's *Tutti a casa* (1960), both describing Italian society during wartime through individualized protagonists, Dino Risi, using his own persuasive style, represented humanity struggling through the years of reconstruction. The script's clever use of both public and private spheres gave the story great stamina, especially with popular audiences that were already familiar with slapstick comedies (a genre that was popularized by the physical expression of Totò, Aldo Fabrizi, and Rascel). Consequently, the main advantage for the new screenwriters was the use of collective historical landmarks and emblematic stories (represented through an individualized protagonist), which at times were able to convey ideas and criticisms more acutely perceived by the public (than it did during the 1950s). *Una vita difficile* came out in theaters on December 19, 1961, with little success among critics at the time (i.e., Alberto Moravia's severe critique in *l'Espresso*[8]); but as time elapsed, some forty years later, the film had reached universal critical acclaim.[9]

The story, covering almost twenty years, begins in Lombardy on the shores of Lake Como during the winter of 1943, following the turning point of September 8, when Silvio Magnozzi (Alberto Sordi), involved in the resistance against the German occupation, is saved by Elena (Lea Massari) at the moment he is to be executed by a German soldier. After the liberation, Silvio and Elena decide to start an exciting and promising life in Rome. As a journalist in a Communist-oriented newspaper *Il lavoratore*, Magnozzi lives, one by one, all of the historic episodes of the nation as they unfold. Elena, by now his wife and mother of his son Paolo, along with Silvio experience the difficulties of marriage and living in a postwar era. Following a first separation with his wife and desperately in search of a publisher for his autobiographical novel, Silvio is reduced to professional beggary. As the film begins to closely mirror real life, Silvio (the protagonist) goes to Cinecittà and asks filmmaker Blasetti and actors Vittorio Gassman and Silvana Mangano to read his manuscript called *Una vita difficile*, but to no avail (the two actors and director appear as themselves in a rather unusual cameo role). In order to regain his life and return to his wife and son, Silvio accepts his longtime feared nightmare: resignation to a life of concession. Reduced to serving a powerful and callous entrepreneur (Claudio Gora), Silvio, with no ideals left in which to believe, has reached the life of compromise against which he had fought for so many years. All of this changes one night after Silvio is

Alberto Sordi (Silvio Magnozzi) and Lea Massari (Elena Pavinato) in
Dino Risi's *A Difficult Life* (*Una vita difficile*, 1961)
Photo courtesy of BIFI

publicly humiliated by his boss during a lavish, high-profile party. The presence of Elena gives him the moral strength to retaliate as he slaps him in the most eloquent manner (in all Italian film history!), sending him into the pool under the watch of bemused guests. Silvio walks away with Elena, his pride and family regained, as well as his difficult life.

The film convincingly investigated the moral and political evolution of postwar Italy followed by the early years of economic boom. Its sequential rhythm was in tandem with key moments of Italy's modern history: the fight of Italian partisans against the army of occupation; the referendum of June 2, 1946, which put an end to the Italian monarchy; the first democratic elections by universal suffrage of April 18, 1948; and the attempted assassination on Communist Party leader Palmiro Togliatti, triggering riots throughout Italy. The story followed almost twenty years of Silvio Magnozzi's life (1943 until 1961) as well as an entire generation of significant moments in postwar Italy that shaped the country. Through an outspoken denunciation of capitalistic exploitation, materialism, and social disequilibrium, the account of the main protagonist was a contemporaneous authentication of the socioeconomic plight of Italians during the first years of cultural change. One of the defining moments of the film was the evident contradiction between two unattainable realities. One clear intention of Risi, and in particular screenwriter Rodolfo Sonego, was to demonstrate the dramatic changes of Italian society and its moral standards, and how idealistic values had been replaced by ephemeral perceptions such as materialism and rapid social success. Magnozzi's countless disillusions represented the sadness of millions of Italian nationals who were left out of the Italian miracle in those years. The bitterness and sadness found a faithful visual expression in the now famous improvised scene (by Alberto Sordi) when Magnozzi stands alone on the avenue of Viareggio, after having been left by his wife Elena, who is now part of the social elite, insulting and spitting on passing cars in the early morning hours of a summer day. From the difficult awakening of the postwar reconstruction as well as years of fascism where everything was planned without discussing orders, Italians had to gain control of their own destiny, for better or for worse.

Unlike most comedies of the economic boom shot in the early sixties, Risi's *Una vita difficile* presented an interesting and consistent subtext, one of an alternative analysis of human behavior versus flamboyant consumerism. Magnozzi, not part of the successful select few who took advantage of the new opportunities, was rather an outsider who refused material temptations and was constantly challenged by the difficulty of upholding moral ideals. While enjoying a rare moment with his son Paolo, Silvio Magnozzi explains to him why he decided long ago never to compromise his ideals: I am not an "unfortunate man," but rather a "man who refuses to seek fortune."

Like most emblematic characters of the comedies of the boom, Silvio Magnozzi shared the ideals of the huge majority of Italians during these early years of postwar Italy. He understood the trouble of a society that, step-by-step, presented itself as the negation of the common good and that failed to reach the ideals born during the time of war. Driven by "anticonformist" symptoms, political opportunism, and a fear of intellectual stagnation, Magnozzi was far from being the stereotypical heroic figure of the comedy Italian style.[10] Unlike most social heroes who lacked moral flaws, Silvio Magnozzi embodied the common man, a flawed hero, with personal aspirations, anxieties, and identifiable limitations shared by millions of Italians. Risi's depiction of a man's solitary fight against society was conveyed through many powerful images, such as the one in the early morning hours in the countryside near Rome when Sordi stopped a shepherd amidst a herd of sheep and asked him, "Tell me shepherd: Are you happy?" or the image of Magnozzi's solitary presence on the crowded summer beach in Viareggio dressed up in a suit (and clearly standing out) in search of his wife and son.

Una vita difficile served not only as a social and political observation but also as an implicit moralistic representation of good and evil under the guise of social decorum. For Silvio Magnozzi, the only device at his disposal to assert himself was his moral willpower, which ultimately would lead him to the final rebellion. A polemic around the ending of the story and its gesture of revolt came about shortly after the release of the film, and it has been suggested that a better ending would have featured a simple humiliation (Silvio's), since many considered that this heroic gesture portrayed him as an unanticipated hero. One could extend this hypothesis by arguing that his heroic moment did not

Jean-Louis Trintignant (Roberto Mariani) and Vittorio Gassman
(Bruno Cortona) in Dino Risi's *The Easy Life* (*Il sorpasso*, 1962)

emerge through his unambiguous act of faith but rather in the countless "difficult" moments of abandonment and despair, all ambushed along the way. The
redemptory slap—which has quickly become a seminal moment of Italian film
history—did not grant Sordi the status of hero as many film critics then noticed,
but rather a reminder that the return to his "difficult life" corresponded with
the actual reality of the time shared by millions of Italians left out of the race for
success. For Aldo Viganò, Risi's satires were not "ontological but phenomenological"[11] and their composition never carried a moralistic tone, since all of the
material came from factual assessment.

As previously mentioned, Risi's concern for the morality of his stories was
secondary; rather the emphasis was placed on cynicism in complex personalities
in order to trigger the spectator's response. Once again, a pervading dimension
of distrust in human nature substituted the inexpert optimism of the postwar
era, bringing to Italian comedies elements of social disenchantment, moral tension, anxiety, repressed needs, and unfulfilled desires.[12] Any new aspiration born
within the years of the reconstruction effort to start a new society was therefore
quickly short-lived by the antique tradition of corruptions, *campanilismo*, and
the art of compromise.

Just a few months after the release of *Una vita difficile,* Dino Risi directed what
is often considered his masterpiece,[13] *The Easy Life* (*Il sorpasso*, 1962). Written by
Ettore Scola and Ruggero Maccari, the film was the biggest box-office hit of the year
in Italy.[14] A prototype of a genre entirely immersed in the novelty of the present day,
this Italian style "road movie" was one of the very first comedies that approached,
in a direct and explicit manner, the noticeable themes of social change initiated
with the economic miracle; at the same time, its sequential narrative paved the

way for the success of the upcoming "episode films" like *The Monsters* (*I mostri*, 1963) and *High Infidelity (Alta infedeltà*, 1963).

The narrative was faithful to the tradition of the *commedia all'italiana*: it was based upon a satirical rendition of contemporary customs with the usual targets of family values, marriage, liberation of sexuality, antiquated social norms, emerging consumerism, and discovery of leisurely pastimes, among others. The comedic value/mechanism, unlike the narration, was produced by the impossible combination of two fundamentally disparate characters: Bruno Cortona (Vittorio Gassman), a contagiously enthusiastic forty-year-old Casanova, and Roberto Mariani (Jean-Louis Trintignant), a young, introverted law student. Unlike many satires of the time, the screenplay made a conscious choice to deliberately avoid a resolute opinion on the character of Bruno and his obvious lack of responsibility; it instead objectively disclosed his moral flaws, emblematic of the many defects of Italian society as it evolved following the economic boom. It was rather the spontaneity of Bruno's actions, and not their content, that triggered the viewers' possibility of critical judgment, since after all, his rash and outrageous behavior was nothing new for the comedic content of the early 1960s (i.e., womanizing, art of getting by, false identity, dodging the law, imitation of regional accents). According to Aldo Viganò, Risi's comedies "assumed the function of catalyst pole, which directed the course of the story and based themselves upon the dialectical contradiction between the represented object and its actual representation."[15] Here the representation of recurring social and human conquests performed by the emblematic Latin lover in question went beyond the habitual rendition of its mythological repertoire; this time it offered an allegorical dimension at the end of the story, suggesting in an unusual epilogue the inherent contradictions of human nature.

During the Italian holiday of *Ferragosto*, in the deserted suburbs of Rome, Bruno Cortona frantically drives his ostentatious "Lancia Aurelia Sport Supercompressa convertible"—also known as "la Spider"—and calls on a stranger, Roberto, whom he sees at his window, to use the phone in his home. To avoid spending the rest of the holiday alone, Bruno presses Roberto to have an aperitif out on the town. The coupe flamboyantly passes through a deserted Piazza di Spagna, Piazza del Popolo, and the Vatican City. Continuing outside the city, speeding toward the nearest port, Civitavecchia, Bruno calls out to passersby, cyclists, and other outdated (much slower) family cars. Roberto, now excited by the animated drive, begins to open up to his new eccentric friend, revealing his love for Valeria, a neighbor, whom he has never formerly met. Later in the afternoon, the two protagonists stop to meet Roberto's aunt and uncle at their country home in Grosseto, Tuscany. Roberto's childhood memories nostalgically come back to him until Bruno explicitly reveals to the young man some unpleasant family details he has just noticed: the secreted homosexuality of the housekeeper ("coincidentally" named Occhiofino),[16] the likely affair his aunt had with the gardener, and finally the lack of consideration the family gives to Roberto as they seem more interested in Bruno's visit rather than their own nephew's. Later in the night and after a tumultuous dinner in a nightclub, they stop at Gianna's house. Gianna (Luciana Angiolillo), Bruno's ex-wife, reluctantly receives them before both men end up sleeping on the beach. Energized by his new friendship and Bruno's encouragement, Roberto, deciding to find Valeria at any cost, drives off with Bruno behind the wheel, to Viareggio where she vacations. In his usual reckless driving style, Bruno engages in a series of dangerous passing moves on the curvy roads and loses control of the vehicle driving over a deadly precipice. By chance, Bruno, thrown from the car, survives the crash and looks at the wreck below him. With a vacant look, he simply answers the policeman asking him for the identity of the casualty: "His name was Roberto, but I do not know his last name. I just met him yesterday morning."[17]

The film was the first Italian style comedy that concluded with the death of one of its central characters (with the exception of Monicelli's *La grande guerra* and its inherent thematic of death). Its presence was punctuated by the many emblematic signs that foretold the imminent danger and consequently heralded the fatal outcome of this sudden friendship: the sticker on the dashboard featuring a photo of Brigitte Bardot inviting caution: "Sii prudente. A casa ti aspetto." ("Be careful. I am waiting for you at home."), the red *corno* (horn) charm hanging,[18] the intrusion in the military cemetery while "chasing" the blond German tourists, the encounter with a fatal truck accident with the covered body laying on the ground. This sword of Damocles, whose menacing presence and imminent punishment were reinforced by the narrative framework, indeed gave more importance and reality to the main character, Bruno, whose shallowness took on an entirely new dimension and depth following the death of Roberto. The dramatic ending of *Il sorpasso* became the trademark of the new style of Italian comedy, with the representation of an ephemeral and superficial present, as Aldo Viganò defined it, a "present that burns out without leaving any marks."[19]

As one of the most notorious and imitated characters of the economic boom of the 1960s, along with Silvio Magnozzi (Alberto Sordi in *Una vita difficile*), Bruno Cortona can be best characterized as socially and morally irresponsible. One of the numerous cliché sequences of the film depicting the art of "getting by" was epitomized by Bruno as he parked his Spider next to an already ticketed car and placed the ticket on his own windshield, justifying his action with a simple—now notoriously famous—statement: "If we drivers don't help each other..." Bruno's emblematic figure was also shaped by a multidimensional characterization centered on narcissism, with a clear obsession to challenge his midlife crisis. Although gifted with an inherent talent for capitalizing on sudden encounters, Bruno, oblivious to traditional responsibilities, embodied the typical free-spirited Italian type thanks to his lack of scruples.[20] Along with his flamboyant personality came the natural extension of his own body: the automobile. The automobile was much more than a pretentious symbol epitomizing a specific social status; it was also a true "metaphorization" of space: the only device that linked the notion of time and space. In other words, the car was the logical solution for a new generation of young Italians to reach any social space in any given time. To extend critic Tullio Kezich's argument,[21] the car was the "pretext of an existentialist act and the projection of a profound imbalance." Surprisingly, the Lancia Aurelia was also, metaphorically speaking, the educational tool for the conservative want-to-be attorney, Roberto: it converted him, against his will, to the carpe diem way of life (the act of "*sorpasso*" becoming each time a modest but genuine conquest on an existence/itinerary already filled with compromise).

The rhetoric of Risi's cynicism conjugated with the art of associating antithetic characters best illustrated the clash and ambivalence of an Italian society in prey of drastic social changes. During the early years of the *commedia all'italiana*, Risi's filmmaking was highly influential on other comedy directors as it faithfully recomposed the social mythology of the Italian miracle. To a certain extent, he established a new collective imaginary, radically different from the one of the immediate postwar Italy and destined to provide symbolic figures to an ever-growing repertoire. On many occasions, the discourse of modernity was emphasized through the lens of cynicism, creating a radical shift with postwar comedies. For example, in the realm of sports and leisure, and in particular cycling, the film significantly accentuated the position of the automobile versus the bicycle. The image of these contrasting vehicles was represented in both visual modes and dialogues as Bruno dashed off, leaving a struggling cyclist far behind, adding: "To me, cycling has never been my thing. Please… it is an anti-aesthetic sport, it makes your thighs look fat…. I'd rather be playing pool." Another source of comic inspiration came from the derisive attitude toward the so-called *film impegnati* or intellectual films. Risi's ironical comment on *auteur* films of the early sixties was a salient intertextual borrowing quite in vogue at the time: while driving off to the coast, Bruno asks Roberto: "Did you see *The Eclipse*? Well I fell asleep, what a bore! Nice filmmaker that Antonioni. He has a Flaminia-Zagato. One time on the Terracina freeway, he made my head spin."[22] Here the reference to a more engaged cinema, one made by intellectuals for intellectuals, was less innocent than it seemed, as it placed audiences in a potentially delicate situation: the viewer ending up being spectator of himself, which explains why the comic lines were almost always accompanied by a feeling of uneasiness, very much characteristic of Risi's cinema.

Risi's comedic style was representative of the years of economic euphoria and its many intrusions in traditional Italy: the speed of his camera movements assisted by fast-paced editing (allowing the spectator to visualize the drivers from different angles, in and outside the car) and the numerous takes from the road interspersed with close-ups of the two main actors gave high energy to the sequencing of the narration. The fluidity and rhythm of the camera also presented a genuine feel of instability (and thus created a suspenseful atmosphere) by indirectly suggesting that Bruno's fate was hanging by a thread. Although present in the visual style, the modernity of the narration also came from the balanced use of scene management and the weight given to both protagonists. While Bruno's disposition dominated the entire storyline by nature of his extroverted and invasive personality, Roberto's space was also protected by his moral dimension thanks to the frequent use of a voice-over (thus communicating his thoughts and apprehension). Finally, Riz Ortolani's insertion of fast-paced jazz music combined with famous Italian songs of the early sixties, such as Edoardo Vianello's *Guarda come dondolo* and *Pinne fucile ed occhiali*, Peppino di Capri's *Per un attimo*, *St. Tropez twist*, and Domenico Modugno's *Vecchio frac*, gave the overall narrative an animated momentum, energizing the comedy to a level rarely before attained (such as in *Il gaucho* in 1964).

Taking a critical distance from its historic perspective, comedy was perhaps the genre through which the description of social changes was most effective. It is no surprise then to notice that one of the strong qualities of the film still today lies in its dual commitment to criticize concomitantly the fossilized social codes of postwar Italian society (i.e., Roberto's aspiration to pursue a conventional career to satisfy his family's expectation) and the illusory magnificence of its economic boom (i.e., Bruno's absence of morality). *Il sorpasso* remains to this day one of the most successful frescoes of a country altered by the sudden uncontrollable effects of the economic boom, as film historian de Gaetano called it, "the story about a masquerade, about the disguise of a destructive impulse that rejects the limits, the rules, the roles, and the forms of social life."[23] It is also considered by film historians to be a valuable source of information about Italian society of the early sixties and its complicated rapport between myths and reality: the exodus of the country toward urban environments, the crisis of family value, the reduction of distances between regions due to the development of private/public transportation (the representations of the city and beach resorts was predominant to the detriment of the countryside's), mass vacations usually taken in August at the beach, and, of course, the advent of consumerism for which every opportunity was a direct invitation to consume new products (cigarettes, vending machines, jukeboxes, public phones, auto radios, night clubs, beach resorts, restaurants). Despite enormous commercial success, *Il sorpasso* was overlooked by critics and was, as a result, neglected for a couple of decades before experiencing a true comeback in Italy and France in the early eighties. Dino Risi's obvious inclination for "politically incorrect" characters coupled with the vitality of an unscrupulous cinema disoriented many critics at the time. Considered by Martin Scorsese as the first road movie of its kind, *Il sorpasso* influenced Dennis Hopper's *Easy Rider* in 1969; it also helped Vittorio Gassman win the Nastro d'argento in 1963 for Best Actor.[24]

Boosted by the enormously popular impact of *Il sorpasso*, Dino Risi continued his filmic investigation of the economic boom with an episode film, *The Monsters* (*I mostri*), in 1963.[25] Originally, the project was a script promised to Alberto Sordi (who by then had practically embodied all existing "monstrous" character types of Italian cinema) and intended to gather into one single feature all of the preceding *Sordiani* characters. The pragmatic actor declined the proposition after realizing the potential discrepancy between screenplay and public expectations and began seeking roles less inclined toward amoralistic considerations. Filmmaker Elio Petri[26] then passed the script to Maccari and Scola as well as Age and Scarpelli, who immediately started to write the screenplay and dialogues with some new elements, especially in light of the popular success of Risi's *Il sorpasso*.

For many film directors interested in developing an expertise in episode films, a booming subgenre of comedy in these early years of the *commedia all'italiana*, the advantage was a tangible one: being able to work within a definite art form with explicit delineations, concentrating on an collective vision of Italian society and reducing its narrative sequencing to a minimum. The filmmaker was not the only beneficiary, as advantages profited all levels of the industry; producers too did not take much risk; actors were less involved while making more money; and in the end films cost less and were making more revenue at the box office for distribution companies. On the comedy level, *I mostri* was to be a continuation of such productions as *Il mattatore* or *Il sorpasso*, but this time, structurally different due to the episode format (episodes varying from a wide range in their lengths: from forty-five seconds to seventeen minutes). Starring Vittorio Gassman and Ugo Tognazzi, *I mostri* was to quickly become the outspoken manifesto of the episode film phenomenon. It was a disconcerting portrayal of Italian society, made of twenty short stories illustrating, with the help of particularly assertive actors, the different facets of a singular metropolitan typology touching all levels of Italian society.

Ugo Tognazzi in the episode "Vernissage" in Dino Risi's
The Monsters (*I mostri*, 1963)

Dino Risi wanted to explore the possibilities of social critique with a new form of narrative format this time: the short novel. The comedy *all'italiana* entered a new phase from this distinctive format with its cold cut fragmentation, and its deconstruction of conventional storytelling. The result could be best described in terms of anecdotes, scenes, skits, or even gags, but in reality the filmmaker's final intentions meant much more. This "extraordinary social laboratory," to paraphrase French film historian Jean Gili,[27] displayed a kaleidoscopic composition on the "Italia brutta" illustrated by a series of crude and cruel social fragments as well as an anatomy of the *homo italicus*. Both content and form of the present episodes underlined the visible evolution of Italian comedies, leaving postwar comedies light-years behind this new comedic prototype. Interestingly, none of the comedic elements, at the basis of comedies of the fifties, were present among the twenty episodes of *I mostri*. The outward signs of farces and slapstick comedies left the center of attention to a subtler pattern of moral uneasiness at the basis of the *commedia all'italiana*. The rapport of the spectator/protagonist also changed, as the days of a distant relationship between actors and viewers had gone away: it was now a more latent complicity that was exerted, creating a tension fuelled by the cruel nature of heartless protagonists. "If the *commedia italiana*," argued Italian film scholar Gianni Canova, "institutionalized absentmindedness and sought a balance through inclusion, the *commedia all'italiana* exorcized anxiety with patterns—similar or different—based on exclusion."[28] The so-called "monsters," by their inherent irresponsibility and malicious nature, always developed into objects of exclusion. Needless to say, the actual monsters Risi styled had nothing to do with any kind of physical considerations or protuberances, but rather were associated to a resemblance with the norm and to the plainness of their lifestyle. The sketches were all taken from raw quotidian life and composed a vibrant behavioral study of normal people: a father and his son, a priest, a congressman, a theatrical actor, a street beggar, a police officer, an award-winning writer, a filmmaker, a Casanova, a soldier on leave, or a former boxer, among others. The clear advantage of the skit's format was the occasion to push the limits of the grotesque beyond socially acceptable terms in order to gain strength for the caricatures in question: misogynous attitudes, egotism, immoralist behavior, adultery, deception, an appalling exhibition of contemporary Italians. However, the characters this time approached reality and furthermore resembled the spectators themselves, which eventually led to a viewer's response: the disturbing resemblance triggered a great deal of curiosity, as the viewer had to relate to the microcosm of real humanity, thus exposed in brief and ephemeral intervals from an almost voyeuristic point of view.

The inaugural episode of *I mostri* is based on the father-son relationship. "L'educazione sentimentale" singularly describes the unusual paternal relationship in which an unscrupulous father (Ugo Tognazzi) raises his ingenuous son (the actor's real son Ricky Tognazzi) to become a deceitful individual in order to succeed in life. The daily "education" first takes them to the bar, where the father teaches how to pay for two coffees and two pastries (while consuming three times more). His recurrent motto is quite direct in its rhetoric: "bisogna farsi furbi" (you've got to be clever in life). On the way to school, the father drives on a one-way street and justifies his action as long as no police officer is in sight. In front of the school, the "benevolent" father gives his son two pieces of advice as he urges him not to share his snack with his schoolmates and always to strike first when bothered by others: "Chi picchia per primo picchia due volte!" ("He who hits first, gets to hit twice!"). Later, at a crowded amusement park, to avoid a long line, the father pretends to be a war invalid in order to dodge the line (with the sympathy of the crowd itself). On the way back home, the father lectures his son on his choices in life and urges him never to trust anyone: "Mai fidarsi di nessuno!" The short story ends ten years later in a brutal flash-forward climax showing a newspaper's headline: "He killed his father after robbing him."

In another episode entitled "Il povero soldato," a young soldier on leave (Ugo Tognazzi), whose sister has been recently murdered, arrives in Rome to help the police investigation. After the discovery of her personal journal revealing her activity as a high-class prostitute, he decides to set the different newspapers of the capital in competition in order to auction the confidential journal, which contains all the names and dates of her prominent clients. The final scene of the episode, a masterpiece in its rendition of human cynicism, shows Tognazzi torn between tears, grief, sorrow, and an explicit desire to sell the document immediately, thus creating a unique emotion at the very heart of Risi's derision.

"Che vitaccia!" ("What a life!") illustrates one of the trademarks of the comedy Italian style of the early sixties, representing through the well-known strategy of "despair" another cruel scene among the poorest of the poor. Vittorio Gassman, father of a family of eight, comes to his house (a *baracca* or famous Roman-style shack) where his hungry children and pregnant wife are trying to make ends meet. Between the cries of despair against misery and misfortune, Gassman cannot even gather enough coins to pay the doctor for his sick child. His wife, despite the obstacles, seems resigned to her own fate, leaving him free to go to his occupation. The place where he wants most to go is nowhere else but the Olympic stadium to see "la Roma" play a soccer game for the *Scudetto*. The final sequence of the episode, through rapid zoom, represents Gassman energized among the delirious screaming crowd of Roma supporters.

"La giornata dell'onorevole," perhaps the masterpiece of the film, is a dire political satire, seemingly aimed toward the prominent Christian Democrat Party, Amintore Fanfani (whose political career included several important participations in various governments at the time) narrates the day of a public figure, presiding over the parliamentary commission on public finance. Following breakfast at the monastery where he temporarily resides, he receives the news that a general is determined to make public a scandal against the state. He has discovered that land sold by the state is about to be bought ten times less than the actual value by crooked entrepreneurs. Because of obvious ties with these business companies, the congressman must avoid the confrontational general, and decides to spend the entire day on official duties: a military parade, a boring discourse at the senate, a lunch at a fancy restaurant with French tourists, a private viewing of a cartoon in a cinema. It is only after dinnertime that the congressman comes back into his office to find the tired and upset general still waiting for him to be heard. He finally can reveal what the congressman already knows: the fraudulent contracts have already been signed and the state has just lost millions in that scandal. The goal is reached, as the statesman appears surprised and shocked by the sudden news as well as upset to have come back too late to prevent the fraud. His morals are safe as well, since he will always be able to say that he found out too late in order denounce it. The general, by now exhausted by the long wait, faints on the very floor. The episode, indirectly intending to denounce the hypocrisy of Christian Democrats and their alleged "motivation" to fight corruption only as a last resort, offered a moral dimension to the film without ever imposing a moralistic deduction. I mostri was evidently a social caricature ahead of its time doomed to exasperate many actors of the political scene, and this may explain the conversation original producer Dino De Laurentiis had with screenwriter Age, who refused to finance the project, saying, "If you want to make this film, ask Togliatti to produce it for you!"[29]

"Latin lovers," one of the shortest sequences of the film, functions as the desacralization of the concept of "Latin lover" by illustrating a homosexual version of a summer beach romance. Homosexuality was here openly depicted as Gassman and Tognazzi joined hands while sunbathing with the soundtrack Abbronzatissima! of famous Italian pop singer Edoardo Vianello filling the background. Here the representation of homosexuality was no longer portrayed through hints and play on words as in Il sorpasso, when the character of Occhiofino comes on screen, but this time the substantiation was purely graphic in its ostentatiously provocative visual style.

"Scenda l'oblio" is a direct allusion to the limits of the neorealism on popular masses during the first years of the new Italian society. Here the target is rather evident as the episode illustrates the irrepressible desire for Italians of the consumerism era to acquire goods and enjoy them immediately, most of the time without any sort of compromise. A couple is watching a war movie in a theater. After a firing squad scene (the German Nazis kill an entire family against a wall), the husband turns to his wife, and with an indolent tone of voice and a nonchalant attitude, asks about her preferences for building a similar wall for their new house. This sequence of obliviousness to the lesson of history was also reemphasized in Roberto Benigni's Life Is Beautiful (La vita è bella) with the engagement scene when the school teacher asks the groom to solve a math problem based on extermination of handicapped persons and Jews. The film reached the limits of uneasiness, leaving viewers between feelings of horror and existentialist will to defeat the displayed monstrosity.

"L'oppio dei popoli" is a brilliant comment on the negative effects of consumerism, and in particular the disastrous consequences of television intruding in the Italian family's or couple's life and its latent destruction of the family nucleus. An unfaithful wife (played by the emblematic French actress Michèle Mercier), using her husband's addiction to late-night thriller series, invites her lover in her apartment while the husband (Ugo Tognazzi) remains glued to the television screen, unable to discern any noise coming from the bedroom. After the broadcasting of the program, the husband goes to bed, and the only words he finally utters are: "Che ti sei persa!" ("You missed a good one!").

In "La nobile arte," Tognazzi, a failing coach desperately in search of a contract, tries to persuade retired Gassman to step up in the ring one last time. The goal is to survive the first round in order to get a cash prize from the tournament organizer. Following a swift and devastating defeat, the former champion, who is clearly out of shape and inferior to his young and skilled opponent, is knocked out before the end of the first round. His injuries are such that he now moves around in a wheelchair, having lost most of his senses. The last scene is notorious in its emblematic sarcasm as the two men experience an unforeseen return to childhood and naively play on the beach with a kite, without a doubt having reached the point of no return: the end of the journey, here represented by the deserted oceanfront, invites a symbolic reading.

I mostri remains perhaps the most brilliant example of this successful subgenre of Italian comedy, as it effectively analyzed and captured the raw realism of the new urbanization that was permeating its humanity, in constant evolution in 1963. As Lino Miccichè explains, Risi's modus operandi illustrated sociological realities rather then contributing to a genre in itself: "The filmmaker chooses comedy not so much as a genre but rather as an ideal language and device to represent the world."[30] Therefore, *I mostri* was exemplary proof that comedy Italian style was still rich in theatrical inventions and that its desperate energy was never resigned to some commercial or ontological limits. With the episode genre, directors were finally able to penetrate into the very heart of the Italian mind: assertive to the point of challenging their most unconditional supporters, and successful in their break from the traditional narrative structure of long feature films. Since then, Dino Risi has explained on many occasions his extended inclination toward the flourishing genre: "I was born with Checkov: he was my master. I particularly like short stories because they eventually end."[31] In addition to the form, the Milanese filmmaker also asserted his preferences about the actual content of the medium:

Technique does not exist. Film directors who supposedly write with the "dolly" make me laugh. That is what critics like to hear: they favor directors who look like writers, because they always have an inferiority complex. My method is not at all a technique. If something interests me, I look at it and develop an interest; when the interest disappears, I give it up. That is why my films are rarely monotonous.[32]

This style of popular filmmaking went against certain principles of the so-called *cinéma de qualité* or even *auteur* film requiring a certain photographic savvy, a genuine intuitive dimension of the art of filmmaking. Instead, it proved that the necessary tools for achieving the description of reality, as cruel as it could get, were simply charismatic actors and accurate scenarios. Regrettably enough for the episode genre, the success of these early films triggered some unfortunate emulations by less talented directors and produced in a seemingly condensed time frame (i.e., *Capriccio all'italiana*, 1964) a detriment to the genre and its appreciation.

Mario Monicelli and Historical Comedies

Along with Risi, Tuscan director Mario Monicelli (b. 1915) could easily be considered the most accomplished filmmaker in the history of Italian film comedies, having authored over eighty films during a long and fertile career. Following an initial period spent as a movie critic in the early 1930s, he entered the world of cinema and launched a film career with his first feature film, *Summer Rain* (*Pioggia d'Estate*, 1937). However, it was only after World War II that Monicelli began to make regular cinematographic contributions beginning with the seminal film *Totò cerca casa*

Mario Monicelli

(1949), which he directed with the collaboration of Steno, followed by other successful motion pictures like *Cops and Robbers* (*Guardie e ladri*, 1951) and *A Hero of Our Times* (*Un eroe dei nostri tempi*, 1955). The major turning point of his career occurred with *Big Deal on Madonna Street* (*I soliti ignoti*, 1958). Despite an overwhelmingly negative critical response from the professionals of the movie industry in Italy, the film experienced a slow but growing triumph in France, especially among local cinémathèques, which indirectly compelled film critics to reconsider their original opinion (see chapter 2). In addition to the innovative thematics involving a less predictable development of the story line (a clever mix of neorealist elements conjugated with a heavy dose of social irony), the film also showed the comical talent of Vittorio Gassman and to a lesser extent confirmed Marcello Mastroianni as a legitimate comic actor. The majority of Italian film historians have credited Monicelli with directing the very first comedy *all'italiana* in history with *I soliti ignoti* (see Chapter 2). Shortly after the delayed success of the film, Monicelli was able to direct (with greater fortune) the historical fresco-comedy style *The Great War* (*La grande guerra*, 1959), identified by many as the director's best film due its innovative denunciation of armed conflict. The film was awarded a shared *Leone d'Oro* at the Venice Film Festival in 1960 and received a nomination for the Academy Award for Best Foreign Language Film. Monicelli continued his successful itinerary with two more nominations in the same competing category at the Academy Awards for *The Organizer* (*I compagni*, 1963) and *The Girl with a Pistol* (*La ragazza con la pistola*, 1968). Perhaps the most successful experience with Italian audiences occurred in 1975 with *My Friends* (*Amici Miei*), featuring French actor Philippe Noiret and Ugo Tognazzi in one of the most accomplished "Tuscan style" comedies of the 1970s, often considered a cult film for its satirical intensity and sardonic humor (see Chapter 6). Monicelli, forefather of the *commedia all'italiana* was also the last to direct a comedy *all'italiana* with the poignant *An Average Little Man* (*Un borghese piccolo piccolo*, 1977). His contribution to Italian cinema, beyond the frontier of the comedy Italian style, was enormous, as he discovered countless acting talents over several generations: Claudia Cardinale, Paolo Villaggio, and, of course, Vittorio Gassman as a comic actor. Following the success of *I soliti ignoti*, Monicelli tackled a more challenging subject for his next picture, *La grande guerra*, with the highly controversial association of humor and Italy's recent military history. While elaborating a supposedly comic scenario, Monicelli concomitantly passed critical judgment on the very nature of the film's subject, indicting military politics and their consequences on individuals and humanity.

La grande guerra narrates the vicissitudes of two foot soldiers during World War I: the extroverted Milanese Giovanni Busacca (Vittorio Gassman) and the less boisterous, yet equally as conniving Roman Oreste Jacovacci (Alberto Sordi), both adept at circumventing duty to avoid the battlefield. The year is 1916 and the story's premise opens with the enrollment line of a military hospital. Busacca, who is actively trying to dodge the draft, approaches hospital assistant

Alberto Sordi (Oreste Jacovacci) and Vittorio Gassman (Giovanni Busacca) in
Mario Monicelli's *The Great War* (*La grande guerra*, 1959)

Jacovacci to offer a bribe, using the pretence of poor health. With no one in sight
to rescue him, Busacca is declared fit for combat and finds himself sent by train
to the front. However, both men cross paths again and realize that from now on,
and despite their differences, their fate is linked, as their own survival in this war
lies on their unanticipated partnership. Their first experience with the army is
a tough one, since they must endure strenuous exercises and countless military
maneuvers, during which they try to find diversion in circumstances that divulge
their evident unawareness about war: volunteering as messengers in order to get
a relief. Following this short period of instruction, their regiment stations them
in a relatively calm zone in the village of Tigliano. One day, an Italian regiment
comes back from the combat zone, with exhausted men, most of them wounded,
their uniforms in rags. Jacovacci, who does not recognize his own fellow soldiers, takes them for Austrian prisoners and unleashes his frustration onto the
incoming troops by insulting them (until someone reveals to him their actual
identity). Distractions are scarce for the men except for the "authorized" visits of
prostitutes like Constantina (Silvana Mangano) with whom Busacca falls in
love. As the war progresses, the Italian army must endure great losses due to
the Austrian army's violent attempts to reach the Veneto region. Again, Busacca
and Jacovacci are entrusted with delivering a vital message from the Italian
headquarters to a remote position located four miles away in the rain. After
delivering the letter, they decide to seek shelter for the night inside farmhouse
stables. But much to their surprise, the Austrians take control of the position
during the same night. To escape unnoticed, they wear enemy uniforms, but
with a twist of misfortune they get caught and are brought to the Austrian officer
in command. Mistaken for Italian spies, they are offered to save their lives in
exchange for revealing strategic information concerning the Italian army's next
move, and in particular the location of a makeshift bridge positioned along the

Piave River. With the arrogance of the Austrian officer, both men regain the strength of their dignity, and in a sudden momentum of self-pride, they defy their executioner and die under the firing squad. The last scene shows the victorious Italian army chasing the fleeing Austrians and passing by the two soldiers' bodies, now anonymous.

The main quality of this epic tale relied on the solid equilibrium between the most authentic characteristic of *commedia all'italiana* combined with the dramatic circumstances of war and its deadly toll. One important artistic achievement was the utilization of World War I as a setting device for comedy, not so much to depict the war with outspoken honesty, but rather to show a true deference to both protagonists and their ultimate sacrifice in facing the firing squad. While the screenplay's primary function (written by Age and Scarpelli, Luciano Vincenzoni, and Mario Monicelli) was to promote a *commedia all'italiana*, mainly inspired by the linguistic differences between Sordi and Gassman (Roman vs. Milanese), it also dwelled on their many similarities and common desire: neither of them wished to be burdened with patriotism or bravery as they stood remotely from any personal or collective commitment. Perhaps the most striking scene using *commedia all'italiana*'s association of both physical and psychological humor found its representation at the hospital scene when after short monetary negotiations, Sordi promises Gassman to put in a good word and secure his discharge. As his turn approaches in the waiting line, Sordi realizes that the present officer in charge of the selection is not the type to do favors, and in order to get out of this quandary, he uses a subterfuge: pretending to point at Gassman while speaking to the medical official, Sordi instead just asks his permission to close a window (one that happens to be just behind the unaware Gassman). Amidst a striking series of elaborate and unpredictable behaviors, it appears that the defining conflict not only manifested itself between the two main protagonists but also between high-ranking officers and ordinary soldiers. One of the many tensions between soldiers and commanders was, for instance, the seriocomic representation of the general in command, making a surprise visit to the troops, which was an unequivocal example of innovative comic relief. As the men wait in line to be served soup, the old general asks Jacovacci (Alberto Sordi), who happened to be the first in line:

> General: "You, taste some of your soup and tell me what you think!"
> Jacovacci: "Sir, yes, sir! Hum… delicious and abundant!"
> General: "No, it is actually disgusting. No fat and too little pasta. This is
>   no food for men who fight."[33]

Later the same general confesses to his second in command that the soup was actually just fine but "sometimes you've got to give men at the front some satisfaction. They just need a little of it." Unfortunately, the future development of the armed conflict will prove that this magnanimous comment was empty rhetoric for most men. In a nutshell, the comedy utilized in *La grande guerra* can be best described as a sardonic mood interrupted by intervals of self-pitying sentimentality that take a clear stance on the side of the common soldier and his hopeless plight. And it was precisely the satirical element of the dialogues that gave the narrative its conducive strength, leaving the solemn and dramatic elements to the battles scenes. At the time of the film's release, movie critic Morando Morandini expressed some reservations about the use of comedy versus history in 1959:

> When it does not become satire, comedy is evidently not the best appropriate means to address themes of great collective dimension; it may succeed as an expedient at the most.[34]

What the critic failed to mention was the magnitude of the innovation brought by humor in order to reexamine the lessons of history. Through its comedic element, satire or not, *La grande guerra* offered suggestions that encouraged a new reflection on the consequences of armed conflict and a look at a possible revision of concept for Italy's national history. According to film historian Claudio Fava, the thematic element centered on World War I was a novelty, "In fact, *The Great War* is the first Italian film that truthfully discusses this period of recent Italian history, an episode almost always avoided by our cinema."[35] In many interviews given at the time, Monicelli's stance always appeared to be a transparent one: he always intended to make an antiheroic film rather than an antipatriotic one and to undo the false myth of a grand and glorious war celebrated profusely by the Fascist regime and beyond.[36] However, at the time of production, the media, newspapers, veteran associations, and the Italian military condemned the project and expressed a severe critique of the use of military personnel as extras for a film that intended, according to them, to take on a derisive attitude toward an Italian institution. The intervention of Giulio Andreotti, at the time Secretary of Defense, was crucial, as it successfully convinced the state commission in charge of supervising cinematographic materials that the screenplay had no intention of offending the Italian state nor its military forces and collective memory. Despite the ongoing media turmoil, Dino de Laurentiis, reluctant for a while, agreed to produce the film. Besides the short-lived polemical debate, the film is best remembered for the portrayal of indifference for human life during wartime, which led the way for many more ambiguous moral lessons in human behavior in films. In an interview given to film critic Cenk Kiral, released in September 1998, screenwriter Luciano Vincenzoni (born in 1928 and also screenwriter for Sergio Leone's *The Good, the Bad and the Ugly* [*Il buono, il brutto, il cattivo*] produced in 1966)[37] revealed the influence of the film after its profitable reception in Italy and the inspiration before writing the screenplay for the celebrated Spaghetti Western:[38]

> I had previously done a movie, which was very successful in the Venice Film Festival in 1959, called *La grande guerra* (*The Great War*) with

Vittorio Gassman. It was based on World War I, and from there I captured the idea to make a Western. Three bums across the Civil War. That's how the idea of *The Good, The Bad and The Ugly* developed.[39]

For many commentators present at the 1959 Venice Film Festival, the socio-logical interest of *La grande guerra* clearly surpassed its own artistic value and still to this date is considered by many historians to be Monicelli's masterpiece. In addition, it included important creative contributions, such as an inspired use of realistic photography. Because of the presence of humor throughout the narrative, and the overpowering theme of war, one could easily neglect the fact that Monicelli brought a keen visual style to the story, using many of his trade-mark shots to bring the epic drama to life. For instance, in a masterfully detailed sequence, which assorted different perspectives, Monicelli allowed spectators to feel the sheer terror of an Austrian spy seconds before his execution by fir-ing squad and at the same time, thanks to deep-focus photography, presented a long dolly shot to include the different accents of Italian dialects indifferent to the looming killing.[40] The view of humanity (i.e., the sociological element illustrated by the many different regional dialects) was at the time shattered and became all of a sudden one bleak portrayal, particularly when focusing on the officers in charge and their inherent disregard for human life (e.g., this time the Austrian officer insults the two Italian prisoners before sending them to their death). Credits must also be given to cinematographers Roberto Gerardi and Giuseppe Rotunno with whom Monicelli was able to elaborate some of the most striking and well-photographed battle sequences in Italian cinema (shot for the great part in the Friuli region in 1959). In his condemnation of war, Monicelli prolonged the tension by offering long tracking shots of the two main protago-nists walking down the line of soldiers clearly unfit for battle. When the time came for them to advance into enemy fire, Monicelli kept his camera trained on the soldiers, earning every single inch of terrain they crossed. These shots of long duration impressed the importance of their subjects upon the spectator-ship at the time: the permanence of trench warfare, the devastation of assaults, the hypocrisy of the ruling commanders, the dread of the condemned men who lacked formal education and awareness about the conflict (in 1915, 70 percent of Italians were still illiterate).[41] Interestingly enough, the confused and dreadful attacks on the Austrian positions, through tangles of barbed wire and the bodies of dead soldiers, contributed to the necessary equilibrium mentioned earlier in its rapport with the comedic element. In reality, unlike many other films classi-fied as antiwar movies (i.e., Stanley Kubrick's *Paths of Glory*, 1957), Monicelli's *La grande guerra* established little visual contrast between the officers' plight and the appalling conditions in the trenches; instead its visual focus was con-veyed by the acute photography of mass destruction from the newly invented industrialized warfare. This could explain the deliberate absence of close-ups during the combat scenes, opening the way to a faceless army of men following each other. Alberto Sordi received the *Nastro d'argento* for his interpretation, and the film conquered the *Leone d'oro* at the 1959 Venice Film Festival, *ex aequo* with Vittorio De Sica's *Il generale della Rovere*. A year later, the film was nominated for Best Foreign Film at the 1960 Academy Awards.

Regional Comedies: Pietro Germi's Style

In the history of Italian film comedies, the case of filmmaker Pietro Germi (1914–74) can very well be considered *un caso a parte* (a special case). Satirical comedies of customs found their best advocate with the Genovese actor turned filmmaker mainly due to the striking directorial qualities of innovation, originality, and visual energy. After studying both acting and directing at Rome's *Centro Sperimentale di Cinematografia* (Italy's national school of cinematography) in 1938, Germi worked as an assistant director for such established filmmakers as Alessandro Blasetti. Shortly afterward, he directed his first film, *Il testimone*, which he also cowrote in 1946. For many years, he was classified as a neorealist, but after over a decade he moved away from social dramas like *The Railroad Man* (*Il ferroviere*, 1956) and other thrillers to enter the field of sardonic comedy with the regional satire of customs as a favorite backdrop. As a matter of fact, the director worked on five feature films in Sicily, including *In the Name of the Law* (*In nome della legge*, 1948), one of the most compelling fictions on the Sicilian Mafia, *The Road to Hope* (*Il cammino della speranza*, 1950), evoking the social theme of Sicilian emigration, and *The Facts of Murder* (*Un maledetto imbroglio*, 1959). Following the enormous success of *Divorce Italian Style* (*Divorzio all'italiana*, 1961) and *Seduced and Abandoned* (*Sedotta e abbandonata*, 1964), Germi became corecipient of the Cannes Festival Best Picture Award for *The Birds, the Bees and the Italians* (*Signore e signori*) in 1966.[42] Pietro Germi's last assignment was entitled *My Friends* (*Amici miei*, 1975), a longtime project that was eventually realized by Mario Monicelli due to Germi's death in December 1974. With Germi's sudden absence, Italian cinema lost one of its most insightful and rigorous directors, unique in his engaged vision of reality.

That *Divorzio all'italiana* was never intended to be written as a comedy is no surprise when considering Germi's experience and commitment to social dramas. While beginning the screenplay, it occurred to the Genovese director that the deployment of comedic devices would be a better segue into taboo subjects, polishing the hard angles of the theme with the use of anecdotal gags instead of dramatization ultimately to outskirt censorship.

> As the screenplay slowly took shape and the film got its tone, we realized that the really comic side would always suffocate the tragic aspect, so it was only natural to pick a grotesque vein, the only one really possible

for these incredible stories of "crimes of honor." It is sad that they lead to blood and mourning; but all the rest, the thoughts, acts and facts that lie behind and around the crime are absolutely foolish, ridiculous.[43]

Germi not only created a successful and convincing comedy, but he also offered valuable critical commentary on the legal institutions and cultural traditions of Italy; the means were as effective as a drama. Like Monicelli's *La grande guerra,* which took a chance by tackling controversial themes on warfare and recent national history, Germi touched the ultra sensitive subject of divorce upon which Italy was still very much divided, as the Demo-Christian governments strove to keep the subject as taboo as possible. Here Pietro Germi explained his selection:

> I chose comedy to challenge a theme that dealt with mentality but not customs. The grotesque is all here: to have confused sex with honor and to have utilized that confusion with an article of law, article 587, to be precise. The crime of honor was a disgrace to be ashamed of.[44]

Divorzio all'italiana, by virtue of dangling its target between farce and satire, offered an ambiguous duplicity that made the categorization of the comic genre even more difficult. More than forty years after its production, the film could be best classified as a master custom satire rather than a grotesque farce, often considered its prototype. The film featured the opposition between the decadent nobility and the overgrowing importance of entrepreneurship of the middle class and its appetite for social success.

While undergoing a midlife crisis, decadent Baron Ferdinando (Fefè) Cefalù (Marcello Mastroianni) is obsessed with driving the wheels of conspiracy to rid himself of Rosalia, his smothering wife (Daniela Rocca). Distant and indolent (with the character's famous dark sunglasses, cigarette holder, slicked-down hair, and nervous tic of the upper lip), the Sicilian baron uses crafty maneuverings to terminate the "holy bond" of marriage—by now twelve years of domestic nightmare. He lives in the antique family palace in Agramonte and uses his leisure time to organize plotted schemes; but to add complication to his enterprise, Rosalia is particularly possessive of her unwilling husband. With a cherubic face, shapely hips, faint mustache (exaggeratedly supplemented for comic effect), and a thunderous cackle, her many affections come unwanted on Fefè especially after his eyes catch sight of a younger and seductive distant cousin named Angela (Stefania Sandrelli). Following a meticulous study of the Italian penal code, Fefè decides to use to his own advantage the so-called *delitto d'onore* (crime of honor) or Article 587,[45] which sanctions the murder of a spouse, daughter, or sister if the discovered illegitimate carnal relation causes an offense to "personal or family honor" and if the ensuing murder is perpetrated in a state of "rage." The article also stipulates a rather clement maximum sentence

Daniela Rocca (Rosalia Cefalù) and Marcello Mastroianni
(Ferdinando Cefalù) in Pietro Germi's *Divorce
Italian Style* (*Divorzio all'italiana*, 1961)
Photo courtesy of Photofest

of three to seven years of imprisonment. Hoping to engage Rosalia in some "intimacy" that will compromise the honor of marriage, he intends to catch her red-handed in adultery and hence have the right to kill her. To achieve his goal, Fefè hires artist Carmelo Patanè (Leopoldo Trieste), also Rosalia's former suitor, to restore the living room frescoes of the family palace in order to push her to temptation and directly in his arms. The coveted experience defeats Fefè's wildest dreams: by indirectly coercing his wife to compromise herself with another man, the two lovers foil his plans by actually eloping by train to a secret location on the island. The self-assured Baron suddenly becomes prey to town gossip, a pathetic caricature of the ultimate label: *cornuto* (cuckold!). With the help of the local Mafia, Fefè catches wind of the remote location and decides to take his destiny into his own hands. Once his spouse is murdered, Fefè goes on trial for murder and receives, as expected, a reduced sentence. After three years in prison, Fefè now enjoys his new relation with Angela. He marries her, but as the last scene reveals, many surprises may occur in the future.

Decadence and unapologetic self-centeredness were the heart of the story's comic tone, and perhaps the most brilliant comic element of the film prevailed within the innovative narrative frame. The visual descriptions of Fefè's own biased account of events, anticipating the discourse of his defense lawyer at his murder trial (once the murder is committed) was all the more comical since it came in the form of neurotic nightmares (Rosalia is variously sent into space, buried alive in quicksand, stabbed and made into soap, and shot in a public square by a Mafia assassin). This ingenious and distinctive comic characterization came on a multitude of occasions within the film. Its outstanding cruelty, which was often heartlessly uproarious until recognizably satirical, was presented as a series of connected sketches, similar to the popular genre of episode films. One of the film's strengths was its ability to offer an endless variety of different satirical moments, all geared toward a different target: Satire of customs that surprisingly enough showed a local chapter of the Communist Party where men were dancing among themselves with an ironic voice-over announcing a certain "road to progress." Satire against religion and the Catholic Church[46] with the "partial" Sunday sermons as the town priest stands in front of the parishioners, recommending them to "vote for a party that was at the same time Christian and democratic!" (leaving of course no ambiguity for their allegiance to the Christian Democrat Party). Satire of the *homo italicus* and his ever eager appetite for erotic and sexual curiosity revealed all the men's reaction while discovering on the big screen the generous features of Anita Ekberg in Fellini's *La dolce vita,* screened for the occasion in Cefalú. Political satire when a representative from the north came to hold a meeting on behalf of the PCI (*Partito Comunista Italiano*), asking the male audience their opinion about an ongoing Cefalù case and the adulterous elopement of Rosalia, and obtained, much to his dismay, the hostility of the men who continued to consider her a "whore." The result, clearly an incisive indictment of Italian machismo and its toll of absurdity, was also a gentle reminder of the slow effects of the economic boom in certain parts of the country.

As film critic Mario Sesti defined it in one of the rare publications in English dedicated to the Genovese director, the implementation of the grotesque was the true function of Germi's comedic dynamics, the foundation without which any attempt to insert an incisive social comment would have been lost among the numerous formulaic dialogues and cliché images of Sicily: "The director's use of the grotesque defines a moral stance which is fundamentally alien to the genre."[47] Germi's handle on the absurdity (and monstrosity in some respect) of Italian traditions and the complicity of the legal institution was therefore a novelty and paved the way for many successive films, such as Dino Risi's *I mostri*.

Defined by Maurizio Grande as *falso coniugale*, the theme of seduction and its difficult rapport with traditional values was explored in the 1950s with films like Nanni Loy's *Il marito*, Dino Risi's *Il vedovo*, Franco Rossi's *Il seduttore*, and Antonio Pietrangeli's *Lo scapolo*. As paradoxical as it may appear, Sicily and southern Italy in general became in these early years of the decade the location par excellence of erotic comedy or drama, at least as it transpired in Germi's rendition, and constituted a completion—or rather a denouement—of decades of literary and theatrical experiments (i.e., Vittorio De Sica's *Marriage Italian Style* [*Matrimonio all'italiana*]; Eduardo de Filippo, Luciano Salce, and Marco Ferreri's *Oggi, domani, dopodomani*; and in a different register, Michelangelo Antonioni's *L'avventura*). Hence, the dawn of a new type of popular "seductors Italian style," and as the backdrop, the coming of the Italian economic boom and its contagious appetite for material goods. However, in Germi's universe, any conceptual image of sex was seen and lived as a continuously delayed fantasy, in a recurring pattern usually combined with comic frustration. Therefore, since the mechanism of Germi's comedy relied on the "consequentiality of facts," the result was also dramatic: eros and sexual desires suddenly vanished when challenged with the weight of traditions and, in particular, the institution of marriage. According to film scholar Peter Bondanella, the film's principal asset was to successfully "dissect the senseless and unwritten codes of behavior governing relationships between the sexes in that male-dominated, insular culture."[48] In fact, by simply rendering a regional vision of human passion, Germi was able to portray an imagined, yet genuine series of sketches on "love and plot" upon the entire Italian sociocultural reality. In many instances, idleness and eros were always intersected with a certain knowledge of the codes of the antique traditions and their legal ramifications, and this was precisely what exacerbated the phantasmagorical evasions of its protagonists, making the story all the more daring for its time. Maurizio Grande explains the conflicting rapport between eros and family value:

> In *Divorce Italian Style* the family habitat makes one with a pathological and excessive human environment in which opposite interests and alien cultures collide. As both worlds run into each other, an insane passion takes shape, generating romantic nightmares of forbidden and criminal love ignoring any law or obstacle, according to the format of Romance literature.[49]

Indeed the chaos of human desire versus the respect (or tolerance) of traditions without age or name became a problem for the literary or cinematographic narration, since much of its manifestation evolved within the realm of incommunicability. The repressed sexuality of Fefè (caught between his repulsion of his wife and his impossible love for Angela) and other characters of the film, women's precarious position in traditional Sicilian society, and the expectation of feminine purity (dictated not only by men but also women), all demonstrated the dire consequences of a premodernist conception of sex and family values in an archaic society in contrast to the advent of new values following the economic boom.

From a technical point of view, besides the visually striking black and white compositions imagined by cinematographer Leonida Barboni, the film heralded many technical features, soon to be imitated in the remainder of the sixties: the recurrent flashbacks and flash-forwards imbedded within the narrative voice-over, the frequent use of close-ups (revealing the stress and dread of protagonists), and the camera moving rapidly in the crowd (expressing the unscrupulousness of the curious gossipers and consequently the despair of the Cefalù family) created an efficient and flexible flow to the film. The screenplay and dialogues represented the other solid core: the circles of social power, in which Baron Fefè Cefalù was entangled, were captured through his own narrative, vision, and fantasies, and it is precisely the "whispered" flashback narration that allowed the viewer to completely penetrate the main protagonist's dark fantasies. Written by Ennio De Concini, Alfredo Giannetti, and assisted by Pietro Germi himself, the script won the Oscar in 1963 for Best Original Screenplay (particularly rare for a foreign film). In addition, the film received several international recognitions such as the Best Comedy Award at the 1962 Cannes Film Festival, and Marcello Mastroianni[50] was nominated for Best Actor (musical or comedy) at the 1962 Golden Globes,[51] as well as for Best Foreign Actor at the British Academy Awards the following year.

With *Seduced and Abandoned* (*Sedotta e abbandonata*, 1964) and the international success of *Divorce Italian Style*, the comedy from the south gradually took shape and producers such as Franco Cristaldi and Luigi Giacosi began to maximize its potential with more realism. Following his worldwide recognition, Germi became one of the comedy Italian style's most predominant exponents (though he did not start out within the comedy genre, he became one of its most renown masters) and attracted the critical comment of many film critics and historians. In 1963, one year before the film's release, Sicilian novelist Leonardo Sciascia commented on the author's contribution:

> Germi's discovery of Sicily corresponds to the discovery of a frontier for Italian history, a sort of new American frontier in Italian history: and let's say with respect to the notion of frontier evolving from history to America, and from the historical theory to cinema: a world of fundamental sentiments that expresses and constitutes a law of its own.[52]

Was *Sedotta e abbandonata* more persuasive than *Divorzio all'italiana*? A sense of maturity was evident, most likely due to a less tolerant predisposition

Saro Urzì (Don Vincenzo Ascalone), Stefania Sandrelli (Agnese Ascalone),
and Aldo Puglisi (Peppino Califano) in Pietro Germi's *Seduced and
Abandoned* (*Sedotta e abbandonata*, 1964)
Photo courtesy of BIFI

concerning the archaic values of Italian society, the outmoded codes of honor
stifling individuality, as well as the fossilized legal system still in place at the
time. These narrated chronicles, enhanced by a strong resolution on the aesthetic level, clearly emanated a sense of emergency, more so than in *Divorzio*.
In addition, the film (using a vindictive sarcasm) displayed, in a rather different
style than *Divorzio*, the dark dimension of human beings. When compared to
its predecessor, *Sedotta e abbandonata*, in many respects, was more capable of
transmitting the devastating effects of a tragic reality, allowing viewers to fully
measure the potential of satire.

Staged in a small town in the province of Caltanissetta, the story begins with
the confessions in church of Agnese (Stefania Sandrelli) as she describes the
(un)expected advances of Peppino (Aldo Puglisi), her sister Matilde's fiancée.
Following the priest's advice, Agnese must "punish her flesh" to atone for her
sin, and seeks redemption by undergoing martyrdom by sleeping with rocks
in her bed rather than speaking to her family. Soon the suspicious parents discover a torn scrap of paper destined to Peppino with the enigmatic "mia colpa
di cedere alla lussuria" (my fault for ceding to lust). Infuriated, the ebullient
patriarch (Saro Urzì) coaxes the truth out of her and scuttles a midwife after
dark in order to have her examined. Following the positive result, Don Vincenzo

Ascalone locks up Agnese in her room. With the result of the medical lab
confirming Agnese's pregnancy, Vincenzo begins his quest to identify the
possible seducer of his daughter since she refuses to reveal his name. After much
reflection and examining all possible malefactors, he comes to the conclusion
that Peppino Califano can be the only possible culprit. In a fit of rage, he rushes
to the Califano's house, interrupting the family's supper, and orders him, in writing, to break off the previous engagement with Matilde (Paola Biggio). However,
the situation gets complicated the next day when Peppino declares to his parents
his refusal to marry the unchaste girl. To ward off Vincenzo's impending vendetta, Peppino seeks refuge in a remote village in the convent of San Giuliano.
Meanwhile, Vincenzo decides to seek legal council from a cousin (Umberto
Spadaro), who asks him at once the nature of the tragedy:

> Lawyer: È cosa grave? (Is it serious matter?)
> Vincenzo: Sì. (Yes.)
> Lawyer: Tumore? (Tumor?)
> Vincenzo: Onore! (Honor!)

According to the cousin, who happens to be a lawyer, the penal code is quite
explicit with Article 530: corruption of a minor. However, the existence of Article
544 offers a remedy.[53] A man who engages in corruption of a minor can avoid jail
time if he marries the minor in question. But Vincenzo does not want Peppino to
marry Agnese simply from that twist in the law nor does he want it to be known
in town. If Vincenzo had killed Peppino immediately out of rage—supposedly
to defend the honor of his family—the sentence would be from three to a maximum of seven years (premeditation foresees twenty years). Don Vincenzo's final
option is to charge a member of his family to kill Peppino, but someone who has
not officially proffered oral intimidations (thus avoiding the accusation of premeditation): his innocuous and pusillanimous son Antonio (Lando Buzzanca).
The assassination is warded off by Agnese, who catching wind of the plot, escapes
from her room and tells Police Chief Polenza (Oreste Palella). Following the
failed assassination, the two families, accompanied by their respective attorneys,
meet at the magistrate's office in order to settle the matter for what is doomed
to be a protracted court battle. No agreement is reached, and Peppino is charged
with corruption of a minor. He must now marry Agnese in order to avoid prison,
but Vincenzo wants Peppino to first endure public humiliation by compelling
him to publicly solicit his daughter's hand. Meanwhile, in order to remediate
Matilde's difficult plight, Vincenzo orchestrates an engagement between her and
penniless Barone Rizieri (Leopoldo Trieste). On his side, Peppino is required to
serenade Agnese one night (so that the whole town can find out about his "genuine" love for Agnese) until Vincenzo purposely fires a gun shot in the air (to put
an end to the serenade as well as to make his refusal known). The saga's final
showdown takes place after both sets of parents secretly agree to stage a false

kidnapping so that Peppino will be "legitimately" compelled to marry Agnese. Peppino, assisted by three accomplices, abducts Agnese in broad daylight during the procession of San Antonio and drives off into the country. A moment later, the couple returns to town and knocks at the door of the Ascalone residence. As Peppino asks for forgiveness in front of a bemused crowd, Don Vincenzo answers with Sicilian poise and style: "First I will slap your face, then you shall kiss my hand and then… I shall forgive you." It seems that the fairytale can come to an end with the impending exchange of vows, but once in front of the judge, Agnese no longer consents to matrimony. Therefore, Peppino is immediately charged with kidnapping and the Ascalone family must return home through the backdoor while the snooping crowd gathers before their house (a kidnapped girl who later refuses her captor is unheard of and can only cast a stain on the family name). While making his way through the mocking throng, Vincenzo is victim of a heart attack. On his deathbed, Vincenzo wants his demise a secret from everyone in town and ironically passes away at the same moment the marriage is celebrated in church (Agnese finally consented to marry Peppino).

The use of humor in *Sedotta e abbandonata* was the predominant element of the film, as Pietro Germi directed certain scenes focusing on visually comic details that ironically served to emphasize realism. Similar to *Divorzio all'italiana*, one notices the insightful use of dramatic zoom lens and close-ups[54] accompanied with a self voice-over; in this case it functions to underscore Don Ascalone's distress as he receives confirmation of Agnese's pregnancy and examines one by one every potential seducer in town (school master? friends of the family? family doctor? the parish priest Don Mariano? her brother Antonio? her sister's fiancée Peppino?). By the time the story reaches its unexpected melodramatic point, the efficiency of his method proves itself to be a capable comic device: the audience is indeed seduced into a belief, the protagonists' cultural universe. The intrusion of modern society and its many temptations appear more palpable to the viewer as it is to the unsuspecting protagonists.

Hidden behind the modern style of its social commentary and the recurrent presence of grotesque undertones, the dynamics of the comedic organization was also based upon an old pattern, used many times in the *commedia dell'arte*: the escalation of comic calamities. Each episode was built upon the ironic and unexpected consequences of the previous ones, thus evermore bringing the tragicomic stake to higher ground. Unlike *Divorzio,* the storyline did not respond to a linear itinerary (Fefè's goal was set from the beginning to the end), since the situation evolved every day without clearly announcing its final outcome. The crescendo of the episodic narrative structure generated a sense of anticipation rarely encountered in comic films (usually dominated by a predictable scenario). Perspectives of assassination, kidnapping, then eventually marriage and possibly death, all emerged from a simple and innocuous love triangle. Hence the inevitable anonymous letters that contained accusations of infidelities as well as the ubiquitous oppression of family values and traditions, this engendered morbid schemes that led to moral obligations of honor, eventually paving the way for the so-called *delitto d'onore,* or crime of honor. Thus, it was no surprise that Police Chief Polenza, exasperated by the constant new twists in the Ascalone saga, especially the new kidnapping in town, put his hand over a map of Italy—hiding Sicily—and in a notorious invective confessed "much better now!"

Another strong aspect of Germi's technique to elicit satirical comedy was an innovative manipulation of montage. The initial and seminal event, upon which the entire saga develops, was reenacted from three different angles. First, the initial courtly love scene while Peppino forcefully seduced Agnese; next Peppino's version of the account depicting an abusive Agnese who purportedly cornered him despite his efforts to ward her off (while trying to read a "Christian Family" magazine!); and finally, Vincenzo's version that eventually leads to the truth. It was therefore that rigorous technique that promoted the strong trademark of Germi's filmmaking as it broke new ground in Italian comedy, always with a concern to push the limits of the socially acceptable, or politically correct, to its full extent.

On a thematic level, the film's comedic elements were mostly generated with the habitual impasse between modernity and secular traditions in Sicily. Giovanni Attolini defines Germi's difficulty to reconcile cinema and comedy as being the "inconceivability between an antiquated way of life with the demands of a society in constant evolution: a contradiction that he had already experienced thanks to the expression of comedy."[55] Concomitantly representing picturesque regional and dialectal atmospheres while portraying the weight of tradition in modern society, Germi was indeed able to offer a key moment in the film that clearly illustrated both sides of the dilemma: Peppino refused to acquiesce to the coerced marriage proposal, and in despair, felt compelled to ask his parents about themselves to find out if his father would have still accepted to marry his mother if she had accepted his advances while engaged.

> Peppino: Papa, Mamma, I do not want Agnese.
> Father: What? How come you don't want her?
> Peppino: I want a virgin wife. Mamma, why should I be denied of this
>   right? Why?
> Father: But didn't you look at Don Vincenzo?
> Peppino: You answer instead, with sincerity. Would you have married
>   mamma if she had behaved like Agnese Ascalone did with me?
> Father: What does this have to do with it?
> Mother: It's not like you didn't try....
> Father: Men have the right to ask and women have the obligation to refuse.
> Peppino: Precisely! That's why I don't want her. Agnese did not refuse.
>   Right? And I don't want a whore for a spouse.
> Father: But I have committed to Don Vincenzo.

Mother: Answer Peppino's question instead. If I had ceded to your
    advances, would you have married me?
Father: Well... (long pause) undeniably, no!

Written by Luciano Vincenzoni, Age and Scarpelli along with Germi himself, the inspired scenario that at times was forthright to say the least, utilized
humor in full irony, painting the social hypocrisy of the local middle bourgeoisie caught between modernization and family values. Germi was able to make
the same discourse on a different level, much less dramatic than the above-
mentioned scene, through the presence of the omnipresent father figure Don
Vincenzo Ascalone,[56] who brought to the screen myriad facets all portraying
the stereotypical image of the *Uomo Siculo* (Sicilian man). He is possessive of
his daughters, leaving his daughter Matilde only "three minutes" to visit her
fiancée Peppino at the door, and jealous, reading aloud the letter of one of his
daughters just received from an admirer at the dinner table. After reading out
loud the nonincriminatory content, he suddenly removes the stamp to discover
the following words secretly written "baci appassionati sulla bocca" (passionate kisses on your lips). Another treasured contribution to the screenplay was
the satire on cultural differences opposing the Trevisan accent and logical mind
versus the Sicilian art of "getting by." Less inclined toward a linguistic distinction between north and south, the plot emphasized the many cultural challenges and ultimately the misunderstandings it created. The police officer who
takes a nap out of town in the country under the shade of a tree does so in
order to leave free rein for the kidnapping to occur, which leaves the northern
colleague bemused and at a loss.

In the 1960s, the thematic of the south with its cultural dichotomy was nothing
new. Previous films on Sicily like Mauro Bolognini's *Il bell'Antonio* (1960), Alberto
Lattuada's *Mafioso* (1962), *Don Giovanni in Sicilia* (1967), Vittorio Caprioli's
Leoni al sole (1961), among others, had been successes at the box office, and both
Divorzio and *Sedotta* did not represent breaking new ground for Italian cinema
even though both offered an unprecedented prism of prevailing social etiquette
and moral values. Although responding to a logic of comedy, *Sedotta e abbandonata* was able to offer a more lucid vision of contemporaneous customs problems
and society in general, principally in a region of Italy where sexual repression
carried its weight of consequences on social behavior and mentality. This element
was definitely its seminal contribution. Therefore a question imposes itself: was
Germi's critical discourse more oriented toward the legal system and all its gender absurdity (i.e., Article 544) or, on the other hand, was it more a portrayal of
an archaic mentality and its dire consequences on everyday people? It seems that
Germi's interest concerned both sides of the problems, as he clearly deplored not
only the existence of such an article of law, but more importantly the fact that
many women were willing to concede marriage even with the former offender.
Commenting on this particular issue, Maurizio Grande notices that in fact "the

protagonists appear cognizant victims of a social role and of a legal condition of love that legitimizes the deception against the opposite sex."[57]

When *Sedotta e abbandonata* came out in theaters in 1964, the film, as paradoxical as it may seem, was welcomed in Sicily, despite the heavy-handed derisive caricature[58] of local customs: the many descriptions of Sicilian mannerisms, the vices of middle-class Sicilians with their furtive glances made behind shutters, shades, curtains, laundry lines (mainly from idleness and inertia). Perhaps the reason for this welcome, in Italy and in particular Sicily, came from the fact that Germi's comedies were able to challenge the definition of provincialism, a theme often neglected by most Italian comedy filmmakers. His personal vision of Sicily and the problem of the south in general was perceived more than ever as an idiosyncratic endeavor, a representation outside the frame of time, illustrating from afar and in a rather subjective manner the effect of society in the wake of the economic boom. As film scholar Jacqueline Reich pointed out:

> The success of these two Sicilian comedies rests precisely on their ability to strike a balance between realism and escapism, between social commentary and recourse to grotesque black comedy, finding humor in such taboo subjects as murder, castration, virginity patrols, and the Sicilian honor code.[59]

Pietro Germi on the set of *The Birds, the Bees and the Italians*
(*Signore & signori*, 1965)
Photo courtesy of photofest

Germi's acerbic tone was a barometer for the health of Italian society, incriminating its most incongruous situations generated by the respect of ancient regulations, and untold codes of family honor, which eventually no one would respect. As Enrico Giacovelli noted, Germi's satires were "true slaps to an obtuse society only able to establish rules that later on will never be respected"[60] (however, one could not accuse Germi of antimeridionalism, since his next project took him to the Veneto region with *The Birds, the Bees and the Italians* [*Signore e Signori*] in 1966). Critically acclaimed in the U.S., especially by fellow filmmaker Billy Wilder, *Sedotta e abbandonata* not only won awards in Italy,[61] such as the *Nastro d'argento* for Best Screenplay, *Nastro d'argento* for Best Actor Saro Urzì (Don Vincenzo Ascalone) as well as *Nastro d'argento* for Best Supporting Actor Leopoldo Trieste (Baron Rienzi), but also abroad at the 1964 Cannes Film Festival with the Award for Best Actor once more to Saro Urzì.

Alberto Lattuada: Between Versatile and Eclectic Comedy

Milanese director Alberto Lattuada (1914–2005) was considered one of the most literary oriented filmmakers. A graduate with a degree in architecture, he first got acquainted with film in 1933 as a set decorator. At the end of the 1930s, along with actor Mario Ferrari and Luigi Comencini, Lattuada founded Italy's first film archive, *Cineteca Italiana*. He started his cinematographic career as scriptwriter and assistant director of Mario Soldati's *Piccolo mondo antico* (1941). Then in 1943, he directed his first movie, *Giacomo l'idealista*. He also codirected with newcomer in the film industry Federico Fellini *Variety Lights* (*Luci del varietà*, 1950). Lattuada, like many film directors in the immediate postwar period, evolved through a neorealist phase with *Bandit* (1946) and *Anna* (1951). He was one of the filmmakers regularly targeted by state censorship in the mid-1950s, especially with films like *The Beach* (*La spiaggia*, 1954), involving an uncommon prostitute (interpreted by French actress Martine Carol), that directed a strong sardonic tone against bourgeois ethics and the preconceived moral code.

In 1962, Alberto Lattuada directed *Mafioso* (1962), a production reminiscent of Dino Risi's *Una vita difficile* for its serious tone, which proved once again that Italian comedies were able to offer valuable prospects in their approach to social critique and consequently that the genre could rival a cinema labeled cinema "impegnato" (engaged), the worthy heir of the neorealist era. Although in its form, Lattuada's film looked at the Sicilian Mafia without making any apparent moral comment of its own, the lesson of the film remained a persuasive description of Sicily in the early sixties—an island trapped between an archaic feudal society and the new pace of modern life coming from the industrialized north—without making the mistake of relying on heavily stereotyped and foreseeable icons.[62] However, Lattuada was not so much attracted by the social critique formed during the postwar years of neorealism, nor was he interested in experimental cinema, and even less in the *auteur*

Alberto Sordi (Antonio Badalamenti) in Alberto Lattuada's *Mafioso* (1962)
Photo courtesy of BIFI

approach. Instead, his starting point was a literary source with solid structured narratives (here a short novel written by Bruno Caruso) in which he was able to insert a perceptive social observation of Sicilian feudal customs, their anachronic morality, and the advent of postwar disillusions and compromises. The value of this film was in placing the Sicilian Mafia in perspective with the sociopolitical cleavages of southern society and announcing—sadly enough with a nonintended premonitory tone—the future events that would take place in the following decades: the changing internal structure and social position of the Sicilian Mafia within the broader context of its growing rapport with its Italian American partners, and the emergence of new crime organizations.

Antonio (Nino) Badalamenti (Alberto Sordi) comes from a small town in Sicily named Càlamo. Eight years earlier, he immigrated to the opulent city of Milan to secure a job in part made possible with the help of a local mobster. Now a dynamic and successful engineer working in the colossal automobile industry, he decides to travel to Sicily to present the family for the first time his "emancipated" Milanese spouse Marta (Norma Bengell) and their two daughters. Just before his departure, he is asked by his manager, an Italian American from New Jersey, what appears to be a simple and innocuous favor: to hand deliver a small package to a "local benefactor" of his hometown—Don Vincenzo (Ugo Attanasio)—in person. Once in Sicily, he delivers the enigmatic parcel and pays his respect to the town godfather. Meanwhile, the Mafia has eyes on the prodigal son and his promising potential for a possible assignment; they send one of their men, Don Liborio (Carmelo Oliviero), to groom the newcomer and hopefully persuade Nino into a special mission. The idea is quite simple: find a way to provide an "act of goodwill" to Nino or his family so as to ask an important "favor" in return. They eventually find their means when they discover that Nino and his father want to acquire some land in the countryside. Both father and son face hostile negotiations with landowner Don Calogero, since the offered price suddenly jumped (from fifty lira to two hundred per square meter). When Don Vincenzo has wind of Nino's financial impasse, he takes advantage of it by using his "persuasion" methods, and swiftly forces Don Calogero to sell to Nino his land at the original price (with some apologies as a coup de grace). Nino, now in a state of ecstasy, reasserts his entire devotion to Don Vincenzo not realizing the nature of the "favor" he will soon be asked to carry out. After having witnessed Nino's flawless shooting abilities, the Mafia chooses him to perform a contractual obligation of a professional killer, and a subterfuge is found: to avoid suspicion from his wife Marta, Nino must be away from her for a couple of days. Under the pretence of a two-day hunting party organized by the local "picciotti" (local mobsters at the service of a boss), Nino is flown under total secrecy to New York City in a cargo case by a night mail carrier to commit a homicide against a rival mob boss. Everyone in town appears to be in the know (e.g., Nino's father embraces his son—Sicilian way—as if he were never to come back). His mission accomplished, he comes back in the middle of the night and silently gets in bed while his wife still sleeps. Nino, who by then is tormented with a sudden attack of guilt, must return to his honest and blissful family life. The next and final sequence shows the workingman back on the job in Milan, his future forever affected by his haunted past.

One of the greatest lessons given by Lattuada's *Mafioso*, despite the seriousness of its tone, was to challenge the narrative mechanisms of Italian comedy in its ability to mix genres and by cleverly switching registers from comedy to reach the ultimate dramatic function: murder. The main comedic mechanism was two-fold: the first one was obviously based on the cultural differences between early 1960s Sicily and the industrialized and liberal north. While on the ferry crossing the Strait of Messina, Nino notices discomfort with Marta. He asks her what is wrong, but she simply sighs a premonitory answer: "Nothing…. I just am looking at Italy moving away." In Càlamo, the cultural adjustment is at first rather delicate for the Milanese family, as cultural obstacles regularly interfere at every stage of the human interactions. When Marta lit her cigarette at the end of the welcome meal, the entire Sicilian family stops eating and stares at her in bewilderment. Nino must rescue her as she begins to resent the awkward silence: "No Marta, it's just because they are not used to seeing a 'female' who smokes."[63] Later on and during their first night, Marta jumps out of bed when she realizes that a hen actually sleeps underneath. The scene where Marta first meets Nino's family is an example of Italian comedy pushed to perfection as everyone hugs in a family uproar in the anarchic style of the Marx Brothers. The second part of the comedic device is a linguistic one, with Nino's contrived northern accent gradually disappearing and becoming an authentic bucolic Sicilian vernacular as the narrative proceeds. Despite the dramatic tone of the denouement, the story manages to end on a comic note, though potentially qualifying as bitter sarcasm, once more underlying the cultural differences between north and south. Nino's accountant, happy to see his pen returned to him (to cap it all by a Sicilian) heckles Nino across the office with a strong Milanese accent: "If everyone were like you, life would be better, I am telling you!"

Along with humor, Lattuada's film also included a strong element of collective drama. As a social commentary, *Mafioso* could be best portrayed as a subjective,[64] yet compelling, testimony on the reality of Mafia and society in Sicily. It offered a glimpse at the organizational structure of the Sicilian underworld and its burden of contradictions and logics ("Sicilian organized crime" being a stock phrase that captured a variety of criminal group activities). One primary focus in this film was on a group whose structure acted in concert with other organized factions in the United States. Interestingly enough, the representation of a local Sicilian mob and its overwhelming psychological and social hold of the middle class over the poor portrayed the Mafia in bleak and uncompromising terms. For instance, the sacred law of *omertà*, the officious code of silence in the Mafia world, here represented by a progressively claustrophobic dimension, prevailed at the end as Nino returned home from New York City and must move on as if nothing had ever happened: "ne visto, ne salutato" as one of Don Vincenzo's lieutenants said. Years later, evoking some of the anecdotes of his career in the early sixties, Alberto Lattuada remembered his obstacle while shooting the film in Sicily:

We were just outside Bagheria and we knew we were being watched. Tonino Cervi wanted to hide the scenario book. Instead I decided to tell the story to the local Mafia boss. From that moment on, the entire town was at our service…. The line which convinced the Mafia gathering was "*Questo fetuso non tiene parola.*" It was referring to the Mafioso that did not respect the rules, and for that ends up killed by Sordi in New York. Having transgressed the code of honor, he was to be killed. I had expressed in this manner their ideology, and from that moment I had total freedom. They also did not know that the film was to generate some dismay, but from their part there was only the approval of the crime.[65]

Another center of interest was on the visible tip of the iceberg. The intention was not only to *divulge* its social and cultural iron grip but also its violence, just as it appeared in the chronics of the time period. Like many comic films, which portrayed the flaws of Italians and Italian society, *Mafioso* was a potential criticism, difficult to digest for the postwar Christian Democrats, who held many films in contempt for emanating negative and reductive representations of Italy's way of life to an audience abroad. Lattuada ultimately gave greater weight to the human drama caused by this archaic, tradition-bound community that led to human failure, especially in the final scene depicting Nino's despondency and remorse; a rather compelling cinematic moment when observed through the lens of the humanist context of neorealism. On a technical level, little has been said, surprisingly enough, on the influential contribution of the music score composed by Piero Piccioni and Nino Rota, who were able to insert some ominous effects as the mounting tension of the suspenseful intrigue repeatedly reappeared. Both composers successfully varied the tone, keeping it light and playful at times, dark and somber at others. Shot in Sicily, the film also benefited from expert cinematographer Armando Nannuzzi,[66] who included shots cleverly utilizing saturated light to enhance the atmosphere of paranoia and suspicion and to keep the tension flowing just as Sicilian sunlight overpowers the island in the summer months. Though the plot could be considered enigmatic at times (it remains unclear who the mobster was that Nino was supposed to murder, or what his connection to the New York Mafia was), its arrangement was quite persuasive due to the continuously escalating storyline. It included a forthright technique and an excellent, subtly nuanced performance for the difficult central role interpreted by Alberto Sordi (a Roman actor, having to impersonate a Sicilian character who after eight years away from home must progressively regain his original accent). In addition, the corrosiveness of Marco Ferreri's humor and the sparkling dialogues written by Age and Scarpelli gave to the film its unremitting stability and balance throughout the narrative (filmmaker Marco Ferreri was supposed to direct the film with an original title: *Viaggio in America*).

On the surface, *Mafioso* may have appeared to be another gangster movie for much of the popular audience, but the story, like the deeply realized characters, was a multilayered one (it was nominated for Best Foreign Film during the 1964 Golden Globes). It fortunately avoided the categorization as another film noir thriller or a good-versus-evil escapade. Nino was credible as the decent family man tortured by a moral dilemma and turned in a performance of rare intensity as the reluctant hit man "connected" against his will. With a successful and serious performance, Alberto Sordi became the quintessential Lattuada hero: a *picciotto* who forgot that he was once one of them, but also and at the same time, a family man turned loner traveling through alien lands in quest of survival.

Though the question of Nino's immediate future remained unanswered, poten-tially leaving spectatorship somewhat perturbed, the strength of *Mafioso* was not only in the gripping intrigue but also in its multileveled social characterizations and powerful performances.

The Newcomers to the *Commedia:* Antonio Pietrangeli and Elio Petri

Unlike Hollywood cinema, the boundaries of the various cinematic genres have always been unclear in Italian cinema of the 1960s. This *maxima* is all the more accurate in that Italian comedies use acute social observation and evolve through different spheres to move seamlessly from satire, parody, melodrama, and ultimately tragedy. Antonio Pietrangeli (1919–68) was one of the early directors to implement as his modus operandi comedies from existing melo-dramatic screenplays. A graduate in medicine (like Dino Risi), Pietrangeli began his career as a movie critic and a strong advocate for the neorealism move-ment, then cowrote film scripts such as Luchino Visconti's *Ossessione* (1942), *La terra trema* (1948), Pietro Germi's *Lost Youth* (*Gioventù perduta*, 1948), and Roberto Rossellini's *No Greater Love* (*Europa '51*, 1952). His directorial debut occurred with *Empty Eyes* (*Il sole negli occhi*, 1953) and rapidly confirmed him as a recognized director of comedies. With commercialized films like *The Bachelor*

Claudia Cardinale (Maria Grazia) and Ugo Tognazzi (Andrea Artusi) in
Antonio Pietrangeli's *The Magnificent Cuckold* (*Il magnifico cornuto*, 1964)
Photo courtesy of BIFI

(*Lo scapolo*, 1955), Pietrangeli was occasionally able to select projects that were more his choice, like *Adua and Company* (*Adua e le compagne*, 1960), *The Girl from Parma* (*La parmigiana*, 1962), and *The Visitor* (*La visita*, 1963), almost always including a careful treatment of female protagonists (i.e., Sandra Milo, Claudia Cardinale, Stefania Sandrelli). A few years after directing his two signature works, *The Magnificent Cuckold* (*Il magnifico cornuto*, 1964) and *I Knew Her Well* (*Io la conoscevo bene*, 1965), Pietrangeli accidentally died by drowning in the sea near Gaeta during the shooting of *How, When and with Whom* (*Come, quando e perché*, 1969), a film later completed by Valerio Zurlini.

Il magnifico cornuto told the story of a man who, driven mad by jealousy, makes life miserable for himself and everyone around him. The film also explored the depths of a disturbed psyche who under the influence of obsessive behavior, orchestrated the gradual dissolution of his marriage. This humorous, yet bleak, depiction of man's unfathomable inner being, told from the point of view of an insanely jealous husband over the alleged infidelities of his wife, was an enthralling study of psychological perversion. Based on the play *Le cocu magnifique*, written in French by Flemish author Fernand Crommelynck,[67] the screenplay (Diego Fabbri, Ruggiero Maccari, Ettore Scola, and Stefano Strucchi) set the narrative trajectory on a downward spiral: the long descent into madness, taking new turns as the truth unfolded with the audience denied any conventional relief. With a pessimistic social comment on the decadent moral and matrimonial values of the newly affluent and industrialized northern Italy, Pietrangeli's comedy served as a forewarning to the possible consequences of social and marital lust.

Andrea (Ugo Tognazzi), a self-absorbed and philandering businessman, is obsessed and convinced that his wife Maria Grazia (Claudia Cardinale) is having an affair. Despite his jealousy, Andrea is the one who falls into an extramarital affair with Christiana (Michèle Girardon) and successfully arranges a surreptitious rendezvous in a hotel. Reflecting on his recent adulterous experiences, Andrea begins to wonder if his own wife may cede to temptation herself. Suspicion and fears, like his own conscience, incite paranoia, which soon accelerates into hysteria. The next day, he experiences his first tangible doubt when he finds out that Maria stopped at an antique shop, supposedly to buy a commode, but whose owner is Gabriele (Paul Guers), one of her known admirers. Soon after, when Andrea finds a brochure of the hotel Emporio (the hotel where he met Cristiana) in Maria's belongings, he cannot help wondering if she knows about his secret relation. He begins to dream about his wife coming to the very same hotel, scantily dressed while a cohort of snooping men watches her. She enters an elevator followed by men who rush to get inside (even a Franciscan monk) who undeniably take great pleasure in contemplating her. She exits the elevator to meet her secret lover (Gian Maria Volonté), who waits for her in a room of the hotel. This fantasy dream sequence, exacerbated by his untamed imagination, confirms the value of his personal quest. Andrea begins by searching her purse and finds a number that appears to be a phone number. He now thinks his quest will soon be over, but after aggressively confronting her, he realizes that the number written on the back of her agenda is simply her own car license plate. Unfortunately, the subjective delusions do not stop here. After secretly checking the unusually excessive mileage on her car, Andrea coerces his associate Belisario (Salvo Randone) to follow Maria Grazia, but the enterprise fails after the colleague loses sight of her (the roles become essentially inverted when the wife, who has recognized Belisario, begins to follow him instead!). At their house-warming party where the upper class of the city attends, Maria Grazia leads a tour of the house to the guests. As the group visits the upstairs bedrooms, Andrea realizes that she is followed by a group of men and engages in another fantasy dream sequence: this time Maria Grazia offers a sensuous strip tease, down to erotic black lingerie, with the enthusiastic admirers all taking a raffle number to select who the "winner" will be.

Therefore, no one seems spared from Andrea's vindictive enterprise. Even the Sicilian gardener undergoes Andrea's severe scrutiny, compelling him to confess his attraction to upper-class women. Andrea takes no chance and decides to fire him the following day. Instead, thinking to have peace of mind, he hires an elderly gardener, unaware that the old chap is still very much an active Casanova. Despite his wife's desperate efforts to convince him of her faithfulness, Andrea continues to torture himself to the point that his mind begins to unravel. One night, he invents a business trip and leaves for the airport in a taxi. A moment later, he exits the taxi and walks back home in order to hide behind the wall of the backyard. Little does he know that his cigarette smoke is betraying him. Exasperated by her husband's latest subterfuge, Maria Grazia leaves in a taxi just to provoke him. Immediately followed, she gets off in the red light district of the city. Andrea's common sense suddenly disappears in a haze of obsession and unanswered questions, and while taking her home he forces her to reveal her lover's name by driving recklessly. In order to be credible, Maria Grazia is forced to invent the name of Gabriele, the antique dealer. Andrea is stunned but reassures her that he feels relieved: "Un cieco è contento di rivedere, non gli importa che cosa vede." (The blind are happy when they see again, they don't care what they see.) Finally, Andrea has proof of his wife's innocence as he overhears a phone conversation between her and Gabriele where she apologizes for having brought his name wrongfully, thus proving that nothing ever happened between them. Following the *coup de théâtre*, Andrea becomes a fulfilled husband, respectful and tolerant, though blissfully unaware that his spouse is now engaging in a relation with his doctor (Philippe Nicaud).

In Pietrangeli's *Il magnifico cornuto,* the cinematographic techniques contributed to the masterful atmosphere, thwarting any logical anticipation from the viewer. The use of *chiaroscuro* lighting was integrated subtly enough so as to avoid making the movie lose all of its grounding reality, thus creating a confusing equilibrium between reality and imagination. With the assistance of brilliant cinematography (Armando Nannuzzi), Pietrangeli was at his analytical best, following his actors around like an invisible voyeur, even at times including difficult intervals of humor, while never looking away from the ugliness and cruelty of the unfolding drama. The editing style also displayed a good amount of energy by using a variety of quick cuts and visual projections of introspective thoughts, which effectively illustrated the subjects' insecurities, recalling the cinematic style of such filmmakers as Pietro Germi or Luigi Zampa. In a similar way, Pietrangeli was known for his unique eye when representing emotional details and for the simplistic style with which he directed the dramatic storylines of his tragicomic films. With this engaging montage, Andrea's lunacy emerges more dominant, the segments get longer, and the time lapsed between each one grows shorter, giving the impression that his mental condition is growing degenerative and gaining momentum. As the film moved toward its final climax, the husband slipped more and more deeply into delusion. But instead of escalating the tension as the dramatic stakes heightened (the conventional themes such as violent separation, murders, etc.), Pietrangeli was able to switch the focus from husband to wife to place its emphasis on the other point of view (Maria Grazia's own perspective). Pietrangeli here presented a film that focused in the first part of the storyline more on the husband's plight, but as the drama unfolded, brought interest to the innocent spouse's position rather than to the adulterer's.

Il magnifico cornuto was a movie about conjugal manners in Italy during the mid-1960s rather than a simple chronicle of modern-time passion. Pietrangeli's nihilistic viewpoint of mankind was here reinforced by the constant downward spiral of the marital union, leading to public outbursts amidst the sardonic bourgeois class in industrialized northern Italy. Andrea's life seems flawless: his surroundings are idyllic; his work is fulfilling and financially rewarding (he is the head of a successful Italian hat company); and his wife is so vivaciously, sensuously alive that all men, young and old, are swept off their feet. But Andrea is also a man whose pride ruins his marriage and his compulsive idolization for Maria Grazia, performed with an inventive and appropriately obsessive behavior, leads him first to boast about her beauty and then to suspect her of being unable to control her sexuality. However, the failing relationship also exists in his professional space, as he begins to abuse his closest associates at work, misinterpreting their reactions and not allowing for any alternate opinions.

In many ways, *Il magnifico cornuto* was a film as much about fidelity as it was infidelity since all the main protagonists are faithful in the fulfillment of their inner desires: their actions make viewers realize that even the most despicable fanaticism can be prearranged to emerge as a rational behavior. The final scene in the night club illustrated this rationalization as Maria Grazia discreetly makes appointments on the dance floor with one of her new lovers, while Andrea at the very same time seems to have definitely joined the clan of "resigned husbands," indolent and unsuspecting of their wives' activities as they talk about their next hunting trip and their new quest for real happiness. Interestingly enough, the film brought noticeable attention to female psychology, influencing productions of films such as *I Knew Her Well* (*Io la conoscevo bene*) with Stefania Sandrelli a year later in 1965. The wittiness of the *commedia all'italiana*, more inclined toward masculine humor, found with Pietrangeli a strong advocate of women's psychology as well as an aspiration for the transformation of what would typically be a supporting role (for Claudia Cardinale) into a leading one. His female protagonist's psychology as well as her performance presented an individual recentering the dramatic function of its role, far from candidness and indolence, to one of manipulation and power. Compelled to use similar weapons as the men, such as hypocrisy and deceit, the female character of Maria Grazia was indeed a rare opportunity for female participation in the plot itself and no longer a minor facet of the plot. Antonio Pietrangeli renewed this experiment of investigation into the female confrontation of a male-dominated society, articulating the fragility and frustration with several of his subsequent works, such as *I Knew Her Well* and *The Visit* (*La visita*, 1966).

Of all the Italian film comedies shot in the 1960s and centered on the reality of the postwar economic boom, Elio Petri's *The Teacher from Vigevano* (*Il maestro di Vigevano*, 1963) stood out for many different reasons. Well known for his politically engaged films, Elio Petri (1929–82), against all odds, successfully fulfilled his assignment with the comedy genre. He began his career in the world of cinema in 1951 as assistant director to Giuseppe de Santis as well as working as film critic for the Communist-oriented daily newspaper *L'Unità*. Other important films include *We Still Kill the Old Way* (*A ciascuno*

Alberto Sordi (Mombeli) and Claire Bloom (Ada) in Elio Petri's *The Teacher from Vigevano* (*Il maestro di Vigevano*, 1963)

il suo, 1967), an adaptation from Leonardo Sciascia's novel; *Investigation of a Private Citizen* (*Indagine su un cittadino al di sopra di ogni sospetto*, 1970), which won the Golden Palm at the 1970 Cannes Film Festival as well as the Oscar for Best Foreign Film at the 1971 Academy Awards; and *Lulu the Tool* (*La classe operaia va in paradiso*, 1971). Determined by an incurable pessimism, Petri denounced in his realistic dramas as well as comedies, violence, the dissolution of the political apparatus facing challenges like the Mafia, corruption and social injustice in general.

Adapted from Lucio Mastronardi's homonymous novel (first noticed by writer and philosopher Italo Calvino, who decided to publish it with Enaudi in 1962), the story of *The Teacher from Vigevano* describes the complex existence of a man caught between two opposite and conflicting spaces: the infectious prosperity of the industrial world and the academe's position fighting for the survival of its humanistic principles. Although similar to mainstream comedies in its thematic approach—a comic tale about consumerism versus family traditions—its tragicomic expression, however, was quite the opposite. The plot covered little new ground, but the material's rhetoric under the lead of Age and Scarpelli was anything but ordinary in its motivation to deviate the original destination of humor with a more politically engaged aim, represented in part by the Manichean conflict of ethics versus immorality. According to film historian Aldo Viganò, director Elio Petri "was able to distinguish with clairvoyance good from evil and when representing the second he was capable of doing it only in the most caricatured, sarcastic and grotesque terms."[68] Therefore, it was no surprise that Petri's narrative style, very much known by an insistence to politicize its content if not its form, as for instance in *Investigation of a Private Citizen* (*Indagine su un cittadino al di sopra di ogni sospetto*, 1970) or *Lulu the Tool* (*La classe operaia va in paradiso*, 1971), included explicit didactical elements, quite the opposite of the previous comedy sensibility (unlike filmmakers such as Dino Risi or Mario Monicelli, Petri was much more involved in expressing moralistic stances).

Antonio Mombelli (Alberto Sordi) is an elementary school teacher in Vigevano, a small town in Lombardy, almost entirely immersed in the shoe industry. Mo-belli has been teaching for nineteen years in the same elementary school, and despite the condescending attitude of the tyrannical and omnipotent headmaster (Vito de Taranto) who takes great pleasure in catching teachers red-handed when late for class, he lives his humble career without much ambition. His beautiful wife Ada (Claire Bloom), however, is the opposite, as she constantly tries to stimulate Antonio's aspiration to change profession in order to access a more comfortable lifestyle and offer their son Rino (Tullio Scavazzi) a "better" future. His teacher's stipend and the private lessons to round out his salary do not allow his family to enjoy the new leisure activities available in Italy after the advent of the economic boom. Due to the ever-increasing momentum, the tension between husband and wife escalates until the relationship slips into a reluctant companionship. Mombelli must endure humiliation from both sides: the ones emanating from the principal, aimed at reminding him that he will always be a simple employee of the state whose mission is to educate children and not take initiative, and the others who have become financially successful through the shoe industry and never miss an occasion to remind him of his mediocre existence. One day, Mr. Bugatti (Piero Mazzarella), father of one of his less brilliant students, comes to see him in the classroom to inform him in front of the class that Ada has asked for a 50,000 lira loan. Under the impression of being railroaded into a shady deal, Bugatti warns him that he may talk to the headmaster if the event reoccurs. Hurt in his pride, Mombelli repays the debt without delay (not without the contemptuous remark of Bugatti, who tells his own son never to follow his teacher's example). For Ada, the material situation at home becomes so unbearable that she decides to work at the shoe factory, facing many humiliations. Pressured by many coworkers who established their own factory from their home, she successfully convinces her husband to resign from his teacher's position and to invest in a small home-based shoe factory, along with her brother Carlo. Indeed, their financial and sentimental situation rapidly improves and both can now proudly make a well-dressed appearance in the city square on Sunday afternoons. At the café with his former colleagues, Antonio boasts about his commercial success and carelessly discloses sensitive information regarding their unorthodox exportation practices. Unfortunately, tax auditors catch wind of their fiscal irregularities, and the next day the small business is sequestered. Now unemployed, Mombelli must take care of his son Rino, since Ada progressively deserts their home, and must retake the difficult examination, which will allow him to regain his position at school. Misfortune seems to hold its grip on Antonio, as he finds out about the infidelity of his wife. As a typical ending for Italian-style comedies, the climax reaches its peak during the last scene as Ada and her lover die in a car accident. The slow descent into solitude starts again for Mombelli, who has no other choice but to go back to his profession, the only place that seems to protect him from the affrays and temptations of modern-day life.

According to Elio Petri, *Il maestro di Vigevano* was supposed to be directed originally by Dino Risi while the episode film *I mostri* was to be Petri's assignment. Following Sordi's rejection for the lead in *I mostri* (reportedly deemed by the actor too negative in its satire of middle-class Italians), Dino de Laurentiis exchanged assignments between the two filmmakers.[69] But a hostile climate rapidly surfaced during the shooting of the movie. Because Mastronardi's novel represented the teaching profession in a less than flattering light, a group of teachers published a vindictive article in the Milanese daily newspaper *Il Corriere della Sera* on September 21, 1963, creating a stir at the time of the shooting of the scenes inside the school in Vigevano. Consequently, the regional school superintendent (*Il Provveditore agli Studi di Pavia*), under pressure, prevented shooting those takes after the teachers of Vigevano protested against Petri's promotion of a novel that explicitly discredited their profession.

Despite the new project, officially far from the social satire, Petri was still able to implement elements of grotesque monstrosity in his socioeconomic and even political satire of the Italy of the boom years. With a background heavily centered on political films, Petri's assignment was logically a challenging one, as he was compelled to create a harmonious marriage between comedy, literary adaptation, and socioeconomic satire. The *maestro di Vigevano* was in fact so exemplary of Petri and Sordi's aptitude to mix genres and skillfully to inject some satire and situational irony in the narrative tone that it was difficult to imagine a similar comedy without the unifying quality of a versatile actor like Alberto Sordi, who alternated comic relief with pathetic decadence. Petri's ability to play humor off the tension, this mixture of opposite ingredients, is best represented by the scene when Mombelli, committed to finding his wife, unsuccessfully attempts to buy a gun due to the required arms permit as well as its prohibitive price. Instead, he manages to buy a humble hammer, which he takes with him to the hotel in order to catch Ada *in flagrante delicto* with her lover, the rich industrialist Bugatti. Interestingly enough, the presence of the grotesque (although never bordering on the farce) was generated by the unforeseen exchange of roles suddenly imposed on the main protagonist as Sordi moved from a reserved individual into a desperate husband ready to commit the unthinkable. As always in the *commedia all'italiana*, the presence of the pathetic manifested itself as the plot was about to reach its climax. That was precisely the case with the character of Mombelli, who entertained a touching friendship with his friend Nannini (Guido Spadea) or with his encounter with the prostitute on the bank of the river Ticino while desperately searching for his wife.

Despite the quality of its technical and artistic cast (original music by Nino Rota and cinematography by Otello Martelli), the film did not receive any significant award. However, by attempting to adapt Mastronardi's homonymous novel and at the same time portray on the screen the difficult economic position of millions of Italians who attempted to endure the frenetic pace of modernization, *Il maestro di Vigevano* reached its ambitious scope: an outspoken condemnation of consumerist fever. Although accused at the time of its release of tackling too much, the film proved by the end of the decade to have produced an accurate illustration of the complexity of the human condition as it fell prey to materialistic temptations. By taking a critical distance, viewers realized that the hero Mombelli was caught between two radically different worlds: the people working for the merciless industry centered on financial profit, and the other made of frustrated school masters, who intend to leave their profession at some point in their lives. The myth of entrepreneurship translated by the obsession of becoming a *padrone a casa sua* was successfully illustrated without any heavy use of moralist devices, making *Il maestro di Vigevano* an authentic example of *commedia all'italiana*.

Notes

[1] Although Sergio Amidei (1904–81) came from the neorealism era, he is considered by many film historians as well as fellow screenwriters as the initiator of comedy Italian style due to his ability to add humor in heavy scripts of neorealism. He was nominated four times for the Oscar for Best Writing, Screenplay. First in 1947 for Roberto Rossellini's *Roma, città aperta* (1945); in 1948 for Vittorio De Sica's *Shoeshine* (*Sciuscià*, 1946); in 1950 for Roberto Rosselini's *Paisà* (1946); and finally in 1962 for Vittorio De Sica's *Il Generale della Rovere* (1959). His career also included screenplays for Luigi Zampa's *Anni ruggenti* (1962) and *Il medico della mutua* (1968) as well as its sequel *Il Prof. Dott. Guido Tersilli, primario della clinica Villa Celeste convenzionata con le mutue* (1969), directed this time by Luciano Salce; Nanni Loy's *Detenuto in attesa di giudizio* (1971); and Mario Monicelli's *An Average Little Man* (*Un borghese piccolo piccolo*, 1977).

[2] Ruggero Maccari (1919–89) can be found in countless comedies *all'italiana*, such as Nanni Loy's *Il marito* (1958); Dino Risi's *Love and Larceny* (*Il mattatore*, 1959), *The Easy Life* (*Il sorpasso*, 1962), *The Monsters* (*I mostri*, 1963), *How Funny Can Sex Be?* (*Sessomatto*, 1973); Antonio Pietrangeli's *Adua and Company* (*Adua e le compagne*, 1960), *The Visitor* (*La visita*, 1963), *The Magificent Cuckold* (*Il magnifico cornuto*, 1964), *I Knew Her Well* (*Io la conoscevo bene*, 1965); and Ettore Scola's *Down and Dirty* (*Brutti sporchi e cattivi*, 1976), and *A Special Day* (*Una giornata particolare*, 1977). Maccari was also nominated in 1976 for the Oscar for Best Writing, Screenplay Adapted From Other Material for Dino Risi's *Scent of a Woman* (*Profumo di donna*, 1974).

[3] Rodolfo Sonego (1921–2000) wrote his screenplays by himself, avoiding what most colleagues did at the time: teamwork. After early works like Alberto Lattuada's *Riviera* (*La spiaggia*, 1954), Sonego wrote many stories tailor-made for Alberto Sordi, such as Dino Risi's *The Widower* (*Il vedovo*, 1959), *A Difficult Life* (*Una vita difficile*, 1961); Luigi Zampa's *Il vigile* (1960); Luigi Comencini's *The Scientific Cardplayer* (*Lo scopone scientifico*, 1972), *Strange Occasion* (*Quelle strane occasioni*, 1976/epidose "L'ascensore"); Alberto Sordi's *Dove vai in vacanza?* (1978/episode "Le vacanze intelligenti").

[4] Luciano Vincenzoni (b. 1926) wrote screenplays for Mario Monicelli's *The Great War* (*La grande guerra*, 1959); Pietro Germi's *Seduced and Abandoned* (*Sedotta e abbandonata*, 1964); and Sergio Leone's *The Good, the Bad and the Ugly* (*Il buono, il brutto, il cattivo*, 1966), and *For a Few Dollars More* (*Per qualche dollaro in più*, 1965).

[5] Ettore Scola (b. 1931) is mostly known as a filmmaker, but a large part of his professional career included screenplays for Nanni Loy's *Il marito* (1958); Dino Risi's *Love and Larceny* (*Il mattatore*, 1959), *The Easy Life* (*Il sorpasso*, 1962), *The Monsters* (*I mostri*, 1963); and Antonio Pietrangeli's *The Magnificent Cuckold* (*Il magnifico cornuto*, 1964). He won the award for Best Screenplay at the 1980 Cannes Film Festival for *La terrazza* (1980) in collaboration with Agenore Incrocci and Furio Scarpelli. He also won the award for Best Director for *Brutti sporchi e cattivi* (1976) at the Cannes Film Festival of the same year.

[6] Peter Bondanella, *Italian Cinema: From Neorealism to the Present* (New York: Continuum, 1996), 158.

[7] Unlike comedies of the sixties, the neorealist experience almost always sustained an element of moralistic value.

[8] Moravia's critique was published in *l'Espresso* on January 7, 1962.

[9] According to Risi, the film was to express a particular subject linked to a particular time of Italian life and heralded some aspects of human nature not linked to a precise moment in time but rather to eternity. Jean Gili, *Effetto commedia* (Rome: Di Giacomo, 1985), 205.

[10] Sordi, unlike many film actors concerned with the level of positive impact on the Italian public, often chose characters little inclined toward positive consideration. Indeed, most of his roles represented egocentric cowards, morally reprehensible and filled with psychological complexes. This important trait of the actor clearly indicated an interest to follow the evolution of Italian custom rather than his own acting career evolution in itself.

[11] Aldo Viganò, *Dino Risi* (Milan: Moizzi Editore, 1977), 54.

[12] Like for *I mostri* two years later, the film was quite prophetical on his presentiment on future material and psychological abuses generated by capitalistic market economy.

[13] Despite a quarrel of the paternity of the subject, as Alberto Sordi and screenwriter Sonego have made claims on the original initiative.

[14] With almost 1.3 million entrances, the film made 1,293,191,000 lira that year.

[15] Viganò, *Dino Risi*, 25.

[16] As Bruno Cortona reminded Roberto, *Occhiofino* was conveniently a witticism for *finocchio*, which is the equivalent of "gay" in Italian slang.

[17] Like for the classical Greek tragedies, the *diegetical* time elapsed was no more than the usual twenty-four hours.

[18] Often mistaken for a red chili pepper, the *corno*, the Greek symbol of good fortune (as well as a protection from ill fortune) is a very popular symbol/object/gesture in Italian popular culture.

[19] Viganò, *Dino Risi*, 36.

[20] *Il sorpasso* was finally the first comedy where Vittorio Gassman was able to act with his real features without the help of heavy make-up and overcharacterization (as opposed to his comedic debut in Mario Monicelli's *Big Deal on Madonna Street*, *The Great War*, and followed by Dino Risi's *Il mattatore*).

[21] Tullio Kezich, "Il momento del film comico italiano," *Sipario* 201 (1963): 34.

[22] Translated by the author from the original Italian dialogue: "L'hai vista *l'Eclisse*? Io ci ho dormito, una bella pennichella! Bel regista Antonioni, c'ha una Flaminia-Zagato. Una volta, sulla fettuccia di Terracina, m'ha fatto allunga' il collo."

[23] Translation by the author from Italian: "*Il sorpasso* è la storia di un mascheramento, del travestimento di una pulsione di distruzione che sconfessa i limiti, le regole, i ruoli e le forma della vita sociale." R. De Gaetano, *Il corpo e la maschera: Il grottesco nel cinema italiano* (Rome: Bulzoni, 1999), 42.

[24] The film was particularly dear to the Genovese actor, as he once declared: "If I had to choose one of my films for some useless, posthumous article, I would pick *Il sorpasso*."

Adriano Aprà and Patrizia Pistagnesi, *Comedy Italian Style 1950–1980 (Catalogo degli incontri internazionali d'arte)* (Turin: Edizioni Rai, 1986), 75.

[25] *The Monsters* can very well be considered Risi's emblematic trademark, as exactly forty years later Risi's autobiographical novel was entitled *I miei mostri (My Monsters*, 2004).

[26] Elio Petri started the *Il maestro di Vigevano* with Alberto Sordi that same year.

[27] Jean Gili, *La comédie italienne* (Paris: Henry Veyrier, 1983), 124.

[28] Translated by the author from Italian: "Se la commedia italiana 'istituzionalizzava la spensieratezza' e cercava l'equilibrio attraverso l'inclusione, la commedia all'italiana esorcizza il disagio con pratiche—uguali e contrarie—basate sull'esclusione." Gianni Canova, "Dalla commedia italiana alla commedia all'italiana," in Lino Micciché, *"Una vita difficile" di Dino Risi: Risate amare nel lungo dopoguerra* (Venice: Marsilio, 2000), 39.

[29] Quoted by Agenore Incroci (Age) in his interview with Lorenzo Codelli, "Entretien avec Age et Scarpelli," *Positif* 193 (May 1977): 8.

[30] Translated by the author from Italian: "Il regista sceglie la commedia non tanto come genere ma come mezzo e linguaggio ideale per rappresentare il mondo." Lino Micciché, *"Una vita difficile" di Dino Risi: Risate amare nel lungo dopoguerra* (Venice: Marsilio, 2000), 53.

[31] Translated by the author from Italian: "Io sono nato con Checov, è stato lui il mio maestro. Le storie brevi mi piacciono molto, perché finiscono." Dino Risi interviewed by Federico Guiglia, *Italiani senza contini* (Florence: Libri Liberal, 2001), 206.

[32] Viganò, *Dino Risi*, 72.

[33] Translated by the author from the film's original dialogues: Generale: "Tu, assaggia il tuo rancio e dimmi che te ne pare." Jacovacci: "signorsi! ottimo e abbondante signor generale." Generale: "invece e uno schifo, niente grassi e poco pasta. Questo non è cibo per uomini che combattono…bisogna portare sodisfazione ai ragazzi.; si accontentano di così poco."

[34] Translated by the author from Italian: "Quando non diventa satira, la comicità non è evidentemente il mezzo più adatto per affrontare temi dì grande impegno collettivo; può riuscire, al più, un espediente." Morando Morandini, "La grande guerra," *Schermi* (October 17, 1959): 279.

[35] Translated by the author from Italian: "In effetti, *La grande guerra* è il primo film italiano che apre veramente un discorso su di un momento della storia recente d'Italia, di cui il cinema nostrano ha quasi sempre taciuto." Claudio Fava, *Alberto Sordi* (Rome: Gremese, 1979), 129–31.

[36] In an interview with Claudio Panella, Monicelli declared his desire to defy "the myth of fabulous war" ("sfatare il mito di una guerra favolosa, del grande slancio eroico dell'Italia di cui si era parlato soprattutto durante il fascismo ma di cui si continuava a parlare"). Claudio Panella, "In viaggio con Monicelli sui luoghi della grande guerra," cinema.dada.net/intersezioni/art12109.html (January 23, 2005).

[37] Luciano Vincenzoni's career as screenwriter and author also included works in Pietro Germi's *Seduced and Abandoned (Sedotta e abbandonata*, 1964) and *The Birds, the Bees*

and the Italians (*Signore e signori,*1966), Sergio Leone's *For a Few Dollars More* (*Per qualche dollaro in più,* 1965), and Mario Camerini's *Killing in Monte Carlo* (*Crimen,* 1960).

[38] Luciano Vincenzoni was also inspired by the short novel *Two Friends* (1882) from Guy de Maupassant.

[39] http://www.fistful–of–leone.com/classic/articles/vince.html

[40] In an interview with Tonino Pinto (the featured documentary of the DVD *La grande guerra*), Monicelli mentioned his preference for that scene.

[41] This high percentage of analphabetism along with the recent unification process of the country, trying to overcome its linguistic and cultural differences, was one of the reasons for which Italy as a nation was not prepared to gather efficient forces against Germany.

[42] Germi's film was co-recipient of the Palme d'or along with French filmmaker Claude Lelouch and *Un homme et une femme.*

[43] Franca Faldini and Goffredo Fofi, *L'avventurosa storia del cinema italiano 1933–1954* (Milan: Feltrinelli, 1979), 128.

[44] Faldini and Fofi, *L'avventurosa storia del cinema italiano,* 128.

[45] Article 587 of the *Penal Code*: "Chiunque cagiona la morte del coniuge, della figlia o della sorella, nell'atto in cui ne scopre la illegittima relazione carnale e nello stato d'ira determinato dall'offesa recata all'onor suo o della famiglia, è punito con la reclusione da tre a sette anni." ("Whoever causes the death of a spouse, daughter, or sister, during the act of an illegitimate carnal relation and in the state of rage caused by the offense to his honor or that of his family, is punishable to three to seven years of prison." Translated from Italian by the author.) The article was abrogated on August 5, 1981.

[46] Divorce was legalized in Italy only in 1970 and confirmed in a popular referendum in 1974. The waiting period between the request for legal separation and the request for divorce, originally five years, was reduced to three in 1987.

[47] Mario Sesti, ed., *Pietro Germi: The Latin Loner* (Milan: Edizioni Olivares, 1999), 106–7.

[48] Peter Bondanella, *Italian Cinema,* 150.

[49] "In *Divorzio all'italiana* l'habitat famigliare fa corpo compatto con un ambiente umano decisamente patologico, eccessivo, in cui si scontrano interessi contrapposti e culture estranee, dove vengono a contatto pulsioni e mondi inconciliabili…. Nel contatto di questi due mondi si fa strada una passione insana, si generano gli incubi romantici dell'amore proibito e criminoso che non conosce leggi o ostacoli, secondo gli schemi della letteratura d'appendice." Translated from Italian by the author. Maurizio Grande, *Abiti nuziali,* 171.

[50] At first, Sordi and Giulietta Masina were considered for the parts, but they turned down the script. Mastroianni, who had just finished embodying a Sicilian character in Mauro Bolognini's *Il bell'Antonio* in Catania a year before, agreed to impersonate the decadent Sicilian baron.

[51] Mastroianni's nomination was all the more impressive in that many talented actors were in competition that year: Jack Lemmon (*Days of Wine and Roses*), Burt Lancaster (*The Birdman of Alcatraz*), and Peter O'Toole (*Lawrence of Arabia*), and the winner for Best Actor Gregory Peck, who received the popular vote for *To Kill a Mockingbird.*

[52] Leonardo Sciascia, *La Sicilia e il cinema. V. Spinazzola (a cura di), Film 1963* (Milan: Feltrinelli, 1963), 26–27.

[53] The article of law (Articolo 530) stipulated that if a man physically abused a woman, he had to go to jail; however, if he married her, his sentence was void, and therefore to be nullified.

[54] For instance, in the oneiric sequence depicting the hypothetical trial, the use of wide-angle lens was able to distort horribly the faces of the jeering crowd and provide the expected claustrophobic environment.

[55] Translated from Italian by the author: "L'inconciliabilità fra modi di vita antiquati con le esigenze di una società in continua evoluzione: una contraddizione di cui egli aveva già sperimentato la particolare traducibilità nei modi della commedia." G. Attollini, *Il cinema italiano degli anni sessanta: Tra commedia e impegno* (Bari: Graphiservice, 1998), 76–77.

[56] Unlike *Divorzio all'italiana,* no leading role appeared to manifest itself in the story, as the scenario offered a large variety of inspired characters.

[57] Grande, *Abiti nuziali,* 166.

[58] The use of self-deprecating humor scoffing at public transportation in Sicily—still very much alive forty years later among Sicilian themselves: "He left with the train? I guess there is time then."

[59] Jacqueline Reich, *Beyond the Latin Lover: Marcello Mastroianni, Masculinity, and Italian Cinema* (Bloomington: Indiana University Press, 2004), 67

[60] Enrico Giacovelli, *La commedia all'italiana* (Rome: Gremese, 1990), 156.

[61] The film sold over one million admissions in 1964.

[62] In all fairness, the film may be entertaining certain stereotyped visions of Sicily and certain preconceived ideas of the Mafia, but only as a corollary device and for the sole purpose of comic relief.

[63] Translated by the author from the film's original dialogues: Marta: "Scusate… disturba il fumo?" Antonio: "Non Marta, non è che disturba. E che non sono abituati a vedere una femmina che fuma." Marta: "Allora se non do fastidio, scusa; ognuno le sue abitudini. Una sigaretta alla fine dei pasti."

[64] Several subjective camera angles gave the viewer a privileged position, allowing a deeper sense of the protagonist's alienation. Both rear shots were presented in a parallel manner, as Antonio Badalamenti was seen from the back at the factory and from the same point of view in New York City just before the killing.

[65] Translated by the author from Italian: "Eravamo a un passo da Bagheria e sapevamo di essere controllati. Tonino Cervi voleva nascondere il copione, io ebbi invece l'idea di raccontarlo al capomafia locale. Da quel momento in poi, tutto il paese è stato al mio servizio…. La frase con la quale ho conquistato una riunione di Mafiosi della zona è stata 'Questo fetuso non tiene parola.' Mi riferivo al mafioso che non aveva rispettato i patti, e per questo viene ucciso da Sordi a New York. Avendo espresso in questo modo la loro ideologia, e da allora in poi ho avuto mano libera. Loro certo che sapevano che il film avrebbe suscitato indignazione: da parte loro c'era solo l'approvazione del delitto." Pietro Pintus, *Commedia all'italiana,* 113.

[66] The cinematographer also collaborated on other important feature films, such as Mauro Bolognini's *Bell'Antonio* (*Il bell'Antonio*, 1960); Vittorio De Sica's *Boccaccio '70* (*Boccaccio '70*, 1962) and *Il boom* (1963); and Antonio Pietrangeli's *The Magnificent Cuckold* (*Il magnifico cornuto*, 1964).

[67] The original play, written by Fernand Crommelynck in 1947, a Flemish playwright who wrote in French, dealt with the author's theme of predilection, the vicissitudes of lust and jealousy, and its predestined itinerary from farce to tragedy. Although the play was of some historical interest, particularly as a precursor of modern "Theater of the absurd," the three-act journey displayed the antirealistic influence of such movements as surrealism and symbolism. This bitterly humorous look at marital relationship did not attract much of the public attention in the 1930s; however, it gained a belated recognition with the emergence of the French *théâtre de l'absurde* in the 1950s, to which its work then was influential.

[68] Translated by the author from Italian: "Petri distingue con la massima chiarezza il Bene dal Male e quando decide di rappresentare il secondo può farlo solo in termini estremamente caricaturali, sarcastici e grotteschi." Aldo Viganò. *Commedia italiana in cento films* (Genoa: Le mani, 1995), 110.

[69] Also recorded in many documents pertaining to the career of Elio Petri was the notorious response of film producer Dino de Laurentis to the filmmaker: "Tu sei comunista, vatti a far produrre questo film da Togliatti!" ("Since you're a communist, go and ask Togliatti to produce this film!")

Part Three

The Final Act of the
Commedia all'Italiana

Chapter 5

Italian Comedy in the 1970s

In the 1970s many influential socioeconomic events took place in Italy and in other Western European countries, which had dramatic consequences for political and societal stability: while the Italian Communist Party was able to seriously contend with the Christian Democrats, Portugal was struggling with a potential revolution; Spain's old Fascist regime ended with the imminent death of Franco; Germany faced extreme-left terrorism; and England sent armed forces to Northern Ireland. Moreover, the expansion of Euro-Communism crossed Italian frontiers to receive a warm welcome in France and Spain.[1] These transitional years were of prime concern for the United States, NATO, and other political entities that feared further political destabilization in Western Europe.

For Italy, the decade (1969–80) brought an unprecedented series of setbacks as extremist political violence became part of quotidian life and affected the face of a nation with significant human loss (more than 600 bomb attacks throughout the peninsula partly responsible for 362 deaths). In response to the emergent social protests and a possible escalation of Communism, Neo-Fascist terrorists directed (with the benediction of an "unorthodox" Masonic lodge and Italian secret service) a series of bombings to destabilize the democratic republic and open the way for an impending authoritarian coup. In return, left-wing extremists organized themselves in local terrorist cells, carrying out assassinations of public officials in the hope of encouraging a mass popular insurrection. This resulted in combined hostilities between opposing terrorist groups and quickly spiraled out of control, as politicians, lawmakers, and police forces were unable to foresee any immediate solution. Interestingly enough, the *Brigate rosse* (Red Brigades), often accused for the totality of the chaos, were responsible for only seventy-five of the fatalities throughout the decade, leaving the large majority of murders to other terrorist organizations from both ends of the terror spectrum (extreme-left and Neo-Fascist organizations).

A Social Climate of Violence: The Lead Years

Looking back in time, the seventies rarely evoke happy moments in Italian national history (Italian film comedies being indisputably an excellent barometer). Unparalleled acts of violence, social tensions, and political unrest all conjugated with a historic economic recession were at the basis of the country's woes. The advent of the so-called *anni di piombo* or "lead years" began to take shape with the disappointment from the disillusion of the 1968 movement and from the *autunno caldo* of 1969 (baptized "restless autumn," it was a short period of social unrest characterized by spontaneous movements among students, workers, and trade unions), the hope it had generated in terms of social reforms, which never engendered the long-awaited cultural revolution.[2] Despite some improvements in the sector of remuneration with equal wage increases in large national companies, and despite the long-awaited introduction of the forty-hour labor week, as well as a noticeable growth of trade union presence in the workplace (whose success was due to the alliance of the three major unions—CGIL, CISL, and UIL), much was yet to be done to bring a peaceful climate to the large northern industries. To make matters worse, the absence of reforms for low-income housing (involving fair rent on a national scale), and for health care, were weighing in the balance. The Italian government was not alone in this uphill battle to restore social consensus in the workplace. Trade unions were also involved in a similar effort to revitalize their influence among the large factories of the north due to the absence of a widespread militancy and mutual solidarity among the lower class. Therefore, the permanent stage of social agitation, which had been at the basis of the revolutionary project of 1968, slowly began to decrease in fervor. In light of the disaffection from the working class for a sustained social agenda and the growing dichotomy between popular and political forces, partial attempts were made by both trade unionists and the Christian Democrat government to mediate the frequent social protests.

Since no foreseeable reforms were announced, much dissatisfaction was still present in the social climate of the turn of the new decade. Consequently, the revolutionary "extra parliamentary" political organizations faced a critical choice: that of continuing the social agenda through a democratic process or using violent demonstrations of force in order to take a shortcut on the course of history. One of the most significant early signs of violence was the bombing at the Fiat stand during the Milan Fair, wounding twenty on April 25, 1969. Then on August 9, several bombs exploded in eight different trains all over Italy, causing twelve wounded. Later, the same year in Milan, on November 19, a police officer was killed during a confrontation with *Unione Comunisti Italiani* demonstrators (Marxists-Leninists). Although these are only a small sample of all the acts of political violence perpetrated that year in Italy, these events illustrated the radical shift in the political horizon and an unpromising sign of the times.

The Strategy of Tension and the Neo-Fascist Groups

Far from remaining simple political observers, the Neo-Fascist organizations anticipated demonstrations of force in the workplace by the newly united trade unions. For this matter, the groups' maneuvering scope was limited, and therefore violent actions were to be swift but carefully planned to stop the growing social unrest in the country. Some of the most prevalent Neo-Fascist groups (i.e., *Ordine Nuovo, Ordine Nero, Fronte Nazionale, Avanguardia Nazionale*, or later *Nuclei Armati Rivoluzionari* known as N.A.R.[3]) became inspired by the successful methods used by the colonels in Greece during the 1967 coup d'état, and counted on the possible exasperation of public opinion in favor of a shift to an authoritarian regime. Italian right-wing paramilitary organizations, often nostalgic for the Fascist regime and its idealized concept of order, employed that theory to potentially destabilize the political order of the country. For the Neo-Fascists, the objective was clearly to destabilize the democratic process in which the Christian Democrat government had committed after the mid-sixties. The so-called "strategy of tension" aimed to foment terror and paranoia in the streets of Italy through carefully prepared violent bomb attacks, all of which led to the belief in a revolutionary coup perpetrated by Communist terrorists and extreme-left radical organizations. The subsequent step was to coerce the Italian government, by then supposedly in a state of panic, to declare a state of emergency and thus implement the first step toward a totalitarian military regime, reminiscent of a nostalgic prewar era, which eventually would remain permanently.

The first act of the conspiracy occurred December 12, 1969, with the bombing inside the Banca Nazionale dell'Agricoltura at the Piazza Fontana in Milan, killing sixteen and wounding eighty-eight. Within the same hour, four more bombings occurred in Rome (with a total of five bombings in fifty-three minutes). At first, the anarchist organizations were immediately singled out by police investigators, mainly the *Autonomia Operaia* (a radical Communist group that promoted total independence of the proletarian forces from capitalistic society). Quickly, several hundred people were arrested; one of them, Giuseppe Pinelli, a railway employee and a known anarchist activist, was held for forty-eight hours by inspectors and incidentally fell from the police station's fourth-floor (charges later were dropped against the officers responsible for the interrogations). The official version of Pinelli's death was suicide, a version contradicted during the trial in Catanzaro six years later, which leaves the true version uncertain.[4] Finally willing to consider evidence they had ruled out previously, police investigators discovered that Neo-Fascist paramilitary organizations orchestrated the bombing hoping to befall responsibility on the extreme-left terrorist cells (*Ordine Nuovo*, a Veneto-based organization whose leaders were Franco Freda and Giovanni Ventura) in direct contact with Guido Giannettini, a colonel of the Italian Secret Service SID (*Servizio Informazioni Difesa*) and MSI (*Movimento*

Sociale Italiano), a Neo-Fascist political party. Even under high criticism by the opposition and the press, the government (the second Mariano Rumor administration whose timid commitment to shed light appeared suspicious) was reluctant to further investigate these suspicious links between paramilitary organizations and right-wing political parties on behalf of national security.[5] In 1981, the three main actors in the above-mentioned bomb attack were finally sentenced to life imprisonment, but all were acquitted the following year after their appeal. Some links with the American CIA and the Gladio network[6] were also brought forth during the investigation and in particular collaboration with the Italian state.[7]

A year later, an attempt of coup d'état organized by Prince Junio Valerio Borghese (a former officer in Mussolini's factions during the Salò Republic) took place on December 7, 1970. Supported by a right-wing paramilitary organization called *Fronte Nazionale* and high-ranked officers of the military, the coup intended to besiege the offices of the Interior and Defense Ministry as well as take control of the RAI offices (including telephone networks). In addition, the head of Italian state Giuseppe Saragat and the head of the police forces were to be kidnapped. The commando succeeded in occupying the Ministry of Interior for part of the evening, before disappearing in the night, without having perpetrated any act of violence. It was only three months later that the coup was made public in the press. At the end of a trial, which involved several generals of the Italian army and Vito Miceli, the head of the secret service, all accused of conspiracy against the state, the actual sentencing was eventually dismissed for lack of evidence. It was only after the trial that light was shed on the so-called *Rosa dei Venti*, a secret Neo-Fascist organization discovered in 1974 that was in contact with NATO. The quaint and rather "cartoonish" attempt led by a few nostalgic men (187 forest guards and a platoon of former paratroopers) inspired filmmaker Mario Monicelli in his 1973 satirical rendition of the event starring Ugo Tognazzi entitled *We Want the Colonels* (*Vogliamo i colonelli*).

The strategy of tension continued with scores of bomb attacks, among which was the bombing during an antiterrorism demonstration aimed at pointing out Neo-Fascist groups, also known as the *Strage di Piazza della Loggia,* orchestrated by a right-wing terrorist group on May 28, 1974, in Brescia, killing eight and wounding ninety. Shortly after, during the same summer on August 4, 1974, a powerful bomb exploded on the express train Roma-Munich in San Benedetto Val di Sambro, near Bologna, causing the death of twelve passengers and wounding forty-four.

The Red Brigades and the Armed Propaganda

Although less "deadly" than the paramilitary Neo-Fascist terrorist cells (when considering the number of causalities), the *Brigate Rosse* are still remembered today as the main players during the lead years. Born from the organization called *Sinistra Proletaria* in 1970 in Reggio Emilia, the Red Brigades were inspired by Marxist-Leninist theories as well as the practices of Latin American guerilla movements. The main goal was imminent socioeconomic and political revolution whose modus operandi was propaganda through immediate action and as a last resort through armed struggle. Unlike the civil movement emanating from 1968 that promoted collective action against the members of the establishment, the terrorist group opted for underground strategies through illegal activities, thus oversimplifying the content of their social observations. But far from accelerating the course of history toward social and political revolution, the Red Brigades' violent actions accelerated the disintegration of the social web and indefinitely postponed long-awaited social reforms.[8]

Along with the *Brigate Rosse* was a myriad of political clandestine organizations such as *Potere Operaio, Lotta Continua, Gruppo XXII Ottobre, Gruppo di Azione Partigiana* (GAP) created by editor Giangiacomo Feltrinelli,[9] *Nuclei Armati Proletari* (NAP), *Collettivo Politico Metropolitano,* and other Maoist groups. The Red Brigades' first kidnapping was perpetrated in 1972 against a manager of the Siemens group, which left him the same day unharmed. This initial action was followed by a series of actions against the so-called "servant of the state": lawmakers, magistrates, high-ranking officers of the military, and even high-profile journalists. In 1974, Alberto Franceschini and Renato Curcio, both cofounders of the *Brigate Rosse,* were arrested due to the new strategy led by the general of the Carabinieri, Carlo Alberto Dalla Chiesa (later assassinated by the Mafia in 1982 in Palermo), and both activists were eventually condemned to eighteen years in prison. Earlier that year, Dalla Chiesa had been appointed to supervise and command the antiterrorism activity in the northern regions, and in the same manner as with the fight against the Mafia, the first "pentiti" were given social treatment and reduced prison sentences in order to acquire valuable information against the clandestine organizations. After 1974, the Red Brigades changed targets and moved from large-scale company managers to more targeted objectives such as political personalities, high-profile judges, and prominent businessmen working for the state. In April 1974, they kidnapped Mario Sossi, a Genovese judge, for a total of thirty-five days. Once again, the victim was released after the categorical rejection from the state to release political prisoners from the *Gruppo XXII Ottobre* close to the Red Brigades. By now, the Italian public opinion had received its first warning that the clandestine organization was able to strike anywhere and at the highest level. However, the Red Brigades were victims of their own success, as Italian police gained considerable ground, thanks to their intelligence services, and were able to infiltrate several networks to arrest the most prominent members by the year 1976. Although winning in their repression against the terrorist cells[10] and their high-profile media success, Italian police committed one of their critical mistakes by underestimating the "re-grouping" ability of the *Brigate rosse*. After 1976, the tracking of terrorists slowed down due to its large-scale accomplishment, which led to the imprisonment of most active members of the Red Brigades. However, the relaxation proved disastrous since many new members reorganized to occupy new spaces. Most likely, less than a hundred executive members, the organization accounted for several thousand supporters, which quickly replaced activists by now imprisoned. One of the early signs of the *Red Brigades'* second wind occurred in 1977 with the intimidation attempt against Indro Montanelli, editor of *Il Giornale Nuovo*, considered a "slave of multinationals," who was shot on his way to the newspaper (two bullets wounding both legs also known under the neologism of "gambizzazione").[11]

In their attempt to eradicate the "servants of the state," the *Brigate Rosse* committed their most infamous action in 1978 with the assassination of former[12] prime minister and Christian Democrat President Aldo Moro. On March 16, a commando of nine terrorists intercepted Aldo Moro's escort in via Fana in Rome while heading to Montecitorio (the Italian parliament) in order to support the new Andreotti government (the first ever to include PCI). The five policemen accompanying the escort and the chauffeur were all killed. Once Moro was kidnapped, the abductors were able to vanish in the crowded street of the capital. Following numerous exchanges in writing, a final ultimatum was sent (the eighth message sent to the Moro family), requesting the liberation of thirteen prisoners close to the Red Brigades in exchange for Moro's life. A difficult dilemma indeed for the Christian Democrat government (DC), caught between personal ties with one of their comrades and president and the conviction to prevent setting a precedent. The Christian Democrat Party was forced to rule out compromise partly due to the strong position taken by the PCI, and to avoid having its opponent as the only political party looking tough against terrorists. After fifty-five days of captivity and the firm refusal from the Andreotti government to negotiate, Aldo Moro was executed. On May 9 in via Michelangelo Caetani, his body was found in a car quickly surrounded by a crowd of police officers and distraught journalists. The abduction, orchestrated principally by activist Mario Moretti, immediately became a high-profile media phenomenon in the press, especially television, maintaining an unbearable tension on a national scale. The photos of Moro in front of the Red Brigades flag accompanied with his letters imploring the government for leniency to secure his release, traumatized an entire nation, regardless of political orientation. In addition, the macabre conditions of Moro's death rebuked national and international public opinions indefinitely, and deprived the organization of the partial popular support they had enjoyed earlier in the decade, which consequently affected their future recruitment. The instant disaffection for the assassination was more and more a reality among supporters of the social revolution and the process of self-isolation began. Following the ordeal, many political commentators, journalists, and members of governments pointed out the irreversible curve that Italian democracy was forced to take. However, looking back with a critical distance of thirty years, one can easily argue that not much has changed in the political life of Italy and in particular between state and society. In the 1980s, many left-wing activists fled to France due to the so-called "Mitterrand Doctrine" implemented in 1985 by the French president, which tolerated the presence of wanted left-wing militants in exchange for a promise to abandon political activity.[13]

The *anni di piombo* took their final "mass destructive" toll with the single deadliest act of terrorism that occurred on Italian soil, on August 2, 1980, inside Bologna's train station, killing eighty-five people and wounding two hundred.[14] During the peak vacation period, a bomb was left in one of the crowded waiting rooms. The magnitude of its explosion destroyed a great part of the station and flipped over a train exiting the station. Once again, as had happened a decade earlier with the bombing of Piazza Fontana, the early allegations were directed toward a possible revitalization of the Red Brigades, but later ongoing investigations revealed the link between extreme-right activists with secret service agents who belonged to the SISMI (*Servizio per le Informazioni e la Sicurezza Militare*). In 1995, Neo-Nazi activists Valerio Fioravanti and Francesca Mambro were condemned to a life sentence. Also sentenced to twelve years of prison were Licio Gelli,[15] *grande maestro* of the Masonic Lodge *Propaganda Due* (P2), Francesco Pazienza, and two officers from SISMI, Pietro Musumeci and Giuseppe Belmonte.

Much has been written about the existence and role of the Masonic lodge in Italy (allegedly responsible for numerous conspiracies, including the failed Borghese coup, the Bologna bombing, the sudden death of Pope John Paul I, the bankruptcy of the Ambrosiano Bank among others), but mystery still persists on the actual role of its members on the course of political history during the postwar years. The main perception is one of political agenda geared toward the destabilization of political order to destitute governments displaying too much leniency with Communist states. Created in 1877, the Italian Masonic lodge was forbidden during the Fascist era, and some of its members met and operated from France. Their political theories and activities were emblematic of an anti-Fascist organization and thus the *Grande Oriente d'Italia* gained considerable credit after 1943 when Mussolini was forced to flee. Under the prestige of the American Masonic order, many postwar political figures were seduced by the prestige of the *Grande Oriente* and were secretly initiated while still remaining faithful to their respective political parties. In 1964, Licio Gelli, a former officer during the Fascist era, was nominated president of the *Loggia Propaganda*, now called P2. Because of the sustained growth of the PCI in Italian political life and its growing collaborative effort with the DC coalition, plans were put on the agenda, such as the reinstitution of the death penalty and new regulations limiting trade union activities in large companies. In March 1981, Italian police discovered a nominative list at Gelli's home in Arezzo, with a total of 932 members, including 44 members of the Italian parliament, 3 members of the current government, 22 generals from the military, many magistrates and high-profile civil servants, as well as journalists and businessmen like Roberto Calvi (found mysteriously hung under a London bridge in 1982), Silvio Berlusconi, Vittorio Emanuele of Savoia, Maurizio Costanzo and Claudio Villa, even members of General Videla's military junta in Argentina.[16] A few months later, Gelli was expelled from the *Grande Oriente d'Italia* in October 1981 following his reluctance to return toward more humanistic perspectives as well as the embarrassment of a potential political scandal.

Economy and Politics

October 1973 was the worst economic crisis since the Great Depression for European nations and in particular for Italy, which was already struggling to overcome its own recession due to the end of the economic boom of the 1960s. Within just a few weeks, OPEC countries quadrupled the price of crude oil to result in several years of a sustained recession that lasted through the second oil crisis of 1978. Many large state-owned industries such as ENI, Fiat, and Siemens were in a difficult financial position, having accumulated a colossal amount of debt following the end of the economic miracle. So when the economic crisis struck in 1973, many of them, avoiding a large gathering of trade unions, began to decentralize their branches into smaller-scale plants in the southern regions where trade union traditions were of lesser importance (also avoiding professional taxes and social security contributions to the *Cassa Integrazione*). In addition, the chronic rise of a galloping inflation spiraled upward to become the highest in Western Europe with a rate between 15 percent and 20 percent for most of the 1970s (a spectacular increase from 5.6 percent in 1972 to 19.4 percent in 1974); worst was the unemployment rate of 20 percent of the active population with a climactic 25 percent in Naples.

The revolutionary message from the *autunno caldo* did not survive much after the 1970s. The anticapitalist conception of the world economy conjugated with radical collectivism did not persist beyond the first years of the new decade, and as the economic conjecture deteriorated following the oil embargo beginning October 1973, many Italian working families adopted a rather individualistic response to economic hardship. According to British historian Paul Ginsborg, "Italy's modernization, as so many others, was not based on collective responsibility or collective action, but on the opportunities it afforded individual families to transform their lives."[17] To make matters worse, the Italian economy was still heavily dependant on a fossilized structure hampered by the sluggishness of its public administration, the expansion of bureaucracy, and the generalization of absenteeism—a chronic problem in large factories. Much like the years of the economic boom, once again the state had carried out no tangible social or economic reforms. This explains why many municipalities took action to resolve social conflicts and invert the deteriorating trend of their local economy.

The 1970s were also the years when, for the first time, local governments (mainly the wealthy northern regions of Emiglia-Romagna, Liguria, Piedmont,

Lombardy, and Tuscany) were headed by Communist and Socialist municipal councils. The years of so-called "national solidarity" were made possible in great part due to local initiatives. Although never officially invested with government responsibilities, the role of the Italian Communist Party was decisive for many aspects of the political life of the 1970s. Following the election of Enrico Berlinguer as its secretary in 1972, the party was at the forefront of the Euro-Communism concept and took advantage of this momentum to reassert a distance with Moscow, which soon was imitated by its French and Spanish counterparts. During these years, the PCI can be considered the only large political party whose primary initiative attempted to change the political horizon of the decade.[18] In 1974, thanks to an inherent gift for political mediation, Berlinguer planned collaboration with the Christian Democrats, a joint venture between Catholics and Communists.[19] In addition to reclaiming public recognition from other parties, the *Compromesso Storico* was also to limit a hypothetical temptation that Christian Democrats shift to a traditionalist right-wing orientation. In the meantime, the growth of the PCI was able to maintain a stronghold in the 1975 regional elections, with a score of 33 percent, thus increasing pressure on the Christian Democracy (DC) to deal with left-wing forces (2 percent short of catching up with the DC, which still remained the first political force of the nation). A year later, in June 1976, the PCI scored its best performance ever with 34.4 percent to the parliamentary election (DC 38.7 percent). The assassination of Aldo Moro in 1978,[20] and the tragic bombing in Bologna in 1980, among other national tragedies, contributed to the failure of the enterprise. This compromise, had it fully achieved its goal, would have been one of epochal magnitude, a political revolution, and at the least recentered the political axis toward a more center-left direction. Although the PSI (*Partito Socialista Italiano*) and PCI could have capitalized from their respective progress, their political agendas did not envisage a political union, which most likely would have changed the course of the nation's history. Instead, the PCI now had to deal with the Christian Democrats' most faithful servant Giulio Andreotti, whose experience in dealing with Communist attacks and criticism was extensive. After this tragic episode, the *Compromesso Storico* no longer existed. Instead, a long-awaited alliance between PCI and the Italian Socialists was next on the agenda, but it came too late, as the latter was going to experience a development with formation of a new government by Bettino Craxi as prime minister in August 1983.

At the end of the decade, the PCI was not the only political party to embark on a slow decline, as the Christian Democrats soon encountered the same fate until its collapse in the late eighties. Because of the Catholic Church's principles on the indissolubility of marriage and its crusade for the salvation of the Italian family, the 1970s saw the beginning of the decline of the Christian Democrats Party (the Catholic Church's main ally), which logically resulted in a series of political setbacks often manifested in lost referendums. Although the most prominent party since the postwar, their defeat over the question of divorce as well as abortion a few years later, hindered by the weight of several financial scandals, and numerous allegations of corruption and connections to the "enigmatic" secret services, accentuated the trend of disaffection.

The Fight for Women's Rights

One of the most decisive changes that occurred in the 1970s was undoubtedly the fight for women's rights following the leadership initiated with the 1960s civil rights movement in America. This collective movement was to involve more women than any time in Italian modern history. Capitalizing on this historical momentum, Italian women, whether at the factory level or magistrates, organized to engage in public life and to become acting components of political decisions.[21] Just like the National Organization of Women in America did a few years earlier in 1966, Italian women began an uphill battle directing their own civil rights fight for the eradication of gender discrimination in the workplace as well as in the private sphere. These initiatives included a wide range of requests such as legalizing divorce and abortion, establishing equal rights between both partners within marriage contracts, promoting awareness for sexual freedom, contraception, and finally the creation of women's commissions in factory councils.

Some of the most visible political groups established a demarcation from traditional political parties, with the exception of the modest Radical Party, well known for its media-orientated campaigns that included anticlerical slogans, antimilitarist initiatives, disarmament, free sexuality, and legalization of soft drugs. These organizations included the *Movimento Liberazione delle Donne* (MLD), created in 1969 during the Radical Party's Convention by Adele Faccio and Maria Adele Teodori. In their footsteps, the *Fronte Italiano Liberazione Femminile* (FILF), created in 1970 and more radical then MLD, proposed a separation from the presence of men even during their political campaigns. In 1970, an autonomous group seceded from the MLD to become *Rivolta Femminile* (RF) and suggested refusing dialogues with men, since it meant accepting their "rules and identity," hence imitating their behavioral attitudes. Their theory stood against the institution of marriage because it was dominated by the male figure for centuries. Another group with national scope (although mostly active in the north and Rome) called *Lotta Femminista* fought for the recognition of housework and demanded financial compensation through the intervention of the state.

This historical movement was much more than the usual *emancipazione della donna* (women's emancipation, which had been discussed in the early years of the postwar era beginning with the right for women to vote in 1946), but this time a true "women's liberation" phenomenon stood against a fossilized patriarchal-dominated society. The first example of significant transformation was the case of adultery and its (mis)conception within the private sphere, as it illustrated the gap between religious code of conduct and an ever distant social reality of the late sixties. In December 1968, women's adultery was finally no longer penalized by the 1930 law (the Penal Code's Article 559 punished women with up to two years of jail sentence for having committed adultery). In addition, the right to immediate separation was consented to by a judge with the proof of adultery committed by the husband.

As related in Chapter 3, the question of divorce took shape in the early sixties and became an actual law a decade later thanks to the leadership of its two main protagonists, Loris Fortuna and Antonio Baslini, who drafted the bill. After two fruitless attempts to propose a vote on Divorce Law in 1954 and 1958, the third attempt proved successful, as the parliament finally voted the new divorce law on November 27, 1969 (Christian Democrats, *Movimento Sociale Italiano,* and Monarchists all voted against). Following the implementation of the new state law (Legge 898) on January 1, 1970, several Catholic organizations quickly collected thousands of signatures in order to present a request for a referendum aimed at consulting the Italian people on the issue and hopefully abrogating the new law. The law was actually a two-step process. First, the legal separation was to be recognized, then and then only was the couple allowed to file for divorce. Along with the implementation of the divorce law came a subsequent sociological aftermath that showed an increase in separations as well as a reduction in the number of children per family. Interestingly, while in the rest of European countries, women were the majority to file for divorce in these early years with "infidelity" as the main reason, Italian men outnumbered Italian women in their request for divorce, invoking most of the time "mutual consent" (a practice that proved faster and less expensive).[22] One of the most clamorous examples proving that *commedia all'italiana* was inspired by everyday life chronicles rather than literary works was the notorious episode of Sophia Loren and Carlo Ponti's tribulations for legalizing their marital status. Since Italy did not have a law on divorce, Carlo Ponti had first to annul his first marriage in 1957, then obtain a Mexican divorce and marry Sophia by proxy. The same year in Italy, Ponti was legally charged with bigamy, since the Catholic Church did not recognize this second marriage, which was annulled in 1962. In 1966, in order to put an end to the continuing saga, Carlo Ponti and his former wife Giuliana obtained French citizenship, and the same year in Paris after almost a decade of tribulations with the Italian state and Church, Carlo Ponti and Sophia Loren were officially and legally married.

On May 12 and 13, 1974, the national referendum on divorce resulted in an unprecedented 87.7 percent participation among which more than 59 percent responded no to the abrogation to the law, therefore reasserting their support to legalize divorce. The popular outcome went beyond any political observers' most pessimistic expectations, which clearly had underestimated the position of the Italian electors. In the wake of the divorce bill, it was clear that many women from all ages had endorsed the movement. After four years of tension and suspense for both political sides, the result was a severe loss for the Christian Democrats, which had based the core of their political program on an ethical and religious platform.

The next and last battle of the decade was the legalization of abortion. At the time of the 1974 referendum, the practice of abortion was punishable by up to a five-year prison sentence (although illegally occurring on a regular basis throughout Italy each year). An active minority of women, anticipating the next battle, began to circulate petitions for the future legalization of abortion (during the divorce referendum, Italian people were also asked their opinion on the necessity of a referendum on abortion, and responded 67.9 percent in favor).[23] In 1975, more than 700,000 signatures[24] were collected with the assistance of the Partito Radicale and under the aegis of Emma Bonino and Marco Pannella. The bill on abortion was presented in January 1977 at the Chamber of Deputies. Because the Senate voted it down later the same year, it only became officially a law in May 1978 (Legge 194). The new legislation consented to women the right to interrupt pregnancy within the first ninety days of gestation (or later if the mother's life was at risk or in cases of fetus malformation). On the other hand, because of the necessity of a medical doctor's approval, in practice finalizing a claim due to the large population of Catholic doctors in Italy was a still a complex procedure.

Another important aspect of the evolution of Italian traditions was the recognition of female sexuality.[25] During the Fascist era, the rare evocations of sexuality were always overshadowed by the matriarchal representation of women and their central role within the family sphere, thus promoting the traditional Catholic family precept. The vivacious propaganda spirit precluded Italian women from assuming their own sexuality, since the myth of virile men and fertile women outpaced any other viewpoints. With the immediate postwar customs, in part brought by the American presence, the situation began to slowly change; the economic boom at the end of the 1950s brought leisure, free time, and vacations that allowed Italians to meet away from home, thus creating new desires for escapism, consumerism, even libertine temptations as illustrated in Fellini's *La dolce vita* (1960). But in these years of social freedom, the Catholic Church still very much promoted a didactic discourse on the evolution of various concepts (marriage, adultery, divorce), as well as sexuality itself (premarital sex, contraceptive devices, extramarital rapport, homosexuality, abortion, and pornography). The double moral standards of the Church, which in theory severely reproved extramarital as well as premarital sex, never attempted to eradicate the presence of the so-called *case di toleranze* and therefore surprisingly "tolerated" their existence.[26] The years of the economic miracle, followed by the evolution toward sexual freedom generated by the hippie movement, coincided with the disaffection of many Italians for the interference on their private lives by a somewhat outmoded religious code of conduct. At the end of the 1960s, women's sexuality was therefore no longer isolated and became a subject of common conversation. It was during these years of sudden sexual freedom that one of the most visible manifestations of the decade began to surface with the advent of graphic eroticism and ultimately pornography (1966 saw the first erotic publication for men in Italy). However, the phenomenon did not explode until the seventies with the first *luci rosse cinema* (red light district theaters began to screen pornographic films in 1977), which eventually deeply divided the feminist movement.

The Italian Film Industry in the 1970s

By the early 1970s, the effects of the boom years and May 1968 had in theory dissipated. Global consumerism appeared as if it would successfully dominate Italian society, which seemed in danger of losing its cultural specificity. By the mid-1970s, Italian culture had freed itself from the rigid hierarchies and social behaviors that previously characterized quotidian life; however, the utopian environment anticipated by the activists in the 1968 movement did not become a reality. In general, the 1970s were marked by disillusionment with social reform and economic change, leading to the rise of individualism in the 1980s and the gradual disappearance of the *commedia all'italiana* spirit.

The dramatic changes of Italian political and social life affected the film industry on an unprecedented level in every aspect of its production. The growing alienation of the individual in a society under the spell of the 1960s hastened modernization and uncontrolled urban development, and the atomization of Italian society all produced an ineluctable consequence: a change of mood from euphoric to pessimist cinema. Moreover, the mood of the national industry was far from displaying exuberant results due to the growing rivalry generated by television, even if production difficulties were nothing new (Lux closed in 1966, Titanus gave up production in 1964 and relocated in the distribution sector).[27] The ruthless competition had already started in the late fifties when Italian associations of producers and distributors (ANICA and AGIS), who had anticipated a possible buy-out of the entire Italian film industry by Hollywood, were able to secure many arrangements with the Motion Picture Association of America (MPAA) to limit American dominance of the market. The most influential decision came from a governmental initiative and was designed to block the growing export of American film revenues earned in Italy. Consequently, large-scale American investments were made with Italian productions due to the difficulty of justifying "financial evasion" to the detriment of the Italian film industry.

For the Italian film industry, the 1970s corresponded with the last years of large-scale national productions. Indeed, in 1972, Italian films accounted for more than 52 percent of the productions distributed in Italy (see figure 1). However, this was the peak of success, as the trend began to follow a downward spiral, reaching only 30 percent of productions in 1980. Part of the conjecture

Figure 1: Italian vs. Foreign Long Feature Films

	Italian Productions	%	Foreign Productions	%	Total
1968	262	43.8	336	56.2	598
1969	247	47.9	269	52.1	516
1970	239	48.4	255	51.6	494
1971	233	47.8	254	52.2	487
1972	280	52.2	256	47.8	536
1973	252	44.6	313	55.4	565
1974	244	44.3	307	55.7	551
1975	205	40.6	300	59.4	505
1976	242	43.4	316	56.6	558
1977	166	36.5	289	63.5	455
1978	139	32.4	290	67.6	429
1979	156	29.2	378	70.8	534
1980	179	30.2	414	69.8	593

source Statistiche 1995, Pubblicazioni S.I.A.E. Roma

that explains the reasons for such competitive performance came from the success of the coproduction system; half of the 280 Italian films produced during the year 1972 were the result of coproductions (the phenomenon goes back to the 1950s, but after the mid-1960s coproductions were going full swing with France and other European film industries).

Although the European movie industry generally experienced a decrease in theater attendance all over the continent (see figure 2), figures of the national distribution were still sound, as Italians remained faithful to Italian productions despite a growing trend to view American films. This result was all the more impressive given that the number of movie theaters shrunk from 7,500 at the beginning of the eighties to around 3,500 twenty-five years later. Interestingly enough, parochial cinemas, despite the significant fall in church attendance on a religious level, were still very much active among the distribution network in the 1970s (see figure 3).[28]

In addition, the price for theater admission in Italy dramatically increased, which rendered statistics based on earned income more and more inaccurate (i.e., in 1958 an entrance ticket equaled 152 lira; two decades later in 1978 the same ticket amounted to around 1,000 lira). In the fabled year of 1955, Italian movie theaters sold a record 819 million tickets, more than eight times the present-day figure (2006 sold 92 million tickets). As the end of the decade closed, the number of box-office entries continued to fall, and by 1980 box-office receipts in Italy for Italian films were significantly less than for their Hollywood counterparts. The strategies and financial incentives promoted by the Italian government during this period insured that Italian filmmaking remained financially healthy;

Figure 2: European Spectatorship (in million per year)

Year	Italy	France	U.K.	West Germany
1958	730	371	754	749
1959	747	353	581	670
1960	744	354	515	604
1961	741	328	449	516
1962	728	311	395	442
1963	697	292	357	366
1964	683	275	342	320
1965	663	257	326	294
1966	632	234	288	257
1967	568	211	264	215
1968	559	203	237	180
1969	550	182	214	180
1970	525	184	193	160
1971	535	177	176	152
1972	553	184	156	149
1973	544	176	134	144
1974	544	179	138	136
1975	513	180	116	128
1976	454	177	103	115
1977	373	170	103	124
1978	318	178	126	135
1979	276	178	111	142
1980	241	174	101	143

source S.I.A.E.

Figure 3: Comparative Study for Italian Distribution

Year	Commercial Theaters	Parochial Theaters	Other Cinemas	Total
1966	7,553	4,404	688	12,645
1977	6,274	3,586	727	10,587

source S.I.A.E.

however, the industry's hold on Italian national pride and culture disappeared. In particular, the younger spectatorship, who had not experienced the birth of the *commedia all'italiana* in the late fifties, was now more interested in foreign productions than in national cinema. So it was no surprise that during these years, Hollywood film gained new ground, further diminishing an audience already depleted by the attractive aura of television. Nevertheless, Italian cinema remained a significant embedded force in Italian culture. Popular comedies such as Mario Monicelli's *My Friends* (*Amici miei*, 1975) starring Ugo Tognazzi and

French actor Philippe Noiret continued to have strong box-office appeal. Even though by the late 1970s Hollywood films systematically outperformed Italian films at the Italian box office, the biggest popular success in terms of distribution and attendance were achieved by comedies of the 1970s and not from comedies of the boom era. Although facing the competition of more cheerful Hollywood comedies, Monicelli's *My Friends* (*Amici miei*, 1975) was without a doubt the best example, as the film later entered into the books as a cult film worshiped by several generations of Italians in spite of its evident melancholic vein of midlife crisis.

The rise of Italian television came in part thanks to a successful portrayal of society, through innovative shows and more powerful news (more immediate than the written press) that related the omnipresent reality of violence. Long feature films were by then no longer the only source of curiosity, surprise, or marvel. Television was able to provide that shocking element for the necessary curiosity inherent in each individual. This trend eventually influenced spectator-ship's desire, evolving ultimately toward a more graphic cinema, and explained the success of erotic productions (Tinto Brass) and the horror genre (i.e., Dario Argento's *Deep Red* [*Profondo Rosso*, 1975]). The effect of television on the big screen was unstoppable, as reminded by Dino Risi:

> The crisis came from a certain malaise of ideas. Television created problems because it lowered the average level, widened the public, and then all the filmmakers were conditioned and unconsciously became victims of the audience's ratings. There was a sort of self-censorship, something that forced them to fly low.[29]

Undoubtedly, the role of cinema in Italian culture changed irrevocably, as it was no longer the primary medium of mass entertainment. By the end of the 1970s, more people watched films on television than in theaters (in 1955, 25,000 Italian families owned a television, and a decade later in 1965 there were more than 6 million regular tele-spectators). Indeed, television as a mass consumption medium affected the notion of community in Italy. After the successful launch-ing of the small screen in 1954, its growth encountered little opposition from other media, and the 1970s saw the final challenge taking place as television sur-passed the performance of the large screen as well as imposed a new vision and requirement on the cinema industry since it cofinanced most of the projects.

While visual consumerism was able to promise instantaneous happiness on the small screen, the long feature films of the same decade were not able to offer the same dreamlike quality (even the comedies had changed tone with, for instance, Mario Monicelli's *An Average Little Man* [*Un borghese piccolo pic-colo*] in 1977). Many films were screened and therefore "consumed" on televi-sion. They were made for and by television. Italians could even take advantage of color coproductions just like in the theaters; on January 1, 1977, the first color broadcast was performed in Italy under the auspices of RAI television. In addition, part of the success of television programming in Italy in the 1970s was an indirect consequence of the effects of terrorism and random bombings in public areas, provoking a sense of self-imposed curfew as well as a sense of security with home-based entertainment (i.e., Dino Risi's *I nuovi mostri*, in 1977, the episode called "exemplary citizen" showing a law-abiding *capo famiglia* Vittorio Gassman, who despite witnessing a murder in front of his apartment building, decides to rush home to enjoy the family supper, in a safe mode while watching his favorite TV show).

In the fifties and sixties, Italian films were screened on television not only through a regular programming policy but more importantly as an artistic and historical device. Films were not simply screened but were gathered around thematics or directors. In the 1970s, films screened on television were always a political choice to partly coproduce films in an industry with financial problems. The first reform of the television organization started at the end of the 1960s and lasted until 1976. During this time period, the large part of production finance was controlled by public and private television companies, thus leaving little space for the cinematographic industry to provide funding for future productions. A pessimistic prospect indeed for young directors. The need to provide new possibilities to filmmakers and producers became imperative through the reform of state television organization.

By the mid-seventies, RAI was much more than a state institution. It had become a large corporation owning an unchallenged monopoly of broadcasting that reached a large audience in Italy, but nothing had been done to adapt the medium to an increasing public (for the year 1975 alone, RAI produced 115 films). In 1974, Silvio Berlusconi inaugurated TeleMilano, a cable network. It was suddenly imperative to have the whole broadcasting system revised. A law passed on April 14, 1975, and confirmed the state monopoly over the air, reinforcing the parliamentary control over radio broadcasting and financing of public networks by both licenses and advertising. Just a year later, in July 1976, an official ruling emanated from the constitutional court went against the law and therefore ended the state monopoly over media broadcasting. From now on, only private television and radio companies (*radio libere*) were allowed to perform local broadcasts. Historian Mary Wood recalled that "the explosion of commercial television made the picture more complicated, with a completely symbiotic relationship between the small and the big screen."[30] The consequent deregulation of broadcasting policies in Italy indirectly became the death warrant of the Italian film industry (in 1976, private television companies totaled sixty-eight, and in 1981 they proliferated to six hundred). The explosion of private commercial television companies served as a promising springboard for Berlusconi's Fininvest group. Like the French film industry, Italian cinema accused television of stealing audiences but at the same time benefited from television's generous rights to capitalize financially in order to coproduce new films.

The opposite of the lawmakers' intentions, the dramatic deregulation led to uncontrolled monopoly from large investment groups, such as the Finivest group already established by Silvio Berlusconi. Rome (RAI) and Milan (Berlusconi) emerged as the principal actors of the new era. In 1980, Berlusconi's *TeleMilano* took a new name, *Canale 5*. The group began to expand, as it bought several television companies such as *Italia 1* (1983) and *Rete 4* (1984). The group exported their activities to France with the creation of *La Cinq* (1986), which experienced a strong opposition from the political class and was forced to close in 1992. Finally, in 1996, it acquired *Mediaset,* becoming the largest media group in Italy. The 1984 Berlusconi decree, which became a law in 1985, legalized the access to national broadcast to private television companies, and ever since, the importance of cinematographic productions became progressively defined by the media themselves and consequently precipitated the Italian film industry to an unprecedented production crisis.

With 241 million spectators in 1980, Italian cinema still incorporated one of the most predominant spectatorships in Europe, making the battle for the control of its industry all the more imperative. However, against all odds, the battle never took place at the political level but rather on an economic level. Italian society, like all capitalistic societies in Europe, was more affected by economic factors than political ones. Cinema was no longer the powerful cultural catalyst it had been in the postwar era. Instead, television was able to offer the most attractive curiosity with the sense of producing a certain "spectacularization" of society through vulgarity and mediocrity, etc.[31] For many Italians, the lure of television sitcoms and game shows remained irresistible. Consequently, the newly created television companies gained considerable power as they were able to influence general audiences in their choice for cultural and entertainment products. Private televisions gave popular audiences what they wanted while at the same time influencing them by creating new behavioral models (usually low-quality products). Subsequently, the question of national mass culture and subculture came into question as the level of popular programs reached an all-time low with the promotion of low-quality prerecorded programs and erotically charged shows (B-series movies, striptease, *televendita* with Vanna Marchi and Roberto da Crema in 1992).

Television not only changed habits among spectators (now also called *telespettatori*), but it also affected the way the cinema industry generated a new generation of actors. If for decades comedy actors came into the spotlight after the usual tedious itinerary of drama schools, *teatro dialettale, avanspettacolo, caffé concerto, teatro di varietà,* then a career in cabaret, this time television gave aspiring actors the possibility of having a more direct access to cinema through its own channel (for better of worse). Actors such as Enrico Montesano, Adriano Celentano, Renato Pozzeto, and Paolo Villaggio were all in different ways involved with cabaret, but their entry into comic cinema (and not *commedia all'italiana*) was due only to their participation in *varietà* programs sponsored by Italian television. The hopeless social outcast made famous by Ugo Fantozzi (Paolo Villaggio) and directed by Luciano Salce in *Fantozzi* (1975) is likely the most flamboyant example of all.

Erotic Comedies "Made in Italy"

Labeled the *filone comico-erotico*, erotic comedies experienced their break-through in the decade of the 1970s, as the visually erotic element pervaded all genres of cinema from comedy to drama without any exception. At the same time, cinematographic censorship policies were slowly discarded (though the X category was created for tax purposes) and the result triggered a prosperous development of erotic cinema also called soft-core pornography (today surprisingly experiencing a revival known as "Italian trash cinema"). One of the early characteristics of the erotic cinema was its element of the so-called "schoolboy point of view," evolving quickly toward a provocative voyeurism. Indeed, the 1970s saw the first sign of graphic female sexuality as well as sexual intercourse, female figures like in Pasolini's *Decameron* (1971). Sadly enough, the uncontrollable wind of B-series productions unscrupulously imitating artistic productions damaged the reputation as well as the future of erotic cinema. British historian Stephen Gundle stated, "The cannibalism of a film industry in crisis made any attempt to promote a progressive conception of tolerance and sexual freedom through the cinema quite impossible."[32] Even Pasolini, disappointed by so many and rapid parodies, disavowed his own work since besmirched by unscrupulous copycat parodies. The reason for this success was partly due to the nature of Italian spectatorship at the time, in large part inclined toward erotically charged images and corresponding with a rather eager desire to swiftly consume a product from a spectator/voyeur point of view.

In the wake of the 1968 social reforms, the implication of censorship was downgraded and the new decade saw the beginning of social and customs changes all over the world. With the hastily imposed modernization and large-scale urbanization, Italian society dealt with new social and cultural innovations, which dramatically affected the seventh art in its graphic representation of female sexuality more than in its content. If the 1960s generated a great deal of improvement in terms of allusion to sexuality, the next decade witnessed a significant evolution for sexual representation, pushing the limits toward and even beyond the taboo frontiers for an audience in search of moderate stimulus. The advent of the erotic element in cinema stemmed from the ongoing liberalization of moral and social custom throughout the country, leading to an unavoidable reevaluation of the actual value system.

Two trends concomitantly developed their own spectatorship. One in *Luci rosse* theaters, more urban, and the other among parochial cinemas, more rural or suburban cinema circuits. The goal was to step further in the direction of the unadulterated space of sexual taboo, in some cases pushing the envelope beyond the physically acceptable, even sustainable. The other goal for the film industry was to "liberate" preconceived ideas in order to gain total artistic freedom. Erotic and pornographic cinemas quickly became a huge part of the film industry revenue (i.e., for the year 1973–74: of 130 Italian films produced, 30 were classified as erotic).[33] Salvatore Samperi's *Grazie zia* with Lisa Gastoni was an example of the forerunner of the so-called erotic *filone*; Pasquale Festa Campanile's *Il merlo maschio* (1970) and Marco Vicario's *Homo eroticus* (1971) were at the very basis of this growing endemic voyeurism trend. The promoted theme of *gallismo siculo* (Sicilian virility confronted to sexual *omertà* Sicilian style) proved to become the driving force of the new subgenre of Italian comedy. Its success influenced the erotic cinema *decamerotico* adapted from literary works, in this case from Boccaccio's short stories. However, the authentic prototype of the *commedia erotica* came with Salvatore Samperi's *Malizia* in 1973. The second wave of soft erotic films included *L'insegnante* (1975), directed by Nando Cicero, reusing the style that a few years earlier made *Malizia* a commercial success, an element also evoked in Fellini's *Amarcord* (1974), Michele Massimo Tarantini's *La liceale* (1975), and Mariano Laurenti's *La compagna di banco* (1976).

One of the frontrunners was Laura Antonelli (b. 1941), as she participated in all the developmental stages of the *commedia erotica*, from early films such as Riccardo Ghione's *La rivoluzione sessuale* (1968) and Massimo Dallamano's *Venere in pelliccia* (filmed in 1969, it was never released because the censorship visa was never granted). Antonelli's major breakthrough came with her provocative role as Angela in Samperi's *Malizia* (1973), a waitress courted by a father and his two sons in a Sicilian background, followed by a quality performance in Dino Risi's *How Funny Can Sex Be?* (*Sessomatto*, 1973). Her highly suggestive pos-

Giancarlo Giannini and Laura Antonelli in the episode "Torna piccina mia" in Dino Risi's *How Funny Can Sex Be?* (*Sessomatto*, 1973)

turing made famous with the film poster at the time, in revealing black stockings while standing on a ladder, was the emblematic image of the entire genre. Along with Laura Antonelli, Edwige Fenech can be considered one of the most famous Italian erotic actresses and certainly, despite her French origins (she was born in Algeria in 1948), one of the most representative of this short-lived genre also called *commedia sexy all'italiana*. Some of her most noticed parts were in Marino Girolami's *Nell'anno della contestazione* (1970), costarring with Franco Franchi and Ciccio Ingrassia; *Giovannona coscialunga, disonorata con onore*, directed by Sergio Martino (1973); *Vedova inconsolabile ringrazia quanti la consolarono* (1973); and *Innocenza e turbamento* (1974). With the growing fascination of Italian popular audiences for erotic female teachers, female doctors or nurses, even nuns at times, Fenech was able to impose herself as a dominant figure of the genre by giving her most memorable interpretation in Nando Cicero's *L'insegnante* (1975), which became like *Malizia* the cult film par excellence of the trash film genre. Fenech's greatest asset as an actress was to strike a natural balance between sensuality and perversion through an emotional seductive power combined with a inherent gift for elegance and comedy. Other popular actors of the seventies included Gloria Guida, Barbara Bouchet, Claudia Koll, Carmen Russo, Agostina Belli, Carmen Villani, Lilli Carati, as well as the emblematic actor Alvaro Vitali, symbol for an entire generation of military service men of Italian erotic comedy. After redundant, graphic incest-related scenes, the genre evolved erotic narratives involving religious protagonists such as priests, nuns, and, of course, novices usually set in the emotional background of an unorthodox convent nicknamed "*filone decameroniano*" by Italian film critique Lorenzo Codelli.[34]

Neglected by film critics for the oversimplicity of its plots and scenarios, the genre began a decisive decline at the end of the seventies, which eventually deteriorated even more with the boom of private television companies as well as the advent of pornographic films distributed in red light theaters. Eventually in the 1980s, Italian television was able to "rescue" some of the main protagonists such as Lino Banfi and Edwige Fenech, but for most, the reconversion of mainstream cinema proved impossible.

The Commedia all'Italiana *in the 1970s*

During the rise and decline of comedy Italian style, many developments occurred for other cinematographic genres. The Peplum (c. 1957–64, also known as "Sword and Sandal" epics) period films about antiquity included major Hollywood stars, such as Kirk Douglas as Mario Camerini's *Ulysses* (*Ulisse*, 1954). The internationally known Spaghetti Westerns (108 films produced between the years 1970 to 1972 and down to 12 during the years 1975 to 1978), a genre born in the early sixties that experienced an unprecedented success in 1964 with Sergio Leone's *A Fistful of Dollars* (*Per un pugno di dollari*, 1964), *For a Few Dollars*

More (*Per qualche dollaro in più*, 1965), and, of course, *The Good, the Bad and the Ugly* (*Il buono, il brutto e il cattivo*, 1966), became almost a rarity by the end of the decade. However, and regardless of the fate and fortune of other contemporary genres, was not due to the success of these genres.

The bitter mood of the early 1970s was due in large part to the social and political ideals, and filmmakers conceptualized that element to its full extent in a very eloquent manner (Monicelli's *Romanzo popolare* in 1974 or Ettore Scola's *C'eravamo tanto amati* that same year, though the latter remained outside of the *commedia all'italiana* movement). What most characterized the continuation of the comedy Italian style in the 1970s was its dimension of bitter satire coming out of the joyful satirical phenomenon of the 1960s, and a sense of disillusioned comedy, evoking subconsciously the missed appointment with history and, for some, the missed "Revolution." On the other hand, not all comedies depicted the bittersweet feeling of the time, the growing malaise of social unrest, and the devastating effects of terrorism (i.e., Albert Sordi's *Stardust* [*Polvere di stelle*, 1973]).

The decline in both quantity and quality of the Italian film industry began in 1975; spectatorship declined in both Italy and abroad, and films were less present in international festivals and competitions, despite some important awards (a Golden Palm at the 1977 Cannes Film Festival with Paolo and Vittorio Taviani's *Father and Master* [*Padre Padrone*] and in 1978 another Golden Palm for Ermanno Olmi's *The Tree of Wooden Clogs* [*L'albero degli zoccoli*]), due to the growing consumption of Hollywood films each year. Comedies, especially comedy Italian style, continued to generate the most revenue for Italian cinema at the box office. However, and regardless of the fate and fortune of other contemporary genres, the reason for the decline of comedy Italian style was not due to the success of these genres.

In a certain way, the hardship of the *commedia all'italiana,* which faced the difficult subjects imposed by the violence of the "lead years," resembled the obstacles French cinema faced during the four years of German occupation. In both cases, despite the constant challenges, both national cinemas were able to produce some of their greatest masterpieces. In a similar manner, and notwithstanding the difficult context of political and social unrest heightened with the unprecedented volume of domestic terrorism, Italian filmmakers and producers continued to specialize in comedy, and eventually spectators continued to support the comedy genre, as figure 4 displays. Despite the low percentage of film comedies (although steady), the Italian film industry was still able to produce a solid number of quality comedy films in the 1970s.

As paradoxical as it may appear, the comedies that had greater success were the ones with an inconsistent, sporadic humor (Monicelli's *Borghese piccolo piccolo*, or *Romanzo popolare*), the famous exception being the mythical *Amici miei* since every scene contained its own famous *battuta*.

The most characteristic evolution of the 1970 comedies was the successful insertion of death as a powerful and inspiring theme (much more promi-

Figure 4: The Presence of Comedies on a National Level

Year	Number of Comedy Films	Italian Films + Coproductions	Percentage of Comedies
59–60	16	116	13.8
60–61	16	150	10.7
61–62	16	159	10.1
62–63	7	156	5.4
63–64	21	158	13.3
64–65	19	174	10.9
65–66	21	208	10.1
66–67	16	225	7.1
67–68	14	274	5.1
68–69	20	257	7.8
69–70	21	285	7.4
70–71	19	255	7.5
71–72	23	269	8.5
72–73	17	334	5.1
73–74	13	265	4.9
74–75	24	271	8.9
75–76	31	291	10.6
76–77	20	239	8.4

source S.I.A.E.

nent than Monicelli's *I soliti ignoti* or Risi's *Il sorpasso*). Death was no longer an outside element in the comedy subordinated to a collateral role. Now it had a regular presence in many comedies, an unavoidable subject matter upon which the entire sequence of events was built (Ferreri's *La grande abbuffata*, Monicelli's *Un borghese piccolo piccolo* and *Amici miei*, Risi's *Profumo di donna*). For Enrico Giacovelli, comedy Italian style had reached complete maturity, as it was able to push the limits of the taboo subjects; he wrote, "Death, which at the time of *Il sorpasso* was still an intrusion, a premonition, was now in vogue."[35] Film scholars Tullio Masoni and Paolo Vecchi concurred that comedy Italian style was a device to "contemplate and exorcize death."[36] However, not everything was subject to laughter, as real-life terrorism and its deadly toll took filmmakers by surprise. With the development of tragic events all over Italy, the choice of comedic subjects became more delicate; for most filmmakers, terrorism and natural disasters were both too contemporary, too close, and too dramatic to employ as comic sources. Two notable exceptions were Dino Risi's *Mordi e fuggi* (1973) and *I nuovi mostri* (1977), with the episode entitled "Senza parole" featuring a bomb smuggled in a airplane following a romantic idyll between a terrorist and a stewardess played by Ornella Muti. Italian comedy included little to no presence of a possible wind of rebellion, with the case of Monicelli's *Vogliamo i colonelli* (1973) being the only exception to the rule.

Should film historians consider the end of the *commedia all'italiana* era as the expression of a natural degeneration of a genre or of a style destined to become unwanted? What remains evident after looking back with a critical distance of some thirty years is the fact that the *commedia all'italiana* was able to impose a cultural change on popular audiences. Pietro Germi's *Divorzio all'italiana* (1961) and *Sedotta e abbandonata* (1964); Dino Risi's *Una vita difficile* (1961); Marco Ferreri's *La grande abbuffata* (1973); Luigi Zampa's *Il medico della mutua* (1968); Luigi Comencini's *Lo scopone scientifico* (1972); Mario Monicelli's *La grande guerra* (1959); and Alberto Lattuada's *Mafioso* (1962) all left their imprint on the collective imagination and cinematic memory, and all possessed the inherent ability of tackling difficult subjects with the powerful device of entertainment and humor.

Ettore Scola and the Discourse of Cynicism

At the turn of the new decade, an imperative need to rejuvenate Italian comedies manifested itself. Many Italian comedy filmmakers gradually realized that the grotesque vein in the seventh art, and in particular, in the genre of comedy, had great promise among general audiences and could potentially become an ideal transition from the comedies of the economic miracle toward a more adventurous and daring cynical realism. In addition, the usual recognizable actors (Ugo Tognazzi, Nino Manfredi, Alberto Sordi, and Vittorio Gassman) had already disclosed a visible propensity for the grotesque vein in their respective repertoire, so it was no surprise to see them able to make an easy transition to this new type of comedy. Following the 1960s' promotion of an individualistic humor came the advent of a comedy based on collective perspectives, and ultimately showed a way to indict Italian society, which by then already faced the gloomy aftermath of the *anni di piombo*. The goal of these new cynical and provocative comedies was to "desacralize" Italian institutions, bureaucracy, corruption, religion, traditional family nucleus—in a nutshell, the fossilized social order. One of the fundamental questions is how to identify the reasons for this unprecedented artistic phenomenon and its function: was the cinematographic grotesque a simple tragicomic deformation of reality through a "monstrous" lens, or did it explore the actual extremity of reality?

According to literary theorist Michail Bachtin and his work on the functions of the grotesque in literature, a plausible definition evokes the "exaggeration, hyperbolism, *démesure* and overabundance" as one of the characteristics of the grotesque style.[37] Whether employed in theater or cinema, grotesque comedies have always been effective devices to approach reality through a human microscope. Italian satirical comedies of the 1970s brought the genre to an unprecedented level of intensity (or outrage for its detractors) thanks to the great attention given to human mannerism and mental perversion. Whether directed by Dino Risi, Mario Monicelli, Luigi Comencini, or Ettore Scola, all of these new comedies had one common denominator of primary importance: that of sharing a perfectly controlled cinematographic tone with humor not exclusively from jokes but also from nuances of phrasing, social behavior, and collective movement. Stripped of any conventional logic, grotesque humor no longer relied on dark comedy but rather on psychological provocation and caricature.

In these early years of the 1970s, the popular trend of grotesque humor was becoming the expression of subjectivity by excellence and as film historian Roberto de Gaetano asserted, the grotesque "was not a genre or a style. It was before anything a vision of the world."[38] Indeed, Lina Wertmüller's *Swept Away* (*Travolti da un insolito destino nell'azzurro mare d'agosto*, 1974); Franco Brusati's *Bread and Chocolate* (*Pane e cioccolata*, 1974); Ettore Scola's *We Loved Each Other So Much* (*C'eravamo tanto amati*, 1974); Dino Risi's *How Funny Can Sex Be?* (*Sessomatto*, 1973); and Mario Monicelli's *My Friends* (*Amici miei*, 1975) were primarily provoking manifestations to address contemporary issues through a satirical lens, this time strengthened by the vitriolic force of the grotesque (absent in the 1960s satirical comedies with the exception of Marco Ferreri's alternative cinema). But in order to fully comprehend the reasons for its sudden expansion, one must take a critical distance to realize that the phenomenon's fundamental nature was nothing new. In classical literature, the grotesque usually adopted a strategy of differentiation between two opposite feelings: splendor and desolation, empathy and disgust. The *commedia dell'arte* frequently resorted to this burlesque approach by creating a visible shift between comic and lyric or between tragedy and pathetic.[39] Therefore, the grotesque in Italian film comedies established the most persuasive link between the expression of hysterical laughter conjugated with the manifestation of the direst pathos.

In addition to the *commedia dell'arte*, the grotesque discourse found a more recent influence in the theatricality of modern-day variety shows, highly popular in postwar Italy, a tradition from which it borrowed the practice of improvisation, bringing a particular freshness, spontaneity, and energy on the screen.[40] Strengthened by the *commedia all'italiana* in the sixties, such as Antonio Pietrangeli's *Il magnifico cornuto* (1964), Vittorio De Sica's *Il boom* (1963), or Franco Giraldi's *La bambolona* (1968), grotesque comedies of the seventies avoided the rules of traditional narration by organizing their plot in a succession of autonomous gags and which in the end fitted together to form a comprehensive narrative strategy. The story usually constituted a pretext for the connection between gags (this explains why the frequency of comic relief was a key factor in grotesque comedies).

Against Establishment, Institution, and Order

What strikes today's contemporary eye is the deep pessimistic imprints that the Italian satires incorporated in their stories' substance rather than in their actual format.[41] In the sixties, the ascending element of Italian comedies focused on the main protagonist's "blind" integration with the new society with its countless cultural changes (a theory according to which the protagonists' main comical function was to integrate society mainly through work and/or marriage).[42] A decade later, that specific discourse appeared rather obsolete. Indeed, the new emergent trend no longer recognized the need to belong to society as the ultimate goal through its visible institutions, but rather to circumvent them through self-reliance and a great dose of realism, even cynicism. The comic protagonists were no longer required to adapt to society, since the latter was manifestly experiencing a process of disintegration and decomposition. Because of the immense popularity of the economic boom comedies, the genre, now entering a new decade, needed new momentum without changing its substance or form. The grotesque dimension naturally provided that missing element and therefore allowed many filmmakers to rejuvenate their satirical repertoire to ensure another prolific decade paved by the successful and lasting impression left by prototype comedies of the 1960s (i.e., Dino Risi's *Il sorpasso* and *I mostri*; Pietro Germi's *Signore & signori*; or Antonio Pietrangeli's *Il magnifico cornuto,* among others).

One of the visible changes that occurred with the new decade was the shift in content, this time more focused on the common sphere of Italian society. With the new type of satirical comedies, especially the ones involving elements of grotesque, the scapegoat rarely corresponded to the single individual (as it used to be in the sixties), though responsible for monstrosities and grotesque actions, but rather this time society itself as the ultimate representation of a destructive labyrinth. The example of *The New Monsters* (*I nuovi mostri*, 1977) written by

Ornella Muti (the stewardess) in the episode "Senza parole"
in Dino Risi's *The New Monsters* (*I nuovi mostri*, 1977)

Agenore Incrocci, Ruggero Maccari, Giuseppe Moccia, and Bernardino Zapponi, also codirected by Dino Risi, Mario Monicelli, and Ettore Scola, epitomized the difficulty for authors to single out and reprobate one "offender" (precisely by the narrative structure of its episode format).

I nuovi mostri is remembered as the most flamboyant experience of the decade in terms of a hyperbolical vision of Italian society. The fourteen episodes combined the meticulous mannerisms of the *homo italicus* type and, as expected, the result was a highly provocative rendition of Italians while simultaneously constructing a social satire. Here the use of the grotesque could be described as a compulsive quest for a particular boundary, a point of no return after which laughter was no longer the appropriate response among spectators (laughter instead becoming a rather uncomfortable experience triggered by an overdose of cynicism). In fact, nothing was spared, as politics, sex, religion, and materialistic ideology were all placed under close scrutiny by the three directors' sensitive eyes. *I nuovi mostri* looked into the darkest corners of the human psyche and never betrayed the original goal: that of indicting a society without structure lost in the tormented aftermath of the economic miracle. The film's representation of a grotesque society devoid of any element of civility offered a unique device for reevaluation of social values imposed too quickly.

In its severe indictment of Italian social and family values, the film was able through the dynamic of short episodes to portray different realities cynically, much more powerfully than a decade before with its prequel *The Monsters* (*I mostri*, 1963). Unquestionably the masterpiece of cynicism came in the episode entitled "Come una regina," showing Franchino (Alberto Sordi) taking his elder mother to the assisted living communities. Pretending to stay in a hotel just for the day, he is finally compelled to confess the truth. At first, the mother is distressed by the suspicious orchestration as well as the unusual number of elderly guests, but ultimately resigns herself to her own fate. As he departs, Alberto Sordi stops, turns around, and, pointing his finger, shouts to the personnel a now famous quote in Italian popular culture: "E trattatela come una regina!" (And treat her like a queen!).[43]

As expected, the characterization of all prominent (and less prominent) protagonists of Italian society took a new twist as everyone in this human comedy went under the contemptuous microscope. If Risi's *I mostri* in 1963 illustrated the *incomunicabilità* (incommunicability) between Italians and the newly imposed cultural model, *I nuovi mostri* now dwelled on the existential disasters emanating from the atomization of Italian society. In its grotesque vein, the film denounced a certain apathy of Italians, the passive acquiescence to social evils (corruption, Mafia, terrorism, individualism, excessive capitalism values, and human alienation), all of which were represented as quotidian nightmares. This "catastrophic" vision of Italian society—even apocalyptic at times—was also a warning to prevent any aspiration of self-destruction and marginalization of Italian individuals in their own society.

Alberto Sordi (Franco) in the episode "Come una regina"
in Dino Risi's *The New Monsters* (*I nuovi mostri*, 1977)

In "L'uccellino della Val Padana," Adriano (Ugo Tognazzi), an impresario husband who manages the struggling singing career of his wife Fiorella (Orietta Berti), deliberately stages an accident to cripple her. The expected result is successful, as it triggers a new interest and sympathy among her decreasing fans. Now singing in a wheelchair, her career experiences new heights. Here, the grotesque element revealed the inhuman nature of beings through a process of psychological close-ups to ultimately disclose the "evil characters" and their disproportionate individualism, narcissism, and hidden monstrosity. Roberto de Gaetano explained that Dino Risi's *I nuovi mostri* epitomized a "world without a face," thus revealing a monstrosity still anonymous to a certain extent. One could also extend this particular argument by pointing out all the humanity displayed in such a small space in time (essentially due to the episode format). Rather, the substantial description generated by the scrupulous scrutiny revealed a face of (in)humanity quite graphic and real. The grotesque for the first time since the *commedia dell'arte* removed the actual mask worn by its protagonists, finally unveiling the existing revulsion that was contained inside the comedic dynamics.

The grotesque register also favored the art of "mode shifting," which consisted of adopting a grotesque tone in a dramatic situation in order to convert it to comedy. This is the case for Ettore Scola's *Down and Dirty* (*Brutti, sporchi e cattivi*, 1976), which exemplified yet another facet of extreme representation of Italian society through the lens of the grotesque. This time, the element of grotesque sexuality among subproletarian classes served as the leading focus. The film narrated the survival and downward spiral of a *Pugliese* family living in the slums of the capital's suburbs. Life is unsympathetic as the only generated income results from stealing, prostitution, or odd jobs in Roman peripheries.

Inside the *baracca* (slum), the situation is no better, with old family antics fueled by the patriarch Giacinto Mazzatella (Nino Manfredi), who has just received a million lira, his insurance compensation for the loss of his left eye. He makes the rest of the family angry as he hides his money everyday in a new location (holes in the wall, water tank, toilet, even underwear). Exasperated by his "domestic despotism," they all plot to get rid of him and eventually intoxicate him during a meal with heavily seasoned rat poison.[44] Giacinto, however, survives the onslaught and decides to avenge himself by setting the family slum on fire.

Among all the outrageous scenes in this human mosaic of despair and violence, the sexually oriented portrayals were the most memorable ones (particularly when considered three decades later). In Scola's universe, the body was no longer a private entity, and was under the spell of primary human impulse, leaving no space and time for desire, code of conduct, civility, or language. The *baracca* was reduced to a space of "pure survival,"[45] offering no privacy and logically no inhibition left with time. Inside the claustrophobic slum, many strange behaviors occur. Giacinto befriends a homeless prostitute, invites her to live with the family and to share his own bed between himself and his wife Matilde. Even in the presence of his numerous family (eighteen in one house!), he cannot help groping women's bottoms just by habit without any real intentions. One morning, Giacinto witnesses Nando, his transvestite son, making love to his daughter-in-law, Dora, while she is washing her hair over the sink. He first thinks he is

Maria Luisa Santella (Iside), Nino Manfredi (Giacinto Mazzatella), and Linda Moretti (Matilde) in Ettore Scola's *Down and Dirty* (*Brutti sporchi e cattivi*, 1976)
Photo courtesy of BIFI

experiencing a hallucinatory vision. But instead of intervening, he later decides to blackmail his daughter-in-law into sexual favors from her in exchange for his silence. Although highly repulsive in its raw representation of human misery, the film was able to explain the precarious conditions compelling humans to live almost like animals or, as Roberto de Gaetano pointed out, the conditions that "make human beings a residue suspended between nature and civilization."[46] Here once again, the raw representation of the dark aspects of human nature was strengthened by the utilization of grotesque humor, elevating the provocation to an unprecedented level of realism. The present tense utilized by Scola's narrative generated a sense of instant nightmares and grotesque forms of desire: social paralysis and a dimension of cruel dissatisfaction of one's own existence. Perhaps the best synopsis of the film came from screenwriter Ruggero Maccari, who once stated in an interview that the poor were "ugly, dirty, nasty, quarrelsome, violent, brutal, and dishonest."

Besides achieving an innovative *commedia all'italiana* (which won the Best Director Award at Cannes in 1976), Ettore Scola's original intention was also to reassess the impact that the populist cinema had in the years of neorealism, as well as drama of the postwar era in general. For the most part, that interval in Italian cinema heavily emphasized a representation of a raw reality made of misery and despair, but at the same time successfully sanitized the psychological nature of its struggling protagonists, eventually able to rebuild their lives for

Ettore Scola
Photo courtesy of Photofest

better tomorrows. Different than the neorealist school, Scola's poor were no longer victimized and frail individuals, humbled by the destruction of the war in search of a new dignity in Italian society (possibly through marriage and labor). Away from any expression of morality, Scola represented selfish individuals, oblivious to the evolution of contemporary society. The epicenter of the universe was the *baraccopoli* where they lived. When comparing the film to Pasolini's *Accattone* (1961), a moral and affective investment from Pasolini's part is obvious, rendering a humane portrayal of proletarian masses; on the other hand, Scola's poor were entirely devoid of humanity, as the filmmaker seemed to maintain a distance between the narration and its protagonists.

In the highly prolific realm of decadent sexuality, Alberto Sordi's *A Common Sense of Modesty* (*Il comune senso del pudore*, 1976) offered an original reflection on middle-age relations, inspired by the growth of the erotic film industry in Italy. The film's narrative emphasized the consequences this mass phenomenon exerted on general audiences and in particular on an uninformed public still mentally "dwelling" in the mold of postwar years. To provide a sense of verisimilitude perspective, Sordi's story was taken from the familiar quotidian chronicles of the seventies, and illustrated the powerlessness of Italians to control the pressure exerted by modern-day society on their private lives, their leisure, and in particular on their sexual orientation. Giacinto (Alberto Sordi) and his wife Erminia (Rossana di Lorenzo) are celebrating their twentieth wedding anniversary and, following a copious meal, decide to spend the afternoon at the movie theater since Erminia has not seen a romantic movie in years. Unfortunately for them, all of the theaters in Rome are only showing either horror or erotic films. After hours of several unsuccessful attempts, the couple thinks they have found the perfect movie. But once again, within minutes of the screening, their expectations fall short, as the film soon features sexually oriented material for which the demure Erminia is not mentally prepared (for a while she attempts to cover her eyes with her scarf and pretends to rearrange her handbag).

The choice for the grotesque ingredient was all the more daring and powerful as it associated on the one hand daring erotically charged scenes with, on the other, the painful experience of an innocent woman, unable to comprehend the changes in Italian society happening around her. In this particular case, Sordi's *Il comune senso del pudore* confirmed that grotesque comedies stood at the forefront for addressing issues of a society deeply affected by cultural changes. Although the erotic phenomenon in the middle of the 1970s did influence the production and distribution of the Italian film industry as well as the behavioral pattern of general audiences at the moment, it is rather impossible to argue that the particular genre was responsible for the behavioral disorientation of Italian society.

If representations of provocative sexual behaviors were the mainstream element of the new comedy of the grotesque, death, as the ultimate act of grotesque humor, was represented in several successful comedies of the 1970s, such as Fausto Tozzi's *Trastevere* (1971), Mario Monicelli's *An Average Little Man* (*Un borghese piccolo piccolo,* 1977), and Franco Brusati's *Pane e cioccolata* (1974). In Mario Monicelli's *Amici miei, atto I* (1975), death was derided in a sardonic mood during the funeral of Giorgio Perozzi (Philippe Noiret), one of the "fraternity" members. To mask their sadness, the four other friends decide to play a trick by telling one of their aspiring new members that they had to "liquidate" him for reasons of treason in the pure "Mafia style": "Era un traditore, abbiamo dovuto eliminarlo" (He was a traitor and had to be eliminated). As the joke convincingly unfolds, they can no longer hold in their laughter and the funeral procession slowly becomes a carnevalesque crowd. The regenerating laughter here was meant to temporarily defy the symbol of death, and the essence of conventional mourning. Similar to medieval popular culture, cynical farce, and the *beffa* Tuscan style dear to Boccaccio, this "liberatory" laughter by regenerating the "cycle of life" effectively functioned as a tool to desacralize death and its daunting subjugation. This particular funeral scene is still today one the trademarks of Monicelli's contribution to comedies of the 1970s.

Marco Ferreri's Grotesque Style

If conventional laughter of the sixties kept a certain dose of control on reality, the grotesque humor of the seventies based on absurdity and irrationality liberated the spectator's mind from moral boundaries. In this type of grotesque comedies, exceptional occurrences constantly made irruption without reason in the protagonists' daily life, and as a result, logic and common sense never had time to take place for the viewers' response.

This type of grotesque comic device, different from the grotesque mentioned earlier, included a dimension of absurd to allow for the coexistence of two opposite concepts, such as the sordid and the sublime, farce and drama, violent sexual behavior with exacerbated romanticism. For instance, in Dino Risi's *Sessomatto* (1973) or Lina Wertmüller's *The Seduction of Mimi* (*Mimì metallurgico ferito nell'onore,* 1972), both narrations ingeniously mixed erotic fantasies and segments of reality, thus carrying the notion of illusion to the extreme. In each case, Giancarlo Giannini (who starred in both films) is a young man obsessed with experiencing a sexual relation with a much older woman until he successfully accomplishes the goal of his neurotic quest.

By reusing medieval and gothic figures, the so-called romantic grotesque evolved toward the manifestation of physical or mental monstrosity rather than carnivalesque icon (i.e., the character of Quasimodo in Victor Hugo's *The Hunchback of Notre Dame*). In this irrational grotesque, laughter was no longer "liberatory" or "reparatory" but rather cynical, perhaps demoniacal in some cases. In Brusati's *Pane e cioccolata,* Nino Garofalo (Nino Manfredi), an unfortunate Italian immigrant in Switzerland desperately in search of a job, ends up in a remote chicken coop where a group of eccentric Neapolitan clandestine workers live in miserable conditions (they live in the chicken coop itself). To make matters worse, he realizes during the welcome dinner that they have all lost their sanity, as they repeatedly act and sound like the chickens they slaughter. Here the grotesque laughter generated by the collective hysteria among immigrants gone mad was the manifestation of a loss of control upon a reality that had all of a sudden become unreal or foreign to the main protagonist in search of his cultural roots. In addition, the extreme manifestation of a subjective reality such as the insanity inside the chicken coop, mixing emotions of laughter and horror, accentuated the immediacy of the grotesque. As Roberto De Gaetano argued, "The reality loses its flexibility and is reduced to a moment without depth: it is an immediate entity of a limitless desire.... The present without plot is the tense of the grotesque."[47] With their inherent eagerness to represent the present moment, the comedies of the 1970s were never closer to the present-day events and contemporary current affairs. It was clear to filmmakers that the decomposition of Italian society was a more pressing and imperative subject when compared to the comedies of the economic boom ten years before.

Often associated with the concept of the grotesque was one of the most prolific filmmakers, Marco Ferreri (1928–97), who regularly explored the realm of romantic irrationality. The Milanese author was without a doubt one of the most nonconformist filmmakers in Italian cinema, and his films are marked by a distinctive originality. Ferreri's major breakthrough[48] occurred in 1962 with the The Conjugal Bed (Una storia moderna: l'ape regina), an anti-Catholic satire denouncing the sacro-saint concept of holy matrimony. The film triggered the wrath of state censorship in addition to the opposition of the Church, ranking him among iconoclast cineastes. These types of ruthless indictments under the form of unprecedented provocation for the Church and the strong censorship resulted in innumerable postproduction cuts, as Ferreri showed little tolerance for self-censorship. With The Ape Woman (La donna scimmia, 1963), a metaphorical representation of the exploitation of men by men, Ferreri chose again the delicate subject of a young woman whose face covered with facial hair becomes the center of attention of her future husband (Ugo Tognazzi), who uses her in order to make a lucrative street spectacle. Also noteworthy was the episode called "Il professore" in Controsesso (1964), and Dillinger Is Dead (Dillinger è morto, 1969), a compelling testimony of solitude in modern capitalistic society. In the seventies, Ferreri proved to be entirely committed to confrontational subjects analyzing the neuroses generated by industrialized society and mass consumption culture.[49] His films were centered on society's decadence, including the ubiquitous role of monstrosity that always leads toward premature death.

In La grande abbuffata (1973), four friends—Marcello (Marcello Mastroianni), an airline pilot; Ugo (Ugo Tognazzi), a restaurant owner; Michel (Michel Piccoli), a television producer; and Philippe (Philippe Noiret), a judge still living with his "lifetime" nurse—meet one weekend in a villa for a gastronomical feast (gradually revealing itself as a collective enterprise of planned

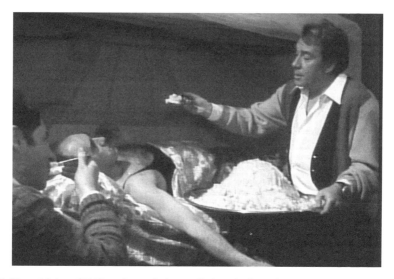

Philippe Noiret (Philippe), Michel Piccoli (Michel), and Ugo Tognazzi (Ugo) in
Marco Ferreri's *La grande bouffe* (*La grande abbuffata*, 1973)

suicide). With the sudden urge for female presence, they also invite three prostitutes along with a schoolteacher, met inadvertently at the last minute, and begin
their euphoric orgy. However, frightened by the turn of events, the female guests
flee in the early morning except for Andréa (Andréa Férreol), the schoolteacher,
mesmerized by the suicidal company of the protagonists, who acts as a substitute
mother until the end. With an idiosyncratic style characterized by a highly corro-
sive and provocative wittiness, *La grande abbuffata* directly appealed to the "wild
impulse" within each spectator. Parody and provocation were the key elements
of this exploration of the human comedy. Here the impulse in question, usually
at the basis of the energy regenerating life, embodied a rather opposite role; one
of self-destruction—from the inside—as all four protagonists intended to commit suicide by eating sumptuous gastronomic dishes to their death. In addition
to the dark lens of Ferreri's "grotesque," the film revealed an extreme form of
hyperrealism, motivated by the actors' exceptional spontaneity, eventually leading their characters to their own fantasies, debauchery, and sexual perversion.

At the basis of the grotesque dimension was the association of antithetic elements such as food and death, laughter and sadness, all becoming immoral at the
end of the feast. As Ugo Tognazzi says to Michel Piccoli, who lays sick on his bed
recovering from overeating, "*Se tu non mangi, tu non puoi morire*" ("If you don't
eat, you cannot die"). Here the association of food and death clearly revealed
the apocalyptical nature of the ongoing ceremony intended to lead them toward
their ultimate quest. The second association was the hyperbolic representation
of "food and sex" that was brought to the extreme in order to trigger a repulsive

effect from spectators (also including sordid scatological details). As Ferreri pictured all four protagonists making love while outrageously consuming food, he also wished to remove any visual pleasure from the audience, expecting it to endure the experience from beginning to end.[50] One could also argue that Ferreri wanted spectators to question their own remorseful and hidden desire and possibly feel a guilty sense of voyeurism while watching the protagonists dying on the screen. The film's distinctive extravagance allowed the spectators to perceive a dark universe beyond reality. In fact, Ferreri's surrealism transcended reality to create a dimension of absurdity, without visible coherence,[51] but whose fragmentation into separate scenes revealed the director's numerous smothered obsessions: solitude, ordinariness and uniformity of quotidian life, midlife crisis, exclusion, eroticism, sexual perversion, and nihilism.

As mentioned above, Ferreri's grotesque comedy was free of any narrative[52] or aesthetic constraints: it was a story without a plot, aimed at destroying the coherence of the characters whose main humoristic dynamics were simply the sequencing of powerful images. His theoretical goal was to have his characters say and show anything necessary in order to represent the human fantasy caught between life and death, reality and imagination. And it was precisely the border between dream and reality that he wished to abolish, adding a greater challenge to this new type of comedy. This explained the reason why the cinema of Marco Ferreri, with the exception of *La grande abbuffata*, a huge popular success, rarely met the expectations of general audiences, perhaps not always prepared for the corrosiveness of the cineaste's comic mind.

Notes

[1] During the same period, the political alliance between Socialists and Communists in France (*Programme Commun*) was also gaining momentum.

[2] Instigated by many extra-parliamentary groups such as *Lotta Continua*.

[3] N.A.R. was active between 1977 and 1981 and responsible for thirty-three homicides.

[4] No less than seven trials were necessary in order to obtain relative closure. The last trial concluded in 2005.

[5] Interestingly enough, most of the information, which surfaced at the time, came as the result of extraordinarily thorough investigative journalism.

[6] The Gladio network was created by the CIA after the wake of World War II. This underground organization under the jurisdiction of NATO was aiming at blocking a possible Soviet infiltration in Western Europe and in case of an invasion, organize from behind the front, sabotaging operations as well as establishing intelligence services.

[7] In 2000, a parliamentary investigation concluded that although no direct link was proven between NATO and Neo-Fascists, the CIA had indeed offered its support to prevent the *Partito Communista Italiano* from accessing the government responsibilities.

[8] P. Ginsborg, *A History of Contemporary Italy: Society and Politics 1943–1988* (London: Penguin, 1990), 361

[9] Giangiacomo Feltrinelli (1926–72) accidentally died while reportedly attempting an act of sabotage in Segrate near Milan.

[10] A large part of the success of the ongoing investigations was the new means bestowed to the police forces. The Reale Law (1975) authorized for the first time since the Fascist regime to perquisite private homes and to arrest individuals without the usual warrant released by a judge, but under the sole basis of allegation emitted from an investigation. In addition, the Cossiga Law, passed in 1979, extended the period of preventive detention for crimes of terrorism and allowed phone tapping.

[11] The criminal activity of the Red Brigades, though less "murderous" than extreme-right terrorist groups in the number of casualties, were still going full swing. In 1976, the Red Brigades killed eight; 1977 seven; 1978 twenty-nine; 1979 twenty-two; 1980 thirty.

[12] By 1978, Aldo Moro had been prime minister five times.

[13] A measure highly unpopular for the entire country, which to this date infuriates the entire political scene in Italy.

[14] Although acts of violence took place after the Bologna tragedy, this disaster marked the last act of violence against the mass population.

[15] Gelli was actually condemned to house arrest for twelve years following the sentence, which found him guilty of fraud in the bankruptcy of the Banco Ambrosiano in 1982.

[16] One of the reasons why the *Loggia P2* cannot be considered a true Masonic lodge comes from the fact that members must normally meet regularly and know each other as in any other type of fraternity, which was not the case there since none of the members included in Gelli's list formerly knew each other.

[17] Ginsborg, *History of Contemporary Italy,* 34

[18] It is important to remember that the stance of the PCI was all the more difficult in a Catholic country where the Church's highest offices continuously stood against its own existence. In 1949 the Holy Office published a document whereby excommunication applied to Communists, and a penalty of apostasy to anyone associated with or who voted for them, as well as to anyone who subscribes to Communist newspapers (in addition, any member of the CGIL trade union).

[19] As the ties between PCI and DC grew stronger, feeling betrayed by their leaders, more youth disengaged from the revolutionary current for a fight that was based on civil rights issues.

[20] Giulio Andreotti organized a new coalition without the Communists following PCI's announcement to separate from any future collaboration.

[21] Under the impetus of women's rights, the acceleration of social mobility for women took place as more female candidates gained access to new professions and reached higher career profiles. At the same time and against common belief, Italian women were proportionally less present in the workplace (and in particular at the factory floor level). If at the turn of the century they accounted for more than 30 percent of the workforce, Italian women were now less than 20 percent in the 1970s. One of the reasons was the

important evolution that took place in the service and education. By now three-quarters of elementary teachers were women, and half at the high school level (although still a very small minority at the university level).

[22] In addition, the law allowed the elimination of the dowry, offered equal responsibility after separation, as well as the right for women to keep her maiden name.

[23] The Mezzogiorno was heavily in favor, surpassing in every southern region 60 percent, with the center and north above 70 percent.

[24] 500,000 signatures were needed to obtain popular consultation.

[25] Because the women's private sphere was at the core of their collective action, the liberalization of their own sexuality, and in particular the legalization of contraceptive pills, occurred not only in pharmacies, but also in the popular mentality. Italy was one of the last countries in Europe to introduce and legalize the use of contraceptive pills, with less than 2 percent of women (of an age to be sexually active) using the device. No doubt that for Italian women this development corresponded to the premise of an eminent sexual revolution, where for the first time they had a feeling of control over their own body.

[26] See Chapter three.

[27] This time competition was less with foreign productions than with the inner phenomenon of the small screen.

[28] Only 1,200 of them are labeled "active theaters," as their economic activity only covers 240 days a year.

[29] Translated by the author from Italian: "La crisi è dovuta a un certo malessere ideativo. La televisione ha fatto danno, perché ha abbassato il livello medio, ha allargato il pubblico, e così tutti i registi sono condizionati e sono inconsciamente diventati anche loro vittime dell'audience, degli ascolti. C'è una specie di autocensura, qualcosa che li obbliga a volare basso." "Dino Risi: Il regista che sorpassa" interviewed by Federico Guiglia, *Italiani senza confini* (Florence: Libri Liberal, 2001), 200.

[30] Mary P. Wood, *Italian Cinema* (New York: Berg, 2005), 43.

[31] Because the television audience wanted to laugh quickly, it indirectly explained the spectacular progression of erotic comedy among a certain part of popular audiences.

[32] Stephen Gundle, "From Neo-Realism to Luci Rosse: Cinema, Politics, Society, 1945-85," in Zygmunt Baranski and Robert Lumley, eds., *Culture and Conflict in Postwar Italy* (London: Macmillan, 1990), 196, 220.

[33] This data includes Italian films with a majority of Italian finance only.

[34] Lorenzo Codelli, "Eros, coups de poings, flics, rigolade et le reste," *Positif* 160 (1974): 51.

[35] Translated by the author from Italian: "La morte, che hai ai tempi del Sorpasso era ancora un'intrusione, una premonizione, adesso è di casa." Enrico Giacovelli, *Non ci resta che ridere: una storia del cinema comico italiano* (Torin: Lindau, 1999), 111.

[36] Tullio Masoni and Paolo Vecchi, "*Degeneri e scostumati: commedia, satira e farsa nel cinema sonoro italiano*," in Ricardo Napoletano, *Commedia all'italiana: Angolazioni controcampi* (Rome: Gangemi, 1986), 79.

[37] Translated by the author from Italian: "L'esagerazione, l'iperbolicità, la smisuratezza e la sovrabbondanza sono, a grandi linee, uno dei caratteristici dello stile grottesco."

Michail Bachtin, *L'opera di Rabelais e la cultura popolare* (Torin: Einaudi, 1995), 332.

[38] Roberto de Gaetano, *Il corpo e la maschera: il grotesco nel cinema italiano* (Rome: Bulzoni, 1999), 7.

[39] Interestingly enough, during the Counter Reformation and classical ages the grotesque was almost absent from any literary productions.

[40] This type of grotesque comedy, also defined as "*grotesco gioioso*" according to De Gaetano (*Il corpo e la maschera*, 22) in the *commedia dell'arte*, with the renewed Greek tradition of the masks, was also promoted beyond its expected scope through the mod-ern–day carnivals (*mascherate*).

[41] The actual predominant trend of episode films was primarily geared toward pure entertainment rather than *cinema impegnato* (politically engaged or militant cinema).

[42] A theory shared by most film historians but best described in Maurizio Grande's works.

[43] Other spectacular representations of cynicism and grotesque included episodes such as "Con i saluti degli amici," where a Sicilian Mafia boss (Gianfranco Barra) is shot in retaliation by a rival gang in broad daylight. As he expires on the sidewalk, a police officer asks him to name his murderers. To respect the sacred saint law of *omertà*, Don Salvatore simply answers with a flaunting smirk on his face: "E che… a me spararono? Quando mai?" (They shot me? When did that happen?). In "Tantum Ergo," a cardinal (Vittorio Gassman) on his way to the Vatican, whose car broke down in a small town, takes advan-tage of unexpected free time to successfully convert a group of parochial "rebels" guided by a Communist priest. At first, the group welcomes the prelate with insults and threats, but as he leaves them following his unorthodox sermon, the same crowd sings the *Ave Maria* with tears in their eyes. The sequence "Pornodiva" includes the painful negotiation between an inexperienced B-series actress and an unscrupulous film producer who suc-cessfully convinces her to accept a nude role in company of a monkey.

[44] Here the episode indirectly conjured up an interesting link with the symbolic device used by Giacinto's family to kill him by poison just like one would do to extermi-nate the presence of rats in a home.

[45] De Gaetano, *Il corpo e la maschera*, 99.

[46] Translated by the author from Italian: "Fa dell'umano un residuo sospeso fra nat-ura e civiltà." De Gaetano, *Il corpo e la maschera,* 100.

[47] Translated by the author from Italian: "Il reale perde la sua distensione e si con-trae in istanti senza spessore: è il tutto e subito di un desiderio che non ha più limiti né confini…. Il presente senza storia è il tempo del grottesco." De Gaetano, *Il corpo e la maschera*, 37.

[48] Ferreri's career actually began in 1953 by coproducing with screenwriter Cesare Zavattini *Love in the City* (*L'amore in città*), directed by Alberto Lattuada, a semidocu-mentary film investigating the lower depths of Italian society and the phenomenon of prostitution, also featuring his very first appearance on the screen as an actor in the episode "Gli italiani si voltano."

[49] Ferreri's other important contributions also included *The Last Woman* (*L'ultima donna*, 1976), *Bye Bye Monkey* (*Ciao maschio*, 1978), and *Tales of Ordinary Madness* (*Storie di ordinaria follia*, 1981).

[50] While making love, Michel Piccoli inadvertently experiences unwanted manifestations of esophagi.

[51] Ferreri, like Buñuel, left a voluntary uncertainty between rational and irrational since they both had an obvious fascination for *illogism*.

[52] Ferreri used the French language as references to literature as well as theater with the sacro saint unity of time and space.

Chapter 6

The Last Protagonists

In the aftermath of the 1968 events and the subsequent social unrest, and despite the call for radical cultural change of already established artistic formats, comedy Italian style survived. Many comedy directors of the 1970s, although experimenting with form and content, never left the *commedia all'italiana* movement, while others, like Lina Wertmüller and Marco Ferreri, remained peripheral figures. Not only was the comedy able to survive this movement, but it was also able to produce some of the most memorable films under these challenging conditions. Because of its enormous success in the preceding decade, many contemporary critics accused filmmakers of repeating already exploited formulae. If their format remained similar to the one used during the boom years, their content experienced a fundamental transformation. The comedies of the 1970s moved away from a humanistic sentiment in the narration and increased the darker elements to become grotesque and cynical, with films like Dino Risi's The New Monsters (*I nuovi mostri,* 1977) and Ettore Scola's *Down and Dirty* (*Brutti, sporchi e cattivi,* 1976). As before, the commedia's laughter was not to distract spectators away from the fatal outcome of a society in perdition caught between violence and despair, but rather to reveal the unfeigned conditions of Italians and their society.

Dino Risi: A Legacy in Evolution

Ever since his international breakthrough in the *commedia all'italiana* with *A Difficult Life* (*Una vita difficile,* 1961), *The Easy Life* (*Il sorpasso,* 1962), and *The Monsters* (*I mostri,* 1963), Dino Risi never looked back on his initial critical and commercial success as he continued to maintain, along with Mario Monicelli, a high profile in the comedy genre unlike the majority of comedy filmmakers who occasionally attempted experiments with other cinematographic genres (i.e., Luigi Comencini's 1972 mini-series for Rai television, *The Adventures of*

Dino Risi on the set of *The Priest's Wife* (*La moglie del prete*, 1971) with
Marcello Mastroianni and Sophia Loren

Pinocchio [*Le avventure di Pinocchio*]). By now recognized by the Italian film
industry as one of the most influential filmmakers of the decade, Risi's strength
was undeniably his ability to offer consistency to the comedy productions and
regular performances at the box office. As far as the content of his films, Risi
made a remarkable transition into the seventies' new style. Having successfully
managed the evolution of the booming 1960s, his humor felt the signs of the
time and implemented a greater dose of cynicism and grotesque in the different
narratives, which resulted in comedies of a new *époque*. As film historian Aldo
Viganò once wrote about Risi's cinema:

The absolute laity of Risi's cinema voluntarily takes the risk of skepticism. However it successfully stays away from the indifference of his agnosticism, by virtue of what he likes to call "measure" and which on the screen results in a complex chemistry between comedy and tragedy.[1]

Between religion (*The Priest's Wife* [*La moglie del prete*, 1971]), corrupted political life (*In the Name of the Italian People* [*In nome del popolo italiano*, 1971]), and terrorism (*Dirty Weekend* [*Mordi e fuggi*, 1973]), Risi reached a wide variety of different targets through a satiric lens, but this time it was energized with the implementation of grotesque and boundless cynicism. The next step was *How Funny Can Sex Be?* (*Sessomatto*, 1973), a comedy on sex and, in particular, the vicissitudes Italians experienced in confronting intimate fantasies with their intimate rapport. Far from developing an interest in erotic cinema, Dino Risi wanted to draw a satire against certain types of sexual behavior that had been conditioned by archaic and moralistic conventions in Italy. *Sessomatto's* greatest interest beyond the comedy itself was tackling the problem of sexual dissatisfaction of millions of Italians at the time, who were caught between a "castigatory" moralist code of conduct and the fast liberalization of social custom. Dino Risi's *Sessomatto* rekindled the tradition of episode films with nine short stories of sex and its deviations that featured the volcanic Giancarlo Giannini and unpredictable Laura Antonelli[2] in each episode. Unlike his successful *I mostri* ten years before, Risi developed this mechanism of episode-based comedy this time by centering on the two actors' interaction. The script, written by Ruggero Maccari and Risi himself, was both inventive and successfully humorous among popular audiences benefiting from the new exposure of sexuality in the media and popular culture (and no longer alluded to as it used to be just a decade before). The segment "Signora sono le otto" opened the series of nine fables. Domenico is a Sicilian servant at the service of Madame Juliette, a rich and beautiful French lady who spends her days at home idle and indolent about everything around her. While laying in the sun or at the swimming pool, she ostentatiously exhibits her sumptuous body under the aroused stare of Domenico. One morning, caught by the surfacing of his long smothered desire, Domenico realizes that his boss sleeps so deeply that she cannot respond to his greetings. Not waiting for the invitation, Domenico makes love to her, which ironically is the only way to slowly wake her up. "Due cuori e una baracca" was similar to the sketch from *I mostri* entitled "Che vitaccia!": a poor couple lives in a slum in Rome with their fourteen children, and their grandmother in a wheelchair. The husband, extremely jealous of his wife's infidelity, comes home and discovers a newspaper. Immediately suspecting that his wife Celeste had a suspicious visit, Cesare begins his violent investigation, which ends in a physical brawl. The next take shows her cleaning her black eye. "Però son contenta, l'omo è omo. Deve menà!" ("I am happy though. A man's got to be a man, and hit!"), she confesses with satisfaction, before finding their reparatory truce in their late-night intimacy. In "Non è mai troppo tardi," Enrico, a young lawyer married to a young attractive model, is physically attracted to Esperia, an old lady who is in her seventies (following the long process of seduction, Esperia accepts his advances until one day she discovers him in the arms of her own decrepit mother). "Viaggio di nozze" tells the story of Lello, a traveling salesman and Grazia who just celebrated their marriage in Venice. Despite his reputation of being an irresistible Casanova, the new husband fails to express his virility on the honeymoon's first night. After several failed attempts the following nights, Grazia discovers that the only way Lello can "function" is when making love in motion. They both rush inside the hotel's elevator and successfully consummate their marriage while waking up the entire hotel. In the final episode called "La vendetta," Risi took the plot to Sicily with a colorful satire of adultery Mafia-style. The widow of a Mafia boss takes her revenge by seducing the rival boss who commanded her husband's murder. Once intimate with him, and aware of his heart's weak condition, she fulfills all his sexual fantasies, thus killing him with a heart attack. On the tomb of her husband, she declares: "Ora la vendetta è fatta. Delitto sessuale fu." ("The vengeance is now complete: sexual felony, it was.")

Giancarlo Giannini achieved a unique feat of skill reminiscent of Vittorio Gassman's performance in *Il mattatore* (1959). This time, however, the dimension of social behavior was different, as the thematic of sexuality was no longer alluded to. The intended goal, besides visual entertainment, as Risi likes to remind film critics, was the satire of vice and sexual alienation occurring in Italy during the years of the so-called sexual freedom of the late sixties. They represented the stereotypes of common Italian individuals, uneducated and highly dependent on a subculture (television and materialistic ideologies) that eventually conditioned the sexual orientation of an entire country, instead of liberating them, as was the intended purpose.

Giancarlo Giannini and Laura Antonelli in the episode "Signora, sono le otto" in Dino Risi's *How Funny Can Sex Be?* (*Sessomatto*, 1973)

Rather typical with comedy-based episode films set up as a series of unrelated skits, the quality varied dramatically from one skit to another: from comedic genius to disappointing physical gags to complete comical failure. One of the most difficult tasks for episode films was to achieve a decent narrative frame necessary by bringing the spectator through a minimal background exposition into the *medias res* of the sequence of events. Although the nature of the episodic film was such that no time was allocated for character development, Risi compensated for this flaw by liberating popular fantasies in a rather audacious manner, by exposing smothered erotic desires and inner impulses of Italian audiences (conjugated, it is true, with a masculine genre). The basis for this movie came from a fertile source of interest: sex, picking up the most common and contemporary concerns filled with smothered desires of sexuality and creating popular fables around them.

The so-called *filone erotico*, which led the big screen to liberalize its conventional portrayal of sexuality—no longer merely suggestive—was a direct consequence of the hastened modernization of the postboom era. *Sessomatto* was one of the more successful and colorful filmic experiences, creating visual and behavioral irreverence throughout much of its time. While the critics were mixed in their assessment of the film, *Sessomatto* hit the pinnacle of comedy as it seduced audiences in Italy and France, making it the second best-selling Italian film of 1973.

Following their spectacular advent at the end of the sixties, Italian erotic comedies strove to secure new sources of inspiration. With Pasquale Festa Campanile's *Il merlo maschio* (1970), Marco Vicario's *Homo eroticus* (1971), and Salvatore Samperi's *Malizia* (1973), reception among popular audiences again confirmed the public's new inclination for a pseudovoyeurism and the need to adopt these images through a derisive lens. This explained the success of "school-boy fantasies" brilliantly and subtlety conjured in Fellini's *Amarcord* (1974) as well as the development (in a radically different register) of ever daring erotic films now called "trash cinema" in Italy (slowly transitioning toward pornographic films). Like any other artistic movement, the phenomenon of erotic cinema in Italy began its slow decline during the mid-seventies, which corresponded directly with the explosion of the *luci rosse* productions, coupled with the implementation of private television companies all over Italy. Caught between its mixed critical reviews and popular endorsement, *Sessomatto* remains Dino Risi's major contribution to the *commedia all'italiana*, even though more than three decades later, it serves as a unique time capsule of the basic elements of the early seventies. According to Jean Gili, "Even in minor works, one can always find the sharp vision that Dino Risi casts on men and on their solitude."[3] This is certainly the case in Risi's next feature film, *Scent of a Woman* (*Profumo di donna*, 1974).

Inspired by Giovanni Arpino's novel *Il buio e il miele* (1969) with a screenplay adapted by Ruggero Maccari and Dino Risi, the story follows retired army

Alessandro Momo (Ciccio) and Vittorio Gassman (Fausto Consolo)
in Dino Risi's *Scent of a Woman* (*Profumo di donna,* 1974)

captain Fausto Consolo (Vittorio Gassman), blind and invalid after a grenade
explosion, and his aide, a young private named Giovanni Bertazzi (Ciccio played
by Alessandro Momo), his personal auxiliary for a week. Although full of vivac-
ity and aristocratic arrogance, his intention is to begin a self-destructive journey
across Italy (from Turin to Naples, through Genova and Rome) and ultimately
put an end to his life with his long time friend and fellow officer Vincenzo (also
blind from a military incident, with whom he has a suicide pact) in Naples. On the
train, Fausto makes scenes with passengers, and when walking on the streets, the
vigorous blind Casanova enjoys great success with Italian women, asking Ciccio
to help him spot beautiful women (he claims that he can scent their perfume at a
distance). The journey takes many twists and turns; in Genoa, Fausto asks Ciccio
to identify a nice prostitute for his enjoyment, and the next day in Rome he visits a cousin priest to discuss existential topics. The aim of the journey is almost
revealed when Ciccio discovers a revolver and a portrait of Sara in the captain's
suitcase. Sara (Agostina Belli) is a longtime family friend who fell madly in love
with Fausto years before the accident, but due to his blindness and disfigura-
tion, he is too proud to accept her love. They finally arrive in Naples and shortly
after the welcome party, Fausto and Vincenzo are left alone for the night by their
respective entourage. Fausto, who misses his shot, ends up wounding his friend
and loses the courage to commit suicide. Hearing the gun shot, Sara and Ciccio
rush back to the house and cover all evidence to make it appear like an accident.
Fausto, resigned to his own fate, continues his life with the help of Sara.

Despite its tragic tone, the film also included numerous comical scenes based
primarily on the utter discrepancy between the two main protagonists. Similar to

the duet in *Il sorpasso* (involving Bruno Cortona also interpreted by Gassman and the young introverted Roberto, the radical opposition in their lifestyle and mentality was at the basis of the spectator reaction), the film was a series of moments when the spectator anticipated Ciccio's reaction after every misdemeanor caused by Fausto. His character regularly indulged in crude, sexual comments and descriptions, and was delighted by the idea of a visit with a prostitute. Not much different were his comments on Ciccio's girlfriend with whom they share a lunch in a restaurant. As she leaves both men, Fausto's verdict is once again intense:

> Fausto: Nice girl, good ideas, good sense.
> Ciccio: She is a clean girl.
> Fausto: And a whore.
> Ciccio: Excuse me?
> Fausto: Wake up, Ciccio. Can't you see? Eighteen years old, cute…What does her dad do?
> Ciccio: Police officer.
> Fausto: See… she goes out with a 400,000 lira purse. Sure, I touched it. It was alligator skin. And the French perfume, at least 40,000 lira the flask. Babysitter… it is an excuse to stay out cavorting until 3am.[4]

As Aldo Viganò wrote, "Fausto discovers with apprehension that the vital instinct of conservation is stronger than will."[5] Paradoxically, the desire to grab life to its full extent can in return become the weight of existence holding back the living uncontrollably. Blindness was somehow a metaphor for the "perception" of one's own limits[6]—a limitation Fausto must deal with every day of his solitary existence, a limit beyond which schizophrenia may be the only way out. On the surface, Fausto was a malicious, bitter villain who physically battered and mentally abused Ciccio. In the end and against all odds, however, a more humane quality emerged to reveal a sensitive, gifted man. Fausto's degenerate lifestyle and crude language were never glamorized, as he was ultimately portrayed as a vanquished human being. Sarcasm, irony, piety, bitterness were all present in the final scene as Fausto, escorted to a remote and abandoned country farm, decided to accept Sara as his guardian. Because of Sara's unexpected patience and concern for her hero, they finally came to respect and care for each other.

Profumo di donna's fortune was unprecedented for a film comedy, as Dino Risi won the prize for Best Director for the David di Donatello. In addition, Vittorio Gassman won an impressive series of awards with a triple award for Best Actor at the 1975 David di Donatello, Nastro d'Argento, and Cannes Film Festival. In the U.S., the film was nominated for Best Foreign Film and Best Screenplay Adapted From Other Material for the Academy Awards in 1976. Moreover, Hollywood's remake *Scent of a Woman* in 1992 starring Al Pacino was a success in Italy as well.

Lina Wertmüller: When Humor Challenges the Rules

Looking at the national success of the *commedia all'italiana,* one cannot help observing that Italian comedies encountered little international success since motion pictures were invented. Surprisingly enough, in a profession dominated by men, one of the very few filmmakers to consistently export comedies abroad and in particular to the U.S. market was Lina Wertmüller. Best known for *Swept Away* (*Travolti da un insolito destino nell'azzurro mare d'agosto,* 1974), Wertmüller brought a new style to the *commedia* and in a certain manner prolonged the existence of the movement until the end of the decade.

Born Arcangela Felice Assunta Wertmüller von Elgg Spanol von Braucich in 1928 in Rome, the filmmaker began her career in 1963 as assistant director on the set of Federico Fellini's 8½, collaborating on the screenplay. That same year, she achieved her first film as director with *I basilischi,* for which she also wrote the subject and screenplay. In 1965, she directed an episode film entitled *Questa volta parliamo di uomini* with Nino Manfredi, who won the Maschera d'Argento for his interpretation. Following the high-profile, long feature films of *Swept Away,* and *Love and Anarchy,* all endowed with an unmistakable style, Wertmüller's comedy style was finally recognized outside Italy with *Seven Beauties* (*Pasqualino settebellezze,* 1975), which received four Oscar nominations (Best Director, Best Foreign Film, Best Screenplay, Best Actor), an unprecedented performance for an Italian filmmaker. Other recent productions include *Ciao, Professore* (*Io speriamo che me la cavo,* 1992) with a Paolo Villaggio light-years away from Ugo Fantozzi, his emblematic character.

Similar to Germi's *Divorzio all'italiana* or *Sedotta e abbandonata,* the Sicilian environment of the early seventies where the protagonists evolved was indeed the

Giancarlo Giannini (Mimì) and Luigi Diberti (Pippino) in Lina Wertmüller's *The Seduction of Mimi* (*Mimì metallurgico, ferito nell'onore,* 1972)

perfect setting for underlying social overtones. Lina Wertmüller's *The Seduction of Mimi* (*Mimì mettalurgio ferito nell'onore*, 1972) offered a deep analysis of the antiquated code of conduct through a humorous yet pungent fresco of the Italian south. In some ways *Mimi* as well as *Love and Anarchy* or *Swept Away* exemplified how environment and individuals came to inspire this filmmakers' varied vision and how soon-to-be cinematic stock elements like sex, church, authority, family, and death were deliberated and defined (as well as a degrading image of women which angered feminists of the seventies).

Carmelo Mardocheo, also called Mimì (Giancarlo Giannini), a Communist metalworker from Catania, loses his job for his opposition to the Mafia. He is then compelled to leave his native Sicily and to separate temporarily from his young wife Rosalia (Agostina Belli) in Turin. He joins the association *Fratelli Siciliani*, which finds him a place to live. He quickly finds out that behind the charity association is a Mafia-owned business. He begins a romantic relation with a northern woman called Fiore (Mariangela Melato), from which a son is born. Once he returns to Catania, Mimì's wife experienced a similar itinerary, as she gave birth to a son from a relation with a police officer (Gianfranco Barra). In order to vindicate his honor, Mimì avenges himself by seducing the obese wife (Elena Fiore) of the police officer in question and attempts to conceive a child.

The film (to be understood as Mimì the metalworker offended in his honor) was a spectacular indictment of the code of honor in patriarchal culture such as Sicily in the early seventies. Again approaching the perennial question of the south, Wertmüller's depiction of a cruel, callous society promulgating humiliation for whoever did not want to follow the rules under the oppression of Mafia organizations rendered the main character sympathetic, despite his extramarital affair, an illegitimate son, and excessive jealousy for his wife's betrayal. More concerned with social roles than sexual identity, Lina Wertmüller's narrative employed a rather complex structure to develop the storyline. Ironically, her narratives are remembered less for their compassionate portrayals of social welfare in the seventies than for their vitriolic approach to graphic and comedic sexuality. The character of Mimì, flawlessly personified by Giannini with a vibrant stylization, was essential to bring the satirical comedy to a deeply political farce. Lina Wertmüller, who won Best Director at the Cannes Film Festival, proved on every occasion to successfully realize sexually charged political comedies whose structure was overloaded with illustrated wonders (i.e., the notorious grotesque love scene between Mimì and Amalia Finocchiaro).

Lina Wertmüller's *Swept Away* (*Travolti da un insolito destino nell'azzurro mare d'agosto*, 1974) also known by its lengthy title *Swept Away… by an Unusual Destiny in the Blue Sea of August* was clearly one of the most untraditional cinematic narratives that emerged during the early 1970s. In its representation of *lotta di classe* (class warfare) and gender roles, *Swept Away* generated a series of interesting dichotomies: north versus south, Lombard accent versus Sicilian dialect, Christian Democrat versus PCI, male versus female, manual labor versus management, bourgeoisie versus lower class. The visible social and political commitment

Giancarlo Giannini, Lina Wertmüller, and Mariangela Melato on the set of *Swept Away* (*Travolti da un insolito destino nell'azzurro mare d'agosto*, 1974)

emanated by this daring subject revealed Wertmüller's iconoclast predisposition and her passion for effectively debating hot topics such as consumerism, capitalism, communism, and even the role of the Vatican in postwar Italy.

Raffaella Pavone Lanzetti (Mariangela Melato), a rich industrial Milanese, spends her vacation on a yacht in the company of her subdued husband and a group of wealthy friends. As they navigate through the Mediterranean sea, the beautiful and opinionated woman of leisure takes much joy in having her whims satisfied and in publicly and systematically humiliating the crewmates and in particular Gennarino (Giancarlo Giannini), a grumpy Sicilian servant (and to cap it all, a Communist). She scolds him for serving tasteless coffee, overdone spaghetti, and wearing smelly shirts while on duty. Raffaela decides to go for a late-night swim and asks Gennarino to drive her on a small inflatable boat. Suddenly the motor stalls, leaving the couple stranded out at sea. After a night of drifting, they reach the shore of a deserted island. Amidst the wilderness and its harsh living conditions, Raffaelle blames Gennarino for their tribulations, increasing his internal frustration. Exasperated by her constant aggression, Gennarino's Sicilian honor suddenly resurfaces and explodes, changing him from a submissive individual to an infuriated rebel. After a storm of mutual insults, they separate on the island in search of food. Soon the social roles reverse, as Raffaela needs Gennarino's expertise to secure her own survival. This time she submits to his dominance, socially and sexually. In addition, she must satisfy his desires, becoming his slave and having to work for the first time in her life.

She must satisfy years of sexual and social repression. This violently passionate relation, however, comes from an atypical romance outside the bonds of society, which abruptly ends with their rescue by French sailors.

Known as a controversial filmmaker rather than a feminist spokesperson, Lina Wertmüller took advantage of the film's background to once again emphasize two of her favorite themes: sex and politics. Instead of picturing an unadventurous battle of the sexes *all'italiana*, the film included a determinant social component to its narrative frame, bringing the experience to a higher level: a hyperbolical fable about bourgeoisie and proletariat, attempting to resolve centuries of social and political frustration through an unanticipated sexual experience. As both protagonists jumped in the ardent power struggle fueled by their desire of survival, a long-awaited sexual tension arose on the screen. The prelude of the fight involved a storm filled with outrageous insults on both sides. Gennarino's condescending nickname for his adversary *Bottana industriale* ("Capitalist whore!" with a Sicilian accent) somehow summarized the double grudge the working class holds in addition to the dominant one (similar to Raffaella comparing Sicilians with Abyssinians).

Their stubbornness slowly developed into a strange and brutal love affair: the more Raffaela submitted, the more ecstasy she seemed to reach. One of the climaxes of the film in terms of humorous sexuality was the moment Raffaela insinuated for Gennarino to venture into some unconventional sexual practices, understandably decadent for any neophytes (whose names are unknown to Gennarino and possibly "against nature," to paraphrase the Sicilian code of conduct). Interestingly, this moment served as a reevaluation of the gender roles, so far dominated by the masculine figure: "La donna è l'oggetto del piacere dell'uomo," Gennarino liked to remind Raffaela ("Women are objects of pleasure for men"). The power of sexual chauvinism was also climactic during the initial "rebellion" scene when Gennarino slapped Raffaella around a sand dune, inflicting punishment for every social injustice generated on Italy's poor (with relative unpredictability, Gennarino even throws his underwear at her, ordering her to wash it). Even during some of the hardly sustainable images of violence, Wertmüller's camera was able to ephemerally pause on Giannini's spectacularly expressive face and, in particular, his evocative eyes toward a woman he has despised too long. For him, the goal is already set as he expects her to recognize his dominance with the very Sicilian "bacia la mano al padrone" (Sicilian way to greet while acknowledging superiority) or "La femmina è un oggetto del piacere, cioè trastulla per il lavoratore" ("Women are an object for pleasure, that is, entertainment for the working man"). However, as the pastoral romance reaches a conclusion, both protagonists express a different wish. Gennarino wants to return to the mainland and challenge the rules of social pressure so that he may test the strength of their newly discovered love, and as Peter Bondanella noticed, "Only Rafaella recognizes that this wish is a foolish one, for the strength of society's class barriers will necessarily destroy the affair that could blossom only beyond social limits."[7] While their existence ultimately settles into idyll, it is Gennarino who flags down a passing ship, needing to know if their newfound relationship would survive a return to their old lives.

The Mediterranean sea was an unusual backdrop for this social comedy since most comedies were set in an urban setting with a predisposition for Rome and its Cinecittà spell. The film's shooting location in Sardegna provided fertile and colorful inspiration for the cinematography under the direction of a group of operators—Giulio Battiferri, Giuseppe Fornari, and Stefano Ricciotti. Wertmüller is also remembered as the first woman to ever be nominated for the Oscar for Best Director in 1977 (with a film entitled *Seven Beauties* [*Pasqualino Settebellezze*, 1975]). As for *Swept Away*, its popular success in America inspired an unfortunate Hollywood remake version directed by British filmmaker Guy Ritchie in 2002. Interestingly enough, Giancarlo Giannini's son Adriano played the part of Gennarino thirty years after his father, with the singer Madonna in the role of Raffaella.

Federico Fellini's Successful Return to Comedy

While Lina Wertmüller, Mario Monicelli, and Dino Risi proved to be faithful to the comedy genre, it was certainly not the case of Federico Fellini, who had

Bruno Zanin (Titta Biondi) and Maria Antonietta Beluzzi (the tobacconist)
in Federico Fellini's *Amarcord* (1974)
Photo courtesy of BIFI

started his directing career with a couple of comedies before investing his expertise in the *auteur* genre. Although Fellini's *Amarcord* (1973) contained all the
necessary characteristics to qualify as a comedy feature film, the subject and
screenplay (written by the director himself and Tonino Guerra) could not be
entirely considered part of the *commedia all'italiana* experience; Fellini's trademark once more offered a strong presence of his artistic touch at every level of
the filmmaking. However, the comic fundamentals (only present during the first
half of the film) clearly displayed all the elements dear to the comedy Italian style
and has been ever since worthy of many studies. Following the success of *The
White Sheik* (*Lo sceicco bianco*, 1952), *I vitelloni* (1953), as well as *The Swindle* (*Il
bidone*, 1955), it comes as no surprise to learn that Fellini's early inclination for
satirical comedies began with his career as a writer for comic screenplays and
satirical papers' columns such as the notorious Marc'Aurelio.

To argue that Fellini's own directorial talent gave a very idiosyncratic touch
to *Amarcord* would be cliché, as much of his cinematic legacy has capitalized on
a unique *auteur* dimension. The greatest contribution of *Amarcord*, perhaps the
most autobiographical tale ever told by Fellini, was its unique storytelling technique: colorful fragmentary compositions, overloaded with illustrated wonders,
hypnotizing dream sequences (beautifully photographed by Giuseppe Rotunno)
along with the intended humanistic approach to the characters, a combination
of grotesque caricatures with melancholic moments, all cadenced by the rhythm
of comical anecdotes. The film included an endless series of oneiric chronicles taken from his childhood memory during the years of Fascism while the
sequence of events, the majority of which were not connected to each other,
narrated an entire year in the town of Rimini, displaying the colorful events that
occurred during four consecutive seasons (the montage successfully created the
impression of the passage of time through each season in order to close the cir-
cular structure of the narrative).

Fellini's primary intention, before making the audience smile and laugh,
was clearly to share his childhood memories in his fictionalized hometown of
Rimini during the 1930s. The phrase *Amarcord*, translated as "my recollection"
(*Mi Ricordo* as spelled in the Emilia-Romagna dialect), carried a warmly nostalgic memory piece of real life, as the young Fellini left Rimini in 1937 to go
to Rome (he eventually returned to his hometown in 1945; much had changed,
to his dismay). Exactly twenty years following the creation of the seminal film *I
vitelloni* (1953), Fellini once again proposed a comic vision in the Romagna of
his childhood (the scenes were actually shot at Rome's Cinecittà studios). While
there was no central character or narrative thread, Titta, interpreted by Bruno
Zanin, served as the pivotal figure instead of Fellini's faithful alter ego Marcello
Mastroianni (*La dolce vita*, 8½, *Una giornata particolare*, *Città delle donne*).
Through the narration of the city's lawyer as the narrator and collective memory
historian (Luigi Rossi), the film presented a remarkable mix of eccentric characters in an avalanche of vibrant caricatures. While on the deserted beach of the

Adriatic or on the main street, the town's lustful teenagers and their tormenting fantasies always put them on the prowl for juvenile entertainment and practical jokes. In a certain sense, Fellini's Rimini was fictionalized into an authentic *paese dei balochi* dear to Collodi's literature: a voluptuous female cigarette vendor endowed with astronomically large breasts; a decadent but attractive prostitute always in search of sexual encounters, whose utterances and moans resembled the ones of a panther rather than a human being; a provocative hairdresser La Gradisca, the unique femme fatale flaunting her delightful curves to her captive audience; as well as old professors who can no longer see the pupils' misdemeanors in class.

Fellini's deliberate choice to concentrate most comical moments inside the narrative of school scenes was a coherent alternative, as the neorealist heritage had always influenced the *commedia all'italiana* by using a child's point of view (i.e., Luigi Comencini's cinema often investigating childhood). Indeed, the school was the collective space par excellence where teenage boys acted with irreverence. Fellini's conceptualization of obsolete education indirectly ridiculed the lessons of the past through profuse satirical vignettes. To the long-established tradition of education mainly based on repetition learning and soporific theory (Fellini's choice for Greek instruction, history of Ancient Rome, Latin, catechism, etc. was not hazardous), the essential lessons of life undoubtedly took a new turn through practical and physical experiences. As if the school was not enough, Fellini's satire of the Catholic Church was portrayed as an incongruity best illustrated by the confessional scene representing the distracted priest Don Balosa (Gianfilippo Carcano). Obsessed with the idea of teens "touching" themselves, the disinterested priest made every effort to investigate their "carnal" sin, as he asks Titta the delicate question: "Commetti atti impuri? Ti tocchi? Lo sai che San Luigi piange quando ti tocchi?" (Do you commit impure acts? Do you touch yourself? You know that San Luigi cries when you touch yourself?) This eloquent derision of the institution of confession, and the generational gap with the post-Vatican II years, was also reminiscent of Pietro Germi's humorous style. Like many comedy films of the decade, the realm of sexuality was often associated with the obsolete code of conduct still upheld in Italy, which stood light-years behind the sixties and seventies, thus creating an irresistible effect of comedy.

Along with the paradigmatic imagery of the school and its inept theatricality, the family nucleus was the other center of interest of the film. Adapted from a collection of remote reminiscences,[8] Titta's home life revolved around a dictatorial father figure who was a rugged construction foreman (Armando Brancia), and an infuriated mother (Pupella Maggio) who continually complained about her husband's political choice and stubbornness (he insists on wearing his Socialist tie to provoke the Fascist militia). Despite being constantly criticized by his wife for his beliefs, Titta's father Aurelio was eventually singled out and physically humiliated by the police, illustrated by the occasion he is forced to drink cod-liver oil. As a genuine film artist, Fellini never overemphasized the political element in his narrative despite dealing with a tormented and oppressive period of the 1930s era himself. Because of the tendency for any given autobiographical account to generate a visible discrepancy between actual past and subjective interpretation, the rendition of Fellini's family life portrayed the problems in his lovingly dysfunctional family with eccentric characters sitting around a rather chaotic table dinner: a mélange of uncouth, bad-tempered, yet colorful and witty characters.

Another element, which can be considered the trademark of the 1970s *commedia all'italiana*, was of course the inescapable satire of sexuality. Representation of sexuality's physicality had always been important to Fellini's filmmaking (i.e., the breakthrough of Swedish actress Anita Ekberg in *La dolce vita*, as well as other actors in films such as *Roma*, *Casanova*, *City of Women*, to name a few), but this time the director offered a mix of meticulous details conjugated with deliberate excessive romanticism. *Amarcord* revealed Fellini as a director qualified to be a protagonist of the *commedia all'italiana* (although primarily a film *auteur*) as he successfully captured a succession of raw humanity through persuasive comedy. These chronicles of teenagers' sexual frustrations in their fantasizing about women was one of the predominant themes of the narrative, and the center of interest of the comedic part of *Amarcord*, as their prolific attention went respectively to the languorous prostitute Volpina (Josiane Tanzilli), the local beauty queen and hairdresser La Gradisca (Magali Noël who Fellini also cast in *La dolce vita* and *Satyricon*), the math teacher who in his dreams roars like a lioness, and of course the incomparable tobacconist (Maria Antonietta Beluzzi) with gargantuan breasts.

The two most stimulating female presences in the film were without a doubt represented by the characters of La Gradisca and Volpina, who stood in radical opposition in their sexual "availability" and how effortlessly they commanded the teenagers' captive attention. La Gradisca, a composed and elegant lady, was beyond reach for the youngsters, and her aspiration eventually went toward her longtime idealized man: an ordinary but handsome police officer. And on the other end, Volpina, who prowled the streets and beaches always in search of new physical encounters with an insatiable sexual appetite, looked rather "soiled" in her grotesque "accessibility." British Film scholar Danielle Hipkins has underlined in a perspicacious manner the tendency among contemporary filmmakers to represent female sexuality under a different light depending on the narrative angle:

> The *narrativization* of the male (schoolboy) gaze upon the female prostitute in comedy of the period following the Legge Merlin, however unruly she may be, and however many '*beffe*' she may carry out, is one that contains her and often hints that she belongs back into the brothel…. However, where the female prostitute does appear outside that framework, she is more likely to express a kind of female subjectivity new to Italian cinema.[9]

Here Fellini's active camera captured through the visual perceptiveness of the "schoolboy gaze" the backside of Gradisca's provocative behind as well as the town's women's behinds as they climb aboard their bicycles (this *filone* proved prolific, as imitations resurfaced years later such as in Giuseppe Tornatore's *Cinema Paradiso* in 1988, or *Malena* in 2000, depicting the relentless sexual impulse among teenagers). Ironically, Titta without scruples displayed his "alphamale" individuality by flirting with the voluptuous tobacconist, only to be "demasculated" during the physicality of the unexpected sexual encounter that, in a way, reduced him to an infant (the woman's breasts physically dominating him).

As usual, Fellini's modus operandi never left much distance between erotic fantasies and oneiric imagery. As Marcia Landy indicated, *Amarcord* "challenges the conventional dichotomy between reality and illusion, calling attention to the ways they are connected rather than separate."[10] Here with comedy, it was precisely the mixture of reality and fantasy that were at the basis of the *felliniesque* humor. The "structureless" composition of the film gave *Amarcord* the appearance of a series of self-contained episodes, including innumerable fantasy scenes (often reminiscent of *La città delle donne* in 1980). One of the most dazzling was the scene where Titta narrates at the confessional his erotic encounter with La Gradisca in a deserted cinema screening a Gary Cooper movie, the actor of her dreams. Since they are the only two spectators inside the theater, Titta carefully circles his "prey" by moving closer, pretending to search for a better seat at every step of the process. Finally reaching the seat next to her, Titta slowly slides his left hand down Gradisca's thigh to be eventually rejected by her humiliating reaction: "Cosa cerchi?" ("Looking for something?"). Faithful to his style, Fellini never intended nor expressed a desire to present any didactic significance on the screen, as most of the erotic fantasies were left open to speculation.

As a film based on childhood memories, *Amarcord* was more concerned with addressing an introspective investigation through comedy impression than offering a re-creation of specific childhood events on the screen. Since Fellini wanted to avoid a certain dose of realism, a consistent trademark of *commedia all'italiana*, he gave his caricatures a substantial oneiric dimension, and rather than shooting on location, the town of his youth was recreated on the Roman stages of Cinecittà under the surrealistic art direction of Danilo Donati. Scenes like Ciccio's wedding with La Gradisca—under the benevolent stare of Mussolini (an obvious critique of the lack of measure in the Fascist *mise-en-scène* turned grotesque)—evolved into internal fantasies becoming almost indistinguishable between reality and the surreal imagery, quintessentially *felliniesque*.

Amarcord was generally well received in Italy, even by popular audiences who as a rule never openly favored Federico Fellini's cinematic style. But in these difficult times, comedy, like all cinematographic genres, was affected by the lead years. As Italian film scholar Lorenzo Codelli pointed out, "Comedy Italian style appeared to be the refuge, or the vanguard, of auteur cinema. *Amarcord's* great success is due to the fact that the spectators link the film with the (best) familiar comedies that entertain them."[11] Unquestionably, the grown-up fantasy world observed by the teenagers' eyes, which inspired the filmmaker during his entire cinematographic career, was this time the common and fruitful denominator with popular spectatorship. In addition, it is fair to remember that the music score of the film, playfully arranged by long-time associate Nino Rota, bestowed the film with an added dimension, and to this date *Amarcord's* music is probably more recognizable than the film itself (very few movies can make such an eloquent statement). Fellini's less accessible films, roughly from the middle of the 1960s through the end of the 1980s, eventually eclipsed his earlier works, which contributed to the idea that the filmmaker was not interested in comedy. Although *Amarcord* was not a comedy per se, it proved just the opposite about its author. *Amarcord* won the Academy Award for Best Foreign Film, the New York Film Critics Circle Awards for Best Picture and Best Director in 1975, and at home it also won the 1974 David di Donatello for Best Director and Best Film, along with three *Nastri d'Argento* for Best Director, Best Original Screenplay, and Best Original Subject.

A Comedy of Frustrations: Franco Brusati

Franco Brusati had a similar relationship to the genre, as the screenwriter turned filmmaker spent his entire career writing scenarios, the majority of which had little to do with *commedia all'italiana*. However, in 1973 Brusati directed and cowrote with Nino Manfredi *Bread and Chocolate* (*Pane e cioccolata*, 1974),[12] one of several films centered on the long-established (although undervalued) theme of Italian immigration abroad. In this picaresque tale of hope and despair,

Nino Manfredi (Nino Garofalo) with a fellow Italian immigrant in Franco Brusati's *Bread and Chocolate* (*Pane e cioccolata,* 1974)
Photo courtesy of BIFI

Brusati drafted a compelling portrayal of solitude and nostalgia. Here the odyssey of a Roman immigrant in search of human values was rife with adversity, indifference, racism, and misunderstanding. The early years of the decade took filmmakers abroad in their own reflection of Italian society filled with economic hardship, making the theme of immigration highly a propos. Francesco Rosi's *I Magliari*, Mario Monicelli's *La ragazza con la pistola*, Luigi Zampa's *The Girl in Australia* (*Bello, onesto, emigrato Australia sposerebbe compaesana illibata*, 1971), starring Alberto Sordi and a convincing Claudia Cardinale, successfully identified the infinite subtleties of racism and indifference. A couple of years later, Brusati's *Bread and Chocolate* took the protagonist much closer to home, to Switzerland. The film was a satire of both the Swiss and the Italians, the former with their sense of order, propriety, and property, and its bourgeoisie loathing the foreigners coming from the south, the latter with its disorganization and feelings of inferiority.

Giovanni (Nino Manfredi) Garofano goes to the land of "chocolate" to do better than his impoverished existence in Italy. He works as a seasonal waiter in a luxurious resort in Switzerland while his family stays behind in Italy. His work is suddenly made difficult due to the fierce competition between him and a Turkish colleague in order to secure long-term employment. When his destiny is about to fulfill his long-awaited dreams, Nino is caught on camera urinating in broad daylight against a city wall. Confronted with this evidence at the police station, he loses his working permit and consequently his job. A long search for a new occupation begins as Nino enters the world of the clandestine. He is temporarily hosted by Elena (Anna Karina), a Greek political activist in exile from the military dictatorship, but the insipient romance between the two is cut short with the presence of Elena's future husband, a police officer. Later, a rich Italian businessman (Johnny Dorelli), in exile in Switzerland for fiscal reasons, recognizes Nino's homesickness and hires him as a butler, but he turns out to be a professional embezzler. The next day following a financial crack, the man commits suicide, leaving Nino on the run once more. He eventually ends up in a remote location among a group of peculiar illegal workers from Naples. Their job in a chicken slaughterhouse is degrading, as they must live yards away from their gruesome work in an empty chicken coop. For entertainment, they watch, through a hole in a wall, a group of young, blond, Swiss women swimming nude in the river—a vision of ecstasy. Pushed by despair, Nino attempts one last try to blend with the Nordic population by dying his hair blond. However the attempt falls short when he is in a bar screening a soccer game between Italy and Switzerland. His national pride overtaking his reason, Nino cannot help but make a "liberatory" scream at the first Italian goal and ends up kicked out on the street. Now escorted by a police officer at the train station to be finally expelled from Switzerland, Nino must say farewell to his host country. As he sits down surrounded by disillusioned fellow Italian immigrants, he expresses disgust about their bitterness and nostalgia. Having heard endless times the same nostalgic folkloric songs evoking for the eternal glory of "mandolins, pizzas, and gondolas," he despises his own condition and begins to have second thoughts, eventually pulling the emergency break of the train under the tunnel leading to Italy. The ultimate image of the final scene showing Giovanni walking on the railroad, alone, his suitcase in his hand, visibly at a loss, is compelling.

One of the centers of interest in the film was the balance achieved between the different tonalities of humor. First, there was a grotesque vein exemplified by several compelling scenes such as the surrealist sequence inside the chicken coop where the workers, mentally damaged by their work and environment, behave like animals themselves. Second are some remnants of physical humor (slapstick comedy style) dear to the American school of the Marx Brothers, but this time "italianized." The art of "getting by" (*L'arte di arrangiarsi* in Chapter three) was once again resuscitated in a successful restaurant scene when Nino must artfully peel an orange in front of a client. He unsuccessfully attempts to cut with style the orange when he notices an artistically cut peel left in the kitchen. As a subterfuge Nino gets rid of the peel "Italian style" and places the orange inside the stylized peel. As the victimized hero, almost a Chaplinesque figure, Nino recognizes against his will a certain inferiority complex among Italians when compared to the civility of the Swiss. Talking about the Swiss to a stranger in a park to break the monotony of his lonely weekends, he says, "Dice son' freddi. Eh no, non son' freddi, son' civili. Che è diverso." (You say they are cold. No, they aren't cold. They are civil. It's different.) Caught between an Italy he does not like and a Switzerland that does not want him, Nino is ready to sacrifice his own identity, ultimately living a continuous moral contradiction: the world of the Swiss—tall, healthy, strong—is a beautiful, clean, and a rich world, but he belongs to the Italian world—which to him seems small, poor, ugly, and dirty. Despite his desire to live inside the first one, his feeling and identity can only be in the second.

As a director, Brusati's choices all seemed prudent and inconspicuous, designed to draw attention to the characters and the story rather than its technical assemblage and much-lauded stars like Manfredi and Karina. The characters and the intimate manner in which their struggles were portrayed was one of the film's most determinant factors in regards to its success among popular audiences. Because of the importance of immigration in Italy (whether abroad or within Italy), the film left few spectators indifferent. The scene of the chicken coop was one of them, as it powerfully depicted the dehumanization of immigrants reduced to live in animalesque conditions while still thanking and praying to the Madonna of Pompeii to keep their providential employment. At the end of a frugal welcome dinner gathering the entire family, Nino asks them an innocent question about what people may think about their hopeless plight. Their answers, exemplifying Italian "sentimental defeatism," comes as a shock: "La gente è invidiosa! E' tutta invidia." (People are jealous; nothing but jealousy.) This whole extended sequence was one of the highlights of the film and demonstrated Brusati's realistic use of architecture and *mise-en-scène* to portray the scene's emotional core.

One of the criticisms that occurred mainly in the U.S. where the film was released in 1978 was that Manfredi maintained a confused optimism of the sort that had the effect of demeaning a character rather than illuminating its own image. It has been said that Brusati personally identified with Nino's character during the drafting of the script, one of constant unhappiness (no matter where he was), a sort of metaphor of his own existentialist itinerary: his aspirations always ending up frustrated and thwarted. Despite his awareness of the hopeless quest, Nino's strength lies in his ability to always start from scratch: his moral strength. The film received a warm international welcome in 1974 and won the Silver Berlin Bear at the Berlin Film Festival, David di Donatello for Best Film and Best Actor (Nino Manfredi), and the New York Film Critics Circle Award for Best Foreign Film in 1978.

Luigi Zampa's Satirical Cinema

Italian immigration took filmmakers even further than its Alpine borders with Switzerland. Luigi Zampa's *A Girl in Australia* (*Bello, onesto, emigrato Australia sposerebbe compaesana illibata*, 1971), starring Alberto Sordi and Claudia Cardinale, took place in Australia and poignantly illustrated the theme of the endless vicissitudes of Italian immigrants struggling to find a better life abroad. Though remotely implicated with the social and political problems for Italians in these difficult years, the film presented a compelling story of identity and despair. This time, the "art of getting by," so prominent in the 1960s, took a new dimension as it involved the mental and psychological well-being of the individual. A couple of years before his Australian adventure, Luigi Zampa directed *Il medico della mutua* (1968), an archetypical example of a successful social satire that touched on the delicate subject dear to all spectators in Italy at that time: the health-care system. From a novel written by Giuseppe D'Agata, and an adaptation signed by Sergio Amidei, one of the early innovative scenarists who provided the initial impetus for the comedy Italian style, the film displayed a human masquerade in full irony, painting the social hypocrisy of the bourgeois standards (the liberal profession) with a well-drawn ensemble cast and convincing dialogues, and displaying the unpleasant reality of Italy's primitive and corrupted health system. The existing bond inside the health-care institution created interdependence between patients and physicians, thus generating an avalanche of abuses, which inspired Zampa in his rendering of the everlasting *arte di arrangiarsi*.

The film narrates the spectacular career of a young doctor, Guido Tersilli (Alberto Sordi), a recent graduate in medicine now looking to establish a practice in a district of Rome. Following the financial sacrifice made by his mother (Nanda Primavera), Guido must succeed at any cost to repay the years of hardship.

The race is on as they begin enrolling as many *mutuati* (registered patients) as possible. Mother and fiancée Teresa (Sara Franchetti) go to local stores and bars in surrounding neighborhoods to provide some indirect publicity for Guido. As they pretend to meet by chance, they praise out loud the merit of Dr. Guido Tersilli, attributing to him some miraculous care and unparalleled competence. As word of mouth begins to pay off, Guido gradually steps on his colleague's toes by stealing their clients (patients) one by one. The growth of his clientele has diverse fortunate twists, as for instance one day, a new patient shows up in his office—an attractive young woman who unexpectedly undresses to start the visit. At the end of a rather unusual "sensual" visit, Guido receives a cold shower when after asking for the honorarium she replies by asking him 10,000 lira for her "service." More fortunate, but no less peculiar, a numerous Sicilian family led by an unemployed father in search of monetary compensations introduce themselves to the doctor. In order to reassure Guido, the father of eleven children promises at least thirty visits a year, thus generating a substantial income for the doctor (25 percent of which he will receive as a bribe): "Vedrai signor dottore, con noi si troverà bene. Noi siamo gente povera ma onesta. E poi, io e mia moglie… mica ci fermiamo qui." ("You'll see doctor, with us you will be all right. We are poor but honest people. And then, me and my wife… we aren't stopping here.") At one point, Guido needs to acquire a lot more patients and ends up courting the spouse of Dr. Bui, a terminally ill patient. After his death, Guido inherits the large group of the late Dr. Bui's patients he had taken care of over the years. Soon his office is crowded with patients seeking treatment for many different reasons (some genuine and some imagined). From now on, the rise of Dr. Tersilli is unstoppable; so is the frequency of patients' visits. One ironic moment of the film occurs as Guido, under the pressure of constant work and exhaustion, collapses one day in his office and is taken to the hospital in an ambulance. Terrified by the idea of seeing his patients stolen by his envious colleagues, Guido escapes from the hospital and returns home to administer care to his patients by telephone.

Behind this colorful comedy, Zampa's intention was the portrayal of the health-care system in Italy that was dramatically lagging behind Western European standards at the end of the sixties. The testimony, though under the form of comedic social satire, was all the more seminal in that the lack of sanitary services was a serious problem in Italy in these days. The ineffectiveness of the health-care organization was indeed generating unprecedented corruption at both ends of the system, and in some cases mass hypochondria (i.e., the Sicilian unemployed father of eleven who asks for 30 percent of his visits).

> Doctor Tersili: What is your profession?
> Sicilian man: Doctor, you can't be serious. You think that with eleven children, a man like me can find time to work?[13]

One important element of the film was the expression of a strong desire to represent the growing discrepancy between bourgeoisie, material greed, and

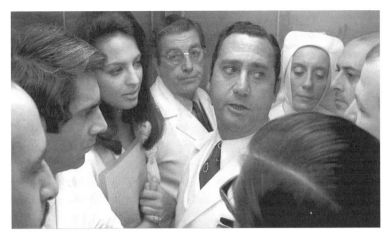

Alberto Sordi (Guido Tersilli) in Luciano Salce's *Il Prof. Dott. Guido Tersilli, primario della clinica Villa Celeste convenzionata con le mutue* (1969)

the working class in Italy, an archaic dual system faithfully represented in terms of health and society. The sequel, entitled *Il prof. dott. Guido Tersilli, primario della clinica Villa Celeste convenzionata con le mutue* (1969), directed by Luciano Salce, experienced a similar fortune, as popular audiences recognized themselves as pseudoprotagonists. Luigi Zampa's success heavily depended upon the performance of Alberto Sordi, as the director often cast him in countless comedies, including *The Art of Getting Along* (*L'arte di arrangiarsi*, 1955); *Ladro lui, ladra lei* (1958); *The Traffic Policeman* (*Il vigile*, 1960); and *A Girl in Australia* (*Bello, onesto, emigrato Australia sposerebbe compaesana illibata*, 1971). Alberto Sordi, one of the greatest Italian comic actors, experienced a rare career both qualitatively and quantitatively, with a total of 150 feature films. The actor's endless repertoire illustrated various types of the average Italian, including a light dose of cynicism, which very quickly became the actor's trademark.

The Human Comedy of Alberto Sordi

Born in the heart of the Trastevere district, Sordi was a true Roman kid. His career began very early in 1936, when he abandoned his studies in Rome to begin his professional career, entering the prestigious *Accademia dei Filodrammatici di Milano*, which discharged him the following year for his excessive dialectal elocution, too rooted in the Roman dialect. In many interviews, Sordi liked to remind everyone that this event encouraged him to keep his *romanesco* accent and exploit the *dialetto*, which eventually became the dynamic of his humor. As paradoxical as it may appear, the actor, whose nickname became *Albertone nazionale*, was only awarded a diploma *honoris causa* in acting from the Milanese

Academy in 1999, some sixty years after his dismissal. In 1937, Sordi won a competition organized by MGM in Italy and consequently became the voice for Oliver Hardy (Ollio) in Italy. In 1950, he cofounded with Vittorio De Sica a company called PFC (Produzione Film Comici) and a year later, his first film as lead actor was Roberto Bavarese's *Mamma mia che impressione* (1951). The encounter with Federico Fellini gave him one of the greatest opportunities of his career, as he was cast for *The White Sheick* (*Lo sceicco bianco*, 1952) and a year later in *I vitelloni* (1953), placing him at the forefront of the future *commedia all'italiana*.

Most of the greatest directors involved with the Italian comedy of the postwar era directed him with great success, due mainly to Sordi's charisma on the screen as well as the premeditated success of the actor among popular audiences. Some of Sordi's most significant contributions for the *commedia all'italiana* included Antonio Pietrangeli's *Lo scapolo* (1955); Luigi Zampa's *Ladro lui, ladra lei* (1958), *Il vigile* (1961), *Il medico della mutua* (1968), followed by the sequel from Luciano Salce entitled *Il prof. dott. Guido Tersilli primario della clinica Villa Celeste convenzionata con le mutue* (1969), and *The Girl in Australia* (*Bello onesto emigrato Australia sposerebbe compaesana illibata*, 1971); Dino Risi's *The Widower* (*Il vedovo*, 1959) and *A Difficult Life* (*Una vita difficile*, 1961); Giorgio Bianchi's *The Moralist* (*Il moralista*, 1959); Francesco Rosi's *I magliari* (1959); Mario Monicelli's *The Great War* (*La grande guerra*, 1959), *Un borghese piccolo piccolo* (1977); Luigi Comencini's *Everybody Go Home* (*Tutti a casa*, 1960), *Il commissario* (1962), *The Scientific Card Game* (*Lo scopone scientifico* 1972), *Quelle strane occasioni* (1976); Alberto Lattuada's *Mafioso* (1962); Vittorio De Sica's *Il boom* (1963); Elio Petri's *Il maestro di Vigevano* (1963); Dino Risi, Franco Rossi, and Luigi Filippo D'Amico's *I complessi*, (1965); Ettore Scola's *Riusciranno i nostri eroi a ritrovare l'amico misteriosamente scomparso in Africa?* (1968); Luigi Magni's *Nell'anno del Signore* (1969); Nanni Loy's *Detenuto in attesa di giudizio*

Alberto Sordi (Romeo Proietti) and Anna Longhi (Augusta Proietti)
in the episode "Le vacanze intelligenti" in Alberto Sordi's
Dove vai in vacanza? (1978)
Photo courtesy of BIFI

(1971); his own *Finché c'è guerra c'è speranza* (1974), his own *Il comune senso del pudore* (1976) and *Dove vai in vacanza?* (1978); Ettore Scola, Mario Monicelli, and Dino Risi's *The New Monsters* (*I nuovi mostri*, 1977); and finally Luigi Comencini's *Bottleneck* (*L'ingorgo—Una storia impossibile*, 1979).

Sordi narrated the stories of an entire city and nation. No other comic actor was able to cover the scope Sordi did as he played a multitude of roles, each one directly portraying the emblematic figures of millions of Italians: magistrate, assassin, *Roma* supporter (football club), physician, widower, lieutenant, police inspector, journalist, schoolteacher, monk, immigrant, surgeon, taxi driver, junk man, idle womanizer, soldier, mafioso, con artist, etc. Sordi possessed a perfect understanding of the Italian people, and in particular, their defects, vices and virtues, contradictions, weaknesses, hopes and disappointments. This explains why as a symbol of Italian people, many of them recognized themselves in him. Sordi received the Golden Lion for lifetime achievement at the Venice Film Festival in 1995 during the one hundredth anniversary of the invention of the cinematograph.

Despite an unparalleled acting career in Italian comedy, Alberto Sordi also managed to conduct a directing career. Though less flamboyant than his acting, and despite a catastrophic first film, *Smoke Over London* (*Fumo di Londra*, 1966), Sordi was able to improve his artistic vision and directing style with *The Couples* (*Le coppie*, 1970, the segment "La camera"), *Stardust* (*Polvere di stelle*, 1973), and *While There's War There's Hope* (*Finché c'è guerra c'è speranza*, 1974). With *A Common Sense of Modesty* (*Il comune senso del pudore*, 1976), Sordi produced a courageous film, as it represented a difficult subject and in particular the immaturity of an Italian public poorly prepared to face the amorality of the pornographic film industry and the subsequent *sottocultura* (mass subculture) it provided. But it was with *Dove vai in vacanza?*, an episode film involving three filmmakers (Mauro Bolognini, Luciano Salce, and himself), that Alberto Sordi reached the level of an accomplished comedy filmmaker. The last and only notable episode worthy of interest was Sordi's segment entitled "Vacanze intelligenti," whose subject and screenplay was assembled by Rodolfo Sonego.

Augusta (Anna Longhi) and Remo (Alberto Sordi) are a couple of *fruttaroli* (Roman dialect for fruit vendors). Their three children, all enrolled in prestigious universities in Rome, have decided to send them on a learning trip in order to enhance their parents' poor general culture, remedy their ignorance, help them get fit by restricting their diet, as well as to remodel the entire family apartment by getting rid of all old furniture and knickknacks considered outdated (principally a *Madonnina*, Gesù bambino, the golden gondola, etc.). While driving their small Fiat 127 through the tortuous roads of Italy, Augusta begins to silently weep, as she knows that she no longer will see her beloved furniture. However, something sheers her up as she pulls out of her bag the only object she was able to salvage: a plastic golden gondola Remo had offered her during their honeymoon. The first stop is a visit to Etruscan tombs in Tarquinia, followed by an austere dinner made up of a bowl of rice and a salad leaf. The next day, they

Alberto Sordi (Giacinto Colonna) and Rossana Di Lorenzo (Erminia Colonna)
in *A Common Sense of Modesty* (*Il comune senso del pudore*, 1976)

arrive in Florence at the Grand Hotel for a diet program based on mineral water,
two olives, and a thin slice of roast beef for dinner. At night, they must attend a
formal contemporary music concert. As the orchestra begins to perform under
the attentive stare of a connoisseur public, Augusta does not realize the nature
of the dodecaphonic music and says out loud: "Che stanno accordando gli stru-
menti?" ("Are they tuning their instruments?") Everyone hushes them, outcast-
ing them from this selective group. The next day, they arrive at the Biennale in
Venice, hoping to relive some sensation of their honeymoon. Following a long
and tedious visit of the modern art exhibits, introduced by an egregious professor whose language goes over their heads, they arrive in St. Mark's Square,
pushed to their limits and famished. After a few seconds of hesitation, they
decide to break the pact they had signed with their children and rush to the
closest bar and buy two enormous sandwiches, which they consume to their
greatest delight on the square. Their gastronomic idyll ends abruptly, as they see
Pasquina, one of their daughters, who unmistakably was spying on them. Angry
to have been caught red-handed, the couple decides to vindicate themselves in a
Venetian restaurant. They order pork sausage, baked beans, red wine, and a large
amount of *pappardelle di lepre*, claiming out loud "E' la fine del mondo!" They
cause a stir inside the restaurant, as all of the snooty clients, witnessing their
jovial appetite, begin one after the other to order the same dishes for themselves.
The scene finishes at the hospital, as both end up intoxicated by the amount of
food consumed in one night. The bewildered doctor asks them the reason for
this gastronomic indulgence, but the only answer he can get from Augusta is: "è
una vendetta… è una vendetta… è una vendetta!" Once back at home in Rome,
they discover with dismay the newly remodeled apartment, bare of furniture
and in a modern style with which they are not accustomed. Fortunately for their

Alberto Sordi

consolation, the children have prepared a gigantic *spaghettata* to celebrate their return. Although inserting a slight dose of moralism, Alberto Sordi was able to successfully portray the clash of generations during the 1970s. The two Italys, one poor and ignorant, having survived the privations of the war as well as the difficult years of the reconstruction of the immediate postwar era, and the other, obsessed with the novelties of art and culture, uncompromisingly oblivious of their parents' daily reality.

Mario Monicelli and the Difficult Years

Along with Dino Risi, Mario Monicelli was able to maintain a high profile in the mutating phase of the *commedia all'italiana*. Following the successful decade of the 1960s, Monicelli kept the same pace in his production. As far as his choices, the Tuscan director did not have the same consistency, especially with sequels (i.e., the popular expectation with the sequel of *L'armata Brancaleone* of 1965 entitled for the occasion *Brancaleone alle crociate*, 1970). Monicelli's *Vogliamo i colonelli* (1973), written by Age and Scarpelli, was inspired by the recent 1967 coup d'état in Greece and rekindled by the missed attempt in Italy in 1970. The film received a mixed reception for its pseudo-*buffonesque* style, which took over the second part of the film. However, in 1975, Monicelli directed his most successful film of the decade with *My Friends* (*Amici miei*). Pietro Germi, who had coscripted the project, fell ill during preproduction and asked Monicelli to take over as director. Following some hesitations from Germi, the plot was actually moved from Bologna to Florence, a city with which Monicelli and screenwriters Leo Benvenuti, Piero De Bernardi, and Tullio Pinelli were more familiar (since all were Tuscans). Germi eventually died on the first day of shooting, leaving Monicelli the difficult task of rising to the occasion (interestingly enough, the film featured "death" as the conclusive point of the story). The story offered an atypical analysis of a Tuscan lifestyle: an epicurean vision of existence shared by five close friends, united in an indissoluble camaraderie and laughter that challenged the excessive gravity of life. Despite the adversity of social and political events in the country, the film focused on the value of unconditional friendship. The year 1975 was also the period that best evoked Italy's disillusion during the lead years, as it revealed one of the major sociological consequences, known as the *disimpegno* (lack of involvement in the community or society).

Mario Monicelli captured the rhythm of Tuscan life and the languor of the protagonists' daily lives in a way similar to Federico Fellini two decades before him with *I vitelloni* (1953). The nucleus of the clan was composed of Giorgio Perozzi,[14] a prominent journalist (French actor Philippe Noiret) working long hours at night; Count Rafaello Mascetti (Ugo Tognazzi), a destitute nobleman who survived the bankruptcy of his estate but can no longer provide for his wife and daughter, despite his inclination for luxury and underage mistresses; Rambaldo Melandri (Gastone Moschin), a municipal architect obsessed with finding the love of his life; and bar owner Guido Necchi (Duilio del Prete in the first act, then Renzo Montagnani for the second and third act). Finally, the last member to join the crew was Professor Sassaroli (Adolfo Celi), a well-off surgeon and unquestionably the most cynical member of the group.

As paradoxically as it may appear, the tribute to friendship also came with a demystification of its own image. In its eulogy of life, as a series of continuous playful moments, *Amici miei* also expressed a serious condemnation of infantilism, making it responsible for the annihilation of the friends' family lives (i.e., Perozzi

Philippe Noiret (Giorgio Perozzi) and Ugo Tognazzi (Lello Mascetti) in
Mario Monicelli's *My Friends* (*Amici miei I*, 1975)
Photo courtesy of BIFI

entertaining a relation with the baker's wife to escape the furies of his disapprov-
ing wife and son). What appeared to be most striking about these characters was
their inherent wariness for responsibility, their refusal to grow and integrate in
society. As best described by Alberto Cattini: "For this reason, the friends' behavior is always similar: defending themselves, against the world and against men,
they crystallized regression."[15] This ambience of pessimism and disillusion was
reinforced by Luigi Kuveiller's cinematography featuring a working class Florence
(light-years away from the sunny tourist postcards). Instead, it showed lead skies
and winter weather, including some authentic footage from the 1966 flood as the
signs of the time, as featured in Monicelli's *Romanzo popolare* two years earlier.

Like many comedy films of the decade, *Amici miei* was a prolific series of
random vignettes, succinct slices of life for this group of friends in search of
unadulterated camaraderie and comic relief. However, in this case, humor was
very much an idiosyncratic production, ruled by inertia, generated by a collective phenomenon: as soon as the protagonists entered the collective sphere,
the group's dynamics made it impossible to keep their sense of responsibility.
But more importantly, the film's humor cultivated (even nurtured at times) the
ancient art of *beffa*, a cruel and cynical practical humor—Tuscan style—going
back to the ancient roots of medieval farce dear to Boccaccio's *Decameron* or
the French *fabliaux*. To the cruelty involved in the development of certain
comic scenes, Monicelli defended his choice for cynical humor: "The lack of

compassion is a sign of intelligence: it is the one that sharpens the mind. This is how, between laughter and tragedy, I chose, and continue to choose, laughter."[16]

The five characters roamed around Florence and the hills of Tuscany, playing adolescent pranks in search of new sensations. Their actions were sequenced by a number of scenes now part of Italian popular culture: the notorious episode at the Florence train station Santa Maria Novella where our five "midlife adolescents" slapped the passengers of departing trains shouting "Buon viaggio!" as the latter look out over the train window. Perhaps the trademark of the film's humor could be best described through the invention of the juvenile art of the *supercazzola* perfected by Ugo Tognazzi in a discourse where nonsensical phrases served as a device to confuse perplexed interlocutors: Half-invented neologisms and half-regular Italian words composed the entire discourse, setting the communication in a state of total confusion. In the following hospital scene, Mascetti successfully manages to use a phone for free by confusing the nurse at the reception:

Mascetti: Mi scusi dei tre telefoni qual'è come se fosse tarapia tapioco che avverto la supercazzola? Dei tre…! Non mi ha capito bene, volevo dire dei tre telefoni qual'è quello col prefisso?(Excuse me, which of these three phones… [unintelligible]? Which one? I didn't make myself clear. I meant… which one to dial out?)

Sorella: Ah; quello lì! (Ah… this one!)

Mascetti: Grazie. Sorella, col tarapia tapioco come se fosse antani la barella anche per due con lo scappellamento a sinistra? No eh…? Pazienza… (Thanks. Sister… [unintelligible]? No? Let's wait….)

The other innovation, which subjugated popular audiences at the time, was known as the *zingarata* (occasional "gypsy" outings). These were aimless wandering escapades without objective, planning, or rules. One day, the protagonists drove to a remote Tuscan village pretending to be surveyors sent by the region of Tuscany. They parked their car on the main square of the village, under the mystified gaze of the local population. As they set up several pieces of survey equipment, exchanging out loud some invented technical jargon in order to guarantee the authenticity of their intervention, they began to slate numerous buildings for demolition to give space for a future interstate. They marked crosses with chalk on the doors of the condemned buildings (even the church was designated to be demolished). As the wind of panic began to swirl among the villagers and town priest, they departed with a sense of mission accomplished. If the neologism *zingarata* was a success on the screen, the label never convinced critics nor the director himself, as Mario Monicelli explained: "I was against the term *zingarata*. It sounded too romantic, but also too silly, since the basic tone of the film was really desperate."[17] Another of the most memorable practical jokes (this time occurring in *Amici miei, atto II*) was the "rescue" of the Tower of Pisa. Once again

The rescue operation of the Tower of Pisa in Mario Monicelli's
My Friends II (*Amici miei, atto II*, 1982)

loaded with equipment and a truck displaying "Servizio Torre," the group pretended to be the official engineering crew of the historical tower. As they arrived on site, they created a chaotic climate of emergency, claiming that the tower was about to collapse. Shouting in their loud speakers, they required immediate assistance from the hundreds of tourists present on site at that moment. To avoid a collapse, they assembled several human lines in a tug-of-war style to pull on ropes in order to invert the inclination. On the other side of the tower, they placed dozens who pushed on long poles. They even succeeded in placing some Japanese tourists inside the tower to counterbalance the inclination. As the police siren closed in, our "heroes" jumped in their truck and vanished in the traffic. Still in the same sequel, the group decided to participate in a voice contest organized by the Music Academy in Arezzo. Once on stage, the quintet began to perform a piece taken from the Barber of Seville. But after the jury and public (among which were dignitaries from the city hall and church) realized that the words had been substituted for highly inappropriate foul language and obscene content, our neophyte singers ran for their lives as the infuriated crowd threatened to call the police.[18] The most sophisticated *zingarata* featured in *Amici miei, atto I* was the forced "enrollment" of Niccolò Righi (French actor Bernard Blier), an introverted retired citizen who regularly took advantage of Necchi's bar by eating pastries without paying for them. To retaliate, the group decided to lure him into their lucrative "drug organization." They presented him to the big boss (Sassaroli) and got him involved in some cocaine smuggling operations (actually bags of sugar) and several fake fire exchanges supposedly involving the rival gang known as the *Marsigliesi*. Once the joke needed to reach its conclusion, they decided to send him away by train to Calabria dressed as a monk, since he was then wanted by the rival drug dealers. Perozzi as head of the chronicles section was able to print a fake page in the newspaper *La Nazione* featuring Righi's mug shot, thus proving he was a wanted man.

Despite the immense popular success, many critics at the time deplored the content of the film's scenario for relentlessly implementing an unnecessary dose of offensive language, which, according to them, affected the quality of the comedy. To this, Monicelli explained the fundamental nature of Tuscan *beffa*:

> The *beffa* is always vulgar…. The Tuscan is vulgar…. A comedy without foul language was unthinkable, by then a part of the common language. To have actors speak with a contrived language would have lessened the strength of the comedy, which starts from the populous and breathes reality. Vulgarity is necessary. It becomes the element around which the protagonists' friendship is built, which makes them establish a camaraderie rite based on a limitless collegiality.[19]

If *Amici miei* offered a high frequency of gags and laughter thanks to its episodic structure and countless pranks, it was at the same time contaminated with numerous traits of melancholy and sadness, and although all the protagonists remained comical to the end, they also possessed an inherent dimension of bitterness and pathos. As every act of rebellion must reach its epilogue, a tangible veil of sadness fell upon the group, as the specter of potential death slowly approached. The need to generate laughter, irony, and cynicism in order to push back the image of death was at the center of the film's rationale. Like many other satirical comedies of the decade, disenchantment and loss of hope, which characterized Italy during these difficult years, permeated the *commedia all'italiana*. Here the complicity of the group dynamics served as a response to the existential crisis generated by the unsympathetic environment. While enjoying the benefits of a comfortable existence, the five characters were, however, experiencing the contradictions of a normal existence versus a nostalgia toward juvenile desires, whose missing gap (the affective one) was provided by the circle of brotherhood often materialized by the escape from family and work. Laughter and tears, irony and anger coexisted in perfect harmony until the last scene of the film. Death was the only "stage of existence" to take seriously, since life did not deserve to be taken seriously. Even the loss of one's own life, to a certain extent, the ultimate solitary act par excellence, was part of a strategy of confrontation as illustrated in the memorable scene when Perozzi, on the brink of death following a heart attack, received from the priest the last sacraments:

> Priest: Dimmi figliolo. (Tell me, my son.)
> Perozzi: Sbiriguda veniale, la supercazzola prematurata. (*Unintelligible.*)
> Priest: Come figliolo? (Pardon me, son?)
> Perozzi: Come fosse antani, con scappellamento a destra. Ostantinato malliti. (*Unintelligible.*)

Priest: Quante volte figliolo? (How many times, son?)

Perozzi: Fifty fifty come fosse mea culpa, alla supercazzola. (*Unintelligible.*)

Priest: Io ti assolvo dai tuoi peccati nel nome del padre, del figlio. (I absolve you, in the name of the father, the son.)

In homage of Germi's legacy, Monicelli pushed the logic even further by upholding the symbol of death with the funeral, but this time through the comic lens. After the mourners exit the church, Righi, who happens to pass by, inquired about Perozzi's fate. Seizing the opportunity, Necchi answers him with the ultimate practical joke: "He was a traitor," and Mascetti adds, "We had to eliminate him." As Righi expresses his profound dismay and emotion, the rest of the group has no choice but to burst into laughter while the rest of the crowd stares at them bemused. For Monicelli, the choice to associate humor with the funeral was obvious: "To me, funerals are the most exhilarating thing there is. I go to my friends' funerals because when I see my other friends, I start to joke about their upcoming mortality. That type of humor is rather amusing, not macabre."[20] To the authors of the film, the act of exorcizing death through humor, whether in real life or on the screen, was the ultimate opportunity for derision—even of the self. In a certain way, it was the obvious device to prolong the state of childhood happiness by dodging the responsibilities and vicissitudes of a dreary adult life, even the grim image of death. Here, the general audience was dealing with a rather uncommon conclusion, the precariousness of a humanity without real prospective, far from the happy ending of the Italian comedies of the 1950s and its customary uplifting dimension.

Could the *commedia all'italiana* come to an end? This question seems to be the conclusion of Monicelli's saga. It is a tradition that comes from the ancient patterns of the *commedia dell'arte* and rejuvenates itself with every generation as long as it continues to describe a genuine reality. Under the façade of a story that many spectators and critics might have perceived as a simple tale of friendship, Monicelli delivered a realistic social analysis of Italy unlike anything contemporary spectators had seen. The film was very well received,[21] and its sequel seven years later (*Amici miei, atto II*, 1982, again directed by Monicelli) experienced the same fortune, unlike the third part (*Amici miei, atto III*, 1985) directed by Nanni Loy, which clearly lacked stamina and inspiration.

The year 1976 saw the progression of the left-wing political forces at the regional and parliamentary elections, thus reflecting a historical decline in the longevity of the Christian Democrats. At the same time, the rise of unemployment among the urban population, and in particular among the youth, consequently generated an unprecedented phenomenon of urban violence. In some ways, the working class on one side and the bourgeoisie and middle class on the other became the major actors of urban settings, especially in light of social conflicts. Monicelli's *An Average Little Man* (*Un borghese piccolo*

Vincenzo Crocitti (Mario Vivaldi) and Alberto Sordi (Giovanni Vivaldi) in
Mario Monicelli's *An Average Little Man* (*Un borghese piccolo piccolo*, 1977)

piccolo, 1977) offered a uniquely genuine fictional rendering of a dramatic
reality through the dark lens of tragicomedy; Monicelli defined it himself as
"a step toward the absurd whose grotesque element coincides with despair and
solitude."[22]

Giovanni Vivaldi (Alberto Sordi), a veteran accountant, has spent an entire
lifetime working for the public administration in Rome,[23] and he is just a few
months away from retirement. With his wife Amalia (Shelley Winters), he hopes
to have their only son Mario (Vincenzo Crocitti) start a career in the same profession. In his numerous attempts to help his son find employment in his administration, Giovanni must go through several delicate initiatives, even enrolling
in a Masonic Lodge without which no promotion would be possible inside the
gigantic administration. During a humiliating and bizarre initiation ritual, he
finds out, much to his dismay, that almost everyone working in the ministry is
a member of this strange but powerful fraternity. He finally secures the promise
to get the subject of the public examination. On the way to the long-awaited
examination, Mario is accidentally killed by bank robbers during a fire exchange
with security forces in broad daylight. Devastated, Giovanni is at a loss, torn
between mourning and hate. To make matters worse, Giovanni's wife, hit by a
stroke, remains an invalid in a wheelchair and can no longer speak. He begins
his solitary enterprise by attending the identification process at the police station. He recognizes his son's murderer but pretends not to, so as to follow the
murderer on his way home and take justice into his own hands. One rainy night,
Giovanni locates the man repairing his car on a parking lot and hits him from
behind with a wrench. He swiftly puts his unconscious victim inside his trunk
and drives off to his countryside cabin, where he attaches him to a chair with

a metallic string around his throat. A few days later, the young man dies by suffocation. Ironically, the day Giovanni is eligible for retirement, his wife passes away, leaving him more isolated than ever. Resigned to his own fate, Giovanni continues his now futile existence, hiding inside his apparently innocuous "Dr. Jekyll and Mr. Hyde" personality, the rage of a recidivist killer.[24]

This dark social comedy was without a doubt Monicelli's most pessimistic and tragic comedy, as the film indirectly reflected some of the violent incidents occurring on a regular basis in the 1970s throughout Italy. Monicelli's personal commitment to include a political element in his comedies was prompted by the growing social deterioration of the second half of the decade (acts of terrorism, kidnapping, and bombings were legion). In addition, Monicelli's desire to take on contemporary social themes within an Italian "commercial" context (as opposed to a more predictable intellectual approach) was convincing enough. The movie was less interested in the direct political implications of the kidnapping than in the way its consequences revealed the relations between Mario and Giovanni, as well as the intricate reasons that pushed an ordinary civil servant to go on a vindictive rampage after losing his only son.[25]

Many film historians until recently had more or less hastily cataloged *Un borghese piccolo piccolo* as the conclusive chapter of a decade of satirical comedies as well as the final testament of the entire *commedia all'italiana* experience. To them, the scarcity of prolific comedic subject was a sign of change. There was no longer any material to laugh about, any character to take into derision, and it was time to turn the page of the comedy Italian style. However, Monicelli never agreed with the statement that his film was the death warrant of the *commedia all'italiana*, but rather underlined the fact that it corresponded, according to him, to a beginning of a long overdue mutation process leading to a brand new type of comic film in the 1980s. Although it may be impossible to argue in favor or against either side of the argument, the irreversible loss of faith in Italian comedies made its possible rejuvenation a difficult task, as the new generation of Italian comic actors and directors took a radically new orientation in the early eighties.

One of the fundamental questions often omitted by film critics was the true disposition of comedy filmmakers in the last years of the decade (Luigi Comencini's *L'ingorgo: una storia impossiblile*, Ettore Scola's *La terrazza*, etc.). Were the comedies purposely including an element of drama, or were the films in question essentially dramas with a reminiscent flavor of a comedy Italian style? Monicelli actually set aside the traditional social satire that had been for years his cinematographic trademark for a more invested goal: *cinema impegnato*. The reason why the film was never classified a drama was simply the overwhelming casual presence of the individuality of Alberto Sordi. In its logic, the choice for the main role was a judicious one in the sense that comic elements and tragic figures have always been an indivisible dimension of his own inherent personality. Vivaldi's character was no exception, but in addition, corresponded to the emblematic figure of Italy's transformation, as his personality evolved from opti-mism to despair, a parallel phenomenon that the entire nation experienced fol-lowing the years of the postboom era and the beginning of the lead years, along with its deadly toll.

In sum, Mario Monicelli's *Un borghese piccolo piccolo* can be considered an important contribution to the *commedia all'italiana,* as it brought an element of diversity in content as well as form. Reminiscent of Dino Risi's *I mostri* (1963), and in particular the episode entitled "Educazione sentimentale" exploring the limits of the father-son relationship, *Un borghese piccolo piccolo* contemplated a similar subject (Ugo Tognazzi in Risi's *I mostri* reminding his seven-year-old son that "I poveri non esistono" ["Poor people don't exist"] or "Chi picchia per prima picchia due volte" ["Whoever hits first, gets to hit twice"], "Mai fidarsi di nes-suno, nemmeno di tuo padre" ["Never trust anyone in life, even your father"]). Alberto Sordi assimilated the discourse of distrust in a similar manner as he reminds his son not to think of others in life and to protect his individualism before anything. The most dominant element of the film's message, beyond the obvious condemnation of blind violence, was the director's ideological critique of an entire country for neglecting the rising social problems, eventually deterio-rating the political climate. The average Italian's absence of social engagement, self-contented by growing *menefreghismo,* inspired Monicelli to direct his attack against excessive individualism generated by the disorganization of social life (also present a few years earlier in Luigi Zampa's *Il medico della mutua,* 1968).

Luigi Comencini: The End of an Era

Like Monicelli, Luigi Comencini's name is often associated with the terminal phase of the *commedia all'italiana.* Along with Monicelli's *Un borghese piccolo piccolo,* Comencini's *Bottleneck (L'ingorgo,* 1979) serves as an illustrative epi-logue of twenty years of affluent comedy, in large part due to the inverted nature of the comedy itself and the overwhelming presence of latent drama, cynicism, and even violence. Born in the notoriously famous city of Salò, near Brescia, in 1916, Comencini, along with filmmakers Alberto Lattuada and Mario Ferrari, founded the *Cineteca Italiana* in Milan in 1947. During the same year, he obtained his first recognition, a Nastro d'Argento, for *Bambini in città,* with Best Italian Short Film. Comencini obtained his very first national success in 1949 with Totò in *L'imperatore di Capri.* Directing many famous Italian actors, such as Vittorio De Sica, Totò, Alberto Sordi, Gina Lollobrigida, and Marcello Mastroianni, Comencini was one of the forefathers of the *neorealismo rosa* (although at times erroneously labeled the creator of the *commedia all'italiana)* with the famous *Bread, Love and Dreams (Pane, amore e fantasia,* 1953) fol-lowed by the sequel *Bread, Love and Jealousy (Pane, amore e gelosia,* 1954). A few years later, he joined the movement of *commedia all'italiana* initiated by

Risi and Monicelli with one of his most important films, *Everybody Go Home* (*Tutti a casa*, 1960), followed by more or less fortunate productions, such as *On the Tiger's Back* (*A cavallo della tigre*, 1961), *Il commissario* (1962), and *L'incompreso* (1967). However, it is in the 1970s that Comencini's contribution to the genre of comedy Italian style proved decisive, as he began to express an inclination toward comedies that included a substantial dose of pessimism, bitterness, even grotesqueness, all inherent of his own style. The manisfesto of the genre, *The Scientific Card Game* (*Lo scopone scientifico*, 1972), paved the way for many imitations of this popular comedy. His next films, *The Sunday Woman* (*La donna della domenica*, 1975), *Strange Occasion* (*Quelle strane occasioni*, 1976), and finally *Bottleneck* (*L'ingorgo: una storia impossibile*, 1979) concluded two decades of an impressive list of comedies, all faithful satires of the Italian people. In 1987, he received the prestigious *Leone d'oro alla carriera* at the Venice Film Festival. Comencini's comedic talent, though under the influence of implicit filmmaking, offered a relentless and persuasive depiction of Italian society, a severe rendering of Italian people and their social flaws, through comedy.

In 1972, Luigi Comencini directed his most successful comedy of the decade. Ten years after the seminal *Tutti a casa*, *Lo scopone scientifico* broke new ground in the realm of cynicism and melodramatic comedy. The metaphor of the card game was the ideal device for narrating the dialectical battle between rich and poor, with the humble ones destined to eternally delude themselves into false hope. Written by screenwriter Rodolfo Sonego and based on an actual event that he had witnessed in Naples in 1947,[26] the narrative privileged the confrontation of human and social contrast. The story is a fable featuring a couple of Roman proletarians who live in a slum of Rome's periphery. A ragman, Peppino (Alberto Sordi), and his wife Antonia (Silvana Mangano)[27] wait impatiently each spring in May for the arrival of Amalia, an old American millionaire (Bette Davis), and her private secretary/chauffeur and ex-husband George (Joseph Cotten who visibly embodied the character of Eric von Stroheim in Billy Wilder's *Sunset Boulevard* in 1950) who regularly spend a few days in Rome in a luxurious villa rented for the occasion. For the past eight years, she invites the naïve couple to play her favorite card game called the *Scopone Scientifico*, a type of *Scopa*, a game based on memory and strategy; but she wins every time, thus shattering their dream of becoming rich. As soon as the millionaire's plane lands in Rome, the entire slum community enters a state of agitation and celebrates the prospect of the future victory. Peppino's dream is to become owner of the junkyard where he works and to give his four children a decent life, access to college, and no longer work for the local funeral homes (assembling funerary crowns and mortuary cleanups). The couple has trained all year for this moment, hoping for payback time. As expected, the old millionaire calls them, and the same evening they arrive in their *Apepiaggio* (motorized tricycle) at the mansion. To appear elegant for the event, Antonia wears an evening gown found the same day in an abandoned basement, and Peppino borrows the black suit from Osvaldo, the town funerary employee. As usual, and in order to get the game started, Amalia grants them an illusory stake of one million lira in order to begin the game. The couple wins several games in a row until they lose one and have no more money to continue. Their dream once more shattered, their only hope is to win the following day. The following evening they lose again, this time 20,000 lire in debt, and Antonia is compelled to ask for a cash advance from Righetto (Domenico Modugno), a former suitor and team partner who is also a highly "unethical" professional card player. The next evening, they finally win seven million until the old Amalia, too weak to continue, decides to withdraw from the game. Back in the slum, the community celebrates Peppino and Antonia and their historical victory. To satisfy the hysterical crowd, Peppino exhibits the 100,000 lira banknotes out of a grocery bag. But the celebration is short-lived, as the local bar receives a phone call: the old millionaire has regained consciousness and wants to continue the game. The dilemma is clear: if they refuse to play and keep the cash, they may no longer be invited to play cards in the future. Pressured by the community, they drive back to the mansion and resume the game with their precarious seven million. The odds seem in their favor as the old lady can barely function and asks to move the game to her own bed since she is too weak to sit in her wheelchair. After an entire night of success (winning 448 million)

Alberto Sordi (Peppino), Silvana Mangano (Antonia),
Bette Davis (Amalia), and Joseph Cotten (George) in Luigi Comencini's
The Scientific Card Player (*Lo scopone scientifico,* 1972)
Photo courtesy of BIFI

and suspense, they eventually lose the whole game due to a gross error from Peppino. In tears, Antonia swears to no longer play with Peppino and teams up with Righetto for a last game before the millionaire's departure back to America. For this last occasion, the community gathers more than one million lira and put its faith in the new team, leaving Peppino dishonored at home. As the game proceeds, news of their skills become known as the new team wins tirelessly 300 million, 400, half a billion, until suddenly no more news from the mansion. An hour later, Righetto attempts suicide in the Tiber river as his honor and reputation are gone following the loss of the game. To make matters worse, Antonia has also even accrued a debt of 300,000 lire that will need to be paid to the American millionaire the day of her departure at the airport, hoping she will refuse. The next day at the gate, the entire family shows up to salute Amalia and George. As Peppino gives her the bagful of coins and bills, Amalia kindly turns down their offer but as Peppino carelessly insists, she offers to gamble the money and takes out a game of cards from her handbag and wins. As the old millionaire says goodbye, Cleopatra, who decided to end the vicious cycle of everlasting misery, offers her a cake she baked filled with rat poison to eat on the plane.

In the *Scopone scientifico*, contrasting characterization was of prime importance. Initially introduced as a rather magnanimous benefactor, Bette Davis' character (the American legend played here one of her very last great film refer) gradually took the shape of cruelty and evil. As the story unfolds, her past existence is slowly revealed. Even on the brink of death, the old millionaire expresses her only wish with a diabolical voice: "I want to play cards!" to the dismay of her entourage. Her ultimate motivation is to accomplish the simple goal of winning and ultimately recuperating the seven million lira that Peppino and Antonia have "taken away" from her safe. Here, Comencini's characters are already conditioned by their inherent desire: the rich do not want to lose their money and the poor do not want to become poorer. In an interview with film scholar Lorenzo Codelli, Comencini explained that the film's spectator was in a certain manner always "attracted by the element of the game, the gain, the loss: it is the emotion of which he identifies with the lottery winner."[28] Here the fable's ultimate message implicitly reminded spectators that the poor, though being wholeheartedly part of a game, will keep losing as long as they keep playing. The film's other screenwriter Rodolfo Sonego[29] once said about the human nature of the story:

> The first thing one learns from the film is that the common man is not rational, but emotional, while the person with power is rational, very good at acting, and therefore an excellent psychologist.[30]

Around the card table, there is no friendship or temporary unity, simply an ephemeral illusion of ownership. Despite the numerous assertions of camaraderie, the poor are obsessed with the millionaire's money, not her friendship nor her personality. At the same time, Amalia does not want to know about their misery, as she is obsessed with winning and indirectly confirming the social order to which she belongs: the poor must lose. As Righetto, the professional card player, explains in the film: the poor will never be able to win, since the rules of the game are imposed in advance by the dominating forces and therefore to its own profit. By accepting the rules, Peppino and Antonia indirectly recognize their announced failure. Since the millionaire has an endless financial reserve, she could afford to lose repeatedly (almost endlessly). As for our two heroes, one mistake and they lose everything. It is their naive honesty that digs their own grave. Only the daughter, Cleopatra, is able to push the fiction's vicious course until the end, with the physical elimination of the American millionaire.

Labeled the *regista dell'infanzia*, Luigi Comencini was usually interested in documentary type productions, especially in comedies that focused on children's potential and their capacity for revolt in order to vindicate parents' frustration. In the *Scopone*, the true protagonists of the film were, as expected, the children with their naive gazes, their disenchanted discourse, and their just vision of reality, unlike the adults: "Qui stamo a lavorà, non stamo mica a giocà!" ("We're here to work, we're not here to play!") The character of Cleopatra (Comencini's favorite in the film), the oldest of Peppino and Antonia's children, symbolized the new generation, different than her parents', having grown up during the difficult years of the war and used to obeying the social order. The new generation was here epitomized in the very last scene of the narrative in a discourse of violence, as Cleopatra emblematically corresponded to the terrorist actions occurring in Italy during the decade; she does not share the same illusions that torment her parents. About the character of Cleopatra, Comencini said:

> The girl is the only one to know the truth. In fact, I paid a great deal of attention to this girl, and I think it is obvious. She has a precise sense of reality; she sees things as they are; she does not live in the same illusion as her family and the entire social web from the slum where she lives: an illusion that drives everyone to insanity.[31]

Often misconstrued as a simple tale about rich versus poor with its powerful allegories against the effect of poverty, *Lo scopone scientifico* also featured a disquieting representation of human tragedy that ran parallel to children's desires to construct their own hopes. With the experience of poverty in the slums of Rome, the image of the four children was represented on the screen with more realism and a total absence of protected environment; the children, and in particular Cleopatra, were the icons of social sufferance. Comencini's visual approach and the screenplay created a convincing arrangement set between documentary, idyllic neorealism, and of course, a *soupcon* of film noir. Sometimes considered too manicheist in its contrast between an intolerant adult world and the innocence of childhood (notably once recentered on the proletarian background), the story denounced the adults, often described as uneducated and careless or literate but cruel (Bette Davis shares her photo album and proudly taunts all the "poor" victims around the world she beat playing cards).

The representation of life, here reduced to the dimension of a card table, offered a rather pessimistic conclusion, as there seemed to be no real recourse to the spiral of power and money. The only hope the poor can have was temporary expedients in order to survive in a capitalistic society. The pernicious power of money and its illusory aura, morally justified by society, created an endless conflict, dividing people from diverse social classes as well as from the same group, jeopardizing family life and trust in others, and leading to lies and deceit for one's own survival. In these early years of the decade, rife with violence and political turmoil throughout Italy, Comencini's film could easily be seen as a metaphor against American imperialism and the power of international finance that seemed to subdue the naïveté of the proletarian and the working class in general.

Looking back in film history, and in particular over the years before Italian neorealism, the character of the child was often the ignorant victim of reality and of the adult world (i.e., Vittorio de Sica's *Children are Watching Us* [*I bambini ci guardano*, 1943]). Then with the advent of neorealism, the image changed toward a new status, one of awareness and determination, without, however, thoroughly losing their identity as children. While the child remained a victim, with neorealism he/she became aware of being victimized (Roberto Rossellini's *Open City* [*Roma, città aperta*, 1945] and *Germany, Year Zero* [*Germania anno zero*, 1947]; Vittorio De Sica's *Shoeshine* [*Sciuscià*, 1946] and *The Bicycle Thief* [*Ladri di biciclette*, 1948]). With Comencini and the *commedia all'italiana*, the

Stefania Sandrelli (Donatella) and Alberto Sordi (Monsignore Ascanio La Costa) in the episode "L'ascensore" in Luigi Comencini's *Quelle strane occasioni* (1976)

representation of children, observed with great meticulousness, opened a new sphere in the realist narration, since the children, in particular Cleopatra, as the eldest, were capable of challenging adults' common sense in a significant way. For Comencini, childhood was one essential domain, a critical point of reference, in both time and space. In contrast to the vision of Italian neorealist directors such as Luchino Visconti (*La terra trema* [*The Earth Trembles*, 1948]), whose representations of children were usually prompted through manicheistic imagery of childhood purity versus adult corruption, Comencini's rendering of youth turned away from the Italian neorealist vision. In its nonsentimentalized revelation of the children's world, the film underscored that while that world may not be as tarnished as the adult's, children's quest for escape would lead them through hazardous paths filled with corruption and cynicism. With an extemporaneous script, the exploration of social misery in the slums of Rome went beyond the innocence of childhood to create a world of freedom according to children's own social observations.

Tragic human experience was represented as a given event, and child protagonists were directed in "optical situations" to its very best. They saw and learned how to see, but were also overwhelmed by what they could not comprehend (or experiment), to which they could only respond with their actions. As the older child, responsible for house chores, Cleopatra was to assimilate the quotidian experience through an exterior eye, the position of a so-called eyewitness. She observed adults without understanding them, but seemed to remember the origins of any given event or movement in the story. Therefore, one of the kinetic functions of the child was to involuntarily carry the burden of signification. This symbolic function of the kinetic child, which has been the subject of much research, usually presented children as a passive being surrounded and even overwhelmed by a world, which observed him/her ruthlessly. With Comencini, the interpretative gaze cannot entirely be unveiled, nor catalogued, much less erased by surrounding adults: the child becomes conscious, active, going so far as to take the family's destiny into her own hands.[32]

A few years later, in an episode of a film entitled *Quelle strane occasioni* (1976), Luigi Comencini's segment "*L'ascensore*" proposed an experimental satirical allegory with a visible dose of anticlericalism very much in tune with contemporary liberalization of sexuality. Similar to *Swept Away*, *Il sorpasso*, and *Profumo di donna*, the scenario involved two radically opposite individuals caught on a journey or in a limited space with a cathartic ending. The most dominant indictment of the film was its derisive dimension toward the priests' presupposed sexual phobia inculcated by twenty centuries of Catholicism.

A bishop, Monsignor Ascanio La Costa (Alberto Sordi), remains stuck inside an elevator in the company of a young attractive woman, Donatella (Stefania Sandrelli), the day before *Ferragosto* (one of Italy's most religious holidays, also illustrated a decade earlier with Dino Risi's *Il sorpasso*). Since no one is present in the apartment building, they must arm themselves with patience. Due to the claustrophobic environment, they both engage in conversation in order to while the time away. At first, Donatella makes no effort to hide her revulsion for the Catholic Church and the hypocrisy of its priests. She blames her misfortune on his own presence: "*Io le corna le ho fatte a questa tonacacia nera che mi ha sempre portata jella*." ("It is your ugly black gown that has always brought bad luck to me.") Suddenly their argument is interrupted by the voice of two car thieves who, while attempting to steal the priest's luxurious Mercedes, pledge to secure help for the two protagonists. Their hope fades when they suddenly hear the alarm of the car going off and understand they are dealing with thieves. Resigned to their own fate, they resume their difficult conversation by sharing Donatella's picnic (originally intended for the day she was to spend on the beach in the company of her boyfriend). While their spirit gets loose and congenial, she opens up, to the priest's greatest delight. And as the temperature rises inside the elevator, she even takes off her clothes, wearing only her bathing suit. Later in the night, they both begin to share the story of their lives, and Donatella eventually narrates her first encounter with her boyfriend, eventually disclosing some intimate details on their first sexual relation. On several occasions, she stops short in her account, realizing the inappropriate nature of the conversation's content. But much to her surprise, the bishop is far from being shocked, as he begs her:

> "Un prete non si stupisce di nulla! Nemmeno se tu mi dici che l'hai assassinato. Avanti sù, che cosa hai fatto a quel ragazzo? Avanti. Dimmi, dimmi, dimmi, dimmi tutto!" (A priest is not surprised by anything! Not even if you told me that you killed him. Come on, what did you do to that young man? Come on, tell me, tell me, tell me everything!)

Later, Donatella narrates a strange event she had witnessed in the apartment building months before. Following the funeral of one of the residents, the widow entertained a guest the very same night. While taking a bath in her apartment located a floor above, Donatella was able to hear their conversation by putting her head under water. While the evening began with casual conversation with the man apparently trying to console the widow, the evening proceeded with far fewer verbal exchanges and long silent intervals (including noises such as the bed creaking and female moaning). Aroused by this erotically charged story, the priest took advantage of a sudden power outage to engage in a physical rapport with Donatella in the dark. As the light comes back, the priest, already pressured by the weight of his sin, engages in a long pseudophilosophical lecture on "free will," making a point that in theory nothing had happened between them. Since caught inside an elevator, and therefore precluded of controlling their destiny, they had lost (in theory and reality) their "free will," unable to decide their actions. Therefore, whatever happened inside the elevator should remain inside the elevator. The priest even goes as far as to offer, "E allora mia cara ragazza, io l'assolvo senza alcuna penitenza" (I absolve you without penitence), leaving the girl quite confused. Finally, the janitor comes and resets the elevator, putting an end to hours of entrapment. As they both depart, the priest makes sure to give Donatella his business card for a possible future rendezvous. The last scene of the story pictures Sordi inside the apartment of his host Signora Adami, no less than the widow featured in Donatella's earlier story. Finding out the details of his elevator predicament, she ventures asking:

> Widow Adami: Senti un pò, con quella lì nell'ascensore cos'è successo? (Tell me something, what happened with that one in the elevator?)
>
> Monsignor La Costa: Niente. Non è successo niente. (Nothing. Nothing happened.)

A few years later, Luigi Comencini directed one of the most important and complex films he ever made: *L'ingorgo: una storia impossibile,* inspired by a short novel from Julio Cortazar entitled *La autopista del sur* (1964). The script, written by Ruggero Maccari and Bernardino Zapponi, along with Comencini himself, offered a broad indictment of consumerism, politics, and everything about capitalistic society in general. Although Comencini's criticisms and observations on materialistic society were nothing unique in Italian comic cinema (see Risi's *Una vita difficile* or Monicelli's *Romanzo popolare*), the narration, made of numerous episodic confrontations, was quite unique in its delivery.

The story did not have a single plot, but rather a myriad of subplots, all interacting with one another during a thirty-six-hour traffic jam somewhere between Rome and Naples. All of the protagonists, representing different classes and regions of Italian society, were the quintessential substance of the story. To illustrate the deep malaise of the Italian consumer society, the narrative frame was organized in a series of confrontations between Rome and Naples, all of which appeared through the rhetoric of myriad situations involving an impressive number of famous actors. The all-star European cast included a corrupt lawyer in search of financial and political power (Alberto Sordi); a famous actor, Montefoschi (Marcello Mastroianni); a midlife couple in search of rejuvenating their relationship (French actress Annie Girardot with her Spanish counterpart Fernando Rey); a *ménage à trois* (Ugo Tognazzi, Miou Miou, Gérard Depardieu); a solitary bachelor (Patrick Dewaere); and a pregnant woman (Stefania Sandrelli) who uses her charms to seduce the famous actor in order to secure a better job at Cinecittà for her husband.

In a certain way, Comencini's episodic style corresponded to a deconstruction of various genres: vaudeville, satire, melodrama, and politically charged chronicles of a difficult decade, all of which were filled with symbolism and toned-down meaning. Indeed, the numerous plot fragmentations appearing throughout the story (betrayals, conspiracies to murder, gang rape, intimate and comic sexual anecdotes) rendered a colorful mix of moral and cultural juxtapositions, underscoring the deep discrepancies present within Italian society of the 1970s.

As an uncompromisingly satirical film, somewhat reminiscent of the anti-bourgeois works of Luis Buñuel, *L'ingorgo* was an explicit indictment of capitalist values. To this date, only a handful of films have been able to effectively capture the vehement rage and brooding resentment toward the modern, excessive consumer society. It was obvious that Comencini battled his feelings about society directly through the camera lens, and one of the best examples was the scene involving the "Communist" priest (José Sacristan), who revealed his major attacks. During the agonizing wait, a patient (Ciccio Ingrassia) in an ambulance dies. A priest is immediately called into the vehicle in order to administer the last sacraments. The liturgy is singular, to say the least.

> Lord, we thank you for calling and sheltering this man, removing him from the disasters of this world. Save us, O lord, from plastic products. Save us from radioactive waste. Save us from the politics of power. Save us from multinationals. Save us from the reason of state. Save us from parades, uniforms, and military marches. Save us from the scorn of the weak. Save us from the myth of efficiency and productivity. Save us from false morality. Save us from lies and propaganda. Respect nature, love life. Copulate carnally in the respect of the next. Fornication is not a sin if done with love, amen.[33]

Interestingly enough, the strongest metaphor of the fiasco and potential fall of capitalism was illustrated through the intricate congestion of its self-generated

Ugo Tognazzi (the professor), Miou-Miou (Angela), and
Gérard Depardieu (Franco) in Luigi Comencini's *Bottleneck*
(*L'ingorgo: una storia impossibile*, 1979)

traffic jam: a bumper-to-bumper carnival of cars, honking, careening, crashing, roaring powerless with their grotesque occupants who, to insure their own survival, will be compelled to consume jars of baby food.

While most road movies were accustomed to wide-open roads (i.e., Dino Risi's *Il sorpasso*), an infinite space of empty road in the midst of nature, Comencini eliminated the freedom and isolation by showing a packed over-crowded highway that was more likely to create trouble than permit escape. The traffic jam was the perfect metaphor for society's nightmares gathered in a single limited space (a sort of modern-day unity of space and time in the style of ancient Greek tragedies). In addition, the car,[34] symbol of social mobility in the 1960s, was here clearly depicted as the place for immobility, selfishness, social protection, and refuge for cowards (it was a deliberate choice to locate the story in front of a junkyard filled with wrecks of cars as well as on a highway, symbol of the economic boom).

The representation of violence in *L'ingorgo* was also innovative in the production design's visual style. With the use of a semirural highway in between abandoned bridge construction, the world all of a sudden became more chaotic, and the film itself became just as anarchic as the violent world it depicted. In addition to the satire of destitute capitalism, the film was a form of satire intense enough to border on sheer brutality. Its message was clear: contemporaneous monsters are among us and also within each one of us. Every hour that passes, the angry crowd gets more and more frustrated, in search of food and therefore increasingly violent, in turn cultivating their own aggressive tendencies. Many people, oblivious to the concerns of the screaming masses around them, honk impatiently at the traffic congestion, blind with rage. Comencini constructed

A scene from Luigi Comencini's *Bottleneck*
(*L'ingorgo: una storia impossibile*, 1979)

a film steeped in violence, not just in subject matter, but in its episodic representation. The climax of violence occurred during a rape scene where three men take advantage of the obscurity to surprise a young woman in her sleep. In this paroxysm of horror, the center of interest lies in the nonreaction of the passengers, all pretending to sleep in order to avoid confrontation with the rapists. As a matter of fact, the young truck driver, the victim's companion, seemed to be the only protagonist with a dose of genuine humanity. He was about to set fire in retaliation to the vehicle of the three men who raped his friend, then stopped short, thinking of the children asleep in the cars next to it.

The monstrous society was caught through the lens of cynicism and, in a certain way, dire pessimism with the scene of the water bottle. Caught by the agonizing wait in the summer heat, businessman and lawmaker De Benedetti (Alberto Sordi) accompanied by Ferretti, his secretary and chauffeur (Orazio Orlando), are in desperate search for water, as they ran out of the champagne usually available in the luxurious Jaguar.[35] As they witness a modest Neapolitan family happily drinking mineral water, Feretti is sent to offer money in exchange for the bottle. Much to his surprise, they offer the bottle amiably, for free. Back inside the car, he explains to his boss the family's refusal to accept any money for the bottle. After pulling up his electric window to get privacy, De Benedetti bursts out in anger:

De Benedetti: Why didn't you pay them? I like to pay for things.
Ferretti: They didn't want anything. They are poor but good people.
De Benedetti : You don't understand a dammed thing if you say poor but good people. Poor people are never good people.
Ferretti: What can I do?
De Benedetti : Anything. They hate us![36]

In concern for equity, Comencini also returned to the rich/poor pattern and proposed a similar scene with the famous actor Marco Montefoschi (Marcello Mastroianni) who, attempting to escape the oppression from admirers and the promiscuity of the crowd, is escorted to a humble dwelling on the side of the road. The couple offers him dinner and a bedroom for him to rest. However, the husband seizes the opportunity to exchange his pregnant wife's favors (Stefania Sandrelli) for a chauffeur's job at the Cinecittà movie studios. The next morning when it is time to depart, the husband indirectly reminded the reluctant actor of his favor. "Non è vero. Io non ci credo. Io vengo a trovarla a Cinecittà dottore. Io la trovo… e io la trovo." ("It's not true. I don't believe it. I'll come and find you, sir. I'll find you.") After exiting the house Montefoschi simply confesses to his chauffeur a gloomy judgment: "l'umanità fa schifo." ("Humankind stinks.") To accentuate the gloomy dimension of the narrative, Luigi Comencini associated sounds and pessimist images with Fiorenzo Carpi's powerful musical score, adding a surrealistic tension to the hallucinatory odyssey of survival for life.

With *L'ingorgo*, produced at the very end of a strenuous decade for Italian society, comedy Italian style found a rather disenchanted Comencini, light-years away from the *neorealismo rosa* of the early fifties. This time, his representation of the humble ones, underlining the contradiction of Italian people, their virtues and defects, was undeniably a work of pessimism, taking spectators inside an apocalyptic world, that of an entire nation exhausted by a decade of violence. Nicknamed by film historians *naufragio della ragione* (wreckage of reason), the film was without a doubt Comencini's most disturbing and controversial film. He commented himself on the relative fortune of his film.

> I wanted *L'ingorgo* to be a "transition" film: starting with situations typically comical and ending in a dramatic, even anxious mode. The audience did not follow me much, nor did the critics. I am convinced, however, that it is one of my best films. But when society is plunged into darkness, watching one's own destiny and its representation, it is not easy to accept.[37]

L'ingorgo was an accumulation of an entire decade of social evils, condensed into just a couple of hours—a rather short time span for such a long and tragic decade. The Italian popular audience perhaps never identified with the humanity portrayed in the two-hour-long feature film. The human acts of mental violence, revealed as psychological self-destruction, in a way deterred the spectator's interest away from the intended and original purpose of the film: that is, comedy.

Notes

[1] Translated by the author from Italian: "L'assoluta laicità del cinema di Risi corre consapevolmente il rischio dello scetticismo. Ma riesce anche a rifuggire sempre dalla freddezza dell'agnostico, in virtù di quella che lui ama chiamare 'misura' e che si concretizza sullo schermo nella forma di una complessa alchimia tra il comico e il tragico." Viganò, *Dino Risi* (Milan: Moizzi Editore, 1977), 33.

[2] Laura Antonelli (1941) became noticed in 1971 with Pasquale Festa Campanile's *Il merlo maschio,* starring Lando Buzzanca. In 1973, she was a sensual waitress in Salvatore Samperi's *Malizia* aside Turi Ferro and Alessandro Momo (mostly known for his role as Ciccio in *Profumo di donna*). A living icon of Italian erotic cinema of the 1970s, the Italian press adulated her with its famous label: "an angel face with a body made for sin." She also featured in important comedies such as Luigi Comencini's *Mio Dio come sono caduta in basso,* 1974; erotic films like Salvatore Samperi's *Peccato Veniale,* 1974; and *auteur* films like Luchino Visconti's *L'innocente,* 1975.

[3] Translated by the author from French: "Même dans les entreprises mineures, on retrouve toujours le regard aigu que Dino Risi pose sur les hommes, sur leur solitude." Jean Gili, "Sexe fou," *Ecran* (June 1974): 66.

[4] Translated by the author from the original screenplay: Fausto: "Simpatica, idee chiare, buon senso." Ciccio: "E una ragazza pulita." Fausto: "E mignota." Ciccio: "Come ha detto prego?" Fausto: "Eh dai svegliati Ciccio. Ma che non ci vedi? 18 anni, carina. Il padre che mestiere fa?" Ciccio: "Maresciallo." Fausto: "Ecco… e lei va in giro con la borsetta da 400.000 lire. E si l'ho toccata, era cocodrillo. E il profumo francese al meno 40.000 il flaconcino. Babysitter. E un pretesto per star fuori a fare marchette fino alle 3 di notte."

[5] Translated by the author from Italian: "scopre con sgomento che il vitale istinto di conservazione è più forte della volontà." Aldo Viganò, *Commedia italiana in cento film* (Genoa: Le mani, 1995), 156.

[6] According to Aldo Viganò, blindness was a persuasive narrative device to exemplify the powerlessness of man on the world: "La cecità del protagonista di Profumo di donna interviene, in fine, a rendere esplicita l'impossibilità umana di dominare il mondo." See *Commedia italiana in cento film*, 33.

[7] Bondanella, *Italian Cinema: From Neorealism to the Present* (New York: Continuum, 1996), 361.

[8] Fellini wrote the script of the film while he was hospitalized in 1967 and was not expected to survive the experience. Therefore the search of memory came logically.

[9] In Danielle Hipkins's article entitled "Fun and the Schoolboy Fantasy: The Prostitute in Italian Film after the Legge Merlin." (Article presented at "Women in the Mass Media in 20th Century Italy" conference, October 2006, University of London.)

[10] Marcia Landy, *Italian Film* (New York: Cambridge University Press, 2000), 118.

[11] Translated by the author from French: "la comédie à l'italienne me parait toujours le refuge, ou l'avant poste du cinéma d'auteur. Le grand succès *d'Amarcord* est sûrement dû au fait que le public le rapproche des comédies (meilleures) auxquelles il est habitué et qui l'amusent." Lorenzo Codelli, "Eros, coups de poings, flics, rigolade et le reste," *Positif* 160 (1974): 54.

[12] Iaia Fiastri and Nino Manfredi also participated in the screenplay.

[13] Translated by the author from the original screenplay: Doctor Tersili: "Scusi che mestiere fa Lei?" Sicilian man: "Dottore mi meraviglio di Lei. Ma le pare che con 11 figli un poveraccio come me trova tempo di lavorare?"

[14] Originally Ugo Tognazzi was supposed to have the role of Perozzi the journalist and Marcello Mastroianni the decadent nobleman. Due to the short distance in time with Ferreri's *La grande abbuffata*, the actor declined the offer, evoking the dark and cynical aspect of his future role. This is how Noiret came to play Perozzi.

[15] Translated by the author from Italian: "Per questo il comportamento degli amici è sempre identico: in difesa di sé stessi, contro il mondo e contro gli uomini, si sono cristallizzati nella regressione." *Amici miei Atto II. Sceneggiatura originale dell'omonimo film di Mario Monicelli con un'analisi del testo di Alberto Cattini*. (Mantua: Publi-Paolini, 1993), 9.

[16] Translated by the author from Italian: "La mancanza di pietà è un tratto intelligente: è quello che aguzza il cervello. Così come, tra il riso e il pianto, io ho scelto e continuo a scegliere il riso." Mario Monicelli, *Autoritratto* (Florence: Edizioni Polistampa, 2002), 21.

[17] Translated by the author from Italian: "Io ero contrario al termine zingarate. Mi suonava troppo romantico, ma anche un pò scemo. Invece il tono di fondo del film è proprio disperato." Sebastiano Mondadori, *La commedia umana: conversazioni con Mario Monicelli* (Milan: Il Saggiatore, 2005), 51.

[18] Their musical theme was taken from Rustichelli (controcanto melanconico of "Bella figlia dell'amore" taken from Verdi's *Rigoletto*).

[19] Translated by the author from Italian: "La beffa è sempre volgare…. Il toscano è volgare…. Era impensabile una commedia priva di parolacce, ormai entrate nel linguaggio comune. Far parlare la gente in maniera fasulla avrebbe significato spuntare la forza stessa della commedia, che nasce dal basso e respira la realtà che la circonda. La volgarità è voluta. Diventa l'elemento intorno al quale si consolida l'amicizia dei protagonisti, che stabiliscono tra di loro una ritualità cameratesca, basata su una goliardia senza freni." Mondadori, *La commedia umana*, 52.

[20] Translated by the author from Italian: "I funerali sono la cosa più esilarante che esista, secondo me. Io vado volentieri ai funerali degli amici, perché mi trovo con altri amici, comincio a scherzare sulla loro prossima morte. Viene fuori una cosa abbastanza divertente, non macabre." Monicelli, *Autoritratto*, 29.

[21] The film was critically acclaimed with a David di Donatello in 1976 for Best Film, as well as one for Best Lead Actor (Ugo Tognazzi).

[22] Translated by the author from Italian: "un ulteriore passo verso l'assurdo, in cui il grottesco coincide con la disperazione e la solitudine." Mondadori, *La commedia umana*, 44.

[23] Rome was often the symbolic location of all excesses: disproportionate bureaucracy, abusive ministries, as well as poor peripheries at times confronted by the urbanization projects of rich politicians and unscrupulous businessmen.

[24] The film differs from the final scene in Vincenzo Cerami's novel as it carries an ominous portent, as Giovanni, insulted by a ruffian, seems to be on the path to kill again.

[25] *Un borghese piccolo piccolo* offered a story of what may or may not be a terrorist kidnapping of the sort that has been making Italian headlines with increasing frequency in these years.

[26] In 1973, Alberto Sordi and Silvana Mangano won the prestigious David di Donatello for Best Acting.

[27] Silvana Mangano's performance recalled the years of dark neorealism.

[28] Interview conducted in Rome (01/05/1973) by Lorenzo Codelli: "Entretien avec Luigi Comencini," *Positif* 156 (1974): 19.

[29] Sonego envisaging his own alter-ego in Alberto Sordi.

[30] Rodolfo Sonego in A. Aprà and P. Pistagnesi, eds., *Comedy Italian Style 1950–1980* (Turin: Edizioni Rai, 1986), 77.

[31] Translated by the author from Italian: "La bambina è l'unica a possedere la verità. Di fatto, ho portato una grande attenzione a questa bambina, e credo che questo si veda… Ha un senso preciso della realtà, vede le cose come sono, non vive nella stessa illusione della sua famiglia e di tutto il tessuto sociale della baraccopoli in cui si trova:

illusione che li porta tutti alla follia." Federico Rossin, "Io scopone scientifico," in Adriano Aprà, *Luigi Comencini* (Venice: Marsilio, 2007), 190.

[32] The films' immediacy and its rendition of realistic details—its kinetic point of view about the human tragedy generated by poverty through the eyes of children—was a compelling exploration of childhood and allowed a rare emancipation of the children's inner emotions. It was precisely the intransigent exteriority of Comencini's viewpoint on childhood that left no one indifferent, not even the critics of the time.

[33] Translated by the author from the original screenplay: "Noi ti ringraziamo signore di aver chiamato a te e accolto nel tuo seno quest'uomo, togliendolo dei disastri del mondo. Salvaci o signore, salvaci dalla plastica. Salvaci dalle scorie radioattive. Salvaci dalla politica di potere. Salvaci dalle multinazionali. Salvaci dalla ragione di stato. Salvaci dalle parate, dalle uniformi e dalle marce militari. Salvaci dal disprezzo per il più debole. Salvaci dal mito dell'efficienza e della produttività. Salvaci dai falsi moralismi. Salvaci dalle menzogne e dalla propaganda. Rispettate la natura, amate la vita. Congiungetevi carnalmente nel rispetto del prossimo. Fornicare non è peccato se è fatto con amore, amen."

[34] One car turns its engine on, then thousands of cars imitate, creating a deafening chaos on a deserted highway.

[35] Sordi loathes the common people and doesn't want them urinating against the tires of his Jaguar.

[36] Translated by the author from the original screenplay: De Benedetti: "Perché non gli ha pagati. A me le cose mi piace pagarle." Ferretti: "Ma non ho voluto niente. Sono buoni poveretti." De Benedetti: "Lei non capisce un cazzo se dice buoni poveretti. O sono buoni o sono poverelli. I poverelli non sono mai buoni." Ferretti: "E che ci posso fare?" De Benedetti: "Di tutto! Ci odiano."

[37] Translated by the author from Italian: "Volevo fare dell'Ingorgo un film 'cerniera': incomincia con situazioni e battute tipicamente umoristiche e scherzose e finisce in modo angoscioso e drammatico. Il pubblico non mi ha seguito molto e la critica nemmeno, sono però convinto che è uno dei miei film migliori. Ma quando la società precipita nel buio, guardare la rappresentazione del proprio destino non è uno spettacolo facilmente accettabile." Pietro Pintus, *Commedia all'italiana: Parlano i protagonisti* (Rome: Gangemi, 1986), 46.

Conclusion

At the end of the 1970s, comedy Italian style as a movement came to an end. Chronicle films, such as Luigi Comencini's *Bottleneck* (*L'ingorgo: una storia impossibile*, 1979), and their emphasis on death anticipated the finality of the movement, which had pushed the tragic-comic element beyond the public and critic's level of tolerance. This fact, compounded with the transfer into a new phase, less creative and glamorous, by comedy Italian style's initiators, like Dino Risi, Mario Monicelli, Luigi Comencini, and Alberto Lattuada, the anticipated evolution of actors, like Vittorio Gassman, Ugo Tognazzi, Nino Manfredi, and Alberto Sordi (who for the most part were soon to reach their sixties), and the absence of any direct heirs, concluded the two prolific and successful decades of the *commedia all'italiana*.

Not only the people involved but also cinematic culture changed dramatically by the end of the 1970s. The Italian film industry was affected by a converging series of irreversible phenomena: a proliferation of private television companies after 1976, the end of the state monopoly over media, the overwhelming power of American distribution in European markets, and finally, the development of a growing subculture among popular audiences that shifted to emphasize highly consumable imagery and emotional modes of expression for both television and cinema. By the 1980s, under the growing influence of media moguls' manipulation and deregulation of media laws, the nature of broadcasting had changed to favor popular culture that required minimal (if any) mental acuity. Ironically, while Italian comedy survived the difficult years of terrorism of the 1970s and preserved its spectatorship, it could not endure the intellectual "alienation" of the 1980s. The minimal government interventions of that decade came too late to alter the interests of Italian audiences, by then accustomed to the newly implemented popular culture goods. As the population of general viewers became television's captive audiences, cinematic culture for filmmakers, authors, and producers became increasingly bound to these new modes of expression, thus forever altering the form and content of Italian film comedies.

While the last comedy films of the 1970s portrayed the turmoil of a disillusioned society through rather pessimistic narratives, the rapid decomposition of the media environment in the 1980s provided the groundwork for a new type of comedy radically different from anything made during the postwar era and the years of the economic boom. Despite the commercial trend to comply with the market's demands for mainstream cinema, several comedy authors were able to produce a new comedy style opposing national trends. Indeed, the end of the 1970s saw the emergence of new directors (all of them featured as actors in their own films) generating a comic cinema based on an egocentricaly vision of the then current Italian reality as opposed to the social vision of the preceding generation. Nanni Moretti was the first noticeable filmmaker who applied his comedic skills in feature films such as *Ecce bombo* (1978) and *Sweet Dreams* (*Sogni d'oro*, 1981). Along with him came Roman transformist Carlo Verdone, who according to many film historians was the only protagonist to present an acting style remotely associated with the *commedia all'italiana* and in particular with Alberto Sordi in films such as *Fun Is Beautiful* (*Un sacco bello*, 1980) and *Bianco, rosso e Verdone* (1981). Other protagonists of the new comedy style post *commedia all'italiana* include the Neapolitan Massimo Troisi with *Ricomincio da tre* (1981) and *Scusate il ritardo* (1982), Maurizio Nichetti' with *Ratataplan* (1979) and *Ho fatto splash* (1980), and of course the Tuscan sensation Roberto Benigni in *Berlinguer: I Love You* (*Berlinguer ti voglio bene*, 1977) and *Seeking Asylum* (*Chiedo asilo*, 1979). By the end of the 1980s Italian comedy was represented by a wide variety of different talents, often standing at different ends of the spectrum from each other in directing style, screenplays, acting performance, as well as the rediscovery of burlesque laughter absent during the two decades of *commedia all'italiana*.

Where does one witness the heritage of comedy Italian style? Did the comedy genre change as a result of *commedia all'italiana* or were subsequent comedies a return to the postwar comic mind? While comedy Italian style may have died as a cinematographic movement at the end of the 1970s, it most certainly continues to exist as a genre today. One such example of a new millennium film based heavily on Italian comedy style is the successful Giovanni Veronesi's *Manual of Love* (*Manuale d'amore*, 2005). Actor/directors such as Roberto Benigni clearly took inspiration from *commedia all'italiana* for difficult subjects, pulling on the strengths of the genre in such films as *Life is Beautiful* (*La vita è bella*, 1997), where the tragic-comic mode successfully combines to illustrate human barbarity along with the loving relationship of a father and son.

The uniqueness of *commedia all'italiana* proved that Italian humor was rarely contained as it pushed the boundaries of comedy to spotlight societal weaknesses. Whether indicting religious institutions, illustrating dire poverty, deprecating urban bureaucracy, or simply representing the cruelty of immigration, the critical analysis of its screenwriting discourses positioned the *commedia* as the best lens to decipher Italian quotidian reality and to reflect on a country in post-war flux. While the commercial trends of the following decades never allowed a continuation of the *commedia* experience, the movement remains a favorite among Italian audiences as it has never been equaled or surpassed in quality and consistency (which has proven to be a sign of strength rather than weakness). Twenty years of cinematic cynicism, social satire, and grotesque caricatures permanently shifted Italian comedy's aesthetic horizons and continues to be celebrated as one of the most important periods in Italian cinematic history. As Dino Risi so poignantly stated, "thanks to *commedia all'italiana*, we have told the [true] story of Italy."[1]

Note

[1] Interview conducted by the author with Dino Risi, June 11, 2005, in Rome.

Abbreviations

ACI	Automobile Club Italia
ANICA	Associazione Nazionale Industrie Cinematografiche Audiovisive e Multimediali
AGIS	Associazione Generale Italiana dello Spettacolo
CGIL	Confederazione Generale Italiana del Lavoro
CIA	Central Intelligence Agency
CISL	Confederazione Italiana Sindacati Lavoratori
DC	Democrazia Cristiana
DS	Democratici di Sinistra
EEC	European Economic Community
ENI	Ente Nazionale Idrocarburi
FILF	Fronte Italiano Liberazione Femminile
GAP	Gruppo di Azione Partigiana
GDP	Gross Domestic Product
MGM	Metro Goldwyn Mayer
MLD	Movimento Liberazione delle Donne
MSI	Movimento Sociale Italiano
MPAA	Motion Picture Association of America
NAR	Nuclei Armati Rivoluzionari
NAP	Nuclei Armati Proletari
NATO	North Atlantic Treaty Organization
PCI	Partito Comunista Italiano
PFC	Produzione Film Comici
PIL	Prodotto Interno Lordo
PLI	Partito Liberale Italiano
PRI	Partito Repubblicano Italiano
PSDI	Partito Socialista Democratico Italiano
PSI	Partito Socialista Italiano

PSLI	Partito Socialista dei Lavoratori Italiani
PSIUP	Partito Socialista Italiano di Unità Proletaria
PSU	Partito Socialista Unificato
RAI	Radio Audizioni Italiane
RF	Rivolta Femminile
SIAE	Società Italiana degli Autori ed Editori
SID	Servizio Informazioni Difesa
SISMI	Servizio per le Informazioni e la Sicurezza Militare
SNGCI	Sindacato Nazionale dei Giornalisti Cinematografici Italiani
UIL	Unione Italiana del Lavoro

Appendix

Academy Awards

Best Foreign Film Award

1948 *Sciuscià* by Vittorio De Sica (win)
1950 *Ladri di biciclette* by Vittorio De Sica (win)
1957 *La strada* by Federico Fellini (win)
1958 *Le notti di Cabiria* by Federico Fellini (win)
1959 *I soliti ignoti* by Mario Monicelli (nomination)
1960 *La grande guerra* by Mario Monicelli (nomination)
1961 *Kapò* by Gillo Pontecorvo (nomination)
1963 *Le quattro giornate di Napoli* by Nanni Loy (nomination)
1964 *8½* by Federico Fellini (win)
1965 *Ieri, oggi, domani* by Vittorio De Sica (win)
1966 *Matrimonio all'Italiana* by Vittorio De Sica (nomination)
1967 *La battaglia di Algeri* by Gillo Pontecorvo (nomination)
1969 *La ragazza con la pistola* by Mario Monicelli (nomination)
1971 *Indagine su un cittadino al di sopra di ogni sospetto* by
        Elio Petri (win)
1972 *Il giardino dei Finzi-Contini* by Vittorio De Sica (win)
1975 *Amarcord* by Federico Fellini (win)
1976 *Profumo di donna* by Dino Risi (nomination)
1977 *Pasqualino Settebellezze* by Lina Wertmüller (nomination)
1978 *Una giornata particolare* by Ettore Scola (nomination)
1979 *I nuovi mostri* by Mario Monicelli, Dino Risi, and Ettore
        Scola (nomination)
1980 *Dimenticare Venezia* by Franco Brusati (nomination)
1982 *Tre fratelli* by Francesco Rosi (nomination)
1988 *La famiglia* by Ettore Scola (nomination)
1990 *Nuovo cinema paradiso* by Giuseppe Tornatore (win)

1991   *Porte aperte* by Gianni Amelio (nomination)
1992   *Mediterraneo* by Gabriele Salvatores (win)
1996   *L'uomo delle stelle* by Giuseppe Tornatore (nomination)
1999   *La vita è bella* by Roberto Benigni (win)
2006   *La bestia nel cuore* by Cristina Comencini (nomination)

Best Actress Award

1956   Anna Magnani for *La rosa tatuata* (win)
1958   Anna Magnani for *Selvaggio è il vento* (nomination)
1962   Sophia Loren for *La ciociara* (win)
1965   Sophia Loren for *Matrimonio all'italiana* (nomination)

Best Actor Award

1963   Marcello Mastroianni for *Divorzio all'italiana* (nomination)
1978   Marcello Mastroianni for *Una giornata particolare* (nomination)
1988   Marcello Mastroianni for *Oci ciornie* (nomination)
1999   Roberto Benigni for *La vita è bella* (win)

Best Director Award

1963   Pietro Germi for *Divorzio all'italiana* (nomination)
1964   Federico Fellini for *8½* (nomination)
1967   Michelangelo Antonioni for *Blow-Up* (nomination)
1969   Gillo Pontecorvo for *La battaglia di Algeri* (nomination)
1971   Federico Fellini for *Fellini Satyricon* (nomination)
1974   Bernardo Bertolucci for *Ultimo tango a Parigi* (nomination)
1976   Federico Fellini for *Amarcord* (nomination)
1977   Lina Wertmüller for *Pasqualino Settebellezze* (nomination)
1988   Bernardo Bertolucci for *L'ultimo imperatore* (win)
1999   Roberto Benigni for *La vita è bella* (nomination)

Cannes Film Festival

1946   Grand Prix: *Roma, città aperta* (*Open City*) by Roberto Rossellini
1949   Best Actress: Isa Miranda for René Clément's *Le mura di Malapaga* (*The Walls of Malapaga*)
1951   Grand prix: *Miracolo a Milano* (*Miracle in Milan*) by Vittorio de Sica *ex aequo* with *Miss Julie* by Alf Sjöberg (Sweden)
1952   Grand prix: *Due soldi di speranza* by Renato Castellani, *ex aequo* with *Othello* by Orson Welles (Morocco)
         Best Screenplay: Piero Tellini for *Guardie e ladri* by Mario Monicelli

1954   International Prize: *Carosello napoletano* by Ettore Giannini

1955   Special Jury Prize: *Continento perduto* by Leonardo Bonzi, Mario Craveri, Enrico Gras, Angelo Francesco Lavagnino, Giorgio Moser

1957   Best Actress: Giulietta Masina for *Le notti di Cabiria* by Federico Fellini

1958   Best Original Screenplay: Pier Paolo Pasolini, Massimo Franciosa, and Pasquale Festa Campanile for Mauro Bolognini's *Giovani mariti* (*Young Husbands*)

1959   Best Comedy Prize: *Policarpo, ufficiale di scrittura* (*Policarpo*) by Mario Soldati

1960   Golden Palm: *La dolce vita* (*La Dolce Vita*) by Federico Fellini

       Jury Prize: *L'avventura* (*L'Avventura*) by Michelangelo Antonioni

1961   Best Actress: Sophia Loren for Vittorio De Sica's *La ciociara* (*Two Women*)

1962   Special Jury Prize: *L'eclisse* (*The Eclipse*) by Michelangelo Antonioni

       Best Comedy Prize: *Divorzio all'italiana* (*Divorce Italian Style*) by Pietro Germi

1963   Golden Palm: *Il gattopardo* (*The Leopard*) by Luchino Visconti

       Best Actress: Marina Vlady for Marco Ferreri's *L'ape regina: una storia moderna* (*The Conjugal Bed*)

1964   Best Actor: Saro Urzì for Pietro Germi's *Sedotta e abbandonata* (*Seduced and Abandoned*)

1966   Sophia Loren, President of the Jury

       Golden Palm: *Signore & signori* (*The Birds, the Bees and the Italians*) by Pietro Germi, *ex aequo* with Claude Lelouch's *Un homme et une femme* (*A Man and a Woman*, France)

       Special Prize for an Acting Career: Antonio de Curtis (Totò)

1967   Alessandro Blasetti, President of the Jury

       Golden Palm: *Blow Up* by Michelangelo Antonioni

       Best Scenario: Elio Petri's *A ciascuno il suo* (*We Still Kill the Old Way*), *ex aequo* with Alain Jessua's *Jeu de massacre* (*The Killing Game*, France)

1969   Luchino Visconti, President of the Jury

1970   Special Jury Prize: *Indagine su un cittadino al di sopra di ogni sospetto* (*Investigation of a Citizen Above Suspicion*) by Elio Petri

       Best Actress: Ottavia Piccolo in Mauro Bolognini's *Metello*

       Best Actor: Marcello Mastroianni in Ettore Scola's *Dramma della gelosia: tutti i particolari in cronaca*

1971   Prix du 25e Anniversaire du Festival International du Film: Luchino Visconti's *Morte a Venezia* (*Death in Venice*) as well as to his career

       Best Actor: Ricardo Cucciolla for Giuliano Montallo's *Sacco e Vanzetti* (*Sacco and Vanzetti*)

       First Film Prize: *Per grazia ricevuta* (*Between Miracles*) by Nino Manfredi

1972   Grand Prix International du Film & Special Prize for Acting to Gian Maria Volonté in Elio Petri's *La classe operaia va in paradiso* (*The Working Class Goes to Heaven*) and in Francesco Rosi's *Il caso Mattei* (*The Mattei Affair*)

1973   Best Actor: Giancarlo Giannini in Lina Wertmüller's *Film d'amore e d'anarchia, ovvero 'stamattina alle 10 in via dei Fiori nella nota casa di tolleranza* (*Love and Anarchy*)

1974   Special Jury Prize: *Il fiore delle mille e una notte* (*Arabian Nights*) by Pier Paolo Pasolini

1975   Best Actor: Vittorio Gassman for Dino Risi's *Profumo di donna* (*Scent of a Woman*)

1976   Best Actress: Dominique Sanda in Mauro Bolognini's *L'eredità Ferramonti* (*The Inheritance*, 1976) and Marie Törocsik in Gyula Maar's *Où êtes-vous madame Déry?*
        Best Directing: Ettore Scola's *Brutti, sporchi e cattivi* (*Down and Dirty*)

1977   Roberto Rossellini, President of the Jury
        Golden Palm: *Padre Padrone* (*Father and Master*) by Paolo and Vittorio Taviani

1978   Golden Palm: *L'albero degli zoccoli* (*The Tree of Wooden Clogs*) by Ermanno Olmi
        Special Jury Prize: *Ciao maschio* (*Bye Bye Monkey*) by Marco Ferreri and Erzy Skolinowski's *The Shout* (U.K.)

1979   Best Actor: Stefano Madia for Dino Risi's *Caro Papà* (*Dear Father*, 1979)

1980   Best Actress: Anouk Aimée for Marco Bellochio's *Salto nel vuoto* (*A Leap in the Dark*, 1980)
        Best Actor: Michel Piccoli for Marco Bellochio's *Salto nel vuoto* (*A Leap in the Dark*, 1980)
        Best Scenario and Dialogues: Ettore Scola, Age, Furio Scarpelli for Ettore Scola's *La Terrazza* (*The Terrace*, 1980)
        Best Supporting Actress: Carla Gravina for Ettore Scola's *La Terrazza* (*The Terrace*, 1980) and Milena Dravic for Goran Paskaljevic's *Poseban tretman* (*Special Treatment*, Yugoslavia)

1981   Best Actor: Ugo Tognazzi for Bernardo Bertolucci's *La tragedia di un uomo ridicolo*

1982   Giorgio Strehler, President of the Jury
        Prix du trente-cinquième anniversaire: Michelangelo Antonioni for *Identification di una donna* (*Identification of a Woman*) and the rest of his career
        Special Jury Prize: *La notte di San Lorenzo*, Paolo and Vittorio Taviani

1983   Best Directing: Andrei Tarkovsky for *Nostalghia*, *ex aequo* with Robert Bresson for *L'argent* (France)
        Best Actress: Hanna Schygulla for Marco Ferreri's *Storia di Piera*

1987   Prix du quarantième anniversaire: *Intervista* by Federico Fellini

1988   Ettore Scola, President of the Jury

1989   *Paradiso* by Giuseppe Tornatore, *ex aequo* with *Too Beautiful For You* by Bertrand Blier (France)

1990   Bernardo Bertolucci, President of the Jury
        Prix du jury œcuménique: *Stanno tutti bene* by Giuseppe Tornatore

1992   Special Jury Prize: *Il ladro di bambini* by Gianni Amelio

1994   Best Directing: *Caro diario* by Nanni Moretti

1998   Grand Prix: *La vita è bella* by Roberto Benigni

2001   Golden Palm for *La stanza del figlio* by Nanni Moretti

2008   Grand Prix: *Gomorra* by Matteo Garrone
        Jury Prize: *Il divo* by Paolo Sorrentino

Venice Film Festival

Best Film

1954   *Giulietta e Romeo* directed by Renato Castellani

1959   *La grande guerra* directed by Mario Monicelli, *ex aequo* with *Il generale della Rovere* directed by Roberto Rossellini

1962 *Cronaca familiare* directed by Valerio Zurlini
1963 *Le mani sulla città* directed by Francesco Rosi
1964 *Deserto Rosso* directed by Michelangelo Antonioni
1965 *Vaghe stelle dell'Orsa* directed by Luchino Visconti
1966 *La battaglia di Algeri* directed by Gillo Pontecorvo
1988 *La leggenda del santo bevitore* directed by Ermanno Olmi
1998 *Così ridevano* directed by Gianni Amelio

Best Actor

1986 Carlo delle Piane for *Regalo di Natale*
1989 Marcello Mastroianni and Massimo Troisi for *Che ora è?*
1993 Fabrizio Bentivoglio for *Un'anima divisa in due*
2001 Luigi Lo Cascio for *Luce dei miei occhi*
2002 Stefano Accorsi for *Un viaggio chiamato amore*

Best Actress

1947 Anna Magnani for *L'Onorevole Angelina*
1958 Sophia Loren for *Orchidea nera*
1968 Laura Betti for *Teorema*
1986 Valeria Golino for *Storia d'amore*
2001 Sandra Ceccarelli for *Luce dei miei occhi*
2005 Giovanna Mezzogiorno for *La bestia nel cuore*

Special Prize for the Career

1982 Alessandro Blasetti, Cesare Zavattini
1983 Michelangelo Antonioni
1985 Federico Fellini
1986 Paolo e Vittorio Taviani
1987 Luigi Comencini
1990 Marcello Mastroianni
1991 Mario Monicelli, Gian Maria Volontè
1992 Paolo Villaggio
1993 Claudia Cardinale
1994 Suso Cecchi D'Amico
1995 Giuseppe De Santis, Goffredo Lombardo, Ennio Morricone, Alberto Sordi, Monica Vitti
1996 Vittorio Gassman
1997 Alida Valli
1998 Sophia Loren
2002 Dino Risi
2003 Dino De Laurentiis
2005 Stefania Sandrelli
2007 Bernardo Bertolucci
2008 Ermanno Olmi

David di Donatello

The David di Donatello Awards is the annual national competition organized by the Italian film industry.

Best Film

1970   *Indagine su un cittadino al di sopra di ogni sospetto* by Elio Petri, *ex aequo* with *Metello* by Mauro Bolognini

1971   *Il conformista* by Bernardo Bertolucci, *ex aequo* with *Il giardino dei Finzi-Contini* by Vittorio De Sica

1972   *La classe operaia va in paradiso* by Elio Petri, *ex aequo* with *Questa specie d'amore* by Alberto Bevilacqua

1973   *Alfredo Alfredo* by Pietro Germi, *ex aequo* with *Ludwig* by Luchino Visconti

1974   *Amarcord* by Federico Fellini, *ex aequo* with *Pane e cioccolata* by Franco Brusati

1975   *Fatti di gente per bene* by Mauro Bolognini, *ex aequo* with *Gruppo di famiglia in un interno* by Luchino Visconti

1976   *Cadaveri eccellenti* by Francesco Rosi

1977   *Il deserto dei Tartari* by Valerio Zurlini, *ex aequo* with *Un borghese piccolo piccolo* by Mario Monicelli

1978   *Il prefetto di ferro* by Pasquale Squitieri, *ex aequo* with *In nome del Papa Re* by Luigi Magni

1979   *Cristo si è fermato a Eboli* by Francesco Rosi, *ex aequo* with *Dimenticare Venezia* by Franco Brusati and *L'albero degli zoccoli* by Ermanno Olmi

1981   *Ricomincio da tre* by Massimo Troisi

1982   *Borotalco* by Carlo Verdone

1983   *La notte di San Lorenzo* by Paolo and Vittorio Taviani

1984   *Ballando ballando* by Ettore Scola, *ex aequo* with *E la nave va* by Federico Fellini

1985   *Carmen* by Francesco Rosi

1986   *Speriamo che sia femmina* by Mario Monicelli

1987   *La famiglia* by Ettore Scola

1988   *L'ultimo imperatore* by Bernardo Bertolucci

1989   *La leggenda del santo bevitore* by Ermanno Olmi

1990   *Porte aperte* by Gianni Amelio

1991   *Mediterraneo* by Gabriele Salvatores, *ex aequo* with *Verso sera* by Francesca Archibugi

1992   *Il ladro di bambini* by Gianni Amelio

1993   *Il grande cocomero* by Francesca Archibugi

1994   *Caro diario* by Nanni Moretti

1995   *La scuola* by Daniele Luchetti

1996   *Ferie d'agosto* by Paolo Virzì

1997   *La tregua* by Francesco Rosi

1998   *La vita è bella* by Roberto Benigni

1999   *Fuori dal mondo* by Giuseppe Piccioni

2000   *Pane e tulipani* by Silvio Soldini

2001   *La stanza del figlio* by Nanni Moretti

2002   *Il mestiere delle armi* by Ermanno Olmi

2003 *La finestra di fronte* by Ferzan Ozpetek
2004 *La meglio gioventù* by Marco Tullio Giordana
2005 *Le conseguenze dell'amore* by Paolo Sorrentino
2006 *Il caimano* by Nanni Moretti
2007 *La sconosciuta* by Giuseppe Tornatore
2008 *La ragazza del lago* by Andrea Molaioli

Best Director

1956 Gianni Franciolini for *Racconti romani*
1957 Federico Fellini for *Le notti di Cabiria*
1959 Alberto Lattuada for *La tempesta*
1960 Federico Fellini for *La dolce vita*
1961 Michelangelo Antonioni for *La notte*
1962 Ermanno Olmi for *Il posto*
1963 Vittorio De Sica for *I sequestrati di Altona*
1964 Pietro Germi for *Sedotta e abbandonata*
1965 Francesco Rosi for *Il momento della verità*, *ex aequo* with Vittorio De Sica for *Matrimonio all'italiana*
1966 Alessandro Blasetti for *Io, io, io... e gli altri*, *ex aequo* with Pietro Germi for *Signore e signori*
1967 Luigi Comencini for *L'incompreso*
1968 Carlo Lizzani for *Banditi a Milano*
1969 Franco Zeffirelli for *Romeo e Giulietta*
1970 Gillo Pontecorvo for *Queimada*
1971 Luchino Visconti for *Morte a Venezia*
1972 Franco Zeffirelli for *Fratello sole, sorella luna*, *ex aequo* with Sergio Leone for *Giù la testa*
1973 Luchino Visconti for *Ludwig*
1974 Federico Fellini for *Amarcord*
1975 Dino Risi for *Profumo di donna*
1976 Mario Monicelli for *Amici miei*, *ex aequo* with Francesco Rosi for *Cadaveri eccellenti*
1977 Valerio Zurlini for *Il deserto dei Tartari*, *ex aequo* with Mario Monicelli for *Un borghese piccolo piccolo*
1978 Ettore Scola for *Una giornata particolare*
1979 Francesco Rosi for *Cristo si è fermato a Eboli*
1980 Gillo Pontecorvo for *Ogro*, *ex aequo* with Marco Bellocchio for *Salto nel vuoto*
1981 Francesco Rosi for *Tre fratelli*
1982 Marco Ferreri for *Storie di ordinaria follia*
1983 Paolo and Vittorio Taviani for *La notte di San Lorenzo*
1984 Ettore Scola for *Ballando ballando*
1985 Francesco Rosi for *Carmen*
1986 Mario Monicelli for *Speriamo che sia femmina*
1987 Ettore Scola for *La famiglia*
1988 Bernardo Bertolucci for *L'ultimo imperatore*
1989 Ermanno Olmi for *La leggenda del santo bevitore*
1990 Mario Monicelli for *Il male oscuro*

1991   Marco Risi for *Ragazzi fuori, ex aequo* with Ricky Tognazzi for *Ultrà*
1992   Gianni Amelio for *Il ladro di bambini*
1993   Roberto Faenza for *Jona che visse nella balena, ex aequo* with Ricky Tognazzi for *La scorta* and Francesca Archibugi for *Il grande cocomero*
1994   Carlo Verdone for *Perdiamoci di vista*
1995   Mario Martone for *L'amore molesto*
1996   Giuseppe Tornatore for *L'uomo delle stelle*
1997   Francesco Rosi for *La tregua*
1998   Roberto Benigni for *La vita è bella*
1999   Giuseppe Tornatore for *La leggenda del pianista sull'oceano*
2000   Silvio Soldini for *Pane e tulipani*
2001   Gabriele Muccino for *L'ultimo bacio*
2002   Ermanno Olmi for *Il mestiere delle armi*
2003   Pupi Avati for *Il cuore altrove*
2004   Marco Tullio Giordana for *La meglio gioventù*
2005   Paolo Sorrentino for *Le conseguenze dell'amore*
2006   Nanni Moretti for *Il caimano*
2007   Giuseppe Tornatore for *La sconosciuta*
2008   Andrea Molaioli for *La ragazza del lago*

Best Screenplay

1975   Age and Scarpelli for *Romanzo popolare*
1976   Alberto Bevilacqua and Nino Manfredi for *Attenti al buffone*
1977   Leo Benvenuti and Piero De Bernardi for *La stanza del vescovo*
1981   Tonino Guerra and Francesco Rosi for *Tre fratelli*
1982   Sergio Amidei and Marco Ferreri for *Storie di ordinaria follia*
1983   Sergio Amidei and Ettore Scola for *Il nuovo mondo*
1984   Federico Fellini and Tonino Guerra for *E la nave va*
1985   Paolo Taviani, Vittorio Taviani, and Tonino Guerra for *Kaos*
1986   Leo Benvenuti, Suso Cecchi D'Amico, Piero De Bernardi, Mario Monicelli, and Tullio Pinelli for *Speriamo che sia femmina*
1987   Ruggero Maccari, Furio Scarpelli, and Ettore Scola for *La famiglia*
1988   Leo Benvenuti, Piero De Bernardi, and Carlo Verdone for *Io e mia sorella, ex aequo* with Bernardo Bertolucci and Mark Peploe for *L'ultimo imperatore*
1989   Francesca Archibugi, Gloria Malatesta, and Claudia Sbarigia for *Mignon è partita*
1990   Pupi Avati for *Storia di ragazzi e di ragazze*
1991   Sandro Petraglia, Stefano Rulli, and Daniele Luchetti for *Il portaborse, ex aequo* with Maurizio Nichetti and Guido Manuli for *Volere volare*
1992   Carlo Verdone and Francesca Marciano for *Maledetto il giorno che t'ho incontrato*
1993   Francesca Archibugi for *Il grande cocomero*
1994   Ugo Chiti and Giovanni Veronesi for *Per amore, solo per amore*
1995   Alessandro D'Alatri for *Senza pelle, ex aequo* with Luigi Magni and Carla Vistarini for *Nemici d'infanzia* and Alessandro Benvenuti, Ugo Chiti, and Nicola Zavagli for *Belle al bar*
1996   Furio Scarpelli, Ugo Pirro, and Carlo Lizzani for *Celluloide*

1997   Fabio Carpi for *Nel profondo paese straniero*
1998   Vincenzo Cerami and Roberto Benigni for *La vita è bella*
1999   Giuseppe Piccioni, Gualtiero Rosella, and Lucia Zei for *Fuori dal mondo*
2000   Doriana Leondeff and Silvio Soldini for *Pane e tulipani*
2001   Claudio Fava, Monica Zapelli, and Marco Tullio Giordana for *I cento passi*
2002   Ermanno Olmi for *Il mestiere delle armi*
2003   Matteo Garrone, Massimo Gaudioso, and Ugo Chiti for *L'imbalsamatore*
2004   Sandro Petraglia and Stefano Rulli for *La meglio gioventù*
2005   Paolo Sorrentino for *Le conseguenze dell'amore*
2006   Stefano Rulli, Sandro Petraglia, Giancarlo De Cataldo, and Michele Placido for *Romanzo criminale*
2007   Daniele Luchetti, Sandro Petraglia, and Stefano Rulli for *Mio fratello è figlio unico*
2008   Sandro Petraylia for *La ragazza del lago*

Best Actress

1956   Gina Lollobrigida for *La donna più bella del mondo*
1958   Anna Magnani for *Selvaggio è il vento* (*Wild Is the Wind*)
1959   Anna Magnani for *Nella città l'inferno*
1961   Sophia Loren for *La ciociara*
1963   Silvana Mangano for *Il processo di Verona*, *ex aequo* with Gina Lollobrigida for *Venere imperiale*
1964   Sophia Loren for *Ieri, oggi, domani*
1965   Sophia Loren for *Matrimonio all'italiana*
1966   Giulietta Masina for *Giulietta degli spiriti*
1967   Silvana Mangano for *Le streghe*
1968   Claudia Cardinale for *Il giorno della civetta*
1969   Gina Lollobrigida for *Buonasera, signora Campbell* (*Buona Sera, Mrs. Campbell*), *ex aequo* with Monica Vitti for *La ragazza con la pistola*
1970   Sophia Loren for *I girasoli*
1971   Florinda Bolkan for *Anonimo veneziano*, *ex aequo* with Monica Vitti for *Ninì Tirabusciò la donna che inventò la mossa*
1972   Claudia Cardinale for *Bello, onesto, emigrato Australia sposerebbe compaesana illibata*
1973   Florinda Bolkan for *Cari genitori*, *ex aequo* with Silvana Mangano for *Lo scopone scientifico*
1974   Sophia Loren for *Il viaggio*, *ex aequo* with Monica Vitti for *Polvere di stelle*
1975   Mariangela Melato for *La poliziotta*
1976   Monica Vitti for *L'anatra all'arancia*
1977   Mariangela Melato for *Caro Michele*
1978   Mariangela Melato for *Il gatto*, *ex aequo* with Sophia Loren for *Una giornata particolare*
1979   Monica Vitti for *Amori miei*
1980   Virna Lisi for *La cicala*
1981   Mariangela Melato for *Aiutami a sognare*, *ex aequo* with Valeria d'Obici for *Passione d'amore*

1982	Eleonora Giorgi for *Borotalco*
1983	Giuliana De Sio for *Io, Chiara e lo scuro*
1984	Lina Sastri for *Mi manda Picone*
1985	Lina Sastri for *Segreti segreti*
1986	Ángela Molina for *Un complicato intrigo di donne vicoli e delitti*
1987	Liv Ullmann for *Mosca addio*
1988	Elena Safonova for *Oci ciornie*
1989	Stefania Sandrelli for *Mignon è partita*
1990	Elena Sofia Ricci for *Ne parliamo lunedì*
1991	Margherita Buy for *La stazione*
1992	Giuliana De Sio for *Cattiva*
1993	Antonella Ponziani for *Verso sud*
1994	Asia Argento for *Perdiamoci di vista*
1995	Anna Bonaiuto for *L'amore molesto*
1996	Valeria Bruni Tedeschi for *La seconda volta*
1997	Asia Argento for *Compagna di viaggio*
1998	Valeria Bruni Tedeschi for *La parola amore esiste*
1999	Margherita Buy for *Fuori dal mondo*
2000	Licia Maglietta for *Pane e tulipani*
2001	Laura Morante for *La stanza del figlio*
2002	Marina Confalone for *Incantesimo napoletano*
2003	Giovanna Mezzogiorno for *La finestra di fronte*
2004	Penélope Cruz for *Non ti muovere*
2005	Barbora Bobulova for *Cuore sacro*
2006	Valeria Golino for *La guerra di Mario*
2007	Ksenia Rappoport for *La sconosciuta*
2008	Margherita Buy for *Giorni e nuvole*

Best Supporting Actress

1982	Alida Valli for *La caduta degli angeli ribelli*
1983	Virna Lisi for *Sapore di mare*, ex aequo with Lina Polito for *Scusate il ritardo*
1984	Elena Fabrizi for *Acqua e sapone*
1985	Marina Confalone for *Così parlò Bellavista*
1986	Athina Cenci for *Speriamo che sia femmina*
1987	Lina Sastri for *L'inchiesta*
1988	Elena Sofia Ricci for *Io e mia sorella*
1989	Athina Cenci for *Compagni di scuola*
1990	Nancy Brilli for *Piccoli equivoci*
1991	Zoe Incrocci for *Verso sera*
1992	Elisabetta Pozzi for *Maledetto il giorno che t'ho incontrato*
1993	Marina Confalone for *Arriva la bufera*
1994	Monica Scattini for *Maniaci sentimentali*
1995	Angela Luce for *L'amore molesto*
1996	Marina Confalone for *La seconda volta*
1997	Barbara Enrichi for *Il ciclone*
1998	Nicoletta Braschi for *Ovosodo*

1999 Cecilia Dazzi for *Matrimoni*
2000 Marina Massironi for *Pane e tulipani*
2001 Stefania Sandrelli for *L'ultimo bacio*
2002 Stefania Sandrelli for *Figli for Hijos*
2003 Piera Degli Esposti for *L'ora di religione*
2004 Margherita Buy for *Caterina va in città*
2005 Margherita Buy for *Manuale d'amore*
2006 Angela Finocchiaro for *La bestia nel cuore*
2007 Ambra Angiolini for *Saturno contro*
2008 Alba Rohrwacher for *Giorni e nuvole*

Best Actor

1956 Vittorio De Sica for *Pane, amore e gelosia*
1960 Vittorio Gassman for *La grande guerra*, *ex aequo* with Alberto Sordi for *La grande guerra*
1961 Alberto Sordi for *Tutti a casa*
1962 Raf Vallone for *Uno sguardo dal ponte*
1963 Vittorio Gassman for *Il sorpasso*
1964 Marcello Mastroianni for *Ieri, oggi, domani*
1965 Vittorio Gassman for *La congiuntura*, *ex aequo* with Marcello Mastroianni for *Matrimonio all'italiana*
1966 Alberto Sordi for *Fumo di Londra*
1967 Vittorio Gassman for *Il tigre*, *ex aequo* with Ugo Tognazzi for *L'immorale*
1968 Franco Nero for *Il giorno della civetta*
1969 Alberto Sordi for *Il medico della mutua*, *ex aequo* with Nino Manfredi for *Vedo nudo*
1970 Gian Maria Volontè for *Indagine su un cittadino al di sopra di ogni sospetto*, *ex aequo* with Nino Manfredi for *Nell'anno del Signore*
1971 Ugo Tognazzi for *La califfa*
1972 Alberto Sordi for *Detenuto in attesa di giudizio*, *ex aequo* with Giancarlo Giannini for *Mimì metallurgico ferito nell'onore*
1973 Alberto Sordi for *Lo scopone scientifico*
1974 Nino Manfredi for *Pane e cioccolata*
1975 Vittorio Gassman for *Profumo di donna*
1976 Ugo Tognazzi for *Amici miei*
1977 Alberto Sordi for *Un borghese piccolo piccolo*
1978 Nino Manfredi for *In nome del Papa Re*
1979 Vittorio Gassman for *Caro papà*
1980 Adriano Celentano for *Mani di velluto*
1981 Massimo Troisi for *Ricomincio da tre*
1982 Carlo Verdone for *Borotalco*
1983 Francesco Nuti for *Io, Chiara e lo scuro*
1984 Giancarlo Giannini for *Mi manda Picone*
1985 Francesco Nuti for *Casablanca, Casablanca*
1986 Marcello Mastroianni for *Ginger e Fred*
1987 Vittorio Gassman for *La famiglia*

1988   Marcello Mastroianni for *Oci ciornie*
1989   Roberto Benigni for *Il piccolo diavolo*
1990   Paolo Villaggio for *La voce della luna*, *ex aequo* with Gian Maria Volonté for *Porte aperte*
1991   Nanni Moretti for *Il portaborse*
1992   Carlo Verdone for *Maledetto il giorno che t'ho incontrato*
1993   Sergio Castellitto for *Il grande cocomero*
1994   Giulio Scarpati for *Il giudice ragazzino*
1995   Marcello Mastroianni for *Sostiene Pereira*
1996   Giancarlo Giannini for *Celluloide*
1997   Fabrizio Bentivoglio for *Testimone a rischio*
1998   Roberto Benigni for *La vita è bella*
1999   Stefano Accorsi for *Radiofreccia*
2000   Bruno Ganz for *Pane e tulipani*
2001   Luigi Lo Cascio for *I cento passi*
2002   Giancarlo Giannini for *Ti voglio bene Eugenio*
2003   Massimo Girotti for *La finestra di fronte*
2004   Sergio Castellitto for *Non ti muovere*
2005   Toni Servillo for *Le conseguenze dell'amore*
2006   Silvio Orlando *for Il caimano*
2007   Elio Germano for *Mio fratello è figlio unico*
2008   Toni Servillo for *la ragazza del lago*

Best Supporting Actor

1981   Charles Vanel for *Tre fratelli*
1982   Angelo Infanti for *Borotalco*
1983   Lello Arena for *Scusate il ritardo*
1984   Carlo Giuffrè for *Son contento*
1985   Ricky Tognazzi for *Qualcosa di biondo*
1986   Bernard Blier for *Speriamo che sia femmina*
1987   Leo Gullotta for *Il camorrista*
1988   Peter O'Toole for *L'ultimo imperatore*
1989   Massimo Dapporto for *Mignon è partita*, *ex aequo* with Carlo Croccolo for *O re*
1990   Sergio Castellitto for *Tre colonne in cronaca*
1991   Ciccio Ingrassia for *Condominio*
1992   Angelo Orlando for *Pensavo fosse amore invece era un calesse*
1993   Claudio Amendola for *Un'altra vita*
1994   Alessandro Haber for *Per amore, solo per amore*
1995   Giancarlo Giannini for *Come due coccodrilli*
1996   Leopoldo Trieste for *L'uomo delle stelle*
1997   Leo Gullotta for *Il carniere*
1998   Silvio Orlando for *Aprile*
1999   Fabrizio Bentivoglio for *Del perduto amore*
2000   Giuseppe Battiston for *Pane e tulipani*, *ex aequo* with Leo Gullotta for *Un uomo perbene* and Emilio Solfrizzi for *Ormai è fatta!*
2001   Tony Sperandeo for *I cento passi*

2002 Libero De Rienzo for *Santa Maradona*
2003 Ernesto Mahieux for *L'imbalsamatore*
2004 Roberto Herlitzka for *Buongiorno, notte*
2005 Carlo Verdone for *Manuale d'amore*
2006 Pierfrancesco Favino for *Romanzo criminale*
2007 Giorgio Colangeli for *L'aria salata*
2008 Alessandro Gassman for *Caos Calmo*

Nastri d'Argento

The *Nastri d'Argento* Awards is the national competition organized by the Italian critics association also called SNGCI/*Sindacato Nazionale dei Giornalisti Cinematografici Italiani* (Italian National Syndicate of Film Journalists).

Best Director

1946 Roberto Rossellini for *Roma città aperta*
1947 Roberto Rossellini for *Paisà*
1948 Pietro Germi for *Gioventù perduta*
1949 Vittorio De Sica for *Ladri di biciclette*
1950 Augusto Genina for *Cielo sulla palude*
1951 Alessandro Blasetti for *Prima comunione*
1952 Renato Castellani for *Due soldi di speranza*
1953 Luigi Zampa for *Processo alla città*
1954 Federico Fellini for *I vitelloni*
1955 Federico Fellini for *La strada*
1956 Michelangelo Antonioni for *Le amiche*
1957 Pietro Germi for *Il ferroviere*
1958 Federico Fellini for *Le notti di Cabiria*
1959 Pietro Germi for *L'uomo di paglia*
1960 Roberto Rossellini for *Il generale della Rovere*
1961 Luchino Visconti for *Rocco e i suoi fratelli*
1962 Michelangelo Antonioni for *La notte*
1963 Nanni Loy for *Le quattro giornate di Napoli*, *ex aequo* with Francesco Rosi for *Salvatore Giuliano*
1964 Federico Fellini for *8½*
1965 Pier Paolo Pasolini for *Il vangelo secondo Matteo*
1966 Antonio Pietrangeli for *Io la conoscevo bene*
1967 Gillo Pontecorvo for *La battaglia di Algeri*
1968 Elio Petri for *A ciascuno il suo*
1969 Franco Zeffirelli for *Romeo e Giulietta*
1970 Luchino Visconti for *La caduta degli déi*
1971 Elio Petri for *Indagine su un cittadino al di sopra di ogni sospetto*
1972 Luchino Visconti for *Morte a Venezia*
1973 Bernardo Bertolucci for *Ultimo tango a Parigi*
1974 Federico Fellini for *Amarcord*
1975 Luchino Visconti for *Gruppo di famiglia in un interno*

1976   Michelangelo Antonioni for *Professione: reporter*
1977   Valerio Zurlini for *Il deserto dei Tartari*
1978   Paolo and Vittorio Taviani for *Padre padrone*
1979   Ermanno Olmi for *L'albero degli zoccoli*
1980   Federico Fellini for *La città delle donne*
1981   Francesco Rosi for *Tre fratelli*
1982   Marco Ferreri for *Storie di ordinaria follia*
1983   Paolo and Vittorio Taviani for *La notte di San Lorenzo*
1984   Pupi Avati for *Una gita scolastica*, ex aequo with Federico Fellini for *E la nave va*
1985   Sergio Leone for *C'era una volta in America*
1986   Mario Monicelli for *Speriamo che sia femmina*
1987   Ettore Scola for *La famiglia*
1988   Bernardo Bertolucci for *L'ultimo imperatore*
1989   Ermanno Olmi for *La leggenda del santo bevitore*
1990   Pupi Avati for *Storia di ragazzi e di ragazze*
1991   Gianni Amelio for *Porte aperte*
1992   Gabriele Salvatores for *Mediterraneo*
1993   Gianni Amelio for *Il ladro di bambini*
1994   Nanni Moretti for *Caro diario*
1995   Gianni Amelio for *Lamerica*
1996   Giuseppe Tornatore for *L'uomo delle stelle*
1997   Maurizio Nichetti for *Luna e l'altra*
1998   Roberto Benigni for *La vita è bella*
1999   Giuseppe Tornatore for *La leggenda del pianista sull'oceano*
2000   Silvio Soldini for *Pane e tulipani*
2001   Nanni Moretti for *La stanza del figlio*
2002   Marco Bellocchio for *L'ora di religione*
2003   Gabriele Salvatores for *Io non ho paura*
2004   Marco Tullio Giordana for *La meglio gioventù*
2005   Gianni Amelio for *Le chiavi di casa*
2006   Michele Placido for *Romanzo criminale*
2007   Giuseppe Tornatore for *La sconosciuta*
2008   Paolo virzì for *Tutta la vita davanti*

Best Actress

1946   Clara Calamai for *L'adultera*
1947   Alida Valli for *Eugenia Grandet*
1948   Anna Magnani for *L'onorevole Angelina*
1949   Anna Magnani for *L'amore*
1951   Pier Angeli for *Domani è troppo tardi*
1952   Anna Magnani for *Bellissima*
1953   Ingrid Bergman for *Europa '51*
1954   Gina Lollobrigida for *Pane, amore e fantasia*
1955   Silvana Mangano for *L'oro di Napoli*
1957   Anna Magnani for *Suor Letizia*
1958   Giulietta Masina for *Le notti di Cabiria*

1960 Eleonora Rossi Drago for *Estate violenta*
1961 Sophia Loren for *La ciociara*
1963 Gina Lollobrigida for *Venere imperiale*
1964 Silvana Mangano for *Il proccesso di Verona*
1965 Claudia Cardinale for *La ragazza di Bube*
1966 Giovanna Ralli for *La fuga*
1967 Lisa Gastoni for *Svegliati e uccidi*
1969 Monica Vitti for *La ragazza con la pistola*
1970 Paola Pitagora for *Senza sapere niente di lei*
1971 Ottavia Piccolo for *Metello*
1972 Mariangela Melato for *La classe operaia va in paradiso*
1973 Mariangela Melato for *Mimì metallurgico ferito nell'onore*
1974 Laura Antonelli for *Malizia*
1975 Lisa Gastoni for *Amore amaro*
1976 Monica Vitti for *L'anatra all'arancia*
1977 Mariangela Melato for *Caro Michele*
1978 Sophia Loren for *Una giornata particolare*
1979 Mariangela Melato for *Dimenticare Venezia*
1980 Ida De Benedetto for *Immacolata e concetta l'altra gelosia*
1981 Mariangela Melato for *Aiutami a sognare*
1982 Eleonora Giorgi for *Borotalco*
1983 Giuliana De Sio for *Io, Chiara e lo scuro*
1984 Lida Broccolino for *Una gita scolastica*
1985 Claudia Cardinale for *Claretta*
1986 Giulietta Masina for *Ginger e Fred*
1987 Valeria Golino for *Storia d'amore*
1988 Ornella Muti for *Io e mia sorella*
1989 Ornella Muti for *Codice privato*
1990 Virna Lisi for *Buon Natale…buon anno*
1991 Margherita Buy for *La stazione*
1992 Francesca Neri for *Pensavo fosse amore invece era un calesse*
1993 Antonella Ponziani for *Verso sud*
1994 Chiara Caselli for *Dove siete? Io sono qui*
1995 Sabrina Ferilli for *La bella vita*
1996 Anna Bonaiuto for *L'amore molesto*
1997 Iaia Forte for *Luna e l'altra, ex aequo* with Virna Lisi for *Va' dove ti porta il cuore*
1998 Francesca Neri for *Carne trémula*
1999 Giovanna Mezzogiorno for *Del perduto amore*
2000 Licia Maglietta for *Pane e tulipani*
2001 Margherita Buy for *Le fate ignoranti*
2002 Valeria Golino for *Respiro*
2003 Giovanna Mezzogiorno for *Il più crudele dei giorni e La finestra di fronte*
2004 Adriana Asti, Sonia Bergamasco, Maya Sansa, Jasmine Trinca for *La meglio gioventù*
2005 Laura Morante for *L'amore è eterno finché dura*
2006 Katia Ricciarelli for *La seconda notte di nozze*
2007 Margherita Buy for *Saturno contro*
2008 Margherita Buy for *Giorni e nuvole*

Best Supporting Actress

1946	Anna Magnani for *Roma città aperta*
1947	Ave Ninchi for *Vivire in pace*
1948	Vivi Gioi for *Caccia tragica*
1949	Giulietta Masina for *Senza pietà*
1951	Giulietta Masina for *Luci del varietà*
1955	Tina Pica for *Pane, amore e gelosia*
1956	Valentina Cortese for *Le amiche*
1957	Marisa Merlini for *Tempo di villeggiatura*
1958	Franca Marzi for *Le notti di Cabiria*
1959	Dorian Gray for *Mogli pericolose*
1960	Cristina Gaioni for *Nella città l'inferno*
1961	Didi Perego for *Kapò*
1962	Monica Vitti for *La notte*
1963	Regina Bianche for *Le quattro giornate di Napoli*
1964	Sandra Milo for *8½*
1965	Tecla Scarano for *Matrimonio all'italiana*
1966	Sandra Milo for *Giulietta degli spiriti*
1967	Olga Villi for *Signore e signori*
1968	Maria Grazia Buccella for *Ti ho sposato per allegria*
1969	Pupella Maggio for *Il medico della mutua*
1971	Francesca Romana Coluzzi for *Venga a prendere il caffè da noi*
1972	Marina Berti for *La califfa, ex aequo* with Silvana Mangano for *Morte a Venezia*
1974	Adriana Asti for *Una breve vacanza*
1975	Giovanna Ralli for *C'eravamo tanto amati*
1976	Maria Teresa Albani for *Per le antiche scale*
1977	Adriana Asti for *L'eredità Ferramonti*
1978	Virna Lisi for *Al di là del bene e del male*
1979	Lea Massari for *Cristo si è fermato a Eboli*
1980	Stefania Sandrelli for *La terrazza*
1981	Ida Di Benedetto for *Fontamara*
1982	Claudia Cardinale for *La pelle*
1983	Virna Lisi for *Sapore di mare*
1984	Monica Scattini for *Lontano da dove*
1985	Marina Confalone for *Così parlò Bellavista*
1986	Isa Danieli for *Un complicato intrigo di donne vicoli e delitti*
1987	Ottavia Piccolo for *La famiglia*
1988	Elena Sofia Ricci for *Io e mia sorella*
1989	Stefania Sandrelli for *Mignon è partita*
1990	Nancy Brilli for *Piccoli equivoci*
1991	Zoe Incrocci for *Verso sera*
1992	Ilaria Occhini for *Benvenuti in casa Gori*
1993	Paola Quattrini for *Fratelli e sorelle*
1994	Milena Vukotic for *Fantozzi in paradiso*
1995	Virna Lisi for *La regina Margot*
1996	Regina Bianchi for *Camerieri*

1997   Lucia Poli for *Albergo Roma*
1998   Entire cast: Mimma De Rosalia, Maria Aliotta, Annamaria Confalone, Adele Aliotta, Francesca Di Cesare, Eleonora Teriaca, Concetta Alfano, Antonia Uzzo for *Tano da morire*
1999   Stefania Sandrelli for *La cena*
2000   Marina Massironi for *Pane e tulipani*
2001   Stefania Sandrelli for *L'ultimo bacio*
2002   Margherita Buy, Virna Lisi, Sandra Ceccarelli for *Il più bel giorno della mia vita*
2003   Monica Bellucci for *Ricordati di me*
2004   Margherita Buy for *Caterina va in città*
2005   Giovanna Mezzogiorno for *L'amore ritorna*
2006   Angela Finocchiaro for *La bestia nel cuore*
2007   Ambra Angiolini for *Saturno contro*
2008   Sabrina Ferilli for *Tutta la vita davanti*

Best Actor

1946   Andrea Checchi for *Due lettere anonime*
1947   Amedeo Nazzari for *Il bandito*
1948   Vittorio De Sica for *Cuore*
1949   Massimo Girotti for *In nome della legge*
1951   Aldo Fabrizi for *Prima comunione*
1952   Totò for *Guardie e ladri*
1953   Renato Rascel for *Il cappotto*
1954   Nino Taranto for *Anni facili*
1955   Marcello Mastroianni for *Giorni d'amore*
1956   Alberto Sordi for *Lo scapolo*
1958   Marcello Mastroianni for *Le notti bianche*
1959   Vittorio Gassman for *I soliti ignoti*
1960   Alberto Sordi for *La grande guerra*
1961   Marcello Mastroianni for *La dolce vita*
1962   Marcello Mastroianni for *Divorzio all'italiana*
1963   Vittorio Gassman for *Il sorpasso*
1964   Ugo Tognazzi for *L'ape regina*
1965   Saro Urzì for *Sedotta e abbandonata*
1966   Nino Manfredi for *Questa volta parliamo di uomini*
1967   Totò for *Uccellacci e uccellini*
1968   Gian Maria Volontè for *A ciascuno il suo*
1969   Ugo Tognazzi for *La bambolona*
1970   Nino Manfredi for *Nell'anno del Signore*
1971   Gian Maria Volontè for *Indagine su un cittadino al di sopra di ogni sospetto*
1972   Riccardo Cucciolla for *Sacco e Vanzetti*
1973   Giancarlo Giannini for *Mimì metallurgico ferito nell'onore*
1975   Vittorio Gassman for *Profumo di donna*
1976   Michele Placido for *Marcia trionfale*
1977   Alberto Sordi for *Un borghese piccolo piccolo*
1978   Nino Manfredi for *In nome del papa re*

1979   Flavio Bucci for *Ligabue*
1980   Nino Manfredi for *Café express*
1981   Vittorio Mezzogiorno for *Tre fratelli*
1982   Ugo Tognazzi for *La tragedia di un uomo ridicolo*
1983   Francesco Nuti for *Io, Chiara e lo scuro*
1984   Carlo Delle Piane for *Una gita scolastica*
1985   Michele Placido for *Pizza connection*
1986   Marcello Mastroianni for *Ginger e Fred*
1987   Roberto Benigni for *Daunbailò*
1988   Marcello Mastroianni for *Oci ciornie*
1989   Gian Maria Volontè for *L'oeuvre au noir*
1990   Vittorio Gassman for *Lo zio indegno*
1991   Marcello Mastroianni for *Verso sera*
1992   Roberto Benigni for *Johnny Stecchino*
1993   Diego Abatantuono for *Puerto escondido*
1994   Paolo Villaggio for *Il segreto del bosco vecchio*
1995   Alessandro Haber for *La vera vita di Antonio H.*
1996   Sergio Castellitto for *L'uomo delle stelle*
1997   Leonardo Pieraccioni for *Il ciclone*
1998   Roberto Benigni for *La vita è bella*
1999   Giancarlo Giannini for *La stanza dello scirocco*
2000   Silvio Orlando for *Preferisco il rumore del mare*
2001   Stefano Accorsi for *Le fate ignoranti*
2002   Sergio Castellitto for *L'ora di religione*
2003   Neri Marcorè for *Il cuore altrove, ex aequo* with Gigi Proietti for *Febbre da cavallo*
2004   Alessio Boni, Fabrizio Gifuni, Luigi Lo Cascio, Andrea Tidona for *La meglio gioventù, ex aequo* with Roberto Herlitzka for *Buongiorno notte*
2005   Toni Servillo for *Le conseguenze dell'amore*
2006   Pierfrancesco Favino, Kim Rossi Stuart, Claudio Santamaria for *Romanzo criminale*
2007   Silvio Orlando for *Il caimano*
2008   Toni Servillo for *La ragazza del lago*

Best Supporting Actor

1946   Gino Cervi for *Le miserie del signor Travet*
1947   Massimo Serato for *Il sole sorge ancora*
1948   Nando Bruno for *Il delitto di Giovanni Episcopo*
1949   Saro Urzì for *In nome della legge*
1951   Umberto Spadaro for *Il brigante Musolino*
1954   Alberto Sordi for *I vitelloni*
1955   Paolo Stoppa for *L'oro di Napoli*
1956   Memmo Carotenuto for *Il bigamo*
1957   Peppino De Filippo for *Totò, Peppino e i…fuorilegge*
1958   Andrea Checchi for *Parola di ladro*
1959   Nino Vingelli for *La sfida*
1960   Claudio Gora for *Un maledetto imbroglio*

1961   Enrico Maria Salerno for *La lunga notte del '43*
1962   Salvo Randone for *L'assassino*
1963   Romolo Valli for *Una storia milanese*
1964   Folco Lulli for *I compagni*
1965   Leopoldo Trieste for *Sedotta e abbandonata*
1966   Ugo Tognazzi for *Io la conoscevo bene*
1967   Gastone Moschin for *Signore e signori*
1968   Gabriele Ferzetti for *A ciascuno il suo*
1969   Ettore Mattia for *La pecora nera*
1970   Umberto Orsini for *La caduta degli dei, ex aequo* with Fanfulla for *Satyricon*
1971   Romolo Valli for *Il giardino dei FinziContini*
1972   Salvo Randone for *La classe operaia va in paradiso*
1973   Mario Carotenuto for *Lo scopone scientifico*
1974   Turri Ferro for *Malizia*
1975   Aldo Fabrizi for *C'eravamo tanto amati*
1976   Ciccio Ingrassia for *Todo modo*
1977   Romolo Valli for *Un borghese piccolo piccolo*
1978   Carlo Bagno for *In nome del papa re*
1979   Vittorio Mezzogiorno for *Il giocattolo*
1980   Tomas Milian for *La luna*
1981   Massimo Girotti for *Passione d'amore*
1982   Paolo Stoppa for *Il marchese del Grillo*
1983   Tino Schirinzi for *Sciopèn*
1984   Leo Gullotta for *Mi manda Picone*
1985   Leopoldo Trieste for *Enrico IV*
1986   Gastone Moschin for *Amici miei atto III*
1987   Diego Abatantuono for *Regalo di natale*
1988   Enzo Cannavale for *32 dicembre*
1989   Fabio Bussotti for *Francesco*
1990   Alessandro Haber for *Willy signori e vengo da lontano*
1991   Ennio Fantastichini for *Porte aperte*
1992   Paolo Bonacelli for *Johnny Stecchino*
1993   Renato Carpentieri for *Puerto Escondido*
1994   Alessandro Haber for *Per amore, solo per amore*
1995   Marco Messeri for *Con gli occhi chiusi*
1996   Leopoldo Trieste for *L'uomo delle stelle*
1997   Gianni Cavina for *Festival*
1998   Giustino Durano for *La vita è bella*
1999   The entire cast: Antonio Catania, Riccardo Garrone, Vittorio Gassman, Giancarlo Giannini, Adalberto Maria Merli, Eros Pagni, Stefano Antonucci, Giorgio Colangeli, Giuseppe Gandini, Valter Lupo, Paolo Merloni, Carlo Molfese, Sergio Nicolai, Corrado Olmi, Mario Patanè, Pier Francesco Poggi, Francesco Siciliano, Giorgio Tirabassi, Venantino Venantini, Andrea Cambi for *La cena*
2000   Felice Andreasi for *Pane e tulipani*
2001   Giancarlo Giannini for *Hannibal*
2002   Gianni Cavina for *La luce negli occhi*
2003   Diego Abatantuono for *Io non ho paura*

2004 Arnoldo Foà for *Gente di Roma*
2005 Raffaele Pisu for *Le conseguenze dell'amore*
2006 Carlo Verdone for *Manuale d'amore*
2007 Alessandro Haber for *La sconosciuta*
2008 Alessandro Gassman for *Caos Calmo*

Italian Comedies at the Box Office

		(1959–78, in million lira)		
1. *Amici miei, atto I*	1975	Mario Monicelli	3,448
2. *Mimì metallurgico...*	1972	Lina Wertmüller	1,816
3. *Un borghese piccolo piccolo*	1977	Mario Monicelli	1,750
4. *Per grazia ricevuta*	1970	Nino Manfredi	1,689
5. *Romanzo popolare*	1974	Mario Monicelli	1,685
6. *Travolti da un insolito destino...*	1974	Lina Wertmüller	1,681
7. *Di che segno sei?*	1975	Sergio Corbucci	1,673
8. *Sessomatto*	1973	Dino Risi	1,576
9. *Amarcord*	1973	Federico Fellini	1,401
10. *Il medico della mutua*	1968	Luigi Zampa	1,224
11. *Pane e cioccolata*	1973	Franco Brusati	1,219
12. *Quelle strane occasioni*	1976	Comencini/Magni/Loy	1,217
13. *Bello onesto immigrato Australia...*	1971	Luigi Zampa	1,180
14. *Alfredo Alfredo*	1972	Pietro Germi	1,173
15. *Profumo di donna*	1974	Dino Risi	1,051
16. *Venga a prendere il caffè da noi*	1970	Alberto Lattuada	1,005
17. *Vedo nudo*	1968	Dino Risi	997
18. *La moglie del prete*	1970	Dino Risi	966
19. *Finché c'è guerra c'è speranza*	1974	Alberto Sordi	948
20. *Matrimonio all'italiana*	1964	Vittorio De Sica	939
21. *Dramma della gelosia*	1969	Ettore Scola	931
22. *Il prof. Dott. Guido Tersili...*	1969	Luciano Salce	908
23. *La ragazza con la pistola*	1968	Mario Monicelli	871
24. *Serafino*	1968	Pietro Germi	871
25. *Amore mio aiutami*	1969	Alberto Sordi	856
26. *Straziami...ma di baci saziami*	1968	Dino Risi	813
27. *Lo scopone scientifico*	1972	Luigi Comencini	761
28. *Il comune senso del pudore*	1976	Alberto Sordi	744
29. *Riusciranno i nostri eroi?*	1968	Ettore Scola	738
30. *Straziami ma di baci saziami*	1968	Dino Risi	725
31. *Brutti, sporchi e cattivi*	1976	Ettore Scola	721
32. *Ieri, oggi, domani*	1963	Vittorio De Sica	675
33. *Signore e signori*	1965	Pietro Germi	605
34. *Anastasia mio fratello*	1973	Steno	575
35. *Operazione San Gennaro*	1966	Dino Risi	567

36. *In nome del popolo italiano*	1971	Dino Risi	532
37. *L'armata Brancaleone*	1966	Mario Monicelli	511
38. *Divorzio all'italiana*	1961	Pietro Germi	473
39. *La più bella serata della mia vita*	1972	Ettore Scola	462
40. *L'arcidiavolo*	1965	Ettore Scola	444
41. *I complessi*	1965	D'amico/Risi/Rossi	441
42. *Il tigre*	1967	Dino Risi	432
43. *La congiuntura*	1964	Ettore Scola	420
44. *Casanova '70*	1965	Mario Monicelli	415
45. *La pecora nera*	1968	Luciano Salce	413
46. *La matriarca*	1968	P.F. Campanile	410
47. *Il magnifico cornuto*	1964	Antonio Pietrangeli	394
48. *La mia signora*	1964	Luigi Comencini	382
49. *I mostri*	1963	Dino Risi	377
50. *Il sorpasso*	1962	Dino Risi	376
51. *Boccaccio 70'*	1962	DeSic/Fell/Moni/Visc	375
52. *La grande guerra*	1959	Mario Monicelli	370
53. *Adulterio all'italiana*	1965	P.F. Campanile	340
54. *Il profeta*	1968	Dino Risi	340
55. *Crimen*	1960	Mario Camerini	338
56. *Tutti a casa*	1960	Luigi Comencini	334
57. *Sedotta e abbandonata*	1964	Pietro Germi	327
58. *La mia signora*	1964	Bolognini	323
59. *Una questione d'onore*	1965	Luigi Zampa	318
60. *Una vita difficile*	1961	Dino Risi	318
61. *La bambolona*	1968	Franco Giraldi	316
62. *Mafioso*	1962	Alberto Lattuada	315
63. *Il federale*	1961	Luciano Salce	310
64. *Il vigile*	1960	Luigi Zampa	292

source Il giornale dello spettacolo (1960–1979)

Bibliography

Various authors. *Dino Risi: Un'Italia allo specchio*. Assisi: ANCCI, 1992.

———. *Viaggio in Italia: Gli anni '60 al cinema*. Rome: Edizione Carte Segrete, 1991.

Abruzzese, Alberto. "Le perle del boom," *Cinema* 60, no. 41 (1964)

Accardo, A. *Age e Scarpelli: La storia si fa commedia*. Rome: ANNCI, 2001.

Accialini, Fuvio, and Lucia Coluccelli. *Marco Ferreri*. Milan: Edizioni il Formichiere, 1979.

Alemanno, Roberto. "Revival nero nella commedia all'italiana," *Cinema Nuovo* 245(January–February 1977).

Allen, Beverly, and Mary Russo, eds. *Revisionning Italy: National Identity and Global Culture*. Minneapolis: University of Minesota Press, 1997.

Allum, Percy. "Italian Society Transformed." Pages 10–41 in Patrick McCarthy (ed.). *Italy Since 1945*. Oxford: Oxford University Press, 2000.

Aprà, Adriano. *Luigi Comencini*. Venezia: Marsilio, 2007.

Aprà, A., and P. Pistagnesi, eds. *Comedy Italian Style 1950–1980 (Catalogo degli incontri internazionali d'arte)*. Turin: Edizioni Rai, 1986.

———. *Pietro Germi, rittrato di un regista all'antico*. Parma: Pratiche Editrice, 1989.

Argentieri, Mino. "Cinema e cultura di massa," *Il Contemporaneo* 69 (1964).

———, ed. *La censura del cinema italiano*. Rome: Editori Riuniti, 1974.

———. *Risate di Regime: la commedia italiana 1930–1944*. Venice: Marsilio, 1991.

Attolini, G. *Il cinema italiano degli anni Sessanta: Tra commedia e impegno*. Bari: Graphiservice, 1998.

———. *Il cinema di Pietro Germi*. Lecce: Elle Edizioni, 1986.

Bachtin, Michail. *L'opera di Rabelais e la cultura popolare*. Turin: Einaudi, 1995.

Balbo, L., and M. P. May. "Woman's Condition: The Case of Postwar Italy," *International Journal of Sociology* 4 (1975/76): 79–102.

Baranski, Zymunt, and Robert Lumley, eds, *Culture and Conflict in Postwar Italy: Essays on Mass and Popular Culture*. London: MacMillan, 1990.

Baroni, M. *Platea in piedi: manifesti, numeri e dati statistici del cinema italiano 1959–1968*. Rome: Bolelli, 1995.

Bellumori, Cinzia. *Dino Risi*. Rome: ANICA, n.d.

Bergson, H. *Il riso. Saggio sul significato del comico*. Bari: Laterza, 1982.

Bernardini, Aldo. *Nino Manfredi*. Rome: Gremese, 1979.

Bernardini, Aldo, and Claudio G. Fava. *Ugo Tognazzi*. Rome: Gremese, 1978.

Bertetto, Paolo. *Il più brutto del mondo: Il cinema italiano oggi*. Milan: Bompiani, 1982.

Bertini, Antonio. *Ettore Scola: Il cinema e io-Conversazione con Antonio Bertini*. Rome: Officina Edizioni Cinecittà Internazionale, 1996.

Bertolino, M., and E. Ridola. *Vizietti all'italiana. L'epoca d'oro della commedia sexy*. Florence: Molino, 1999.

Bevilacqua, A. *I grandi comici: Le battute, le scene, gli sketch che vi hanno divertito negli ultimi vent'anni*. Milan: Rizzoli, 1965.

Bizzari, Libero. *Il cinema italiano: industria, mercato, pubblico*. Rome: Edizioni Gullivet, 1987.

Bizzari, Libero, and Liberto Solaroli. *L'industria cinematografica italiana*. Florence: Parenti Editore, 1958.

Boarini, Vittorio, ed. *Erotismo, eversione, merce*. Bologna: Cappelli, 1974.

Bolzoni, Francesco, and Mario Foglietti. *Le stagioni del cinema: Trenta registi si raccontano*. Messina: Rubbetino, 2000.

Bondanella, Peter. *Italian Cinema: From Neorealism to the Present*. New York: Continuum, 1996.

———. "La comedie métacinématographique d'Ettore Scola," in Michel Serceau, ed., "La comédie italienne de Don Camillo a Berlusconi," *CinemAction* 42 (1987): 91–99.

Boneschi, M. *Poveri ma belli: inostri anni cinquanta*. Milan: Mondadori, 1995.

Borghini, Fabrizio. *Mario Monicelli: cinquant'anni di cinema*. Pisa: Edizioni Master, 1985.

———. *Mario Monicelli*. Viareggio: Improbe, 1985.

Brunetta, G. P. *Cent'anni di cinema italiano*. 2 vols. Rome-Bari: Laterza, 2006.

———. "Introduzione," in Jean Gili, *Arrivano i mostri*. Bologna: Cappelli, 1980.

———. *Storia del cinema italiano*. 4 vols. Rome: Riuniti, 1993.

Bruno, G., and M. Nadotti, eds. *Off Screen: Women and Film in Italy*. London: Routledge, 1988.

Buss, Robin. *Italian Films*. London: B. T. Batsford Ltd., 1989.

Caldiron, Orio. *Mario Monicelli*. Rome: ANICA, 1980.

———. *Totò*. Rome: Gremese, 1980.

Caldwell, L. *Italian Family Matters*. Basingstoke: MacMillan, 1991.

Camerini, Claudio. *Alberto Lattuada*. Florence: La Nuova Italia, 1981.

Cammarota, Domenico. *Il Cinema Peplum*. Rome: Fanucci, 1987.

———. *Il cinema di Totò*. Rome: Fanucci, 1986.

Campari, Roberto. *Il fantasma del bello: iconologia del cinema italiano*. Venice: Marsilio, 1994.

———. *Hollywood-Cinecittà: il racconto che cambia*. Milan: Feltrinelli, 1980.

Canova, Gianni. "Dalla commedia italiana alla commedia all'italiana," in *"Una vita difficile" di Dino Risi: Risate amare nel lungo dopoguerra*. Ed. Lino Micciché. Venice: Marsilio, 2000, Pages 29–40.

Caprara, Valerio, ed. *Dino Risi, Maestro per caso*. Rome: Gremese, 1993.

———. *Mordi e fuggi: La commedia secondo Dino Risi*. Venice: Marsilio, 1993.

Capriolo, Vittorio. *Alberto Sordi*. Milan: Feltrinelli, 1962.

Carcassone, Philippe, Villien Bruno, Roulet Claude, Cuel François, de Lara Philippe. "Dossier: Cinéma italien et culture populaire," *Cinématographe* 30 (September 1977).

Carrano, Patrizia. "Divismo." Pages 229–47 in *Schermi ed ombre: Gli italiani e il cinema del dopoguerra*. Edited by Marino Livolsi. Florence: La Nuova Italia, 1988.

———. *Malafemmina: la donna nel cinema italiano*. Florence: Guaraldi Editore, 1977.

Cattini, Alberto. *Amici miei Atto II. Sceneggiatura originale dell'omonimo film di Mario Monicelli con un'analisi del testo di Alberto Cattini*. Publi-Paolini: Mantova, 1993.

Cesareo, Giovanni. "Le commedie del boom" In *Film 1964*. Milan: Feltrinelli, 1964.

Ciment, Michel, "Entretien avec Ettore Scola," *Positif* 543 (May 2006): 92.

Causo, Massimo. *Tognazzi: L'alter Ugo del cinema italiano*. Lecce: BESA, 2001.

Clark, M., D. Hine, and R. Irving. "Divorce Italian Style," *Parliamentary Affairs* 27 (Summer 1974): 333–58.

Codelli, Lorenzo. *Dino Risi*. Turin: Pungolo, 1974–75.

———. "Entretien avec Age et Scarpelli," *Positif* 193 (1977): 2–9.

———. "Entretien avec Luigi Comencini." *Positif* 156 (1974): 19.

———. "Entretien avec Rodolfo Sonego," *Positif* 216 (March 1979).

———. "Eros, coups de poings, flics, rigolade et le reste," *Positif* 160 (1974): 51.

———. "Hypothèses sur l'oeuvre du scénariste Sergio Amidei," *Positif* 253 (April 1982).

———. "La partie cachée de l'iceberg: la comédie italienne aujoud'hui," *Positif* 129 (July–August 1971): 18–34.

———. "Au nom des monstres italiens" (on Dino Risi), *Positif* 142 (September 1972).

Codelli, Lorenzo, and Jean Gili. *Mario Monicelli*. Grenoble: Institut culturel italien, 1985.

Comand, Mariapia. *Dino Risi: Il sorpasso*. Turin: Lindau, 2002.

Comencini, Luigi. *Luigi Comencini: Infanzia, vocazione, esperienza di un regista*. Milan: Baldini & Castoldi, 1999.

Corsi, B. *Con qualche dollaro di meno: Storia economica del cinema italiano*. Rome: Editori Riuniti, 2001.

Cosulich, Callisto. *I film di Alberto Lattuada*. Rome: Gremese, 1985,

Crainz, Guido. *Storia del miracolo italiano: Culture, identità, trasformazioni fra anni cinquanta e sessanta*. Rome: Donzelli, 1996.

D'agostini, Paolo. *Dino Risi*. Rome: Il Castoro Cinema, 1995.

———. *Romanzo popolare: Il cinema di Age e Scarpelli*. Rome: Edizioni Scientifiche Italiane, 1991.

D'Amico, M. *La commedia all'italiana: Il cinema comico in Italia dal 1945 al 1975*. Milan: Mondadori, 1985.

De Fornari, O. *Il sorpasso: 1962–1992. I filobus sono pieni di gente onesta*. Rome: Edizioni Carte Segrete, 1992.

De Franceschi, Leonardo. *Lo sguardo eclettico: Il cinema di Mario Monicelli*. Venice: Marsilio, 2001.

De Gaetano, R. *Il corpo e la maschera: Il grotesco nel cinema italiano*. Rome: Bulzoni, 1999.

Degiovanni, Bernard. *Vittorio Gassman*. Paris: Editions PAC, 1980.

Del Buono, Oreste, and Lietta Tornabuoni, eds. *Era Cinecittà: vita, morte e miracoli di una fabbrica di film*. Milan: Bompiani, 1979.

———. *Le persone che hanno fatto grande Milano: Dino Risi*. Milan: Catalogo della mostra omonima, 1985.

Della Casa, Stefano. *Mario Monicelli*. Rome: Il Castoro, 1987.

Della Fornace, Luciana. *Il film in Italia dalla ideazione alla proiezione: Strutture e processi dell'industria cinematografica*. Rome: Bulzoni, 1978.

Delli Colli, Laura. *Monica Vitti*. Rome: Gremese Editore, 1987.

De Santi, Pier Marco, and Rossano Vittori. *I film di Ettore Scola*. Rome: Gremese Editore, 1987.

Di Giammateo, Fernando. *Dizionario del cinema italiano: Dall'inizio del secolo a oggi, i film che hanno segnato la storia del nostro cinema*. Rome: Riuniti, 1995.

———. "I film comici italiani," *Rivista del cinema italiano* 3 (March 1954).

"Italian in commedia." In *Prima della Rivoluzione. Schermi italiani 1960–1969*. Venice: Marsilio, 1984.

Dorigo, Francesco. *Mistica del peccato in Rivista del cinematografo* 6–7 (1963).

Duggan, C., and C. Wagstaff, eds. *Italy in the Cold War: Politics, Culture and Society 1948–58*. Oxford: Berg, 1995.

Ellero, Roberto. *Ettore Scola*. Florence: La Nuova Italia, 1988.

Erenstein, Robert. "The Humour of the Commedia dell'Arte." Pages 118–40 in *The Commedia dell'Arte from the Renaissance to Dario Fo*. Edited by Christopher Cairns. Lewiston, ME: Mellen Press, 1988.

Faldini, Franca, and Goffredo Fofi. *Il cinema italiano oggi 1970–1984: Raccontato dai suoi protagonisti 1960–1969*. Milan: Feltrinelli, 1981.

———, *L'avventurosa storia del cinema italiano 1933–1954*. Milan: Feltrinelli, 1979.

———. *Totò: l'uomo e la maschera*. Milan: Feltrinelli, 1977.

Fava, Claudio G. *Alberto Sordi*. Rome: Gremese, 1979.

Fava, Claudio G., and Matilde Hochkofler. *Marcello Mastroianni*. Rome: Gremese, 1980.

Ferlita, Ernest, and John R. May. *The Parables of Lina Wertmüller*. New York: Paulist Press, 1977.

Ferme, Valerio C. "Ingegno and Morality in the New Social Order: The Role of the Beffa in Boccaccio's Decameron." *RLA: Romance Languages Annual* 4 (1992): 248–53.

Ferroni, G. *Il comico nelle teorie contemporanee*. Rome: Bulzoni, 1974.

Ferroni, G., and F. Faldini. *Totò: l'uomo e la maschera*. Rome: Feltrinelli, 1977.

Fofi, Goffredo. "La comédie du miracle," *Positif* 60 (1964).

Forgacs, D. "Cultural Consumption, 1940s to 1990s." Pages 273–90 in *Italian Cultural Studies: An Introduction*. Edited by David Forgacs and Robert Lumley. New York and Oxford: Oxford University Press, 1996.

———. *Italian Cultural Studies: An Introduction*. Oxford: Oxford University Press, 1996.

———. *Italian Culture in the Industrial Era 1880–1980: Industries, Politics and the Public*. Manchester: Manchester University Press, 1990.

Fulci, L. *Miei mostri adorati*. Bologna: Pendragon, 1995.

Gambetti, Giacomo. *Vittorio Gassman*. Rome: Gremese, 1982.

Garel, Alain. "La comédie italienne et la critique," *La revue du cinéma* 316 (April 1977).

Gassman, Vittorio. *Un grande avvenire dietro le spalle: vita, amori e miracoli di un mattatore narrati da lui stesso*. Milan: Longanesi, 1981.

Giacovelli, Enrico. *La commedia all'italiana*. Rome: Gremese, 1990.

———. *Non ci resta che ridere: una storia del cinema comico italiano*. Turin: Lindau, 1999.

———. *Pietro Germi*. Milan: Il castoro, 1991.

Gili, Jean A. *Arrivano i mostri. I volti della commedia italiana*. Bologna: Cappelli, 1980.

———. "Entretien avec Furio Scarpelli: L'ironie fait partie du drame de la vie," *Positif* 543 (May 2006): 96.

———. *Italian Filmmakers. Self portraits: A Selection of Interviews*. Rome: Gremese, 1998.

———. *Le cinema italien*. Paris: Union Générales d'édition, 1978.

———. *La comédie italienne*. Paris: Henry Veyrier, 1983.

———. *Luigi Comencini*. Paris: Edilig, 1981.

———. *Parigi-Roma: 50 anni di coproduzioni italo-francesi*. Milan: Il Castoro, 1995.

———. *Prima della Rivoluzione: Schermi italiano 1960–1969*. Venice: Marsilio, 1984.

———. "Sexe fou," *Ecran* 26 (1974): 66.

Gili, Jean A., and Lorenzo Codelli. *Mario Monicelli*. Grenoble: Institut Culturel Italien, 1985.

Ginsborg, P. *A History of Contemporary Italy: Society and Politics 1943–1988*. London, Penguin, 1990.

Giordano, Michele. *La commedia erotica italiana*. Rome: Gremese, 2000.

Gosetti Giorgio. *Comencini. Il Castoro cinema*. Florence: La Nuova Italia, 1988.

Governi, G. *Alberto Sordi: Un italiano come noi. Biografia, testi, filmografia*. Milan: Milano Libri Edizioni, 1979.

Grande, Maurizio. *Abiti nuziali e biglietti di banca: La società della commedia nel cinema italiano*. Rome: Bulzoni, 1986.

———. *Il cinema di Saturno: Commedia e malinconia*. Rome: Bulzoni, 1992.

———. "Le istituzioni del comico e la forma commedia." Pages 37–54 in Riccardo Napolitano, *Commedia all'italiana: Angolazioni controcampi*. Rome: Gangemi, 1986.

———. *Marco Ferreri*. Florence: La Nuova Italia, 1974.

Grazzini, Giovanni. *Eva dopo Eva: La donna nel cinema italiano dagli anni Sessanta a oggi*. Rome: Laterza, 1980.

———. *Gli anni Sessanta in cento film*. Bari: Laterza, 1988.

Grmek Germani, Sergio. *Mario Camerini*. Florence: La Nuova Italia, 1980.

Guiglia, Federico. *Italiani senza contini*. Florence: Libri Liberal, 2001.

Gundle, Stephen. "From Neo-Realism to Luci Rosse: Cinema, Politics, Society, 1945–85," in Zygmunt Baranski and Robert Lumley, eds., *Culture and Conflict in Postwar Italy*. London: Macmillan, 1990. Pages 195–224.

Günsberg, Maggie. *Italian Cinema; Gender and Genre*. Basingstoke: Macmillan, 2005.

Horton, A.S., ed. *Comedy/Cinema/Theory*. Berkeley: University of California Press, 1991.

Harris, Warren G. *Sophia Loren: A Biography*. Milan: Longanesi, 1981.

Kezich, Tullio. "Il momento del film comico italiano," *Sipario* 201 (1963).

Landy, Marcia. *Italian Film*. New York: Cambridge University Press, 2000.

Laura, Ernesto. *Comedy Italian Style*. Rome: ANICA/National Association of Motion Pictures, 1981.

———. *I nuovi mostri*. Turin: Assessorato alla cultura della Regione Piemonte, 1982.

Liehm, M. *Passion and Defiance: Film in Italy from 1942 to the Present*. Los Angeles: University of California Press, 1984.

Lizzani, Carlo. *Il cinema italiano 1895–1979*. Rome: Riuniti, 1979.

Lucano, Angelo. "Perché in Italia questo cinema comico?" *Rivista del cinematografo,* parte I: n. 7 (July 1965); parte II: n. 10 (October 1965).

Macry, Paolo. "Rethinking a Stereotype: Territorial Differences and Family Models in the Modernization of Italy," *Journal of Modern Italian Studies* 2, no. 2 (Summer 1997): 188–214.

Magrelli, Enrico G., ed. *Sull'industria cinematografica italiana.* Venice: Marsilio, 1986.

Maraldi, Antonio. "I film e le sceneggiature di Ettore Scola." *Centro Cinema di Cesena. Quaderno* 6 (October 1982).

———. *Pietrangeli.* Florence: Il Castoro Cinema, 1991.

Marinucci, Vincio. *Ettore Scola.* Rome: ANICA, 1977.

Masi, Stefano, and Enrico Lancia. *Italian Movie Godesses: Over 80 of the Greatest Women in the Italian Cinema.* Rome: Gremese International, 1997.

Masoni, Tullio, and Paolo Vecchi. *Luigi Comencini autore popolare.* Reggio Emilia: Comune di Reggio Emilia, 1982.

Massaro, Gianni. *L'occhio impuro: cinema, censura e moralizzatori nell'Italia degli anni Settanta.* Milan: Sugar, 1976.

Mast, Gerald. *The Comic Mind: Comedy and the Movies.* Indianapolis: Bobbs-Merrill, 1973.

McCarthy, P. *Italy Since 1945.* Oxford: Oxford University Press, 2000.

Miccichè, Lino. *Cinema italiano: Gli anni '60 e oltre.* Venice: Marsilio, 1998.

———. *Cinema italiano degli anni '70.* Venice: Marsilio, 1989.

———. *Pane, amore e fantasia.* Turin: Lindau, 1997.

———. *"Una vita difficile" di Dino Risi: Risate amare nel lungo dopoguerra.* Venice: Marsilio, 2000.

Monaco, E. *L'industria cinematografica.* Rome: Romana, 1966.

Mondadori, Sebastiano. *La commedia umana: conversazioni con Mario Monicelli.* Milan: Il Saggiatore, 2005.

Monicelli, Mario. *Autoritratto.* Florence: Edizioni Polistampa, 2002.

———. *Cinema italiano: Ma cos'è questa crisi?* Bari: Laterza, 1979.

———. *L'arte della commedia. A cura di Lorenzo Codelli. Prefazione di Tullio Pinelli.* Bari: Edizioni Dedalo, 1986.

Morandini, Morando. "La grande guerra: recensione." *Schermi* (October 1959): 279.

Mughini, Giampietro. "Aspetti ed episodi del cinema italiano" *Giovane Critica* 3 (1964).

Napolitano, Ricardo. *Commedia all'italiana: Angolazioni controcampi.* Rome: Gangemi, 1986.

Nowell-Smith, Geoffrey. *The Companion to Italian Cinema.* London: Cassell, 1996.

Olmoti, G. *Il boom 1954–1967.* Rome: Editori Riuniti, 1998.

Panero, A. *Carlo Verdone: Un bel giorno mi imbarcai su un cargo battente bandiera liberiana…* Rome: Gremese, 1998.

Parigi, Stefania. *I film di Dino Risi.* Pesaro: Ente Nazionale del Nuovo Cinema, 1993.

Pecori, Franco. *Vittorio De Sica.* Florence: La Nuova Italia, 1980.

Pellizzari, Lorenzo. *Critica alla critica: Contributi a una storia della critica cinematografica italiana.* Rome: Bulzoni, 1999.

———. "Dal cinismo al civismo e ritorno. Libera escursione nel cinema "romano" tra eventi, ceti, classi e personaggi." In *Commedia all'italiana: Angolazioni controcampi.* Edited by Riccardo Napolitano. Rome: Gangemi, 1986.

Perrella, G. *L'economico e il semiotico del cinema italiano.* Rome: Theorema, 1981.

Pillitteri, P. *Cinema come politica: Una commedia all'italiana*. Milan: Franco Angeli, 1992.

Pintus, Pietro. *Commedia all'italiana. Parlano i protagonisti*. Rome: Gangemi, 1986.

———. *Storia e film: Trent'anni di cinema italiano (1945–1975)*. Rome: Bulzoni, 1980.

Pistagnesi, Patrizia. "Risi, Comencini, e altri: La dialettica delle maschere," *Cinema e Cinema* 7–8 (April–September 1976).

Porro, Maurizio. *Alberto Sordi: Profilo critico, recitazione, filmografia completa*. Milan: Il Formichiere, 1979.

Prudenzi A., and C. Scognamillo. *Dino Risi: Maestro dell'equilibrio e della leggerezza*. Rome: Fondazione Scuola Nazionale di Cinema, 2002.

Quaglietti, Lorenzo. *Storia economico-politica del cinema italiano 1945–1980*. Rome: Editori Riuniti, 1980.

Questerbert, Marie-Christine. *Les scénaristes italiens: 50 ans d'écriture cinématographique*. Paris: Hatier, 1988.

Reich, Jacqueline. *Beyond the Latin Lover: Marcello Mastroianni, Masculinity, and Italian Cinema*. Bloomington: Indiana University Press, 2004.

Risi, Dino. *I miei mostri*. Milan: Mondadori, 2004.

Rossitti, Marco. *Il film a episodi in Italia tra gli anni Cinquanta e Sessanta*. Bologna: Alberto Perdisa editore, 2005.

Sabatini, Mariano, and Oriana Maerini. *Intervista a Mario Monicelli: La sostenibile leggerezza del cinema*. Naples: Edizioni Scientifiche Italiane, 2001.

Salizzato, Claver, and Vito Zagarrio, eds. *Effetto commedia: teoria, generi, paesaggi della commedia cinematografica*. Rome: Di Giacomo Editore, 1985.

Sassoon, D. *Contemporary Italy: Politics, Economy & Society since 1945*. London: Longman, 1986.

Sciascia, Leonardo. *La Sicilia e il cinema. V. Spinazzola (a cura di), Film 1963*. Milan: Feltrinelli, 1963.

Serceau, Michel. "La comédie italienne de Don Camillo à Berlusconi." *CinémAction* 42 (1987).

———. "Voleurs et delinquents" *CinémAction* 42 (1987).

Sesti, Mario, ed. *Pietro Germi: The Latin Loner*. Milan: Edizioni Olivares, 1999.

———. *Tutto il cinema di Pietro Germi*. Milan: Baldini and Castoldi, 1997.

S.I.A.E. *Lo spettacolo in Italia, Statistiche 1995*. Rome: Pubblicazione SIAE, 1995.

Sola, P. "Quattro passi nel supermercato della commedia all'italiana," *Rivista del cinematografo* 5 (May 1980).

Sorlin, Pierre. "Popular Film or Industrial Byproducts?" *The Italian Melodrama of the 1950s. Historical Journal of Film, Radio and Television* 15 (3 August 1995): 349–359.

———. *Italian National Cinema 1896–1996*. London: Routledge, 1996.

Spinazzola, Vittorio. *Cinema e pubblico. Lo spettatore filmico in Italia 1945–1965*. Milan: Bompiani, 1974.

Spinazzola, Vittorio (ed). *La Sicilia e il cinema*. Milan: Feltrinelli, 1963.

Stewart, John. *Italian Film: A Who's Who*. Jefferson, NC: McFarland & Company, 1994.

Tassone, Aldo. "La comédie italienne vue par ses auteurs," *La revue du cinema* 137 (May 1977).

———. *Parla il cinema italiano*. 2 vols. Milan: Il Formichiere, 1979.

Terzano, Enzo. "L'evoluzione della commedia all'italiana," *Sipario* 408 (January 1982).

Tinazzi, Giorgio. *Il cinema italiano degli anni '50*. Venice: Marsilio, 1979.

Trionfera, Claudio, ed. *Age & Scarpelli in commedia.* Rome: Di Giacomo Editore, 1990.

———. *Italian directors: Luigi Comencini.* Rome: ANICA, n.d.

Turigliatto, R. *I film di Dino Risi.* Venice: Marsilio, 1993.

Turroni, Giuseppe. *Alberto Lattuada.* Milan: Moizzi Editore, 1977.

Valeri, A. *Pubblicità italiana: Storia, protagonisiti e tendenze di cento anni di comunicazi-one.* Milan: Edizioni del Sole 24 Ore, 1986.

Viganò, Aldo. *Commedia Italiana in cento film.* Genoa: Le Mani, 1995.

———. *Dino Risi.* Milan: Moizzi Editore, 1977.

———. *Mordi e fuggi.* Venice: Marsilio, 1993.

———. *I film di Pietro Germi.* Genova: Comune di Genova, 1994.

Villa, F. *Il narratore essenziale della commedia cinematografica italiana degli anni Cinquanta.* Pisa: ETS, 1999.

Vitti, Antonio. *Incontri con il cinema italiano.* Rome: Salvatore Sciascia Editore, 2003.

Volpi, Gianni. "Entretien avec Alberto Lattuada," *Positif* 210/11 (September–October 1978)

———. "Notes sur Alberto Lattuada," *Positif* 207 (June 1978).

Wagstaff, C. "Italy in the Postwar International Cinema Market."Pages 89–115 in C. *Italy in the Cold War: Politics, Culture and Society 1948–58.* Edited by Duggan and C. Wagstaff. Oxford: Berg, 1995.

Wertmüller, Lina. *The Screenplays of Lina Wertmüller.* Translated by Steven Wagner. New York: Quadrangle, 1977.

Wood, Mary, P. *Italian Cinema.* New York: Berg, 2005.

Zagarrio, Vito, ed. *Dietro lo schermo: ragionamenti sui modi di produzione cinematografici in Italia.* Venice: Marsilio, 1988.

Index